O N E

I've got lower back pain. It's a lot better now, but I've still gotta be careful!

—ONE

Manga creator ONE began *One-Punch Man* as a webcomic, which quickly went viral, garnering over 10 million hits. In addition to *One-Punch Man*, ONE writes and draws the series *Mob Psycho 100* and *Makai no Ossan*.

Y U S U K E M U R A T A

For the most part, I get to draw action scenes however I want. Thinking about how to handle the flow of action is fun.

—Yusuke Murata

A highly decorated and skilled artist best known for his work on *Eyeshield 21*, Yusuke Murata won the 122nd Hop Step Award (1995) for *Partner* and placed second in the 51st Akatsuka Award (1998) for *Samui Hanashi*.

ONE-PUNCH MAN 15

ONE + YUSUKE MURATA

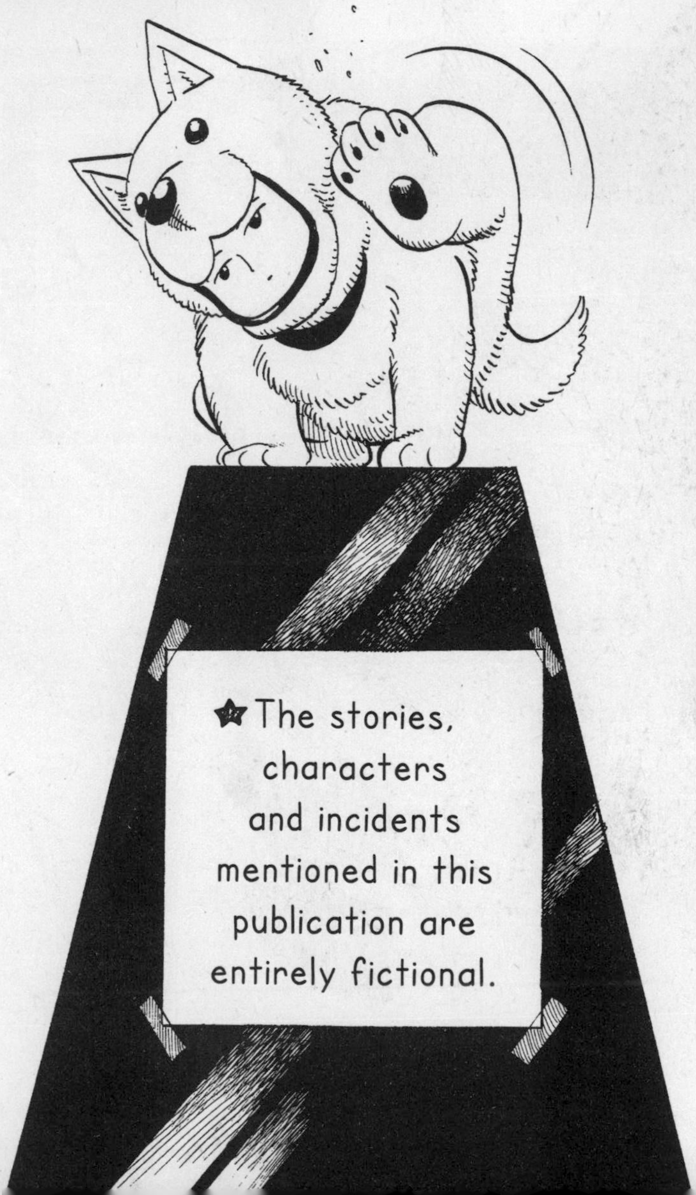
★The stories, characters and incidents mentioned in this publication are entirely fictional.

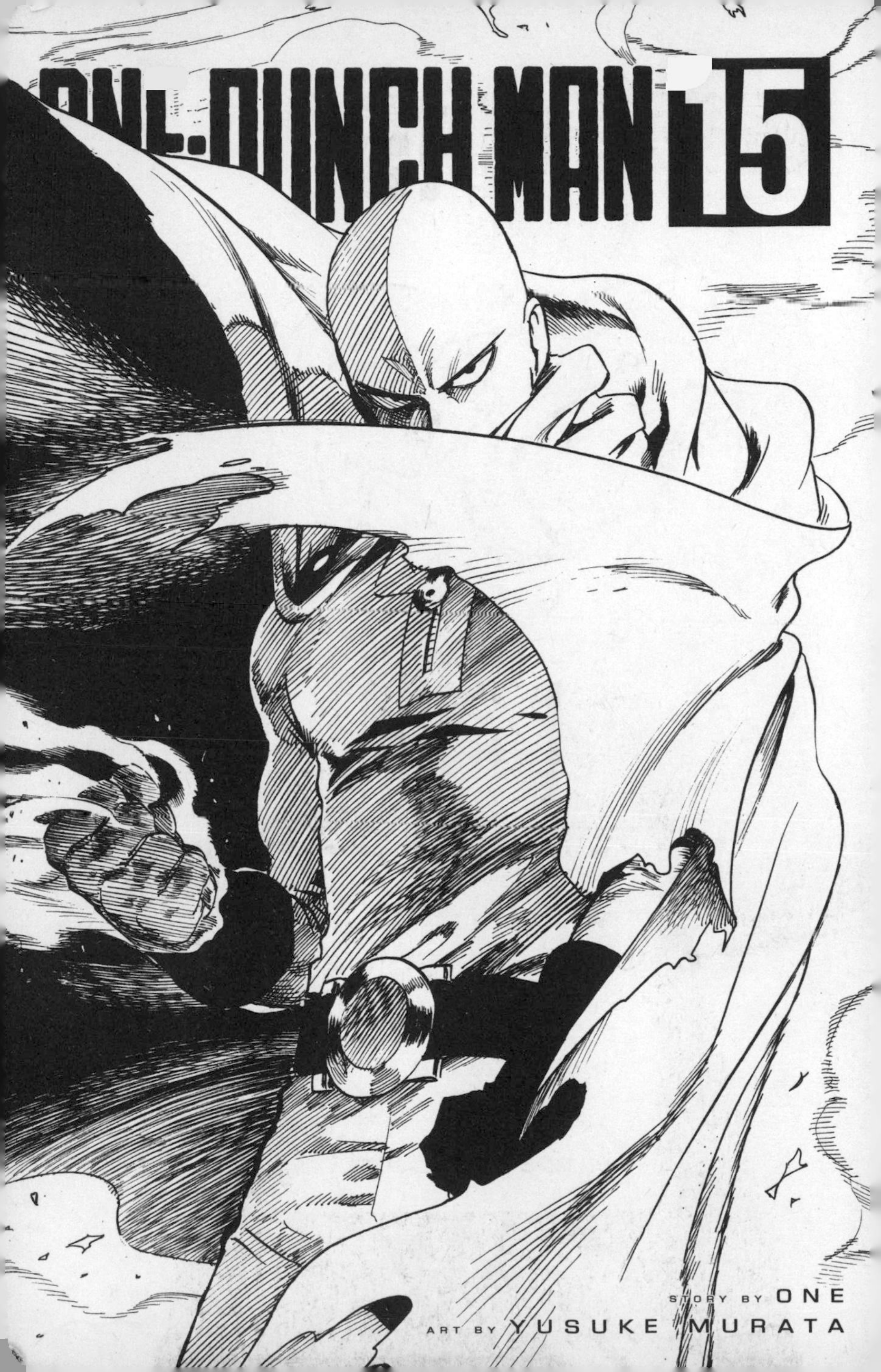
ONE-PUNCH MAN 15
STORY BY ONE
ART BY YUSUKE MURATA

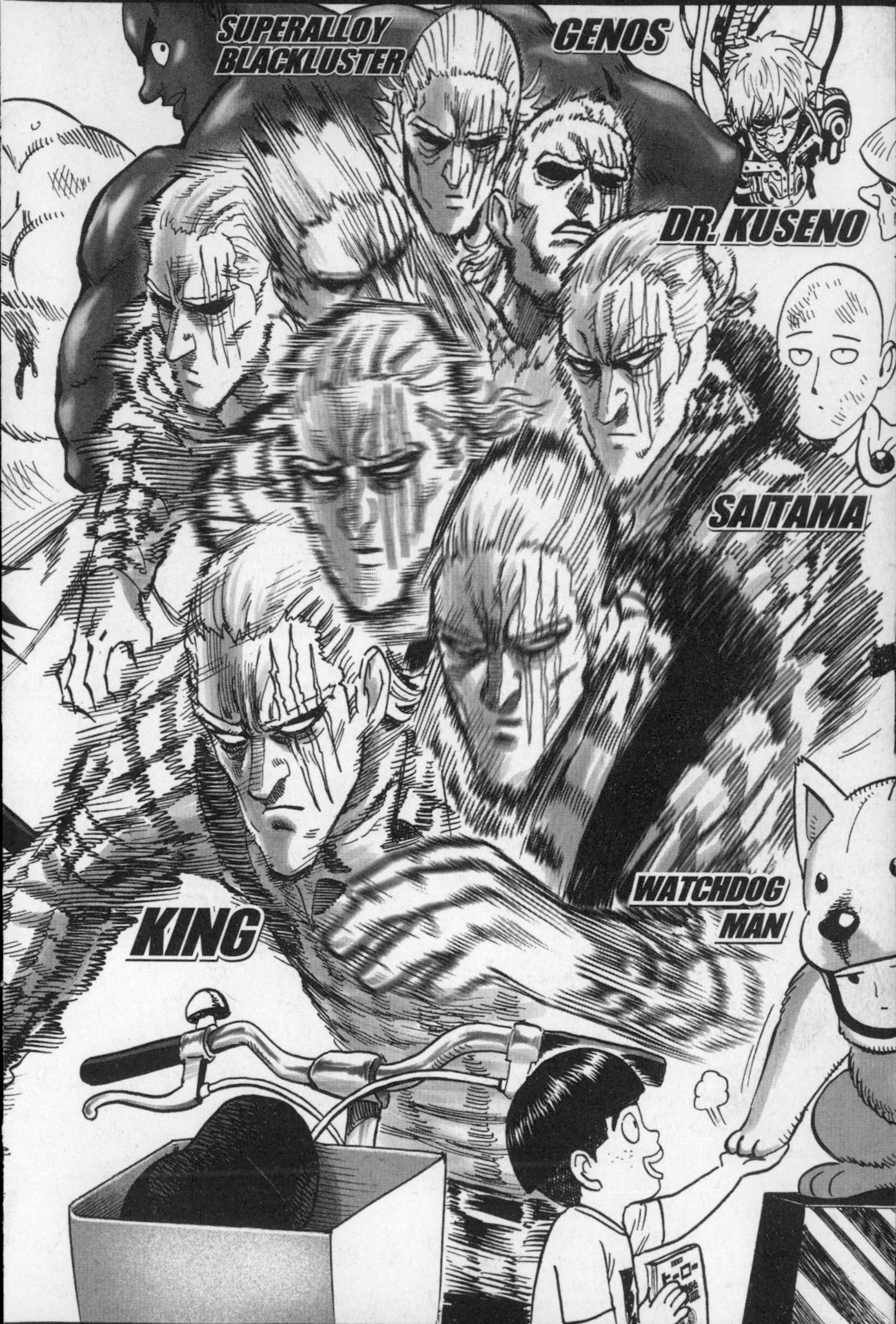
GENOS
SUPERALLOY BLACKLUSTER
DR. KUSENO
SAITAMA
WATCHDOG MAN
KING

CHARACTERS

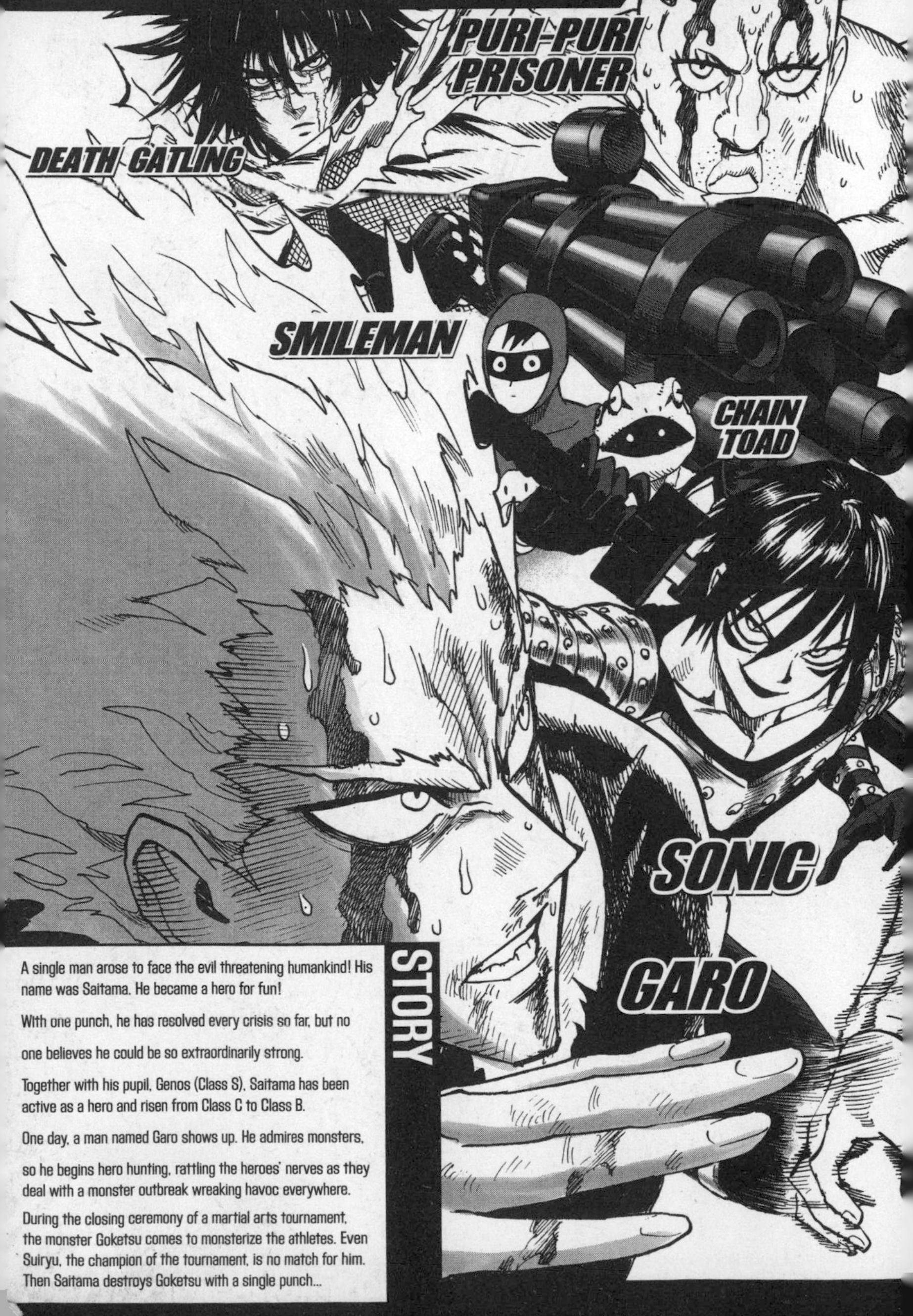
PURI-PURI PRISONER
DEATH GATLING
SMILEMAN
CHAIN TOAD
SONIC
GARO

STORY

A single man arose to face the evil threatening humankind! His name was Saitama. He became a hero for fun!

With one punch, he has resolved every crisis so far, but no one believes he could be so extraordinarily strong.

Together with his pupil, Genos (Class S), Saitama has been active as a hero and risen from Class C to Class B.

One day, a man named Garo shows up. He admires monsters, so he begins hero hunting, rattling the heroes' nerves as they deal with a monster outbreak wreaking havoc everywhere.

During the closing ceremony of a martial arts tournament, the monster Goketsu comes to monsterize the athletes. Even Suiryu, the champion of the tournament, is no match for him. Then Saitama destroys Goketsu with a single punch...

CONTENTS

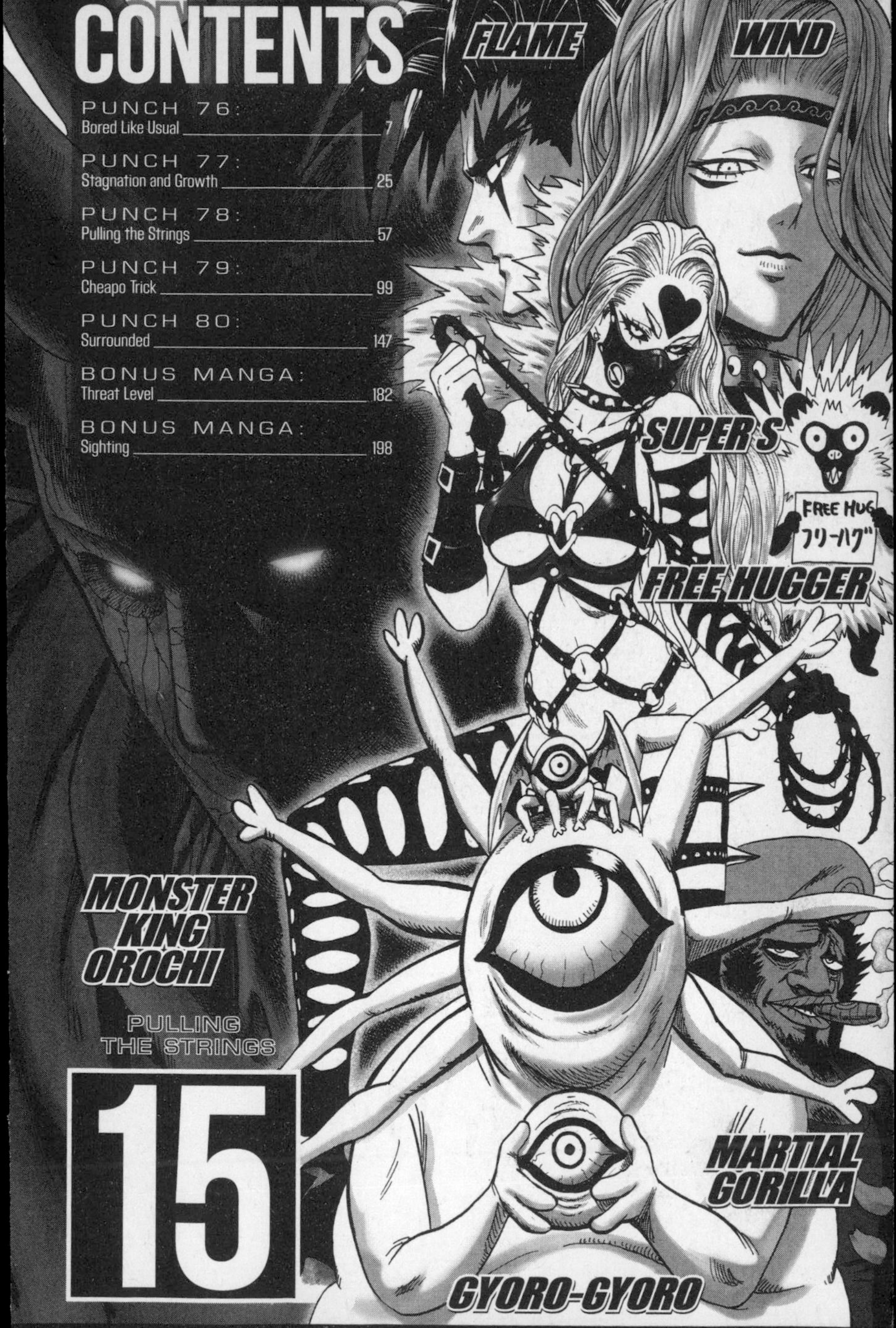

FLAME
WIND
SUPER S
FREE HUG
フリーハグ
FREE HUGGER
MONSTER KING OROCHI
MARTIAL GORILLA
GYORO-GYORO

PULLING THE STRINGS

15

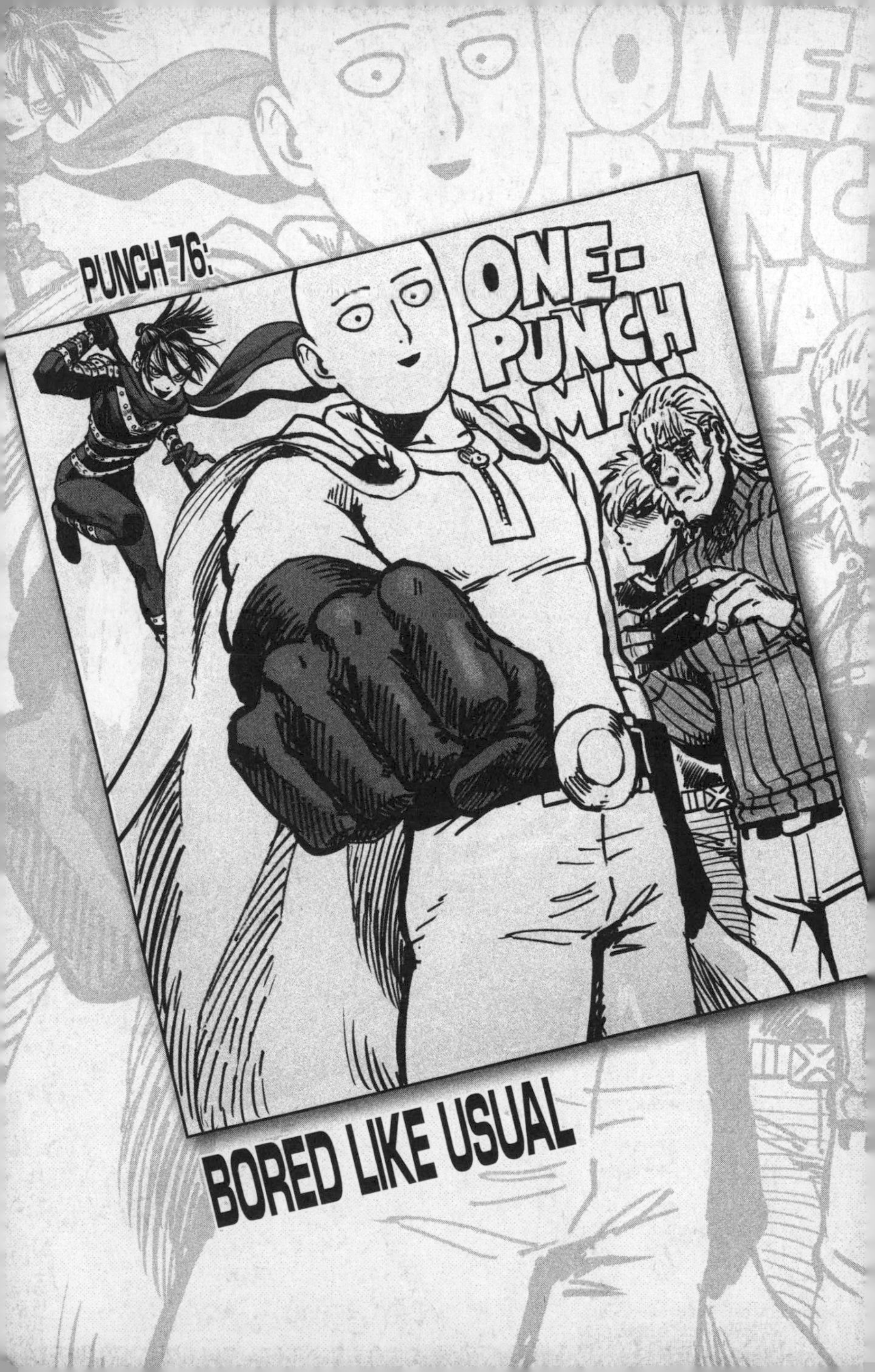
PUNCH 76:
ONE-PUNCH MAN
BORED LIKE USUAL

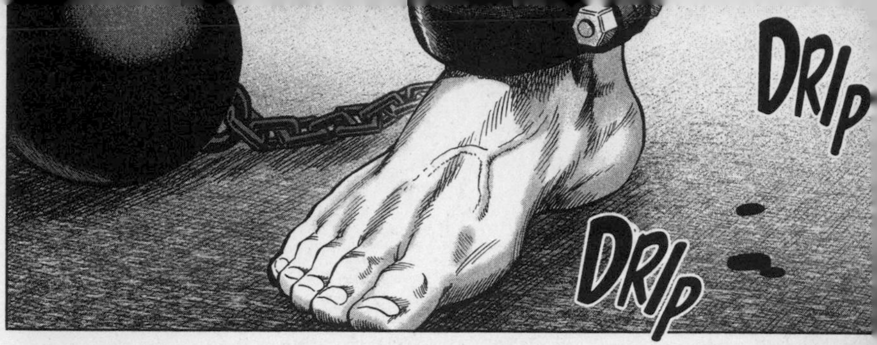
DRIP
DRIP

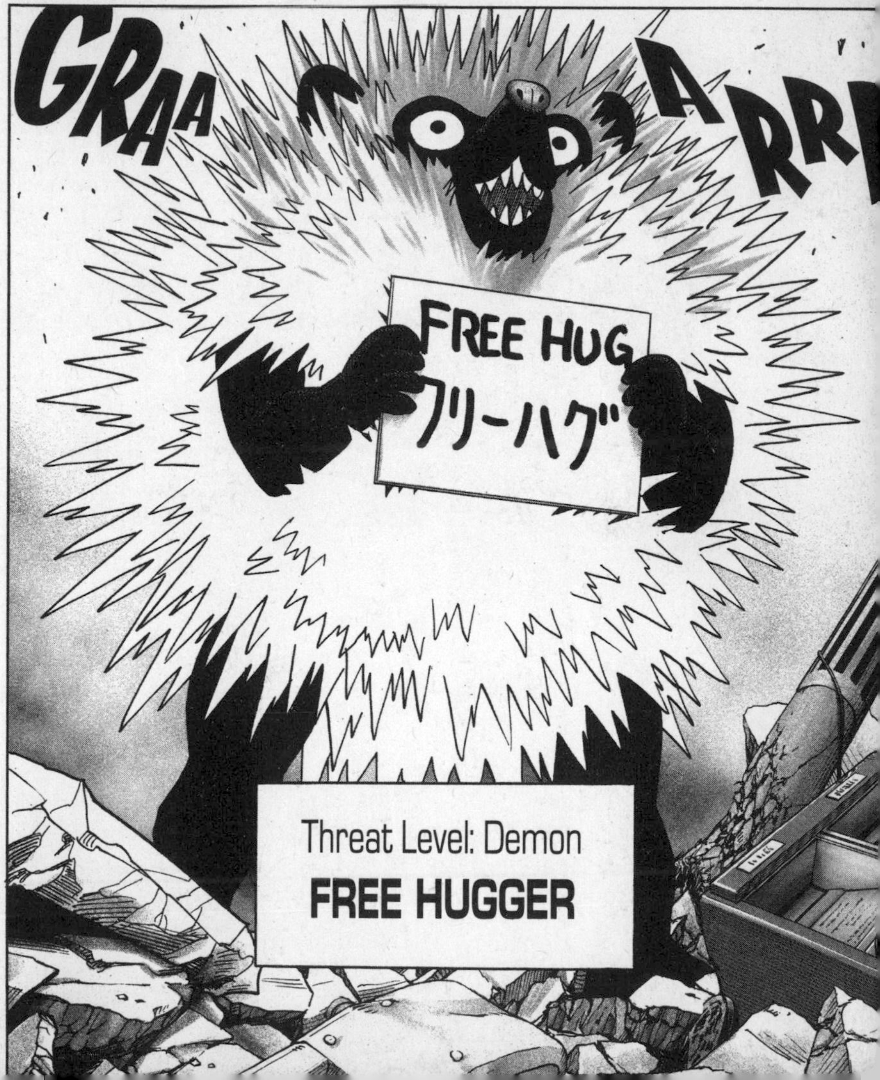
GRAAARRR
FREE HUG
フリーハグ
Threat Level: Demon
FREE HUGGER

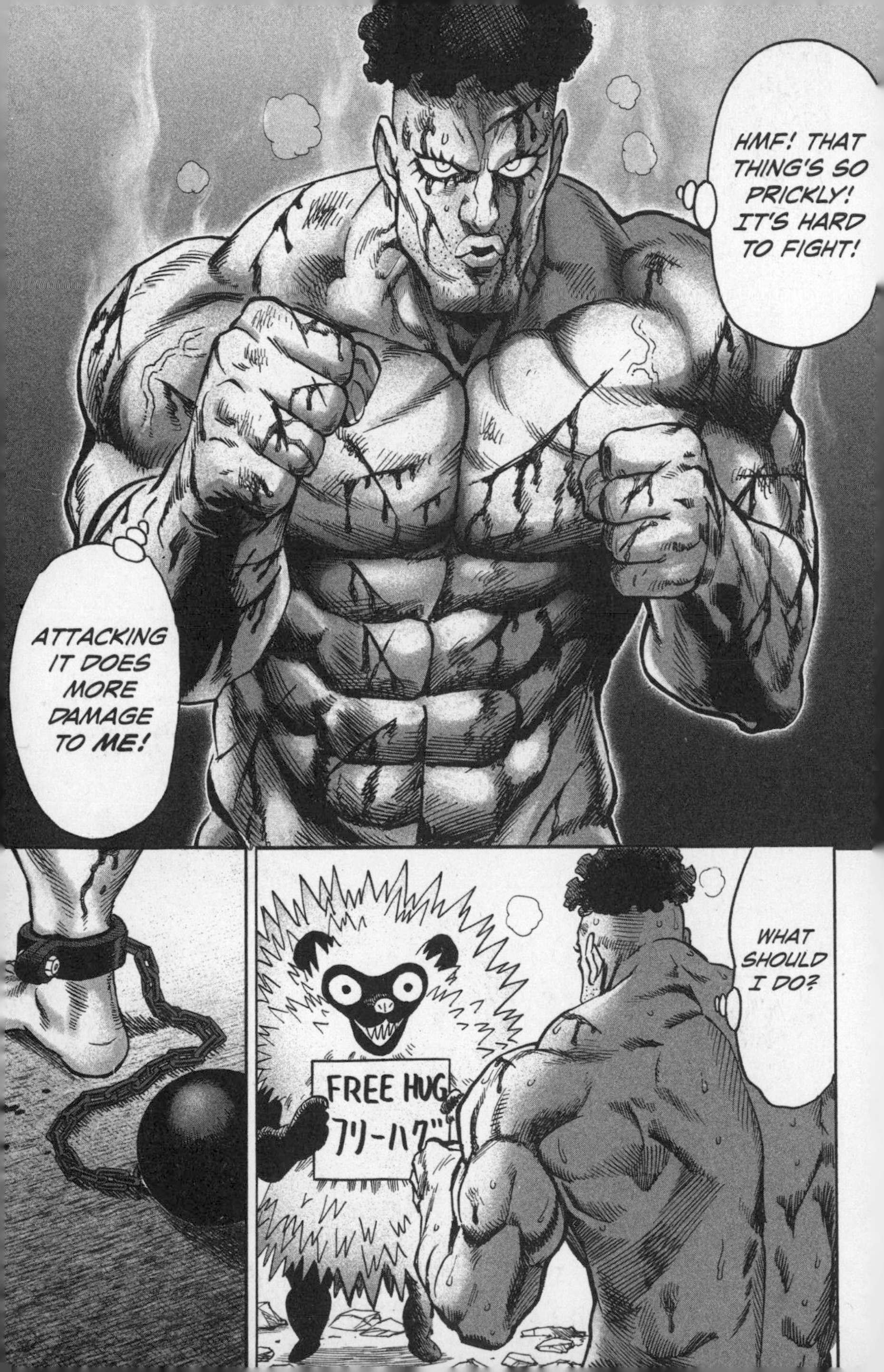
HMF! THAT THING'S SO PRICKLY! IT'S HARD TO FIGHT!
ATTACKING IT DOES MORE DAMAGE TO ME!
WHAT SHOULD I DO?
FREE HUG
フリーハグ

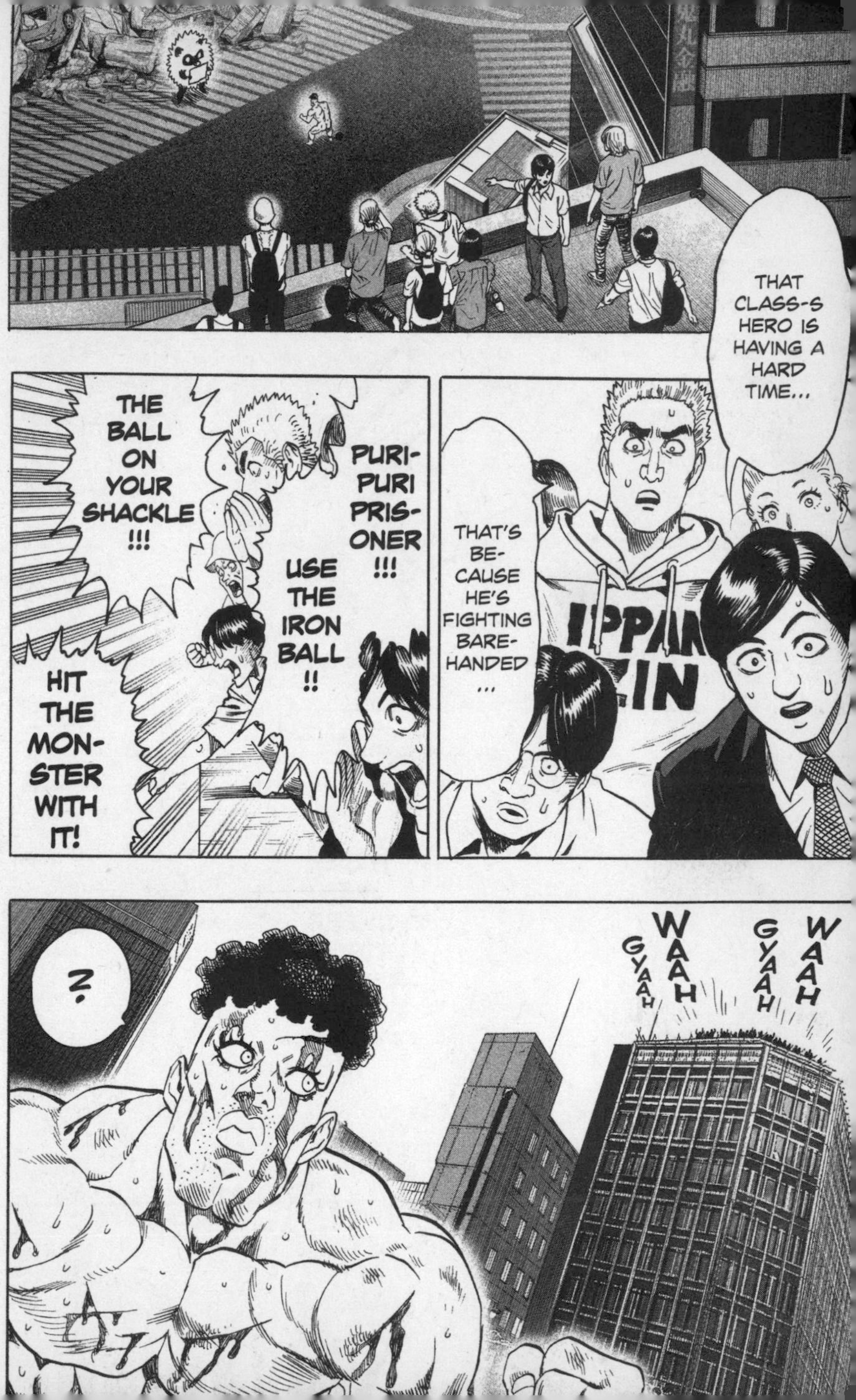
THAT CLASS-S HERO IS HAVING A HARD TIME...
THAT'S BE-CAUSE HE'S FIGHTING BARE-HANDED...
PURI-PURI PRIS-ONER!!!
USE THE IRON BALL!!
THE BALL ON YOUR SHACKLE!!!
HIT THE MON-STER WITH IT!
WAAH GYAAH
WAAH GYAAH
?

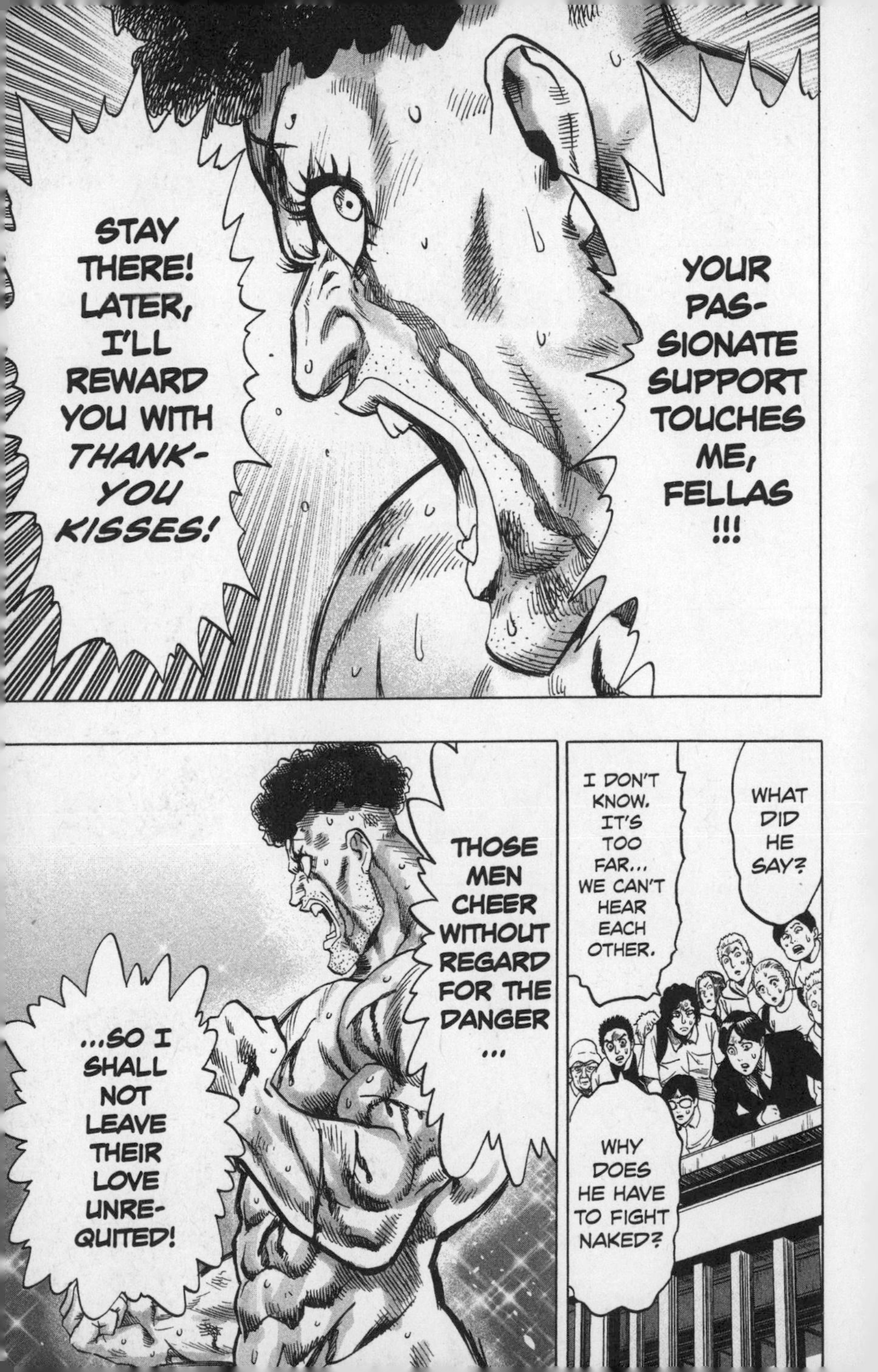
YOUR PASSIONATE SUPPORT TOUCHES ME, FELLAS!!!
STAY THERE! LATER, I'LL REWARD YOU WITH *THANK-YOU KISSES!*
WHAT DID HE SAY?
I DON'T KNOW. IT'S TOO FAR... WE CAN'T HEAR EACH OTHER.
WHY DOES HE HAVE TO FIGHT NAKED?
THOSE MEN CHEER WITHOUT REGARD FOR THE DANGER...
...SO I SHALL NOT LEAVE THEIR LOVE UNREQUITED!

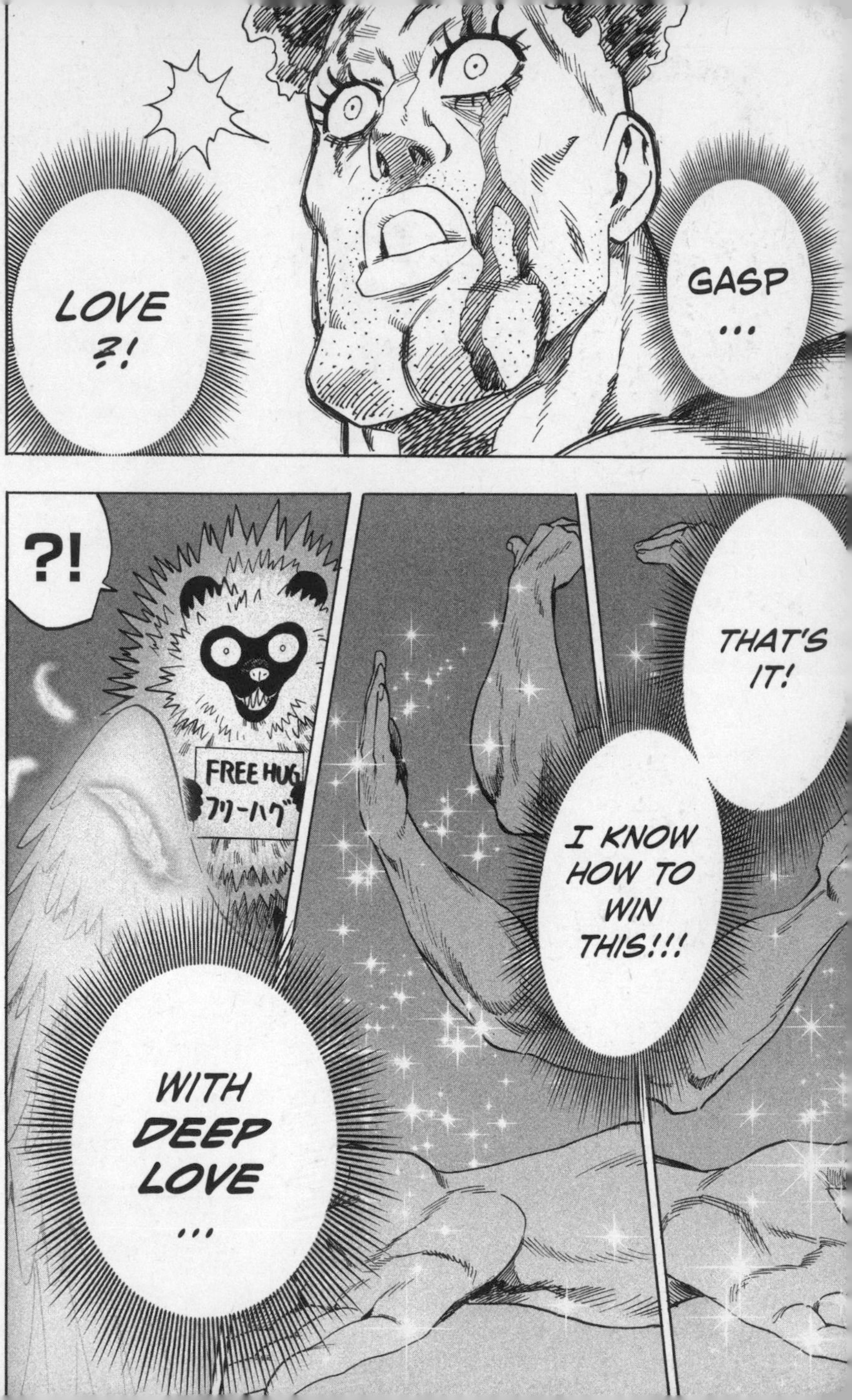
GASP ...
LOVE ?!
THAT'S IT!
I KNOW HOW TO WIN THIS!!!
?!
FREE HUG
フリーハグ
WITH DEEP LOVE ...

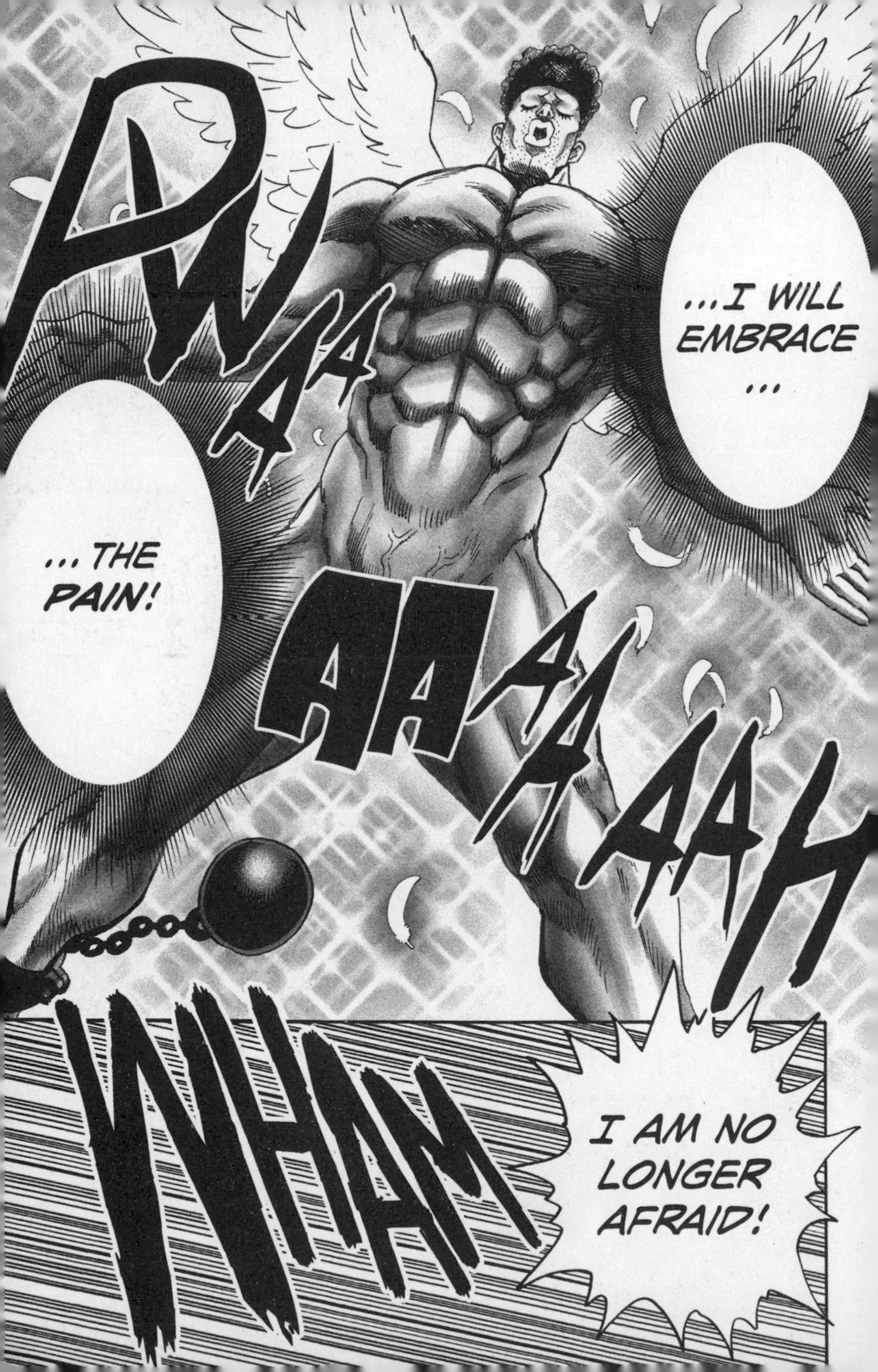
...I WILL EMBRACE ...
... THE PAIN!
PWAAAAAAAAH
I AM NO LONGER AFRAID!
WHAM

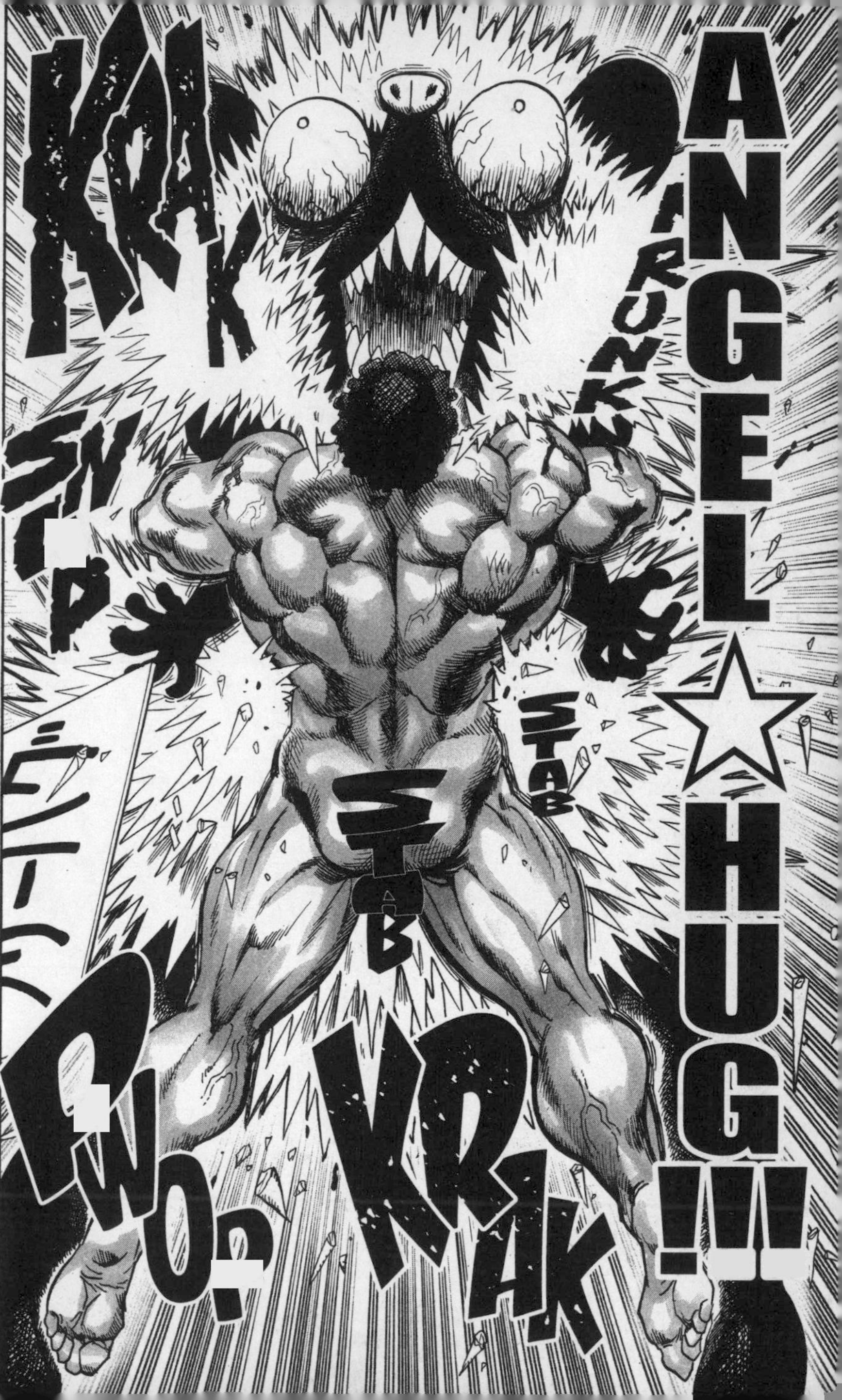
ANGEL☆HUG!!!
KRAK
STAB
STAB

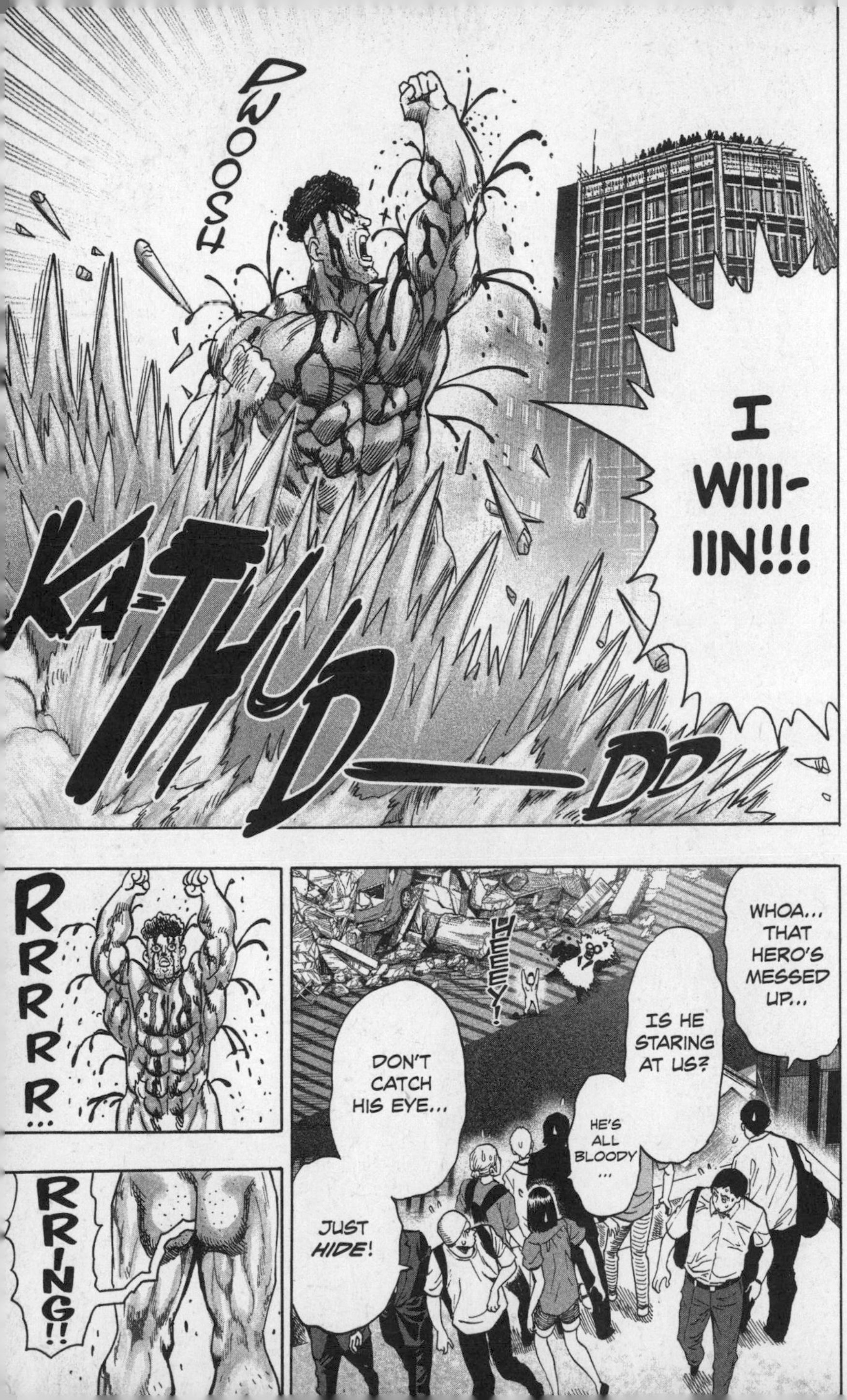
I WIII-IIN!!!
DWOOOSH
KA-THUD—DD
WHOA... THAT HERO'S MESSED UP...
HEEEY!
IS HE STARING AT US?
HE'S ALL BLOODY...
DON'T CATCH HIS EYE...
JUST HIDE!
RRRRR..
RRING!!

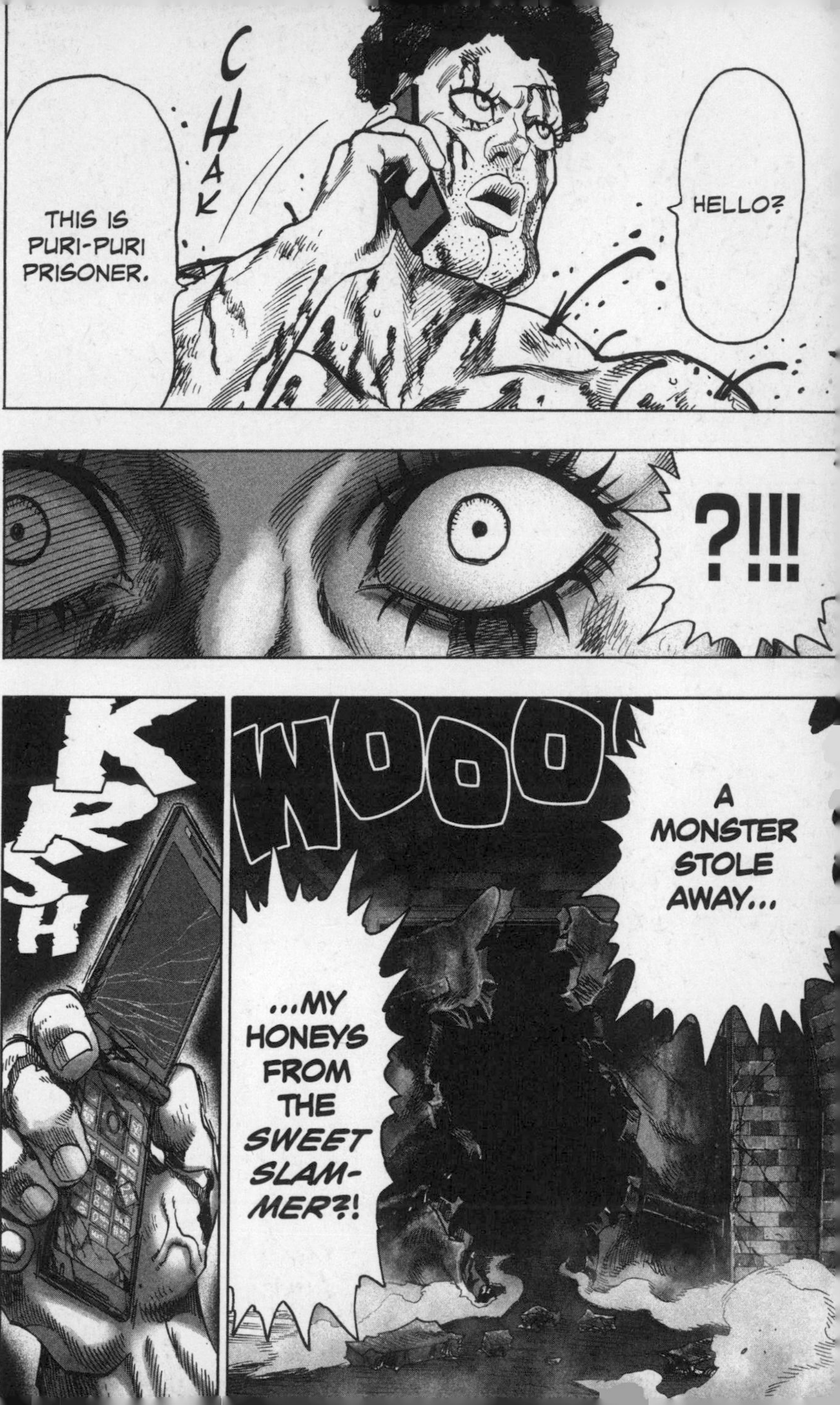

HELLO?
CHAK
THIS IS PURI-PURI PRISONER.
?!!!
WOOO
A MONSTER STOLE AWAY...
...MY HONEYS FROM THE SWEET SLAM-MER?!
KRSH

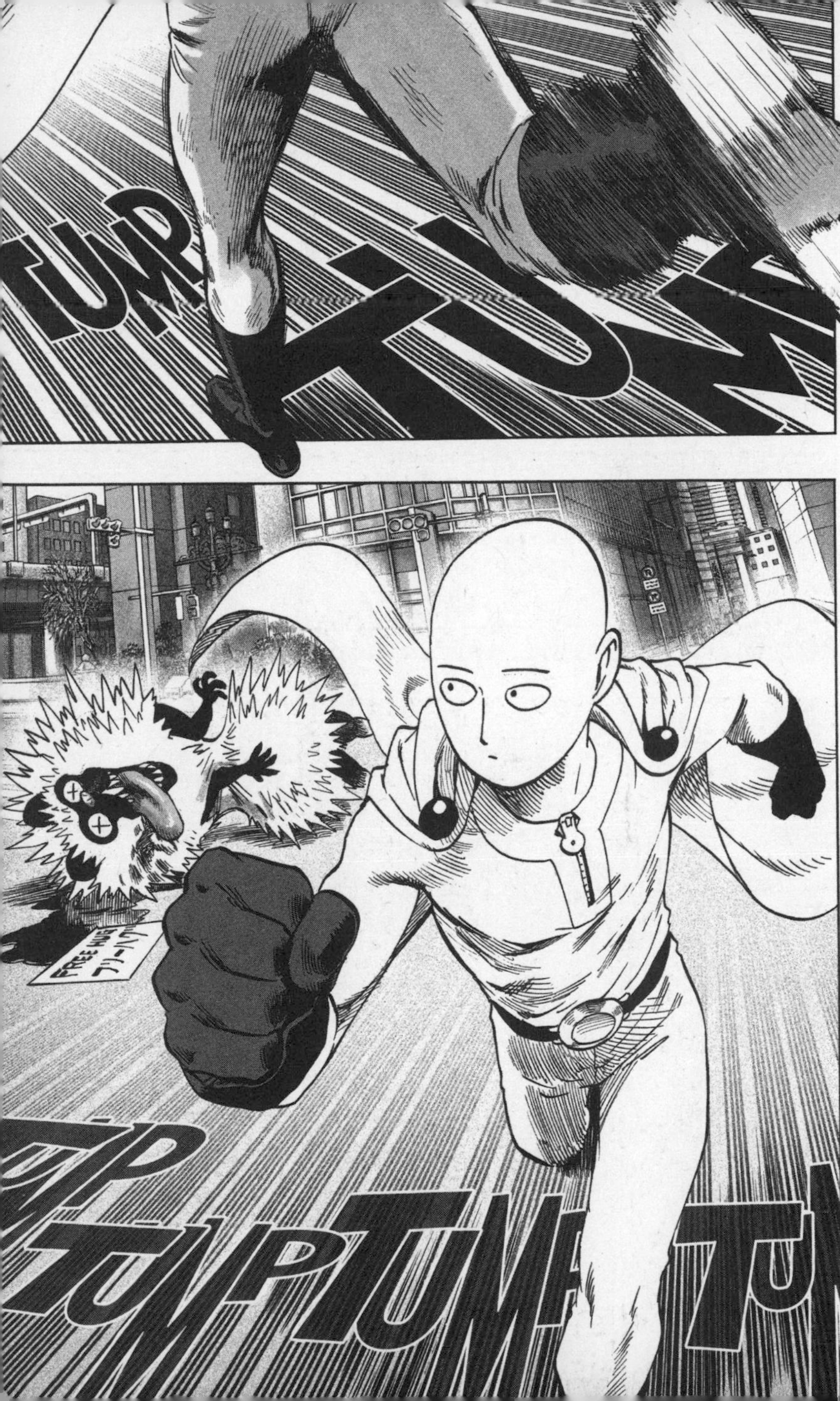
TUP
TUM
FREE HUG
フリーハグ
TUP
TUMP
TUM
TUM

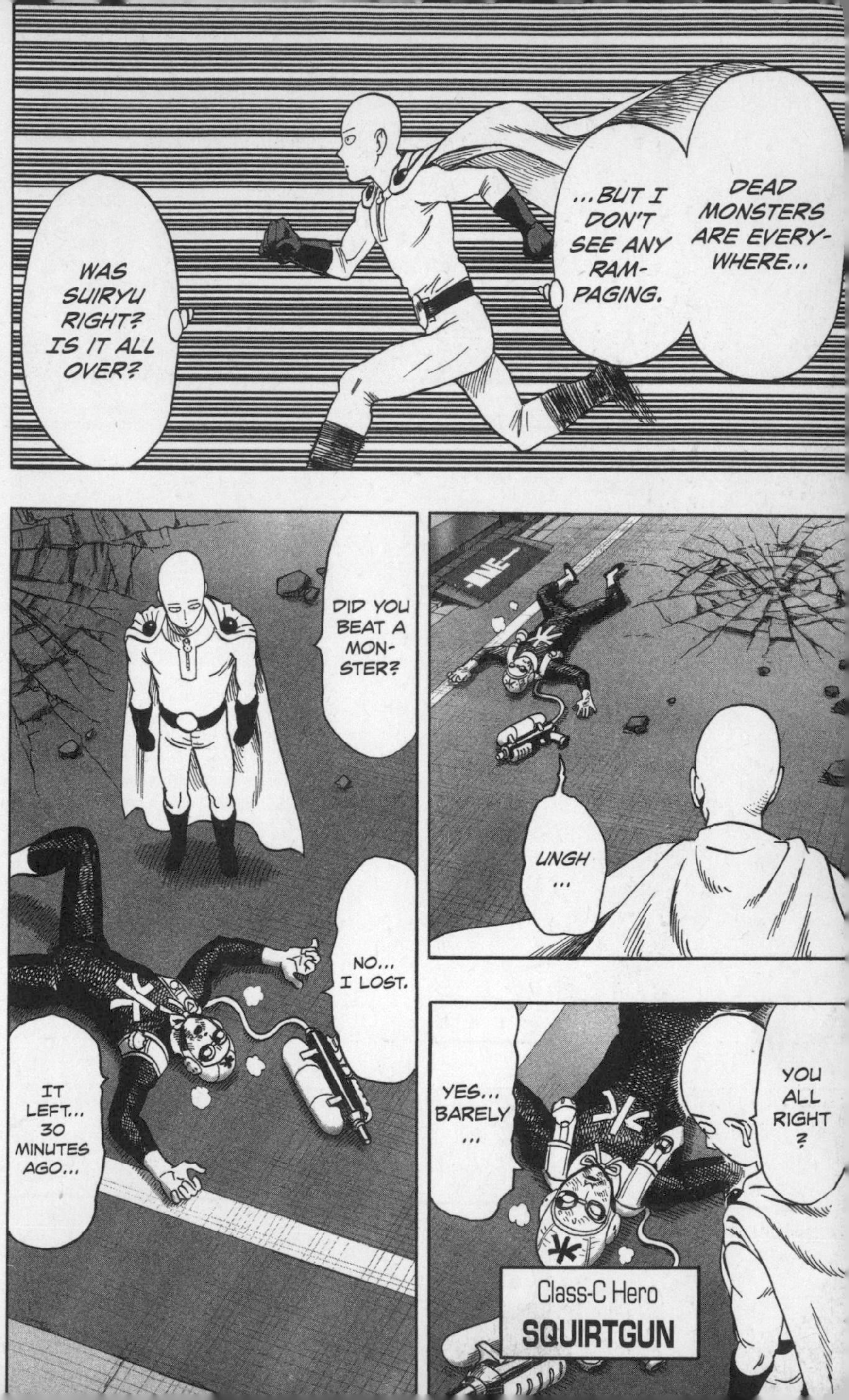
DEAD MONSTERS ARE EVERYWHERE...
...BUT I DON'T SEE ANY RAMPAGING.
WAS SUIRYU RIGHT? IS IT ALL OVER?
UNGH ...
YOU ALL RIGHT?
YES... BARELY ...
Class-C Hero
SQUIRTGUN
DID YOU BEAT A MONSTER?
NO... I LOST.
IT LEFT... 30 MINUTES AGO...

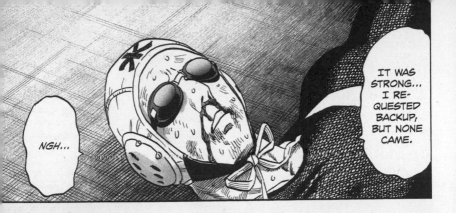

IT WAS STRONG... I RE-QUESTED BACKUP, BUT NONE CAME.
NGH...
THE MONSTERS APPEARED ALL AT ONCE AND DISAP-PEARED ALL AT ONCE...
...IN JUST ABOUT THREE OR FOUR HOURS.
...
BUT WHY?
DARN IT...
SCRITCH
SCRITCH
I MISSED THE WHOLE THING!
NOTHING EVER GOES MY WAY...

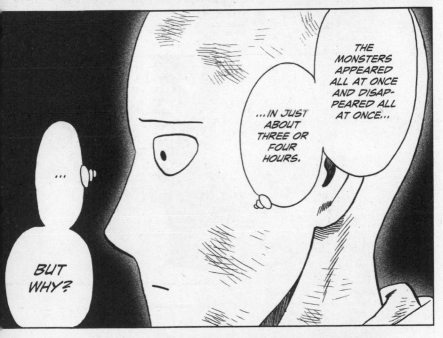

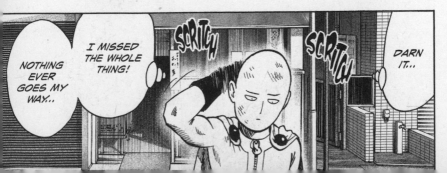

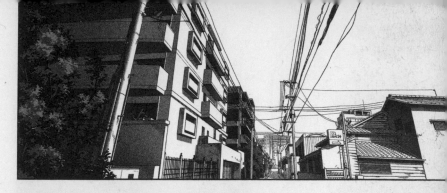

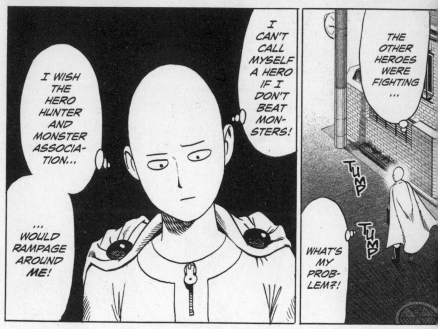

THE OTHER HEROES WERE FIGHTING ...
TUMP
TUMP
WHAT'S MY PROBLEM?!
I CAN'T CALL MYSELF A HERO IF I DON'T BEAT MONSTERS!
I WISH THE HERO HUNTER AND MONSTER ASSOCIATION...
... WOULD RAMPAGE AROUND ME!
HM? NO, WAIT...
I DON'T FIGHT MONSTERS BECAUSE I WANT TO CALL MYSELF A HERO.

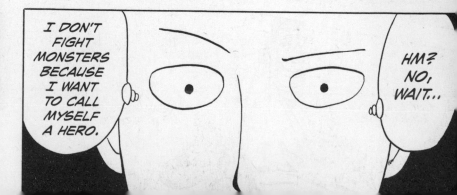

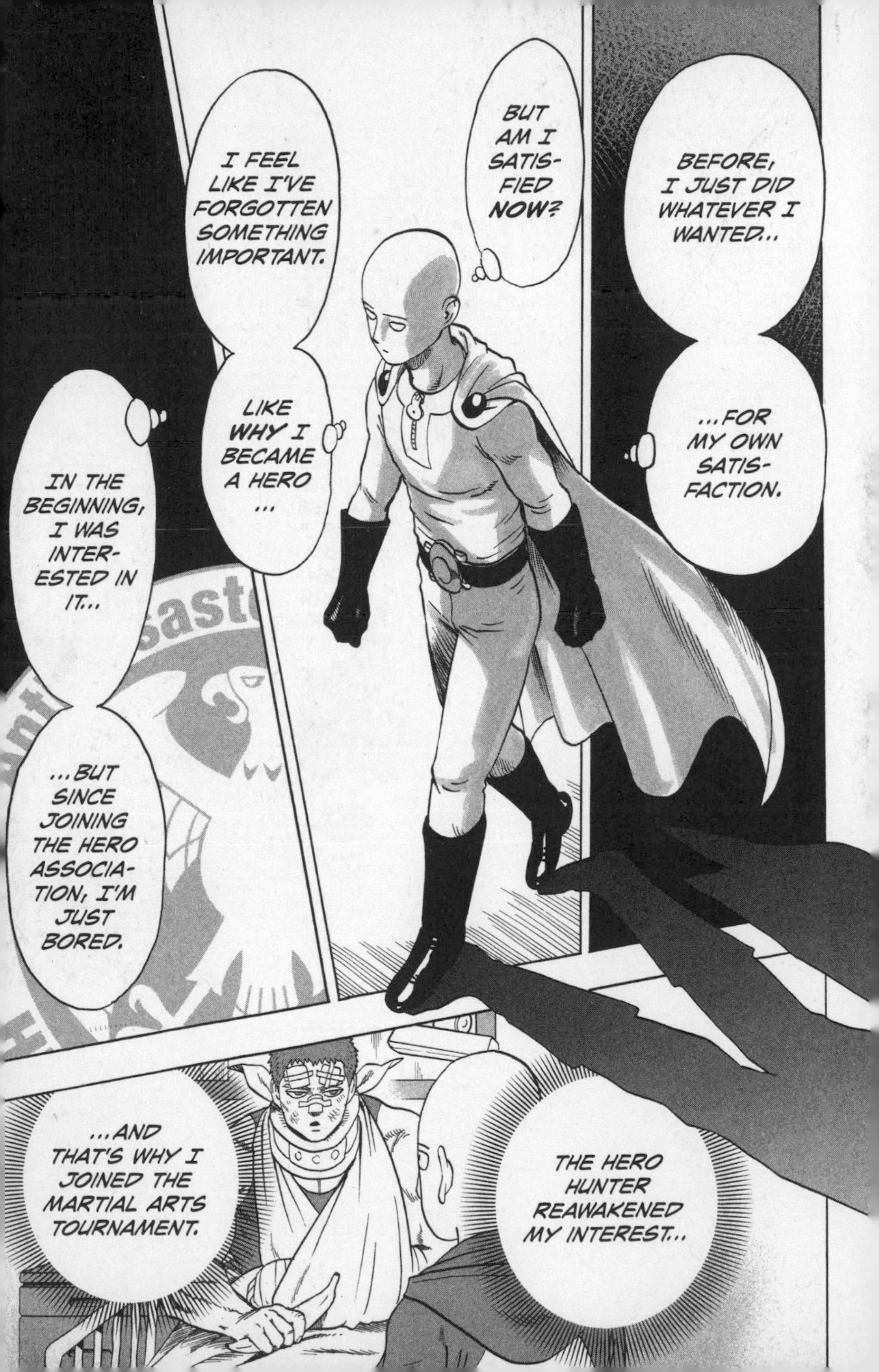
BEFORE, I JUST DID WHATEVER I WANTED...
...FOR MY OWN SATISFACTION.
BUT AM I SATISFIED **NOW?**
I FEEL LIKE I'VE FORGOTTEN SOMETHING IMPORTANT.
LIKE **WHY** I BECAME A HERO...
IN THE BEGINNING, I WAS INTERESTED IN IT...
...BUT SINCE JOINING THE HERO ASSOCIATION, I'M JUST BORED.
THE HERO HUNTER REAWAKENED MY INTEREST...
...AND THAT'S WHY I JOINED THE MARTIAL ARTS TOURNAMENT.

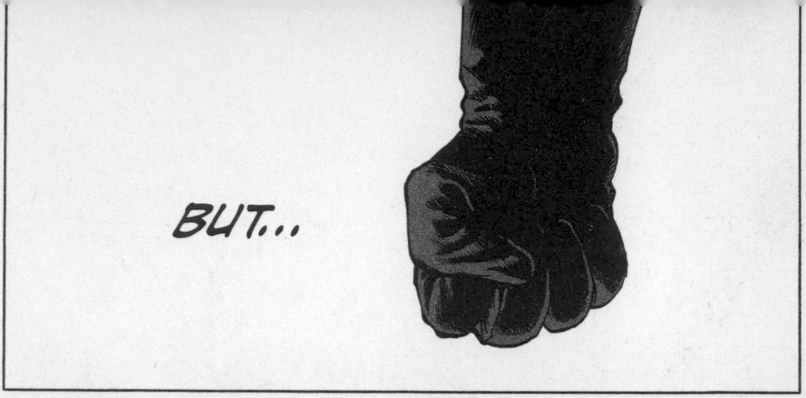
BUT...

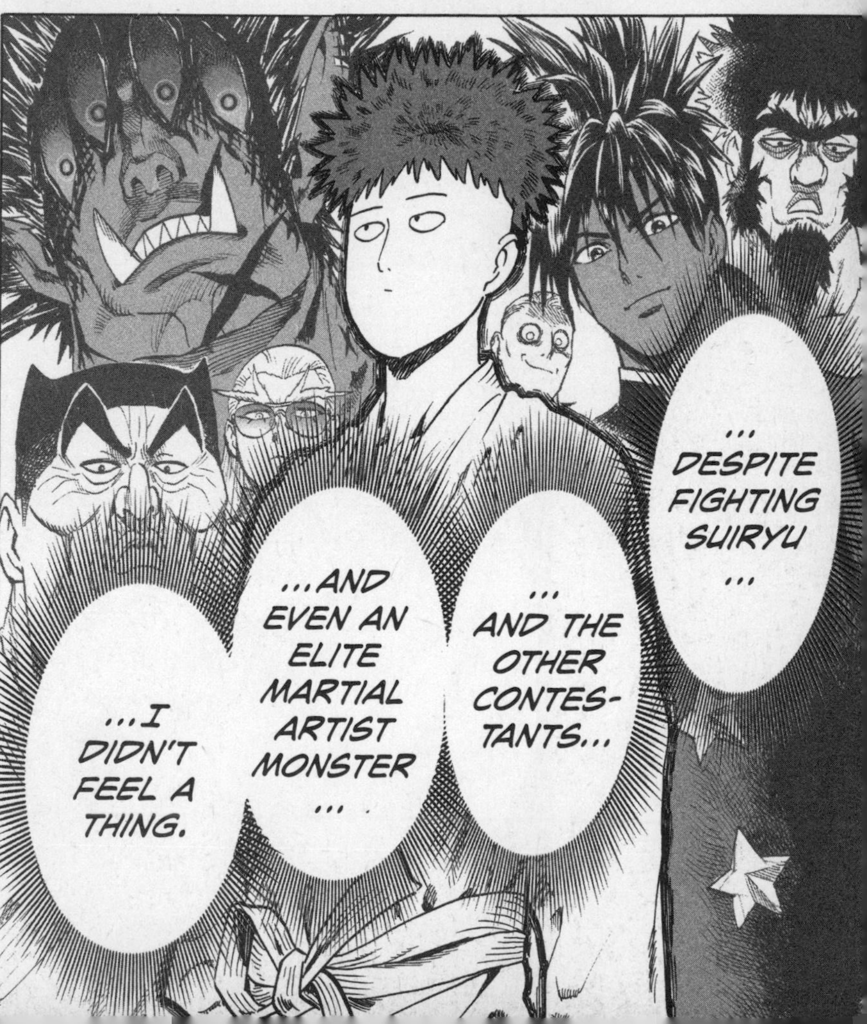
...DESPITE FIGHTING SUIRYU ...
... AND THE OTHER CONTES-TANTS...
...AND EVEN AN ELITE MARTIAL ARTIST MONSTER ...
...I DIDN'T FEEL A THING.

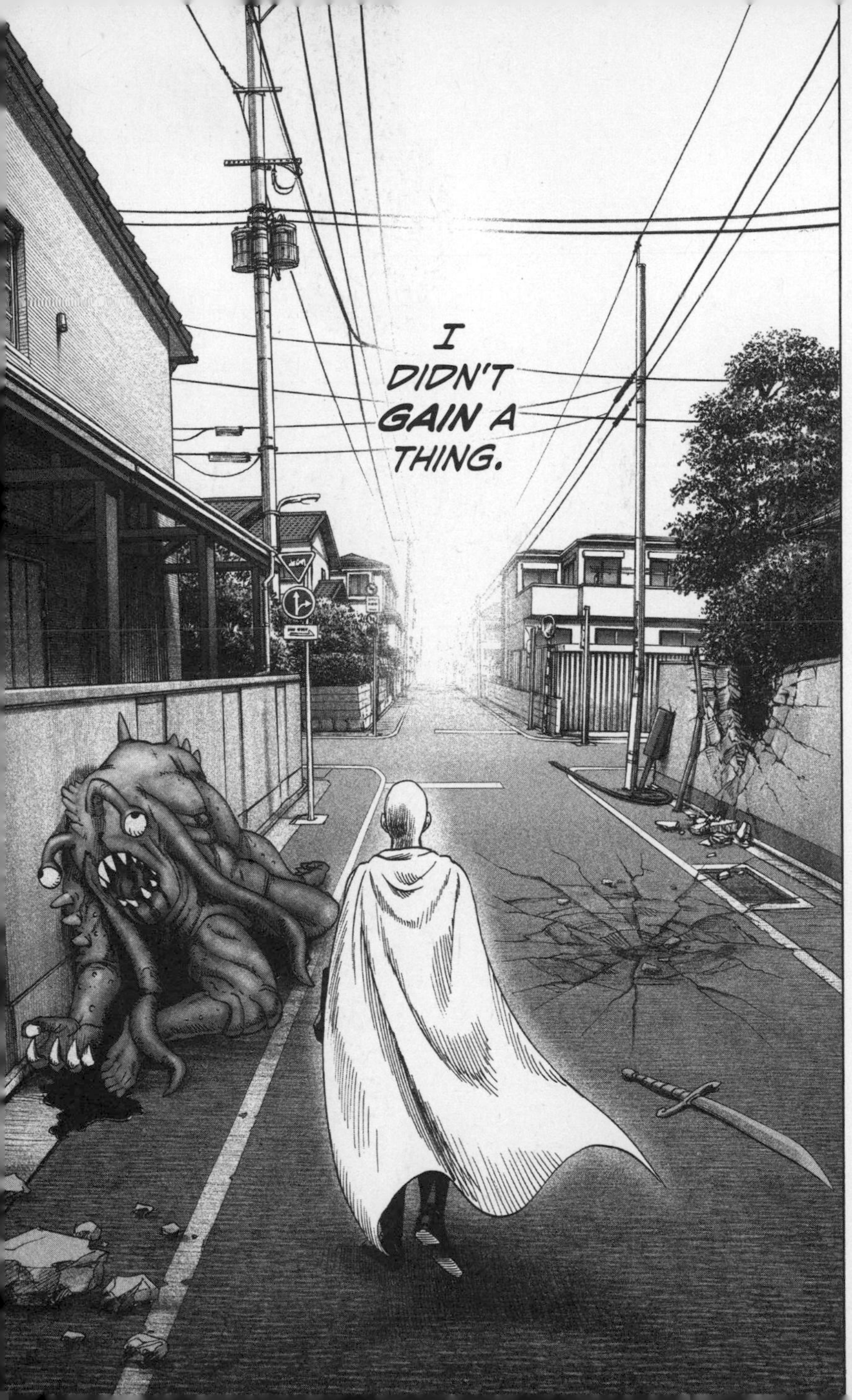
I DIDN'T GAIN A THING.

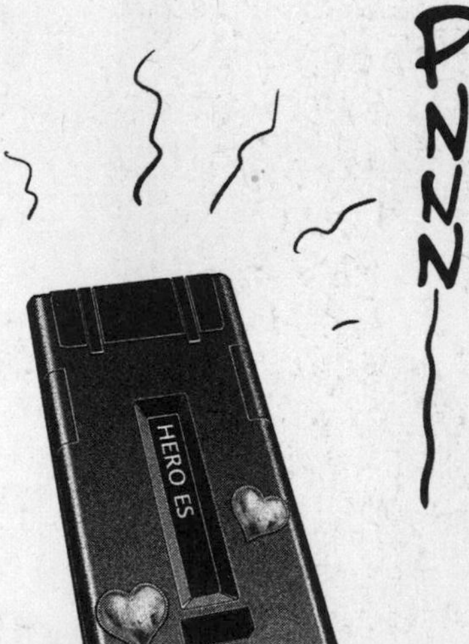
PNNN—
HERO ES

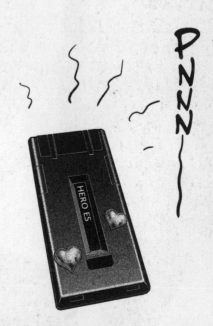

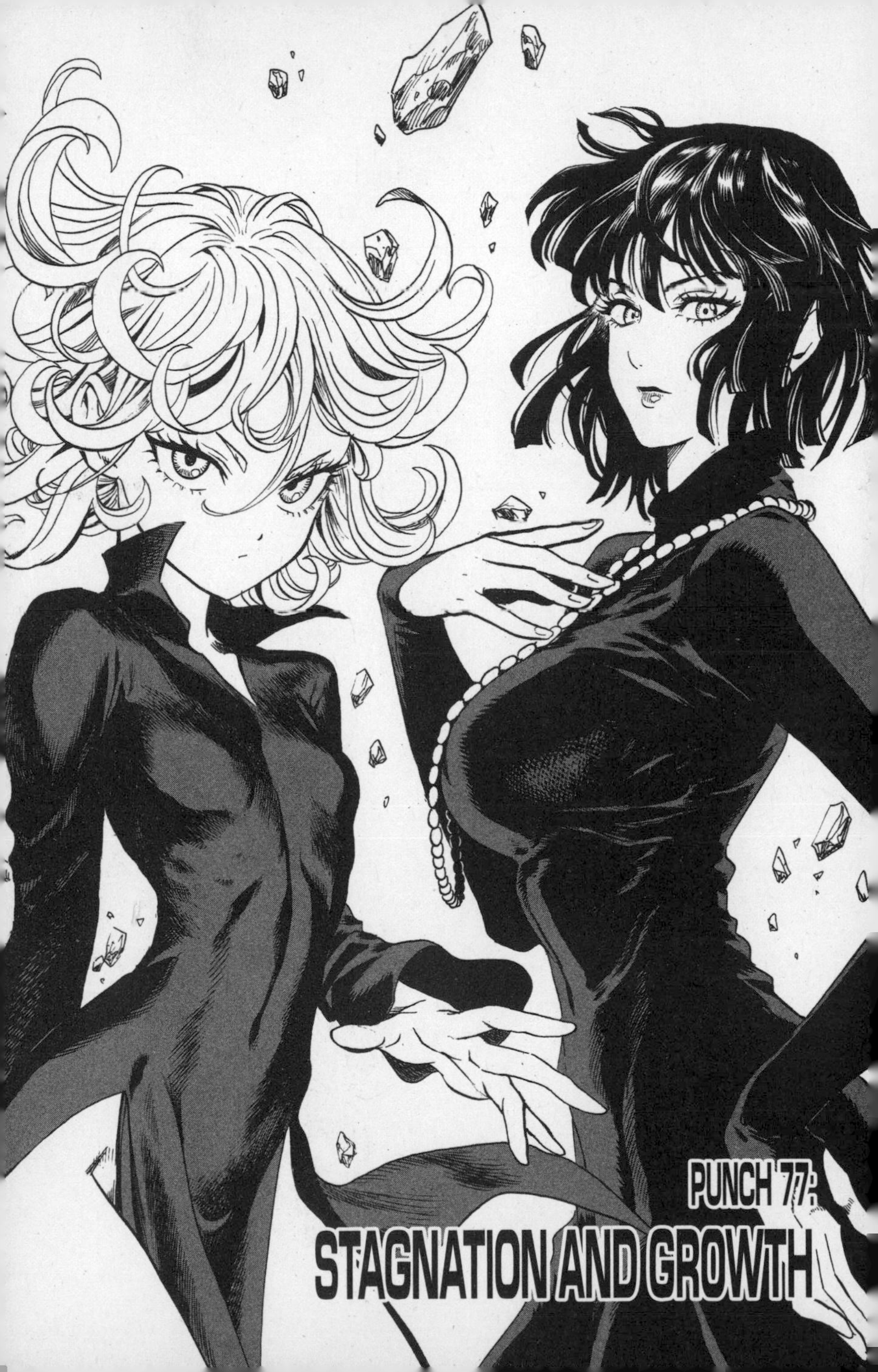
PUNCH 77:
STAGNATION AND GROWTH

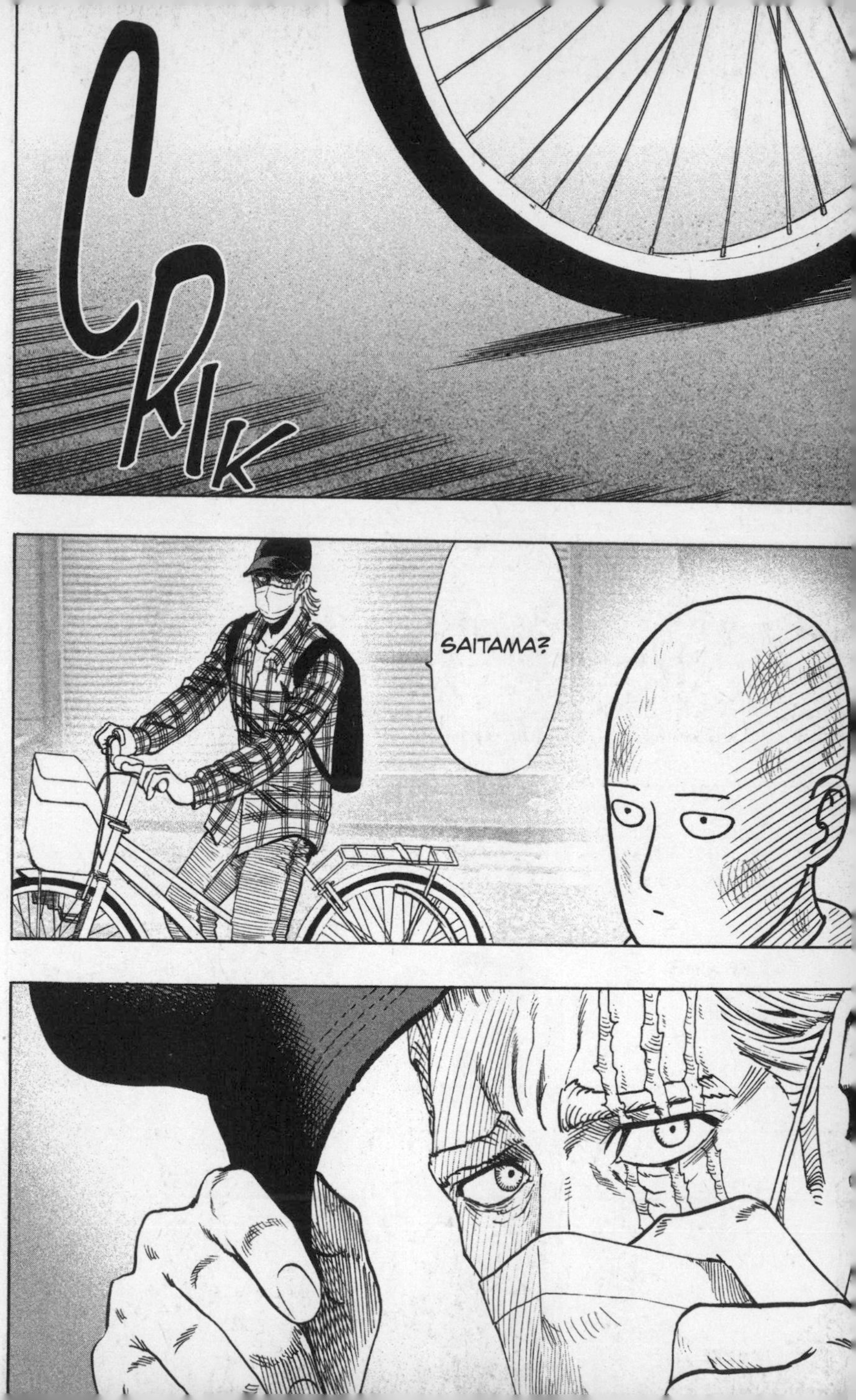
CRIK
SAITAMA?

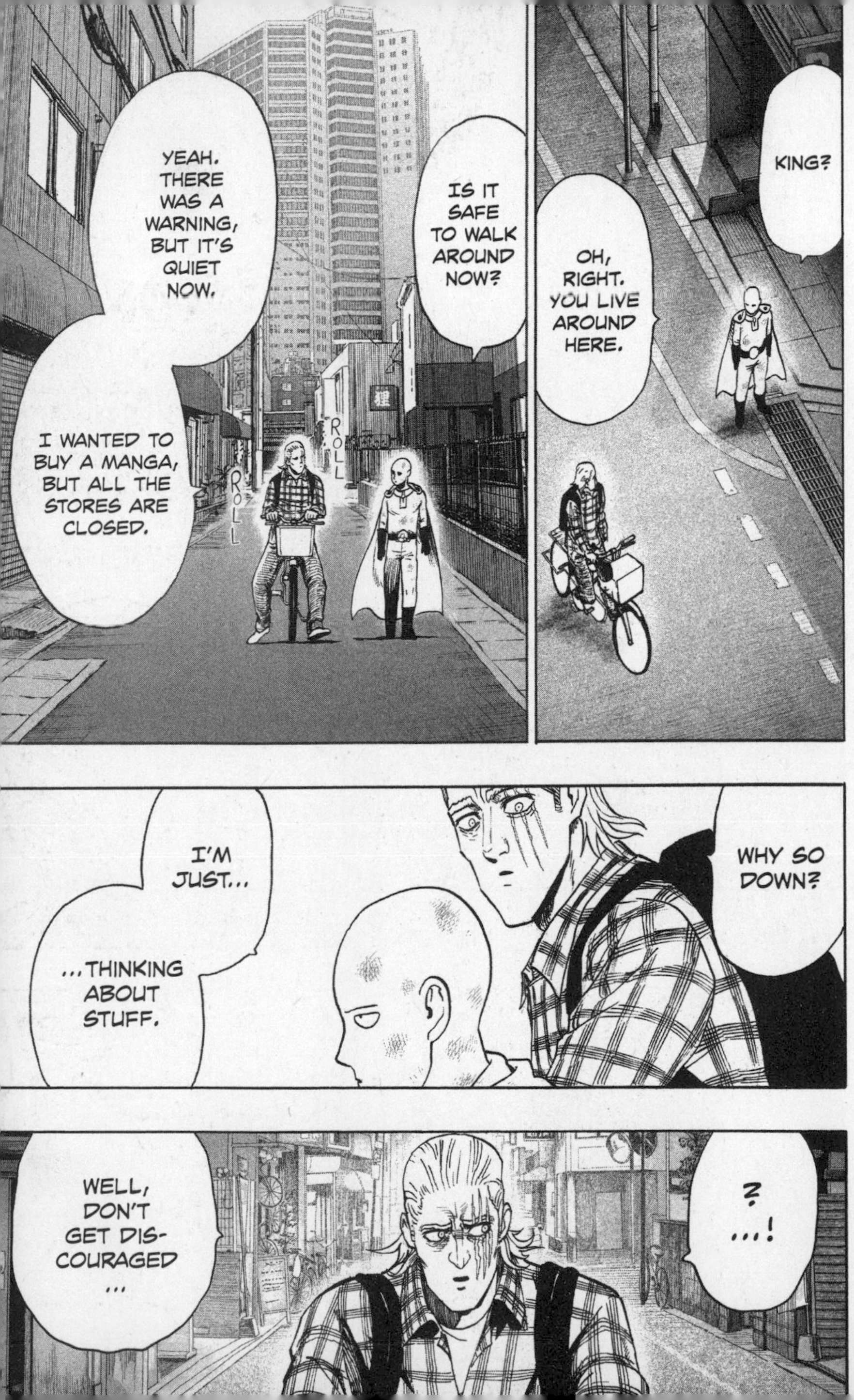
KING?
OH, RIGHT. YOU LIVE AROUND HERE.
IS IT SAFE TO WALK AROUND NOW?
ROLL
ROLL
YEAH. THERE WAS A WARNING, BUT IT'S QUIET NOW.
I WANTED TO BUY A MANGA, BUT ALL THE STORES ARE CLOSED.
WHY SO DOWN?
I'M JUST...
...THINKING ABOUT STUFF.
?
...!
WELL, DON'T GET DIS-COURAGED ...

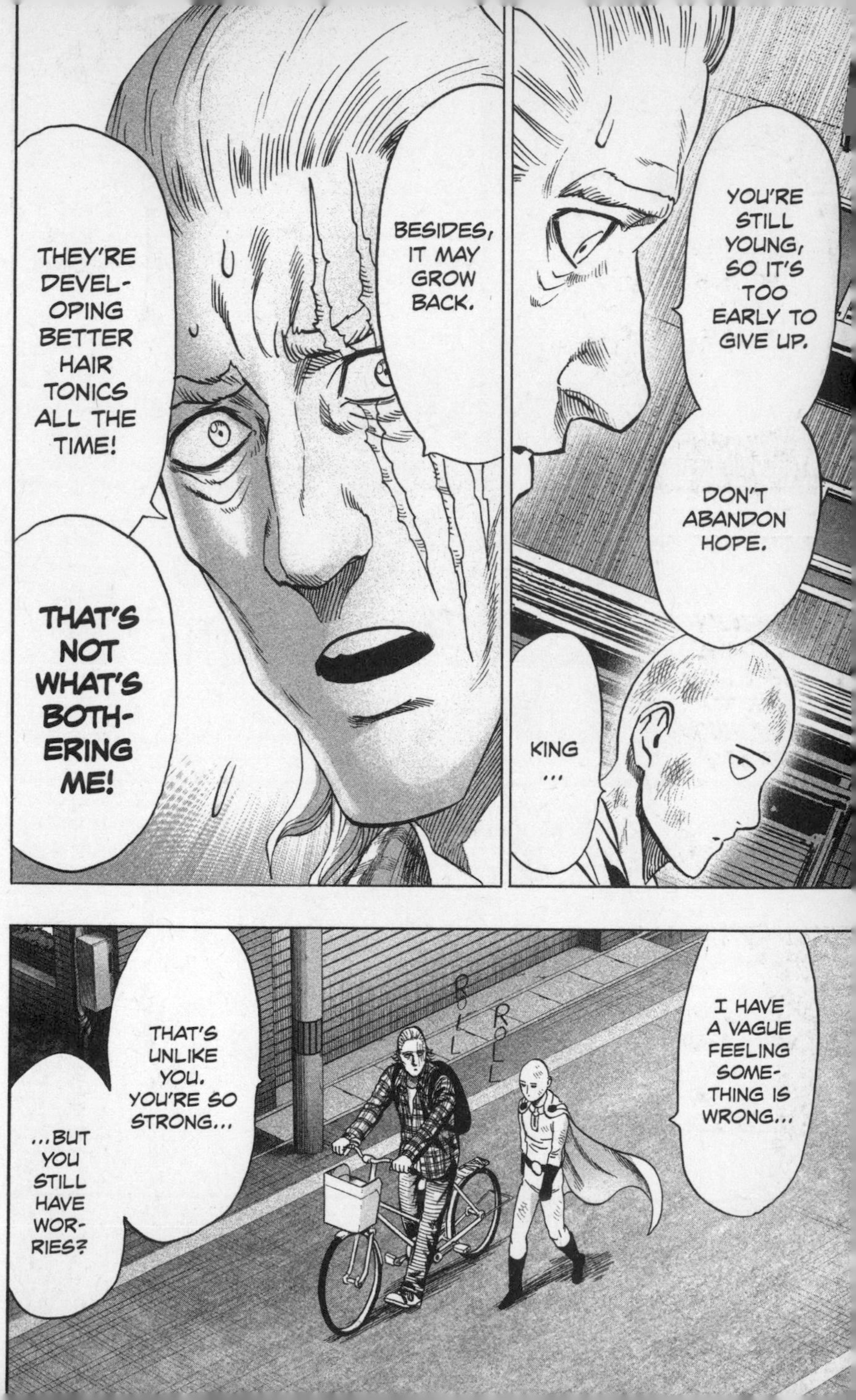
YOU'RE STILL YOUNG, SO IT'S TOO EARLY TO GIVE UP.
DON'T ABANDON HOPE.
KING ...
BESIDES, IT MAY GROW BACK.
THEY'RE DEVEL-OPING BETTER HAIR TONICS ALL THE TIME!
THAT'S NOT WHAT'S BOTH-ERING ME!
I HAVE A VAGUE FEELING SOME-THING IS WRONG...
ROLL
ROLL
THAT'S UNLIKE YOU. YOU'RE SO STRONG...
...BUT YOU STILL HAVE WOR-RIES?

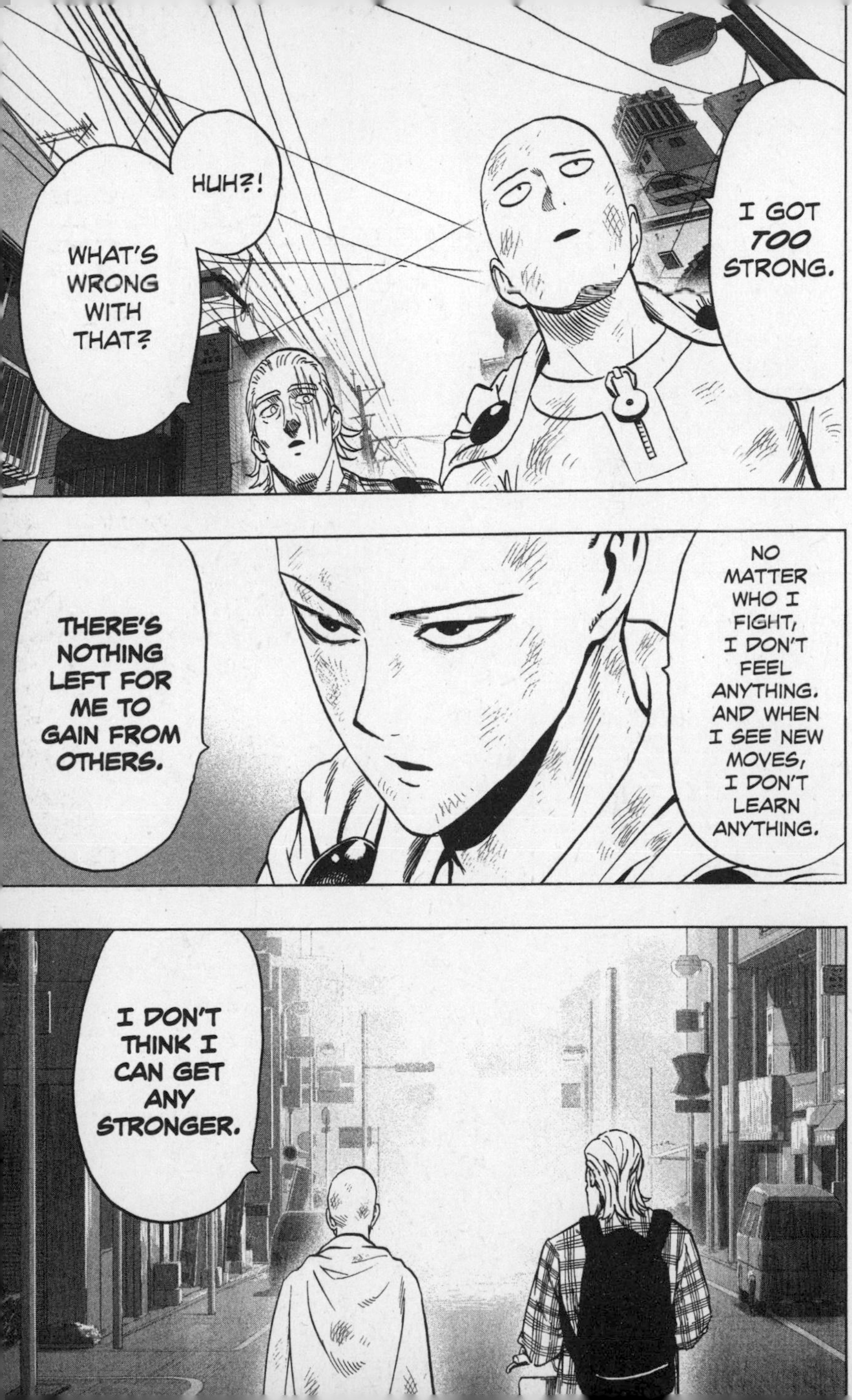
I GOT *TOO* STRONG.
HUH?! WHAT'S WRONG WITH THAT?
NO MATTER WHO I FIGHT, I DON'T FEEL ANYTHING. AND WHEN I SEE NEW MOVES, I DON'T LEARN ANYTHING.
THERE'S NOTHING LEFT FOR ME TO GAIN FROM OTHERS.
I DON'T THINK I CAN GET ANY STRONGER.

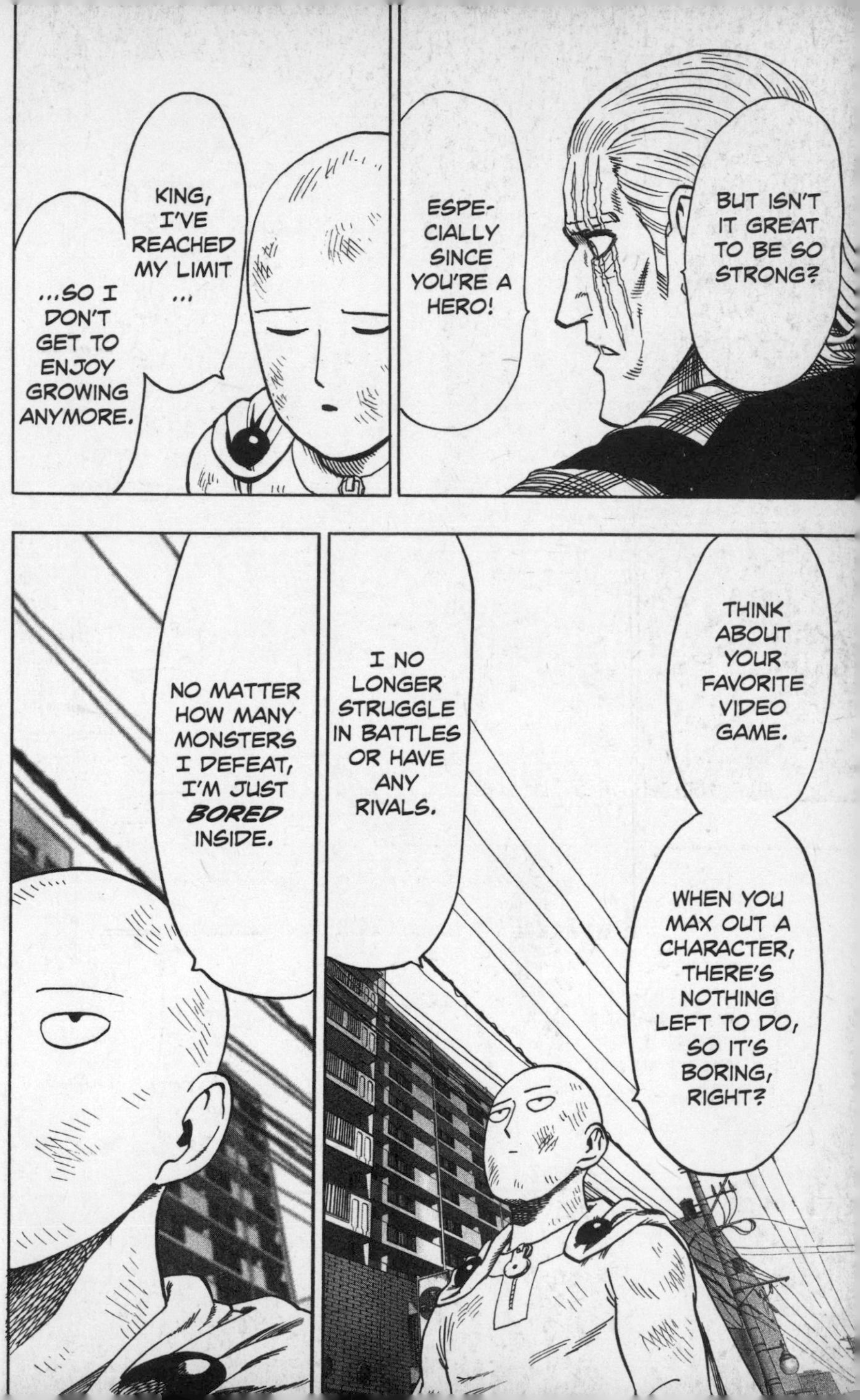
BUT ISN'T IT GREAT TO BE SO STRONG?
ESPE-CIALLY SINCE YOU'RE A HERO!
KING, I'VE REACHED MY LIMIT ...
...SO I DON'T GET TO ENJOY GROWING ANYMORE.
THINK ABOUT YOUR FAVORITE VIDEO GAME.
WHEN YOU MAX OUT A CHARACTER, THERE'S NOTHING LEFT TO DO, SO IT'S BORING, RIGHT?
I NO LONGER STRUGGLE IN BATTLES OR HAVE ANY RIVALS.
NO MATTER HOW MANY MONSTERS I DEFEAT, I'M JUST *BORED* INSIDE.

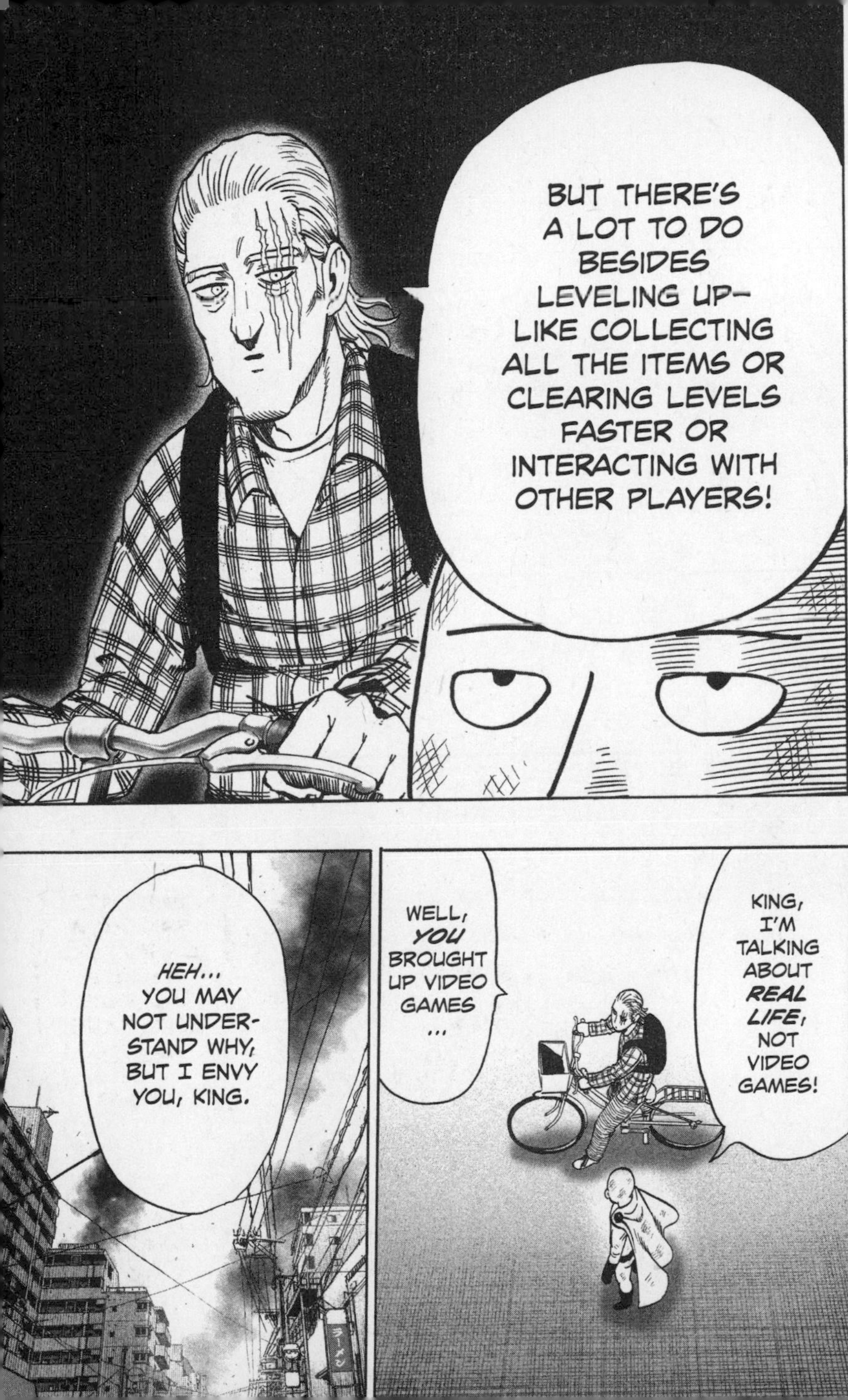
BUT THERE'S A LOT TO DO BESIDES LEVELING UP— LIKE COLLECTING ALL THE ITEMS OR CLEARING LEVELS FASTER OR INTERACTING WITH OTHER PLAYERS!
KING, I'M TALKING ABOUT *REAL LIFE*, NOT VIDEO GAMES!
WELL, *YOU* BROUGHT UP VIDEO GAMES ...
HEH... YOU MAY NOT UNDER-STAND WHY, BUT I ENVY YOU, KING.

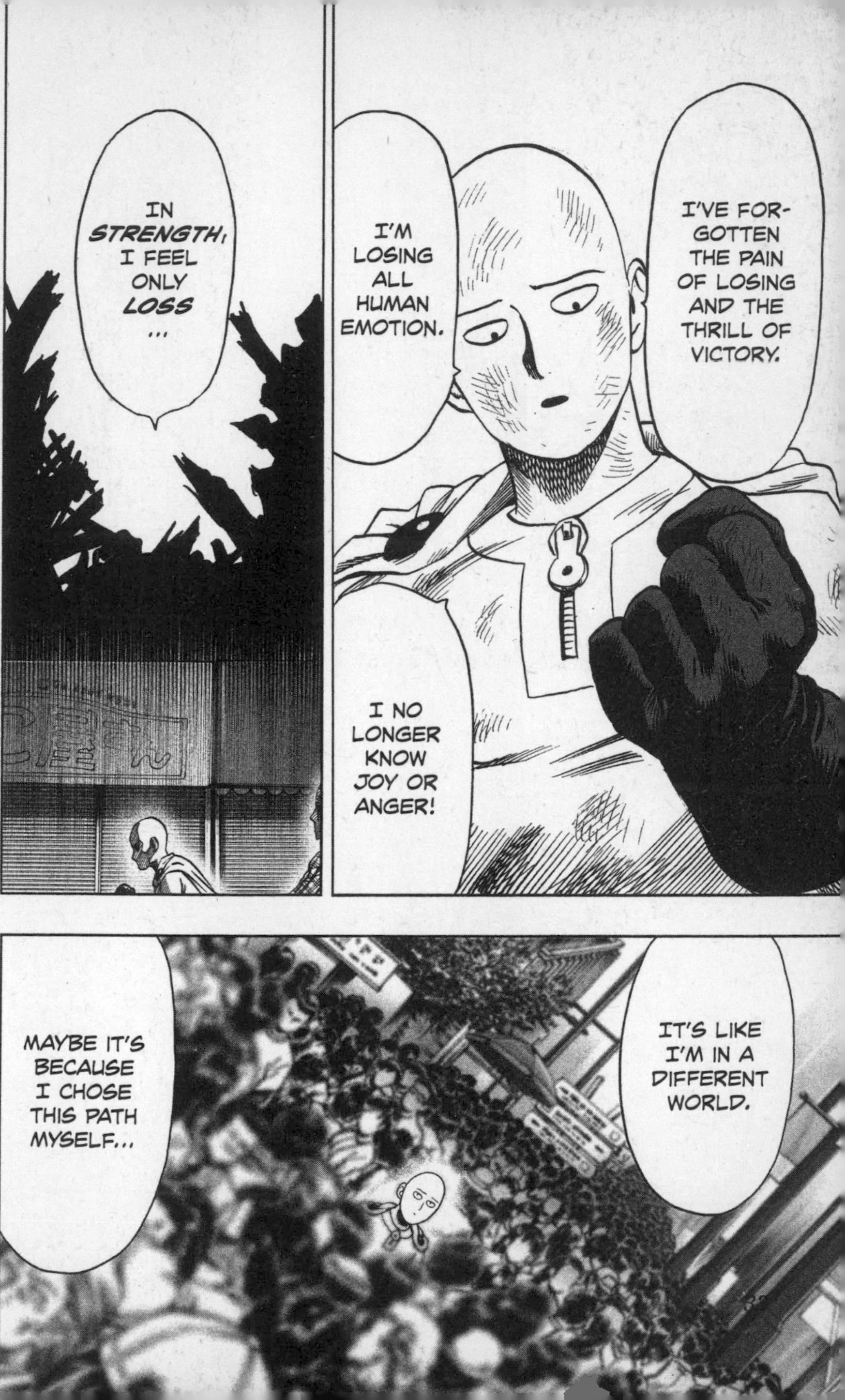
I'VE FOR-GOTTEN THE PAIN OF LOSING AND THE THRILL OF VICTORY.
I'M LOSING ALL HUMAN EMOTION.
I NO LONGER KNOW JOY OR ANGER!
IN *STRENGTH*, I FEEL ONLY *LOSS* ...
IT'S LIKE I'M IN A DIFFERENT WORLD.
MAYBE IT'S BECAUSE I CHOSE THIS PATH MYSELF...

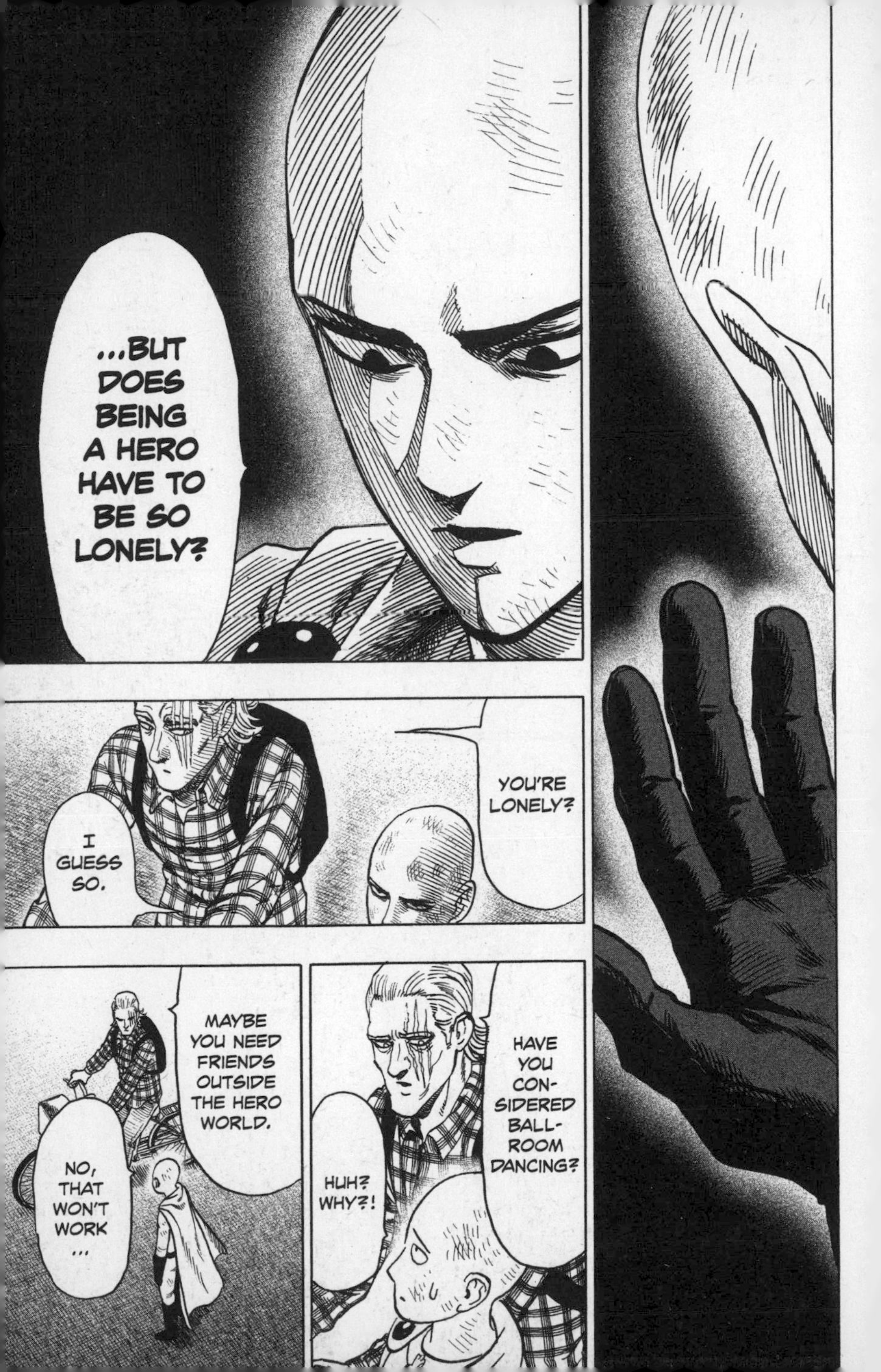
...BUT DOES BEING A HERO HAVE TO BE SO LONELY?
YOU'RE LONELY?
I GUESS SO.
HAVE YOU CON-SIDERED BALL-ROOM DANCING?
HUH? WHY?!
MAYBE YOU NEED FRIENDS OUTSIDE THE HERO WORLD.
NO, THAT WON'T WORK ...

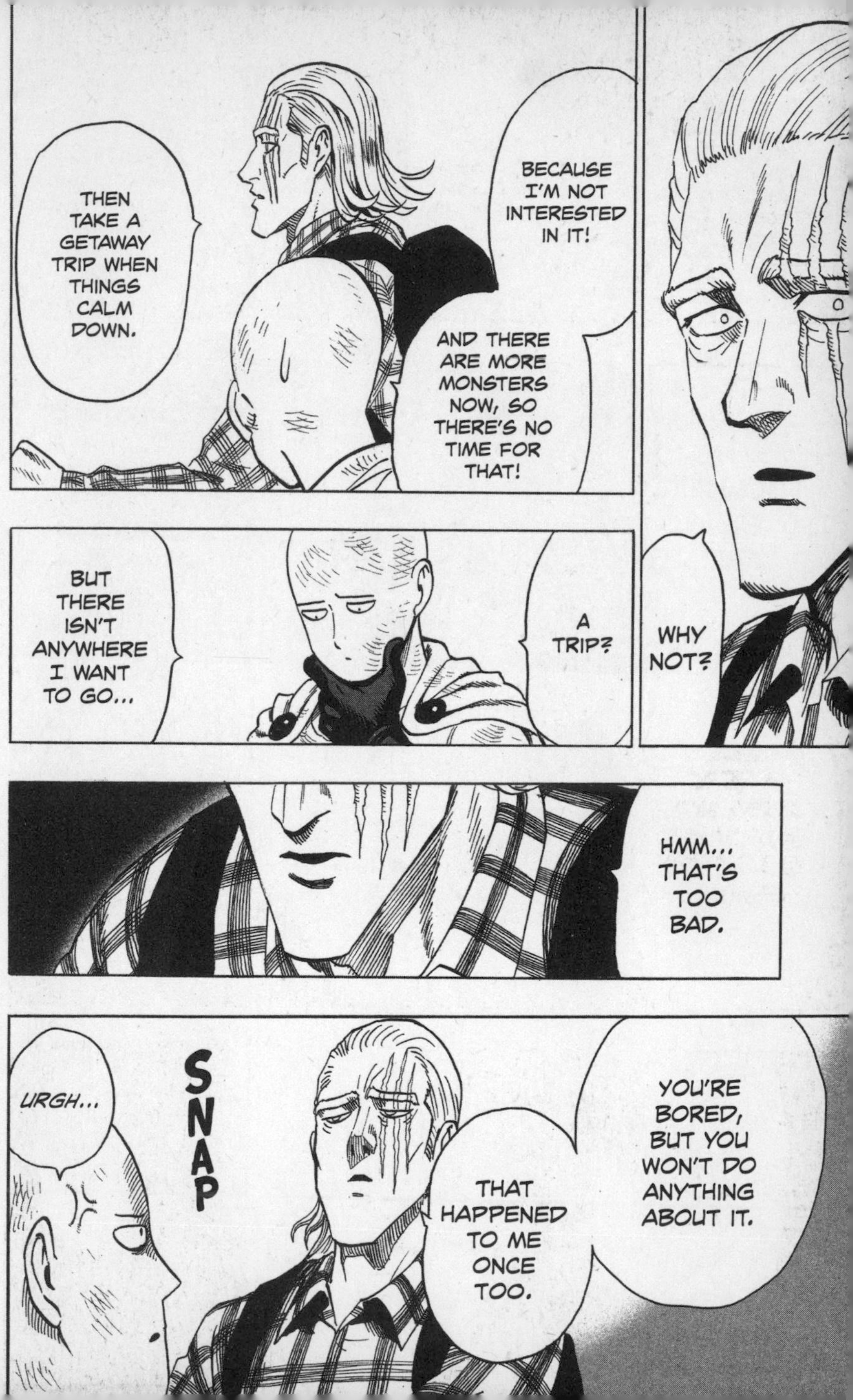
WHY NOT?
BECAUSE I'M NOT INTERESTED IN IT!
AND THERE ARE MORE MONSTERS NOW, SO THERE'S NO TIME FOR THAT!
THEN TAKE A GETAWAY TRIP WHEN THINGS CALM DOWN.
A TRIP?
BUT THERE ISN'T ANYWHERE I WANT TO GO...
HMM... THAT'S TOO BAD.
YOU'RE BORED, BUT YOU WON'T DO ANYTHING ABOUT IT.
THAT HAPPENED TO ME ONCE TOO.
SNAP
URGH...

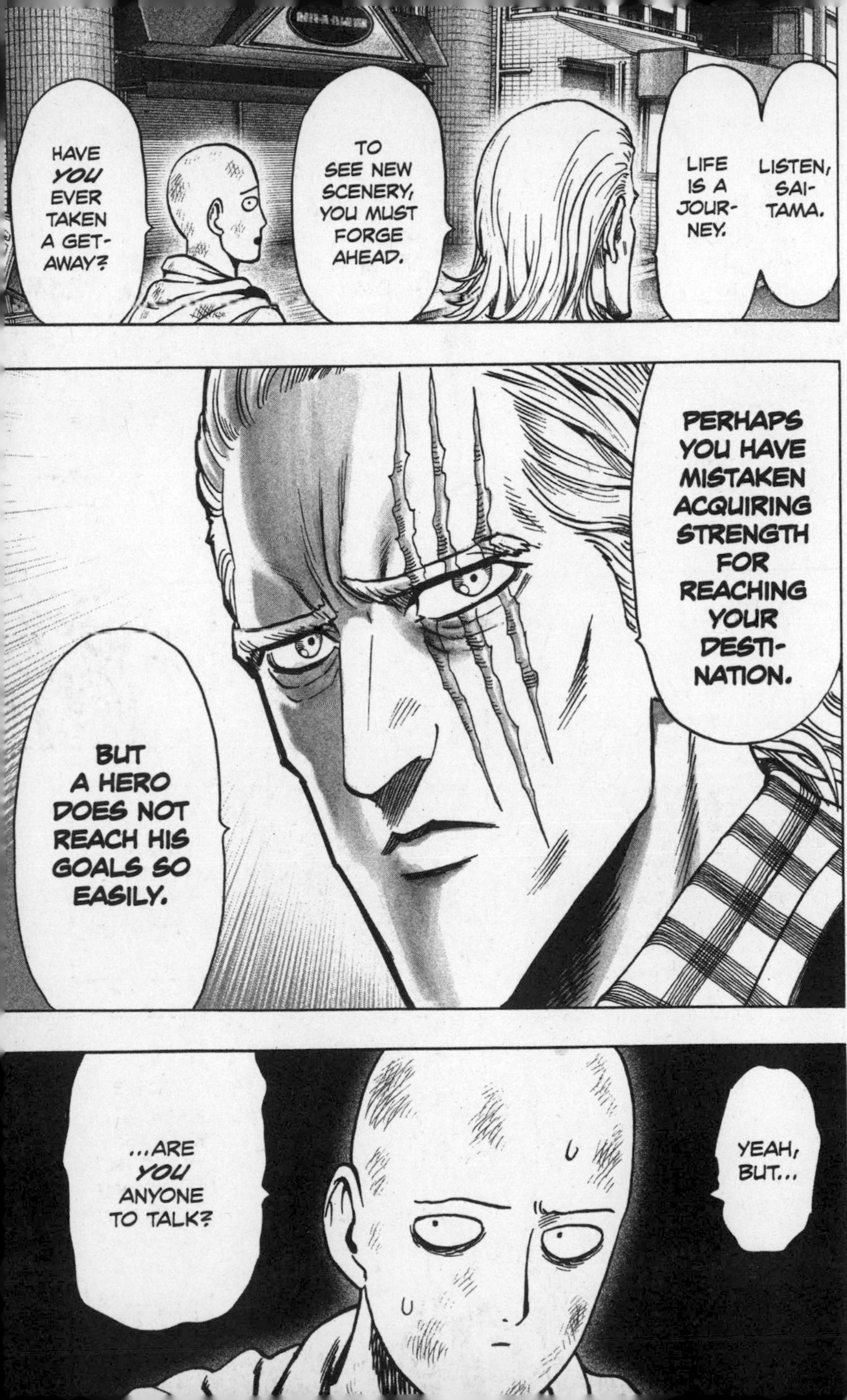
LISTEN, SAI-TAMA.
LIFE IS A JOUR-NEY.
TO SEE NEW SCENERY, YOU MUST FORGE AHEAD.
HAVE *YOU* EVER TAKEN A GET-AWAY?
PERHAPS YOU HAVE MISTAKEN ACQUIRING STRENGTH FOR REACHING YOUR DESTI-NATION.
BUT A HERO DOES NOT REACH HIS GOALS SO EASILY.
YEAH, BUT...
...ARE *YOU* ANYONE TO TALK?

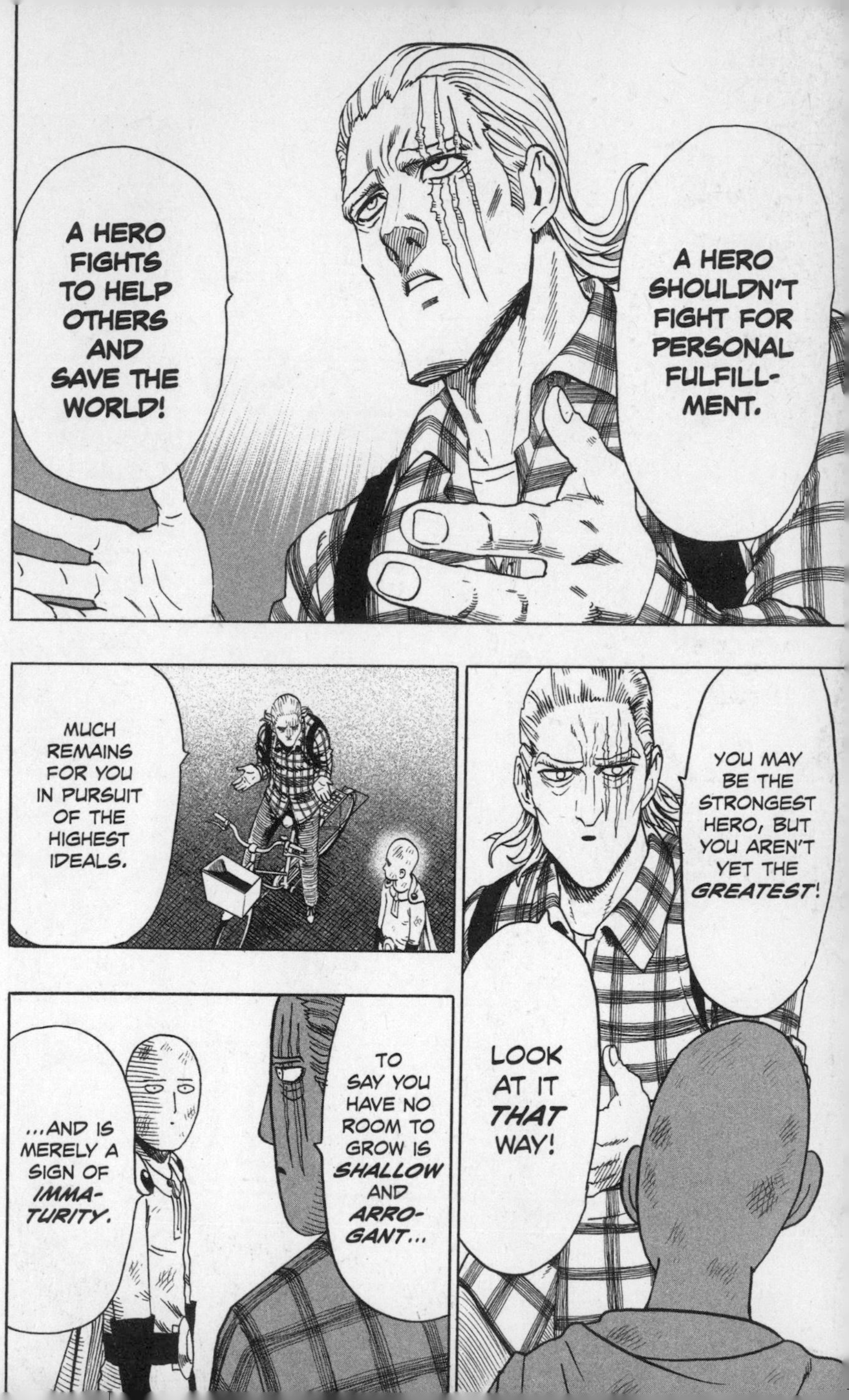
A HERO SHOULDN'T FIGHT FOR PERSONAL FULFILL-MENT.
A HERO FIGHTS TO HELP OTHERS AND SAVE THE WORLD!
YOU MAY BE THE STRONGEST HERO, BUT YOU AREN'T YET THE *GREATEST*!
LOOK AT IT *THAT* WAY!
MUCH REMAINS FOR YOU IN PURSUIT OF THE HIGHEST IDEALS.
TO SAY YOU HAVE NO ROOM TO GROW IS *SHALLOW* AND *ARRO-GANT*...
...AND IS MERELY A SIGN OF *IMMA-TURITY*.

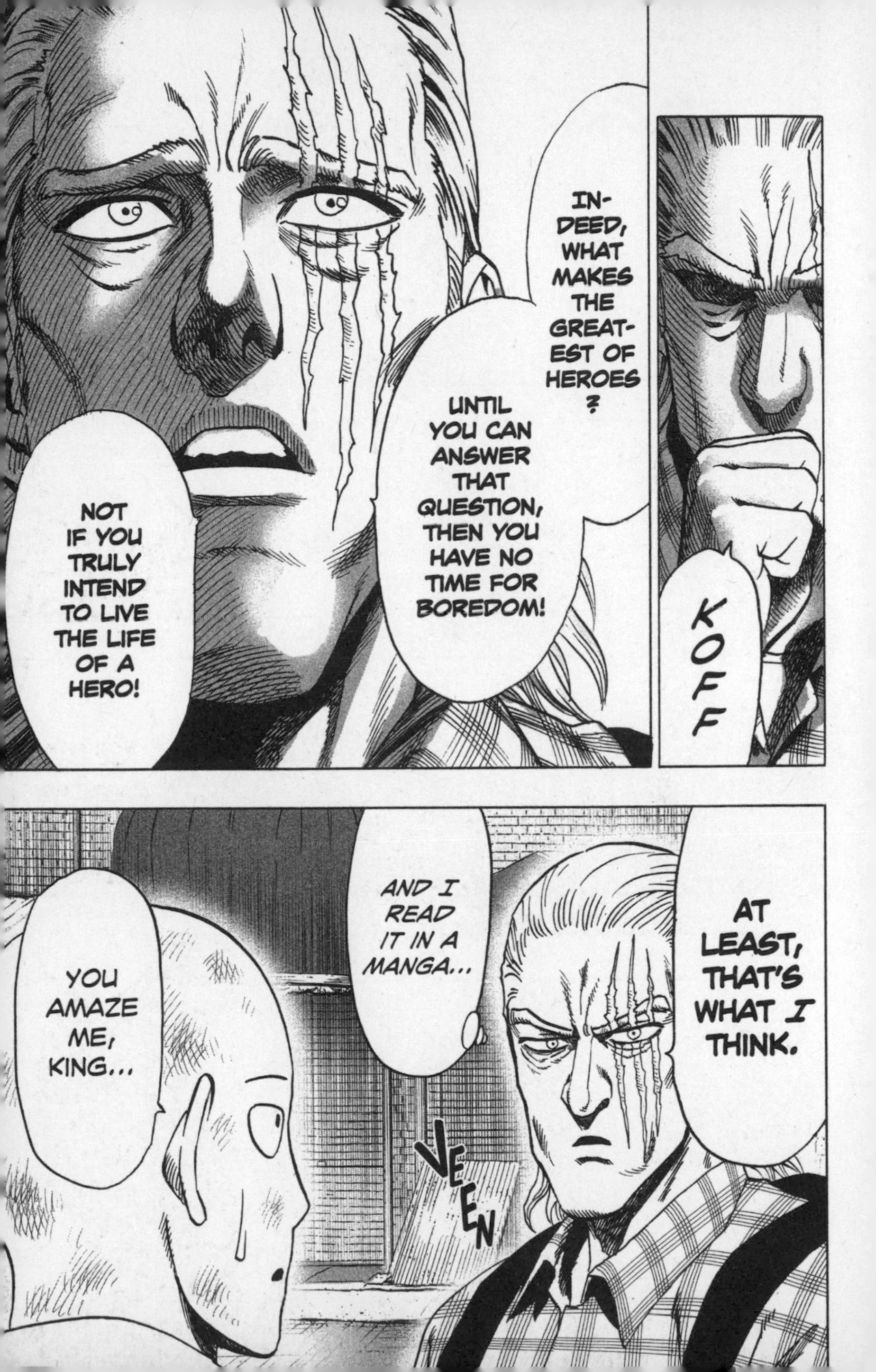
KOFF
INDEED, WHAT MAKES THE GREATEST OF HEROES?
UNTIL YOU CAN ANSWER THAT QUESTION, THEN YOU HAVE NO TIME FOR BOREDOM!
NOT IF YOU TRULY INTEND TO LIVE THE LIFE OF A HERO!
AT LEAST, THAT'S WHAT I THINK.
AND I READ IT IN A MANGA...
VEEEN
YOU AMAZE ME, KING...

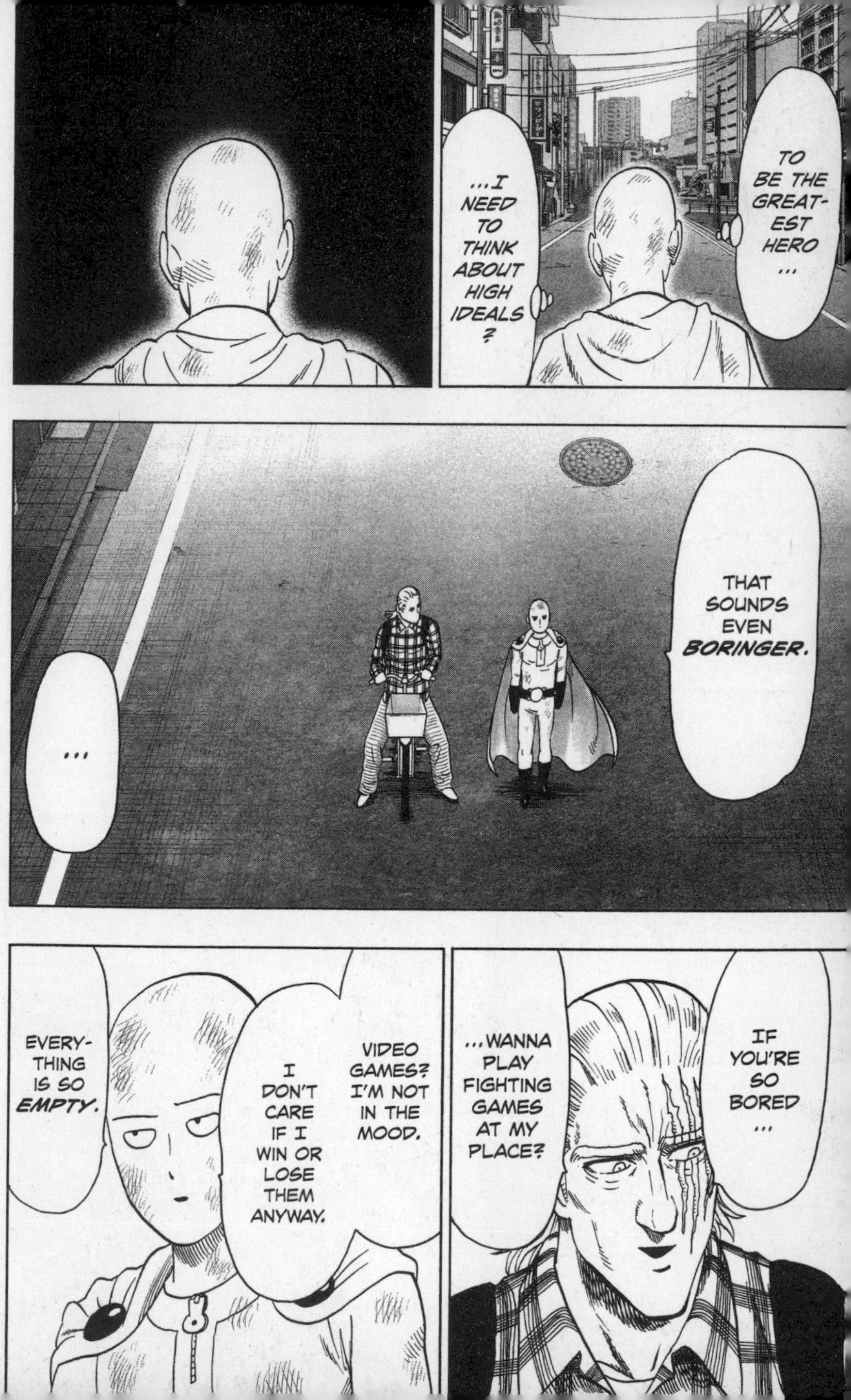
TO BE THE GREATEST HERO...
...I NEED TO THINK ABOUT HIGH IDEALS?
THAT SOUNDS EVEN BORINGER.
...
IF YOU'RE SO BORED...
...WANNA PLAY FIGHTING GAMES AT MY PLACE?
VIDEO GAMES? I'M NOT IN THE MOOD.
I DON'T CARE IF I WIN OR LOSE THEM ANYWAY.
EVERYTHING IS SO EMPTY.

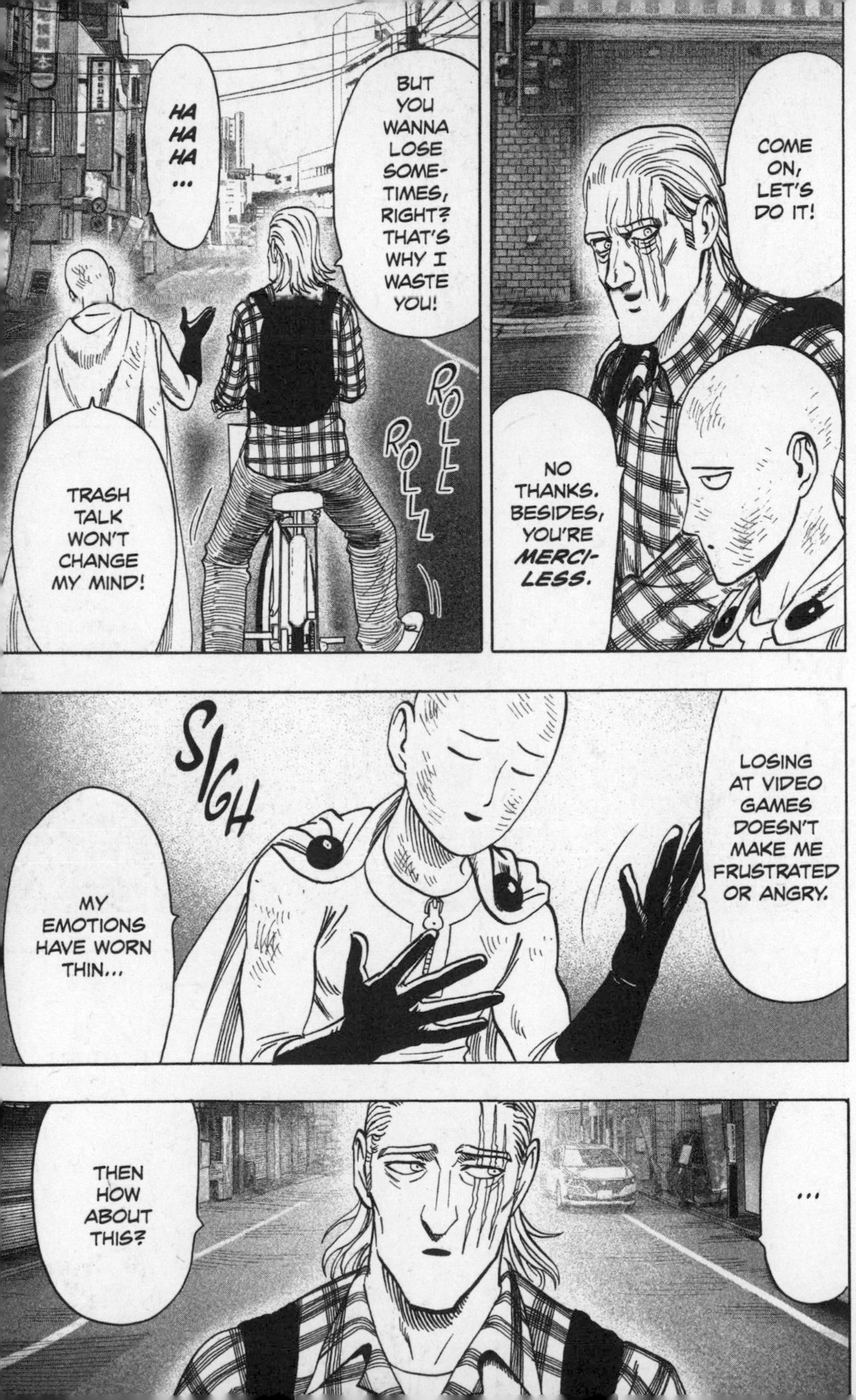
COME ON, LET'S DO IT!
NO THANKS. BESIDES, YOU'RE *MERCILESS.*
BUT YOU WANNA LOSE SOMETIMES, RIGHT? THAT'S WHY I WASTE YOU!
HA HA HA ...
ROLL
ROLL
TRASH TALK WON'T CHANGE MY MIND!
LOSING AT VIDEO GAMES DOESN'T MAKE ME FRUSTRATED OR ANGRY.
SIGH
MY EMOTIONS HAVE WORN THIN...
...
THEN HOW ABOUT THIS?

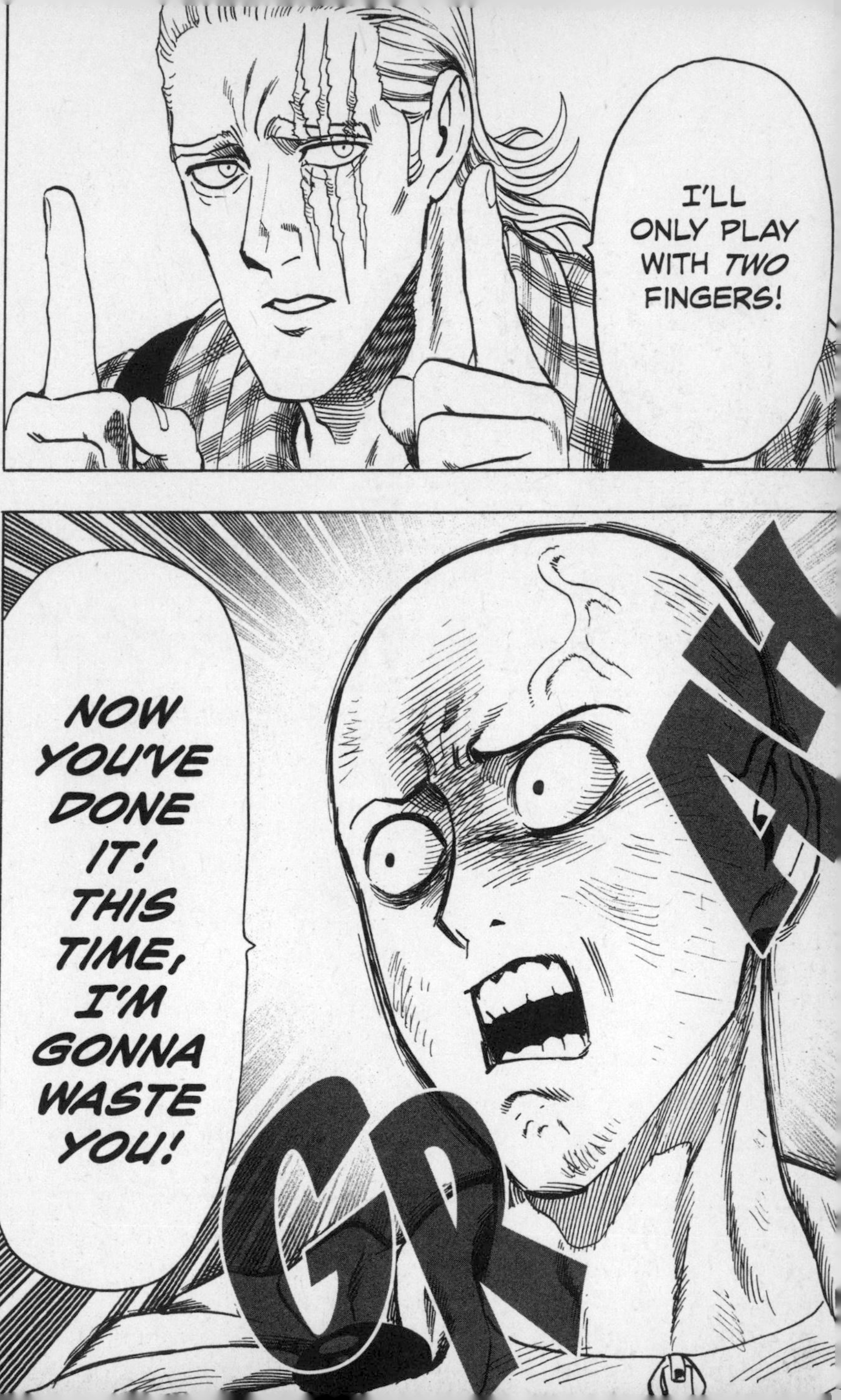
I'LL ONLY PLAY WITH *TWO* FINGERS!
NOW YOU'VE DONE IT! THIS TIME, I'M GONNA WASTE YOU!

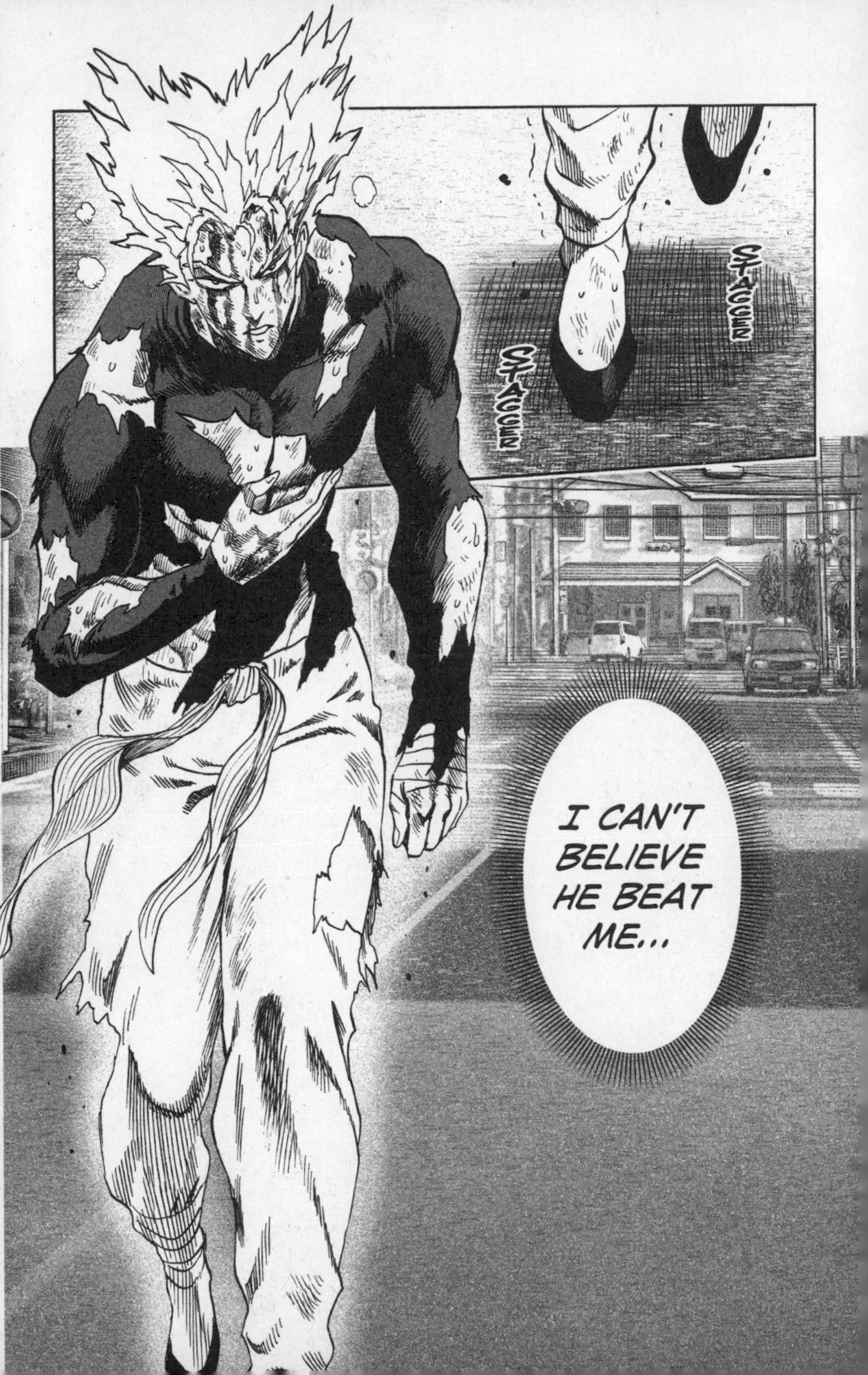
STAGGER
STAGGER
I CAN'T BELIEVE HE BEAT ME...

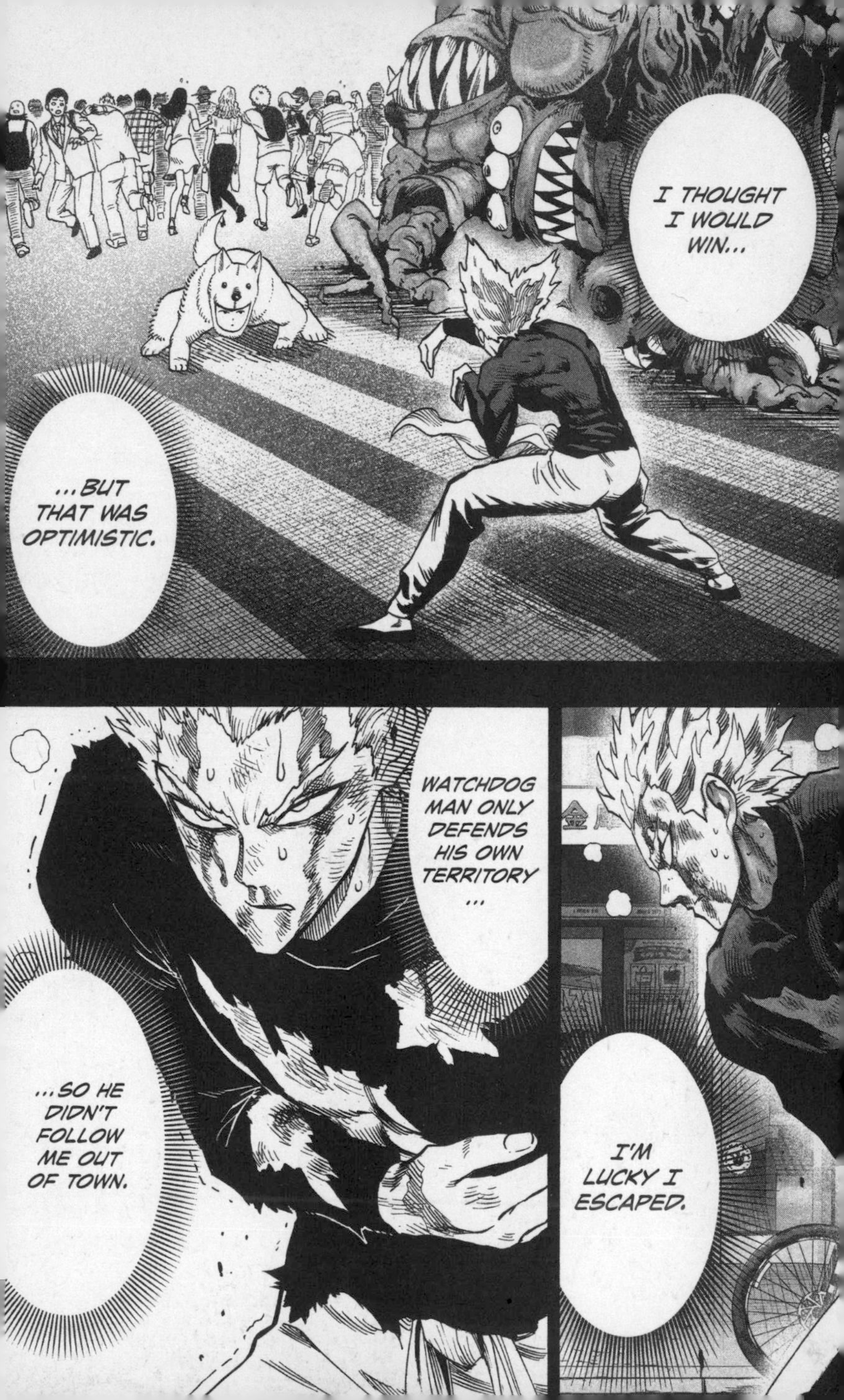
I THOUGHT I WOULD WIN...
...BUT THAT WAS OPTIMISTIC.
I'M LUCKY I ESCAPED.
WATCHDOG MAN ONLY DEFENDS HIS OWN TERRITORY ...
...SO HE DIDN'T FOLLOW ME OUT OF TOWN.

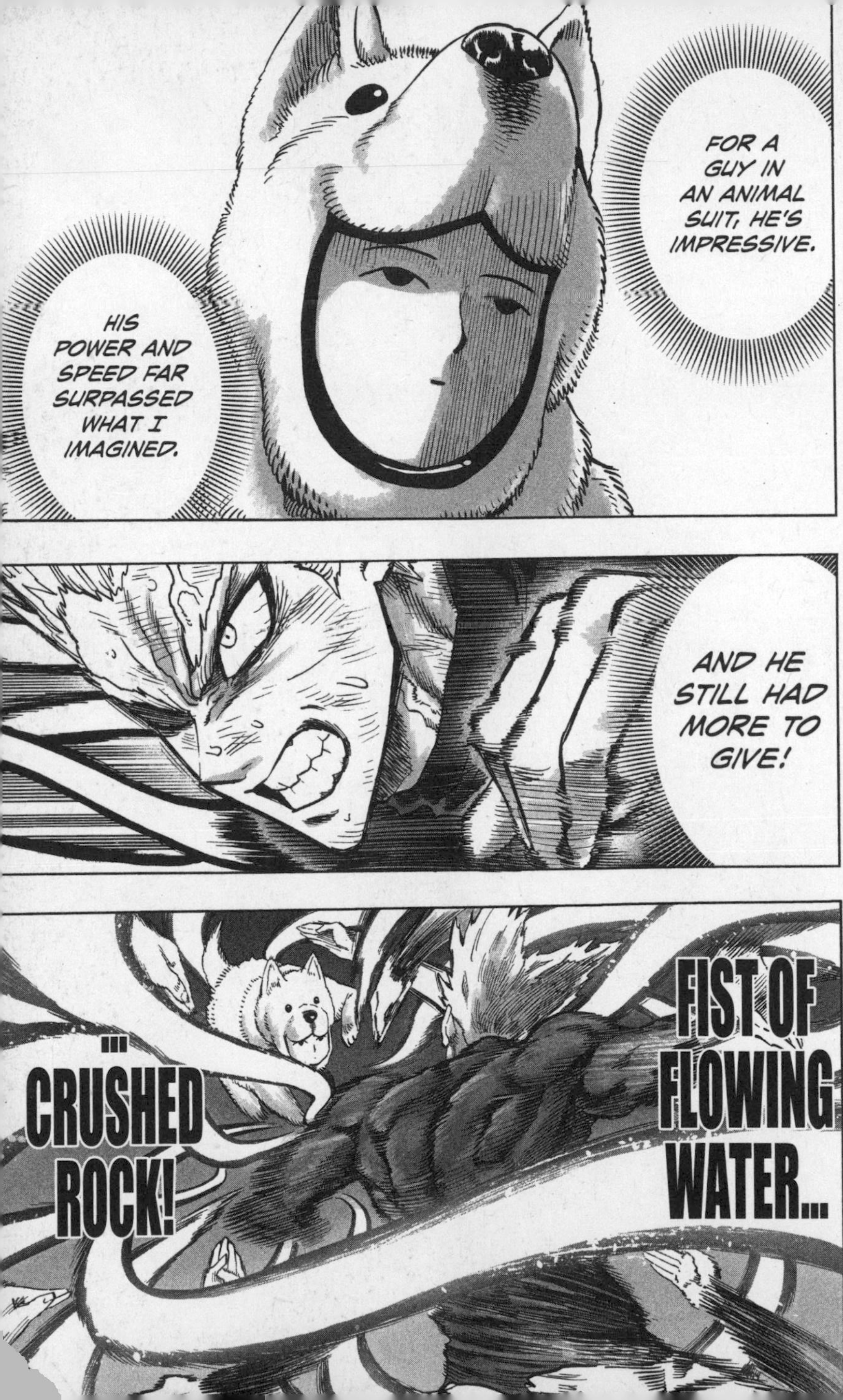
FOR A GUY IN AN ANIMAL SUIT, HE'S IMPRESSIVE.
HIS POWER AND SPEED FAR SURPASSED WHAT I IMAGINED.
AND HE STILL HAD MORE TO GIVE!
FIST OF FLOWING WATER...
...CRUSHED ROCK!

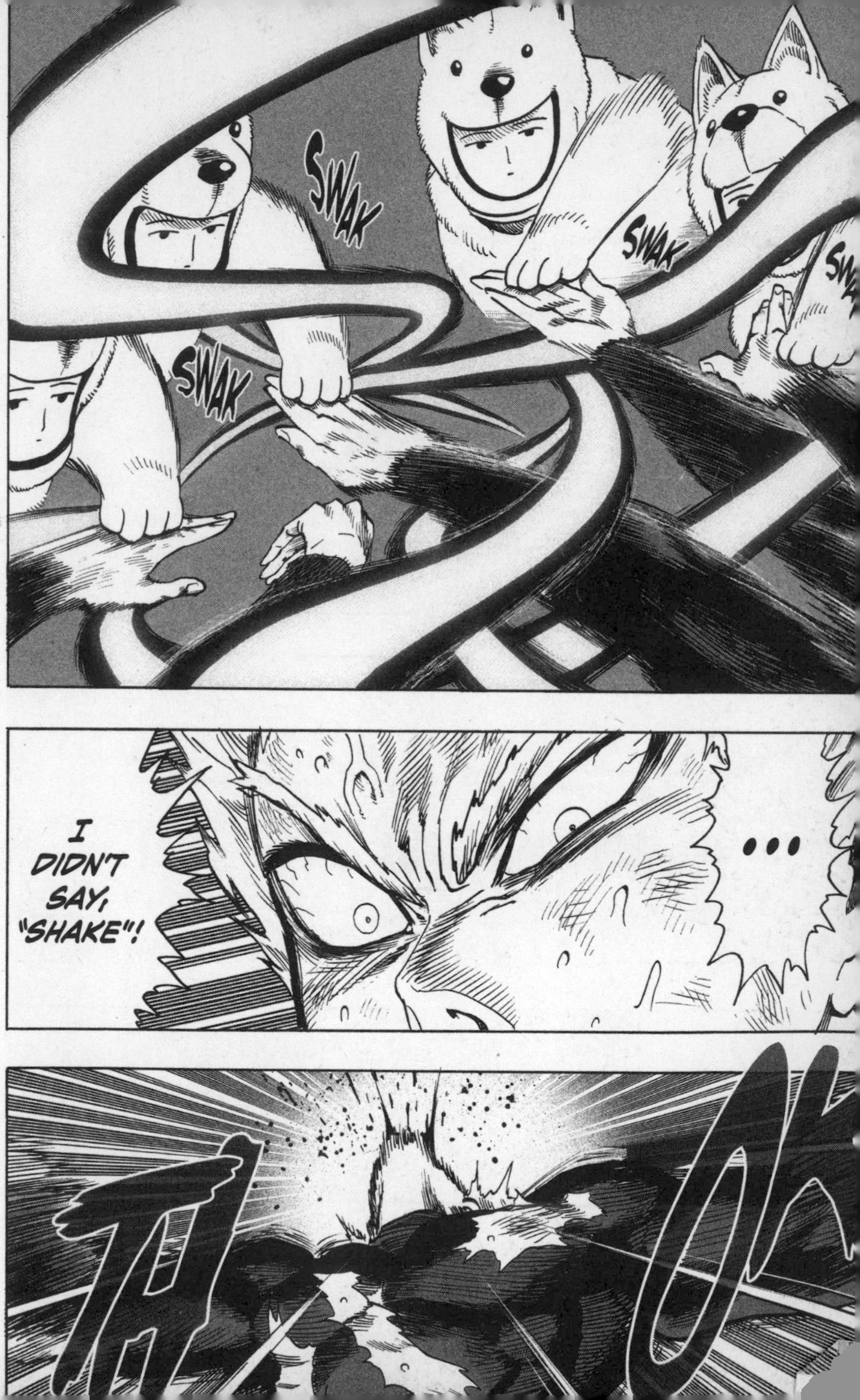
SWAK
SWAK
SWAK
...
I DIDN'T SAY, "SHAKE"!

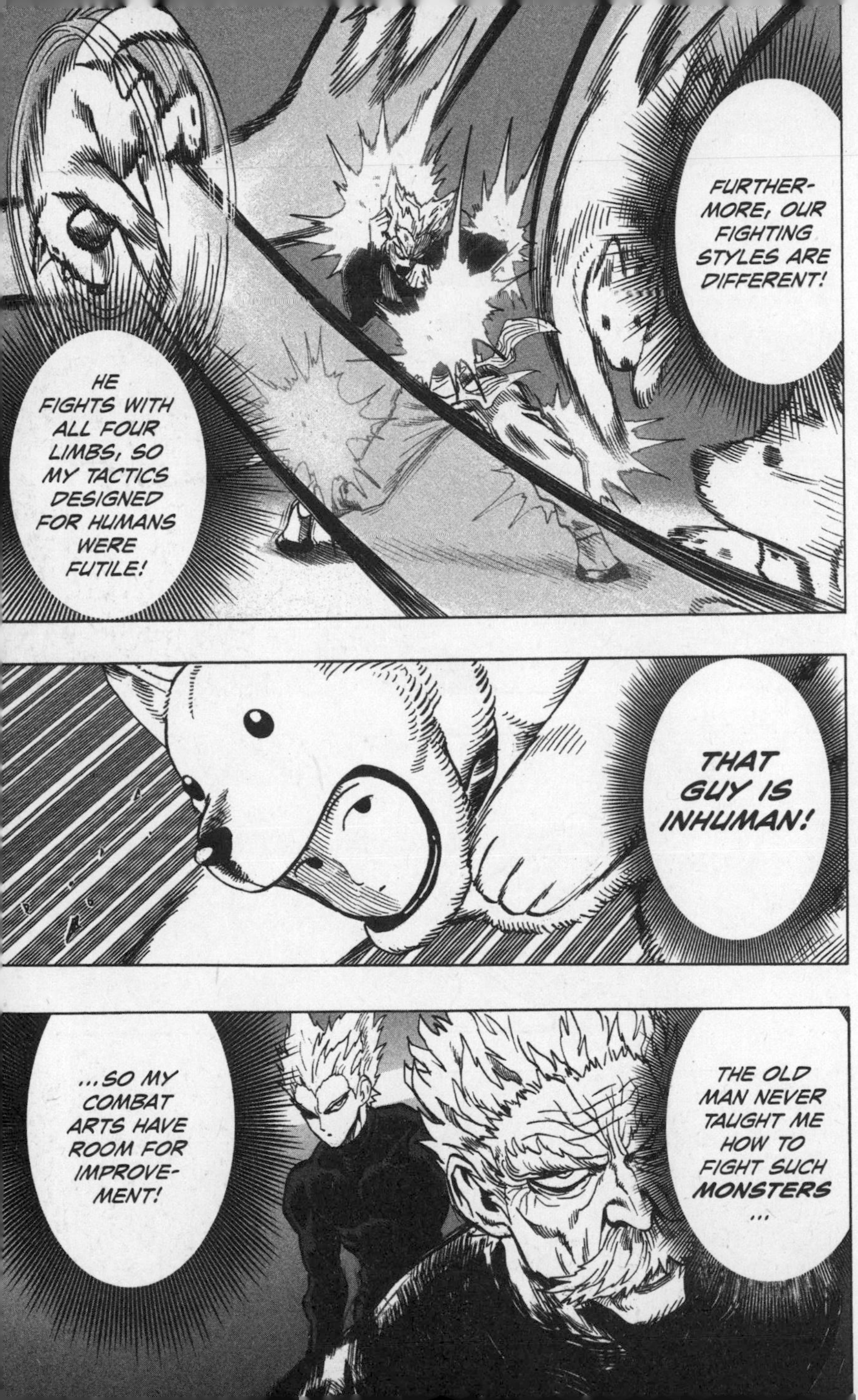
FURTHERMORE, OUR FIGHTING STYLES ARE DIFFERENT!
HE FIGHTS WITH ALL FOUR LIMBS, SO MY TACTICS DESIGNED FOR HUMANS WERE FUTILE!
THAT GUY IS INHUMAN!
THE OLD MAN NEVER TAUGHT ME HOW TO FIGHT SUCH MONSTERS...
...SO MY COMBAT ARTS HAVE ROOM FOR IMPROVEMENT!

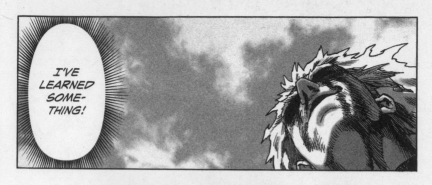

I'VE LEARNED SOME-THING!
ARGH... I GOT BEAT UP...
...BUT NOW I'M STOKED!
HEH HEH HEH ...

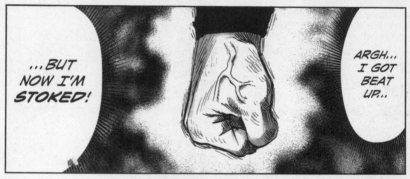

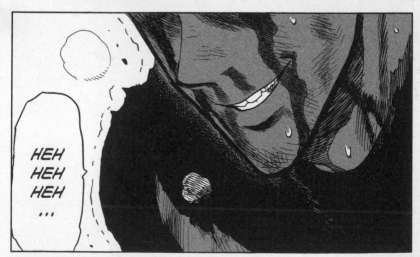

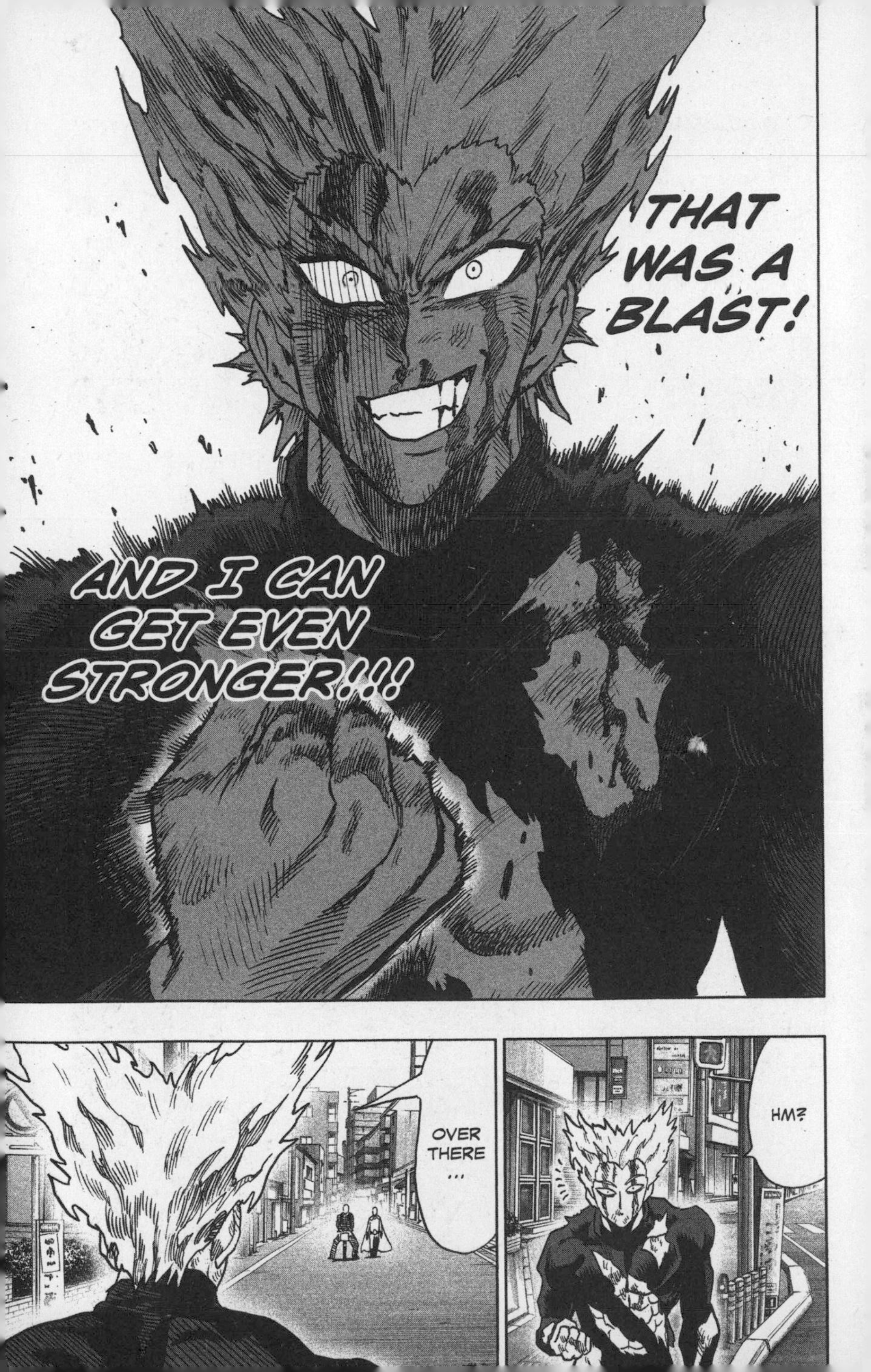
THAT WAS A BLAST!
AND I CAN GET EVEN STRONGER!!!
HM?
OVER THERE ...

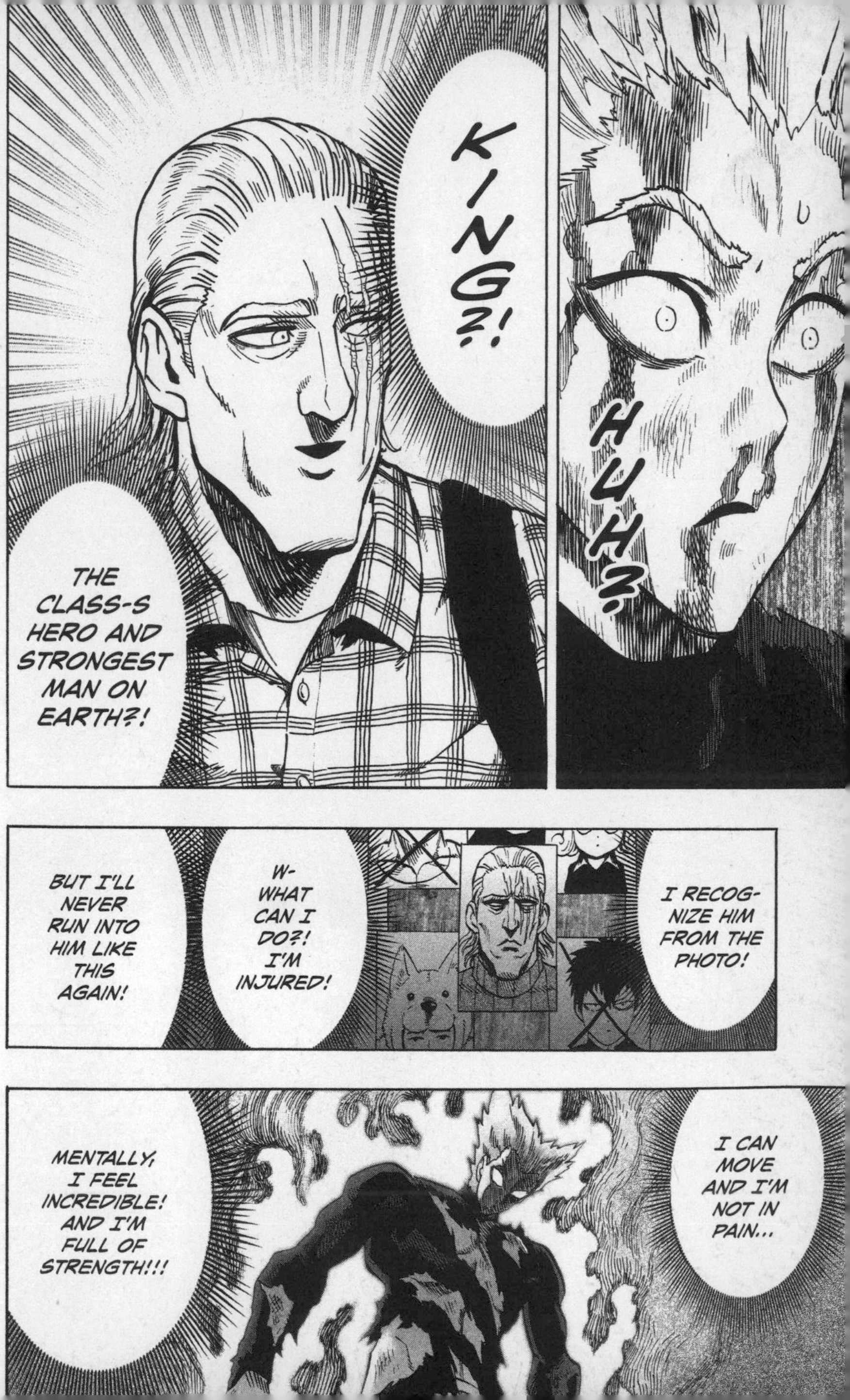
HUH?!
KING?!
THE CLASS-S HERO AND STRONGEST MAN ON EARTH?!
I RECOGNIZE HIM FROM THE PHOTO!
W-WHAT CAN I DO?! I'M INJURED!
BUT I'LL NEVER RUN INTO HIM LIKE THIS AGAIN!
I CAN MOVE AND I'M NOT IN PAIN...
MENTALLY, I FEEL INCREDIBLE! AND I'M FULL OF STRENGTH!!!

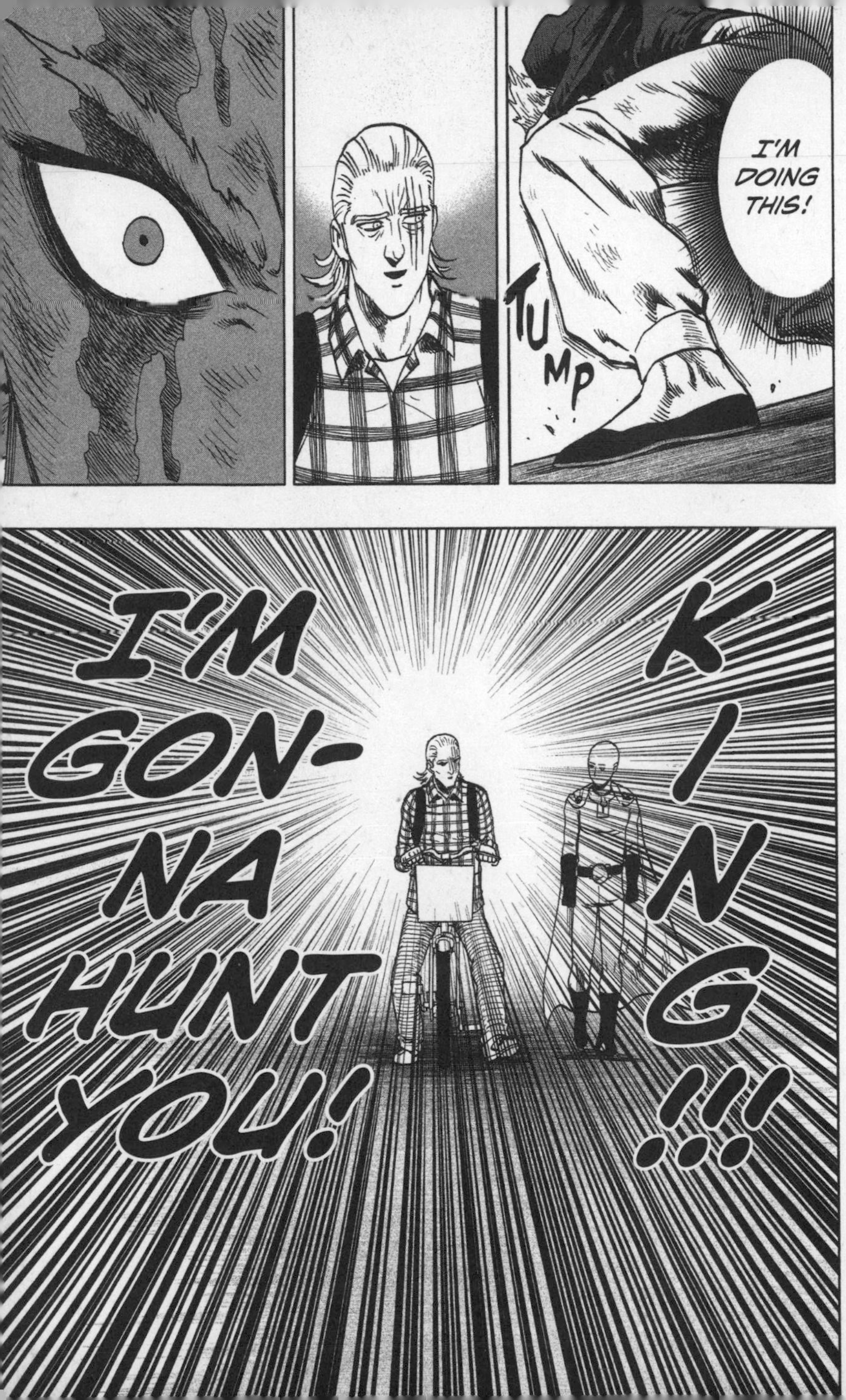
I'M DOING THIS!
TUMP
KING!!!
I'M GONNA HUNT YOU!

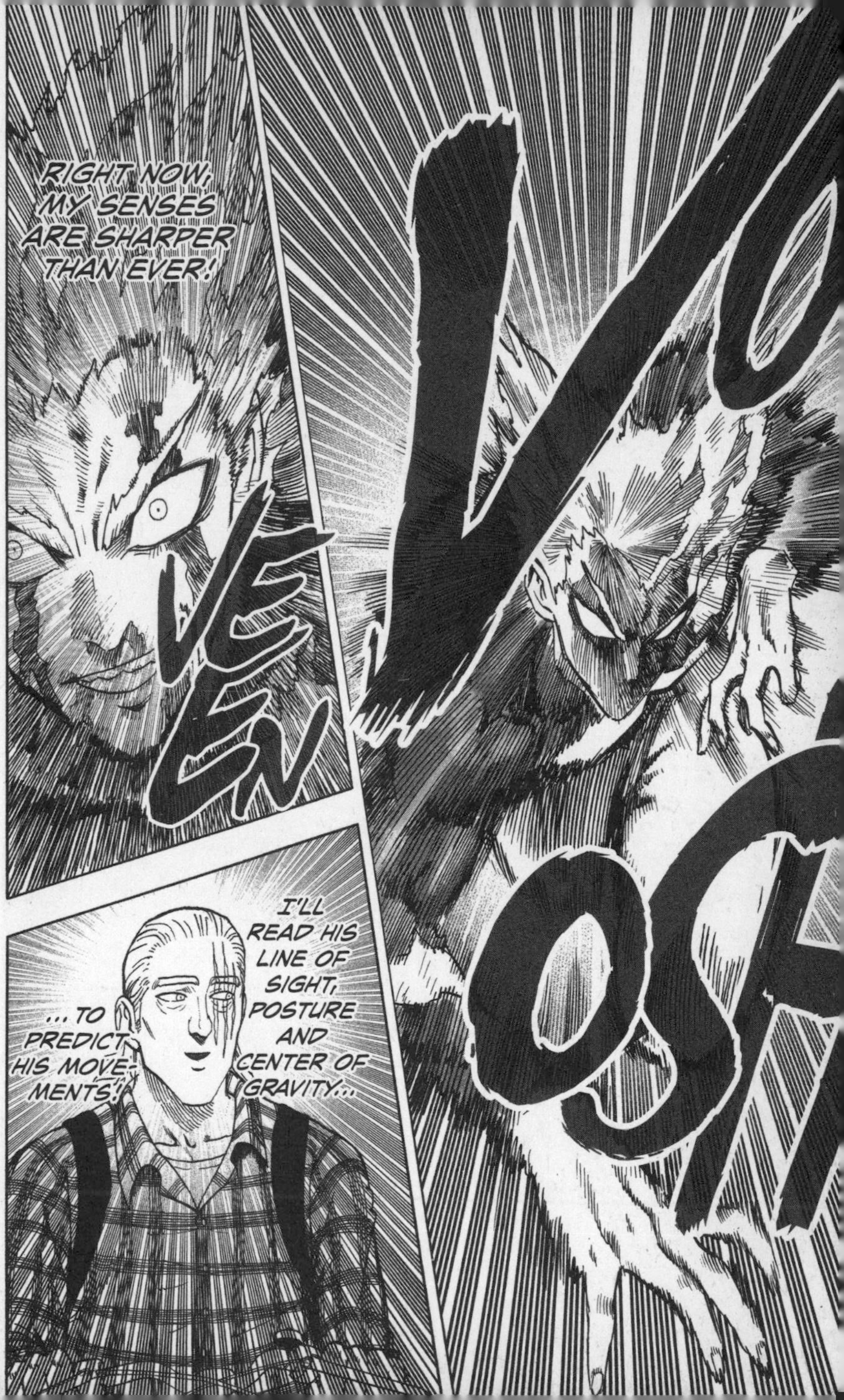
RIGHT NOW, MY SENSES ARE SHARPER THAN EVER!
I'LL READ HIS LINE OF SIGHT, POSTURE AND CENTER OF GRAVITY...
...TO PREDICT HIS MOVE-MENTS!

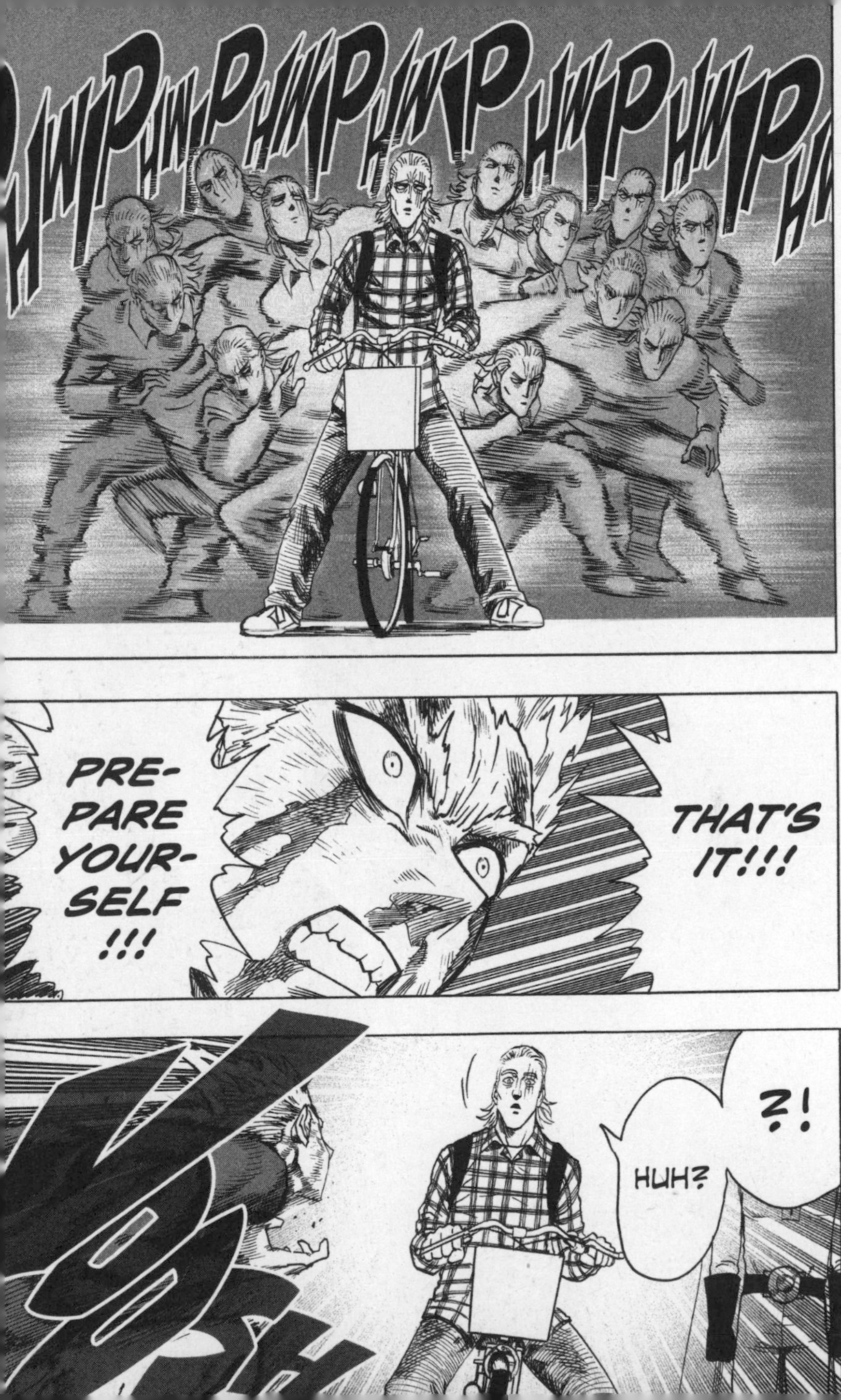
THAT'S IT!!!
PRE-PARE YOUR-SELF!!!
?!
HUH?

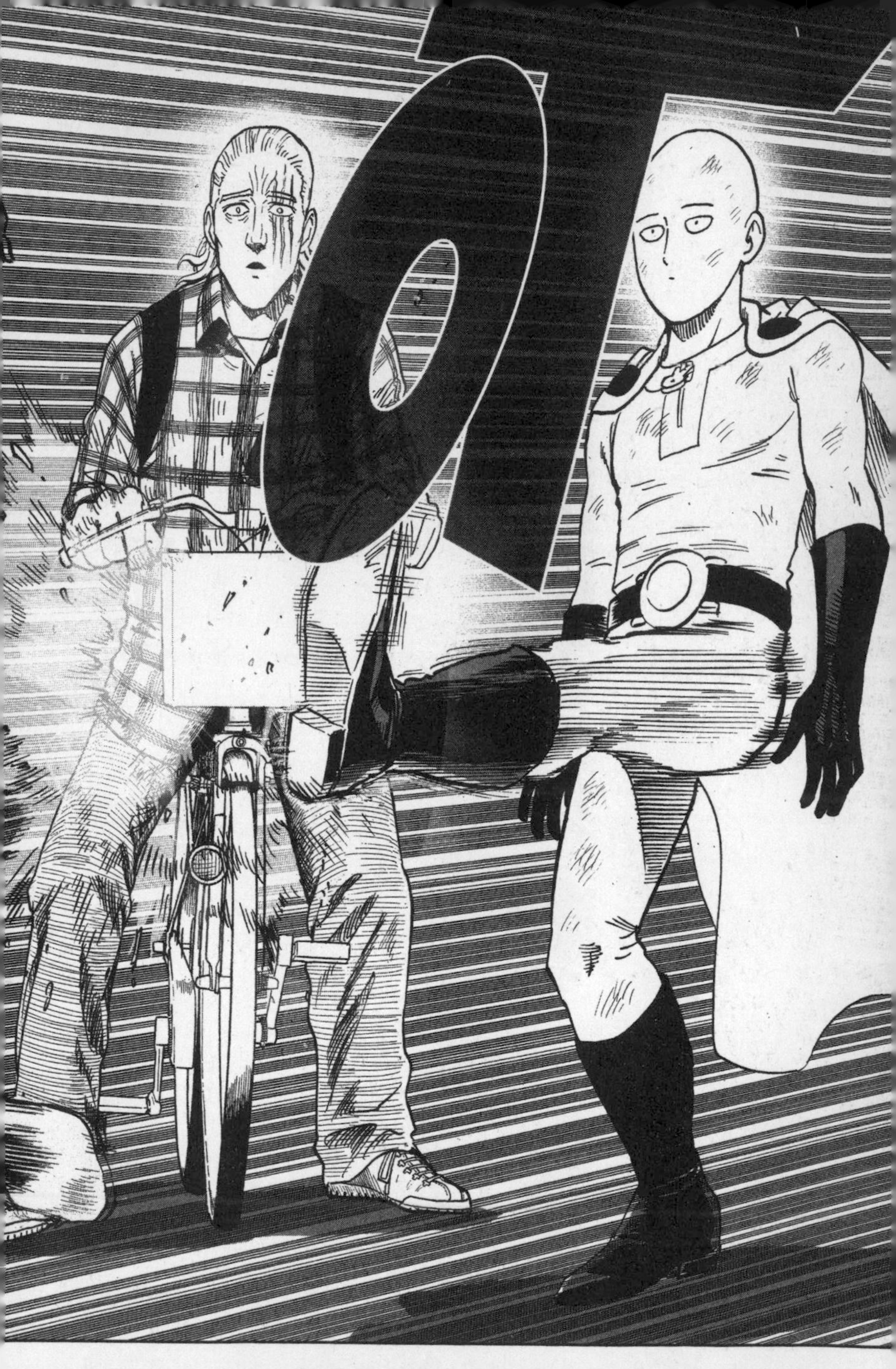
OT

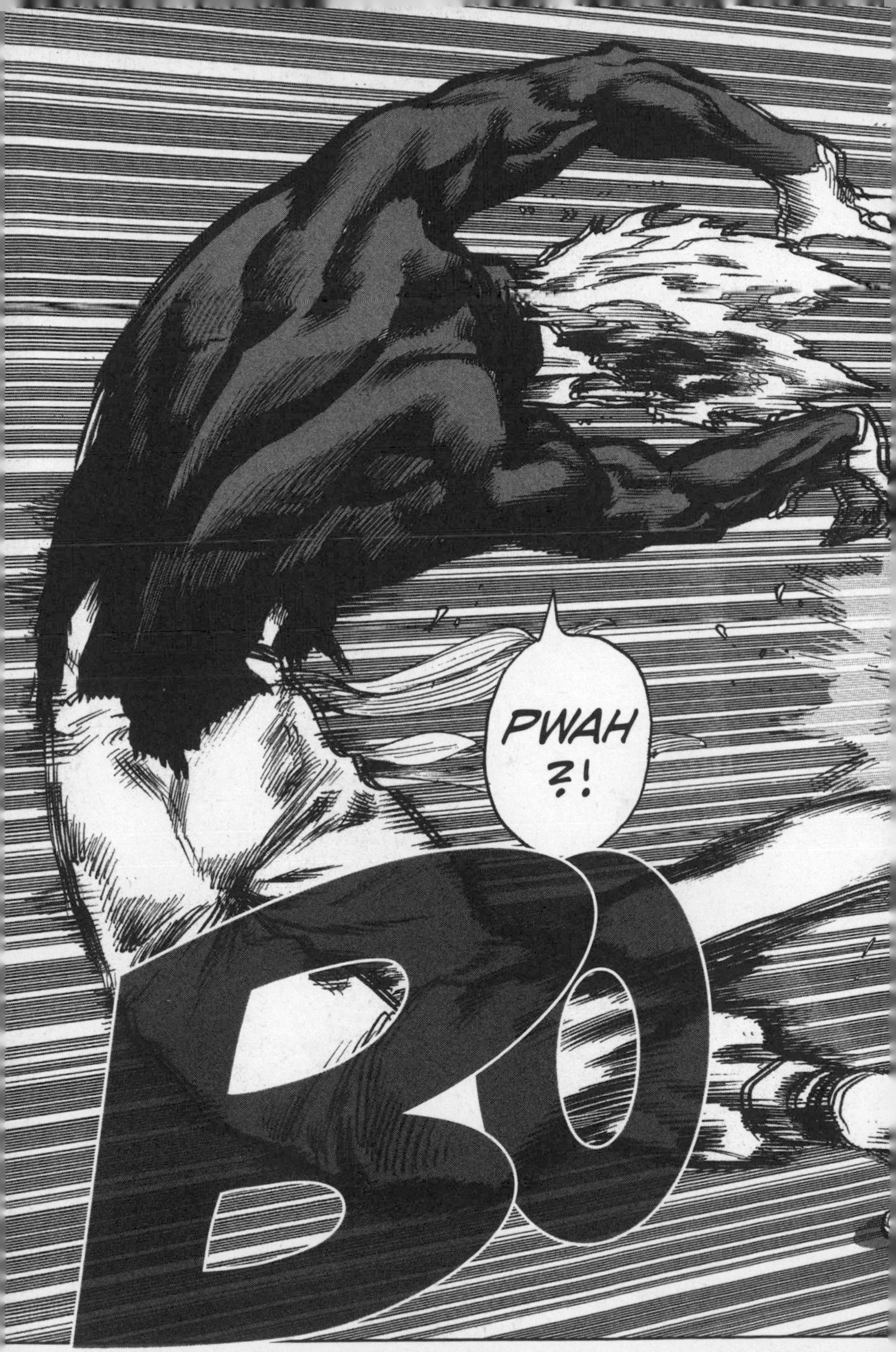
PWAH ?!
BO

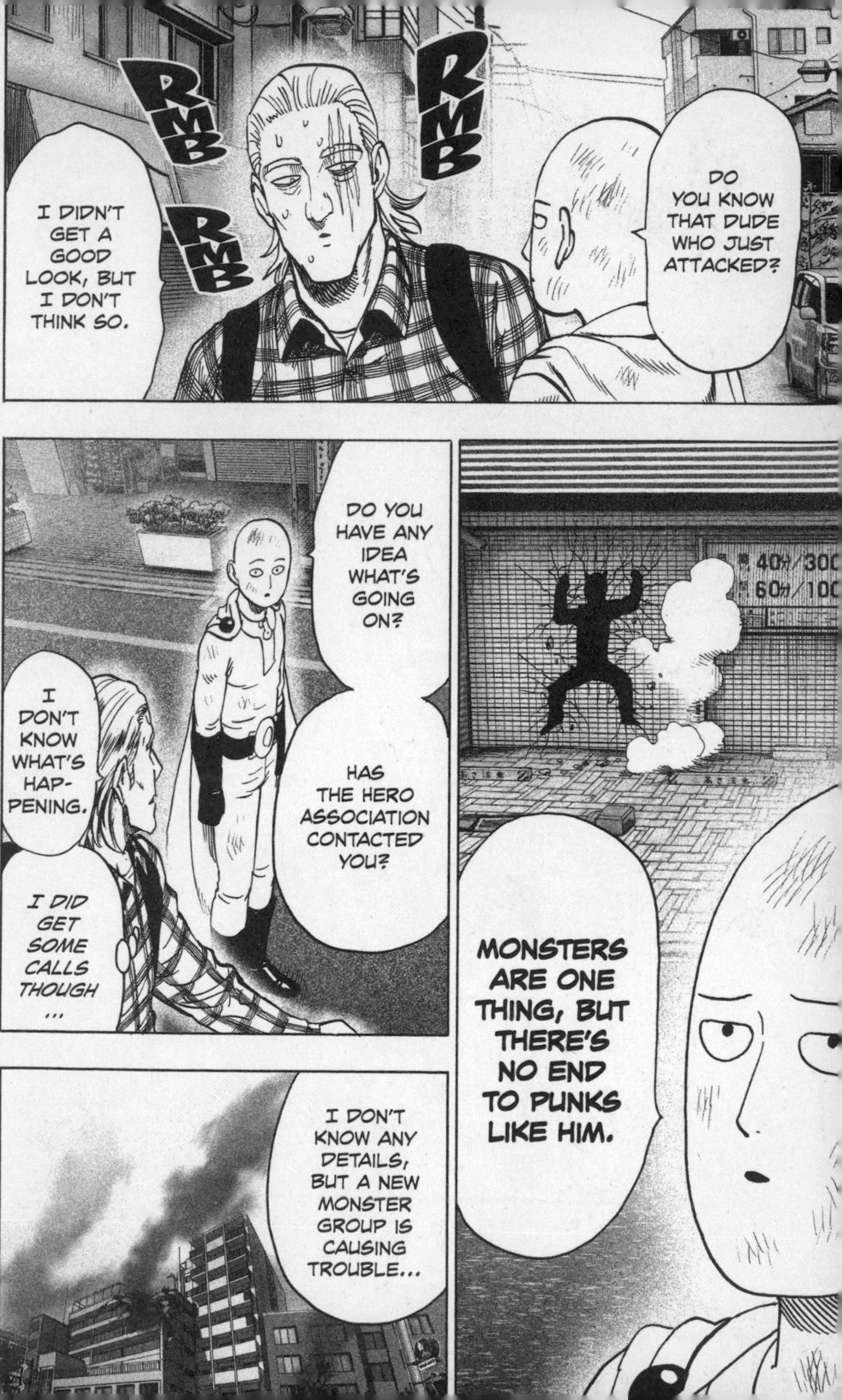
DO YOU KNOW THAT DUDE WHO JUST ATTACKED?
RMB
RMB
RMB
I DIDN'T GET A GOOD LOOK, BUT I DON'T THINK SO.
MONSTERS ARE ONE THING, BUT THERE'S NO END TO PUNKS LIKE HIM.
DO YOU HAVE ANY IDEA WHAT'S GOING ON?
I DON'T KNOW WHAT'S HAP-PENING.
HAS THE HERO ASSOCIATION CONTACTED YOU?
I DID GET SOME CALLS THOUGH ...
I DON'T KNOW ANY DETAILS, BUT A NEW MONSTER GROUP IS CAUSING TROUBLE...

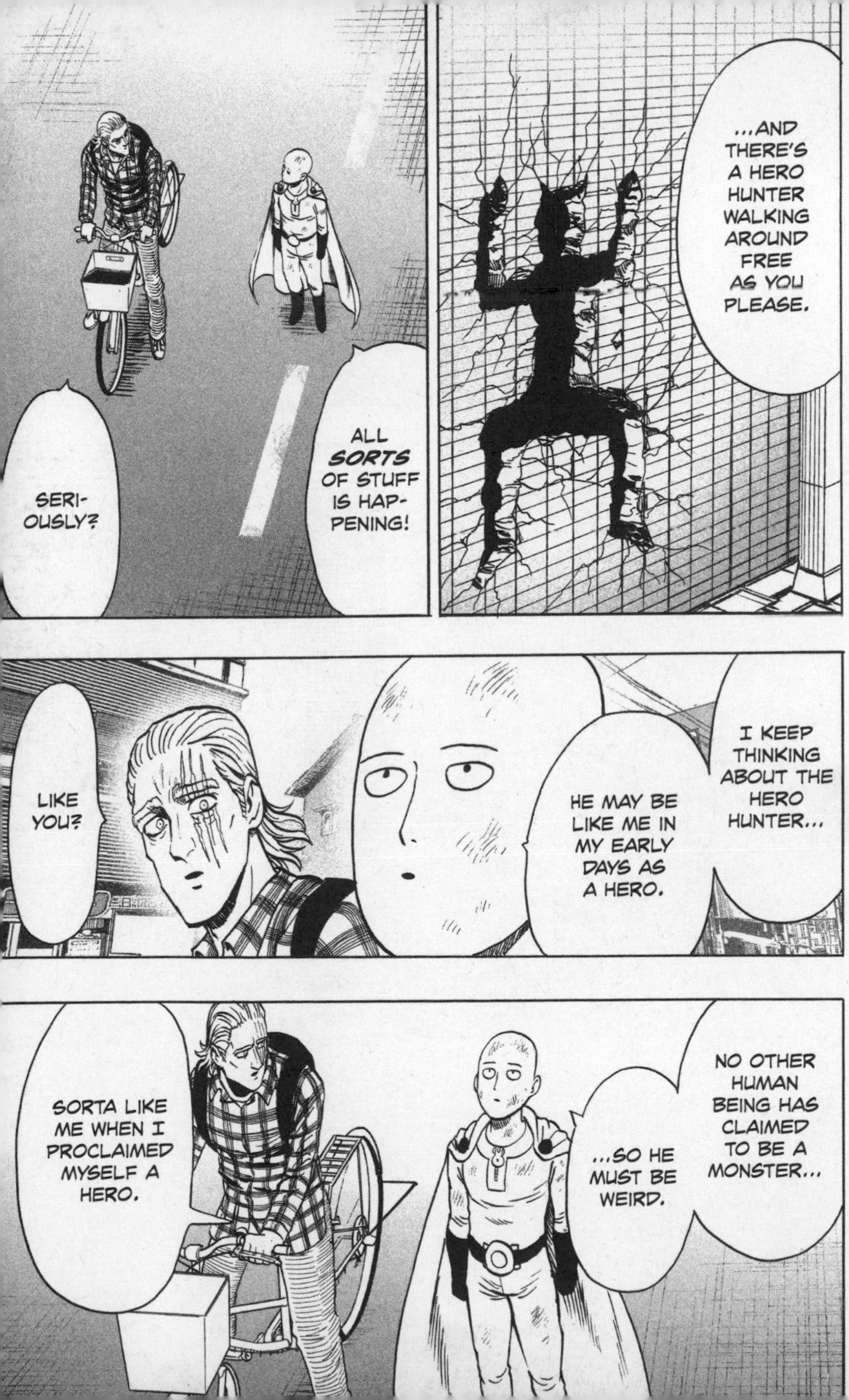
...AND THERE'S A HERO HUNTER WALKING AROUND FREE AS YOU PLEASE.
ALL *SORTS* OF STUFF IS HAP-PENING!
SERI-OUSLY?
I KEEP THINKING ABOUT THE HERO HUNTER...
HE MAY BE LIKE ME IN MY EARLY DAYS AS A HERO.
LIKE YOU?
NO OTHER HUMAN BEING HAS CLAIMED TO BE A MONSTER...
...SO HE MUST BE WEIRD.
SORTA LIKE ME WHEN I PROCLAIMED MYSELF A HERO.

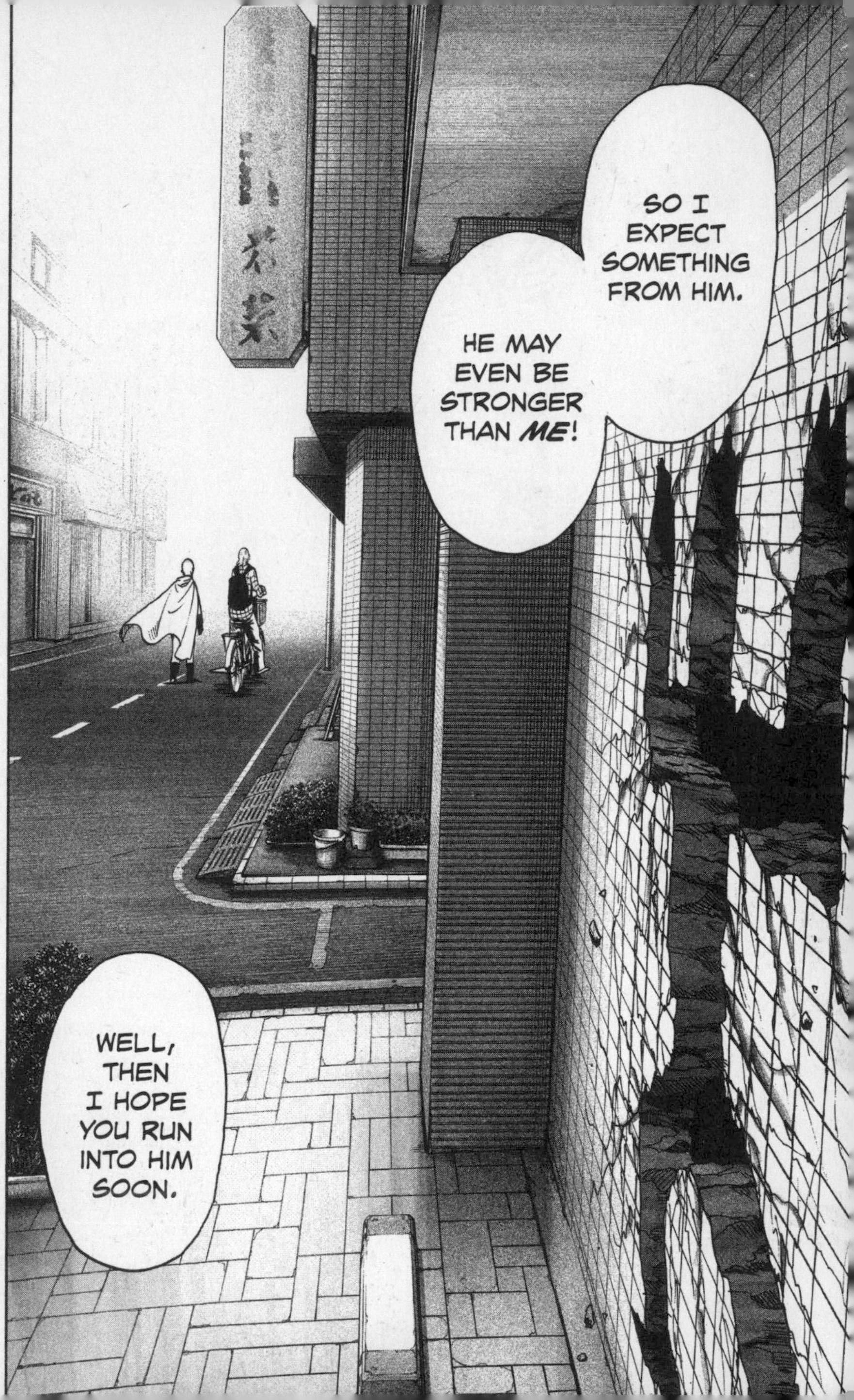
SO I EXPECT SOMETHING FROM HIM.
HE MAY EVEN BE STRONGER THAN *ME*!
WELL, THEN I HOPE YOU RUN INTO HIM SOON.

PUNCH 78: PULLING THE STRINGS

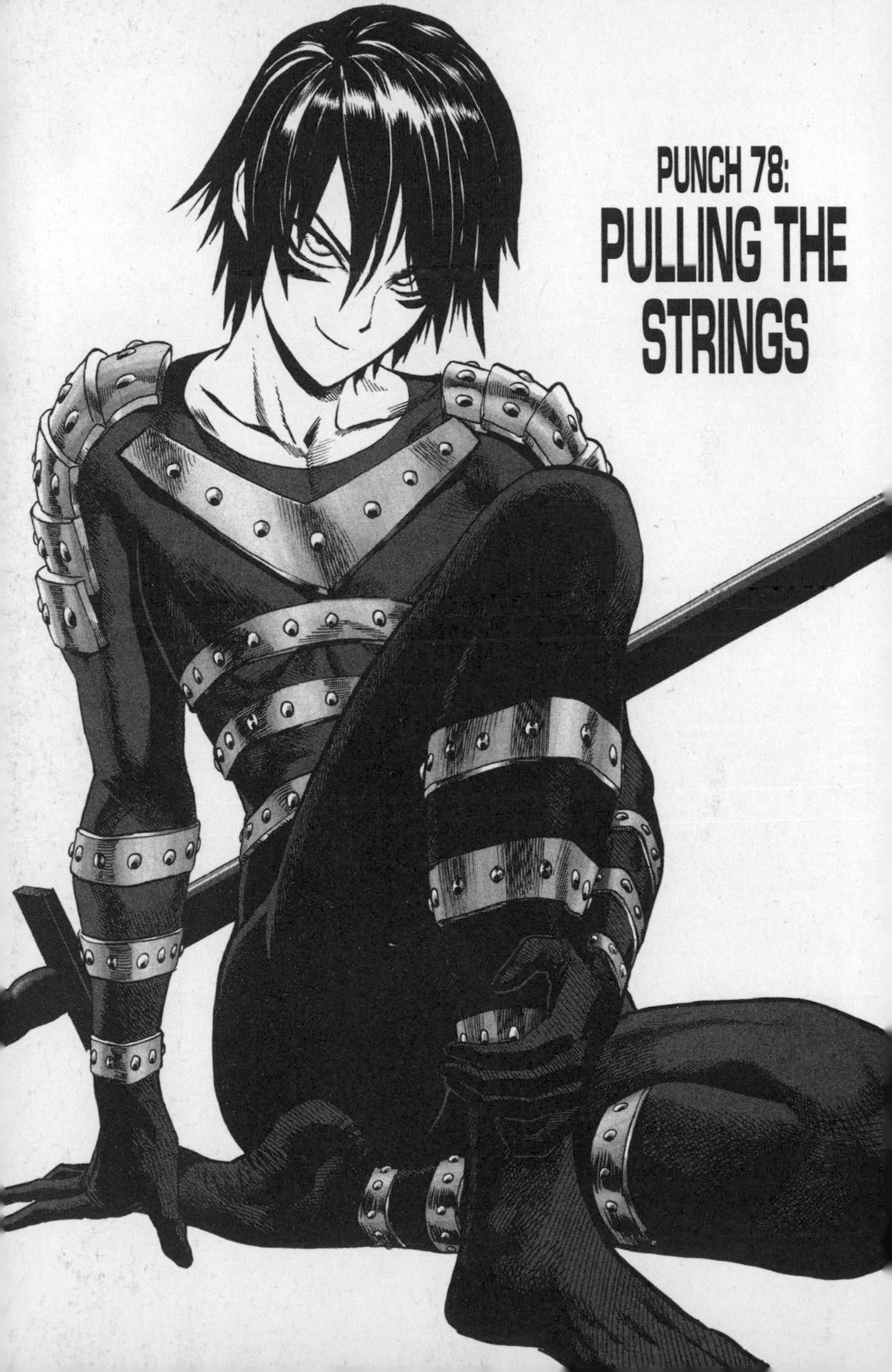

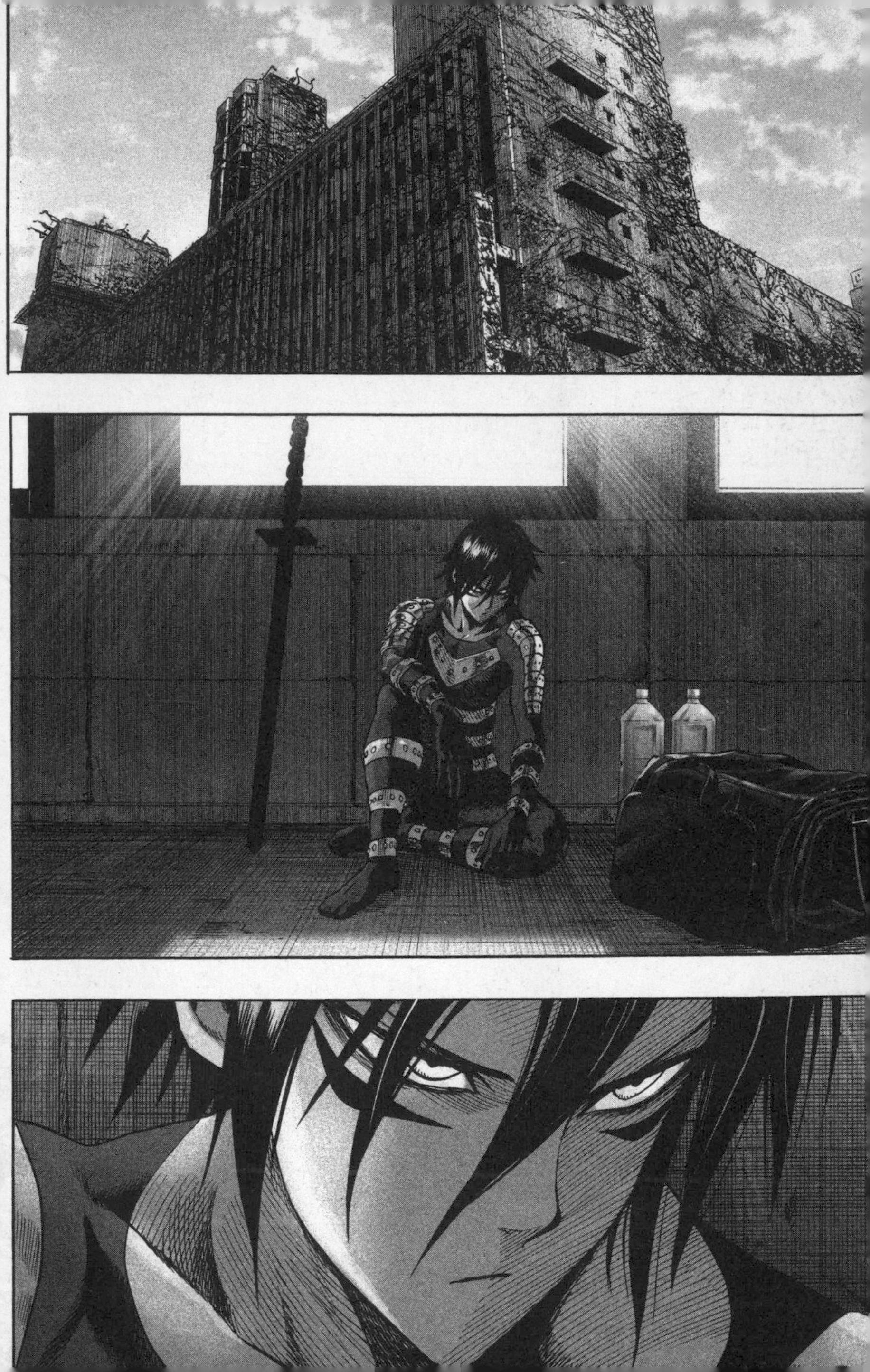

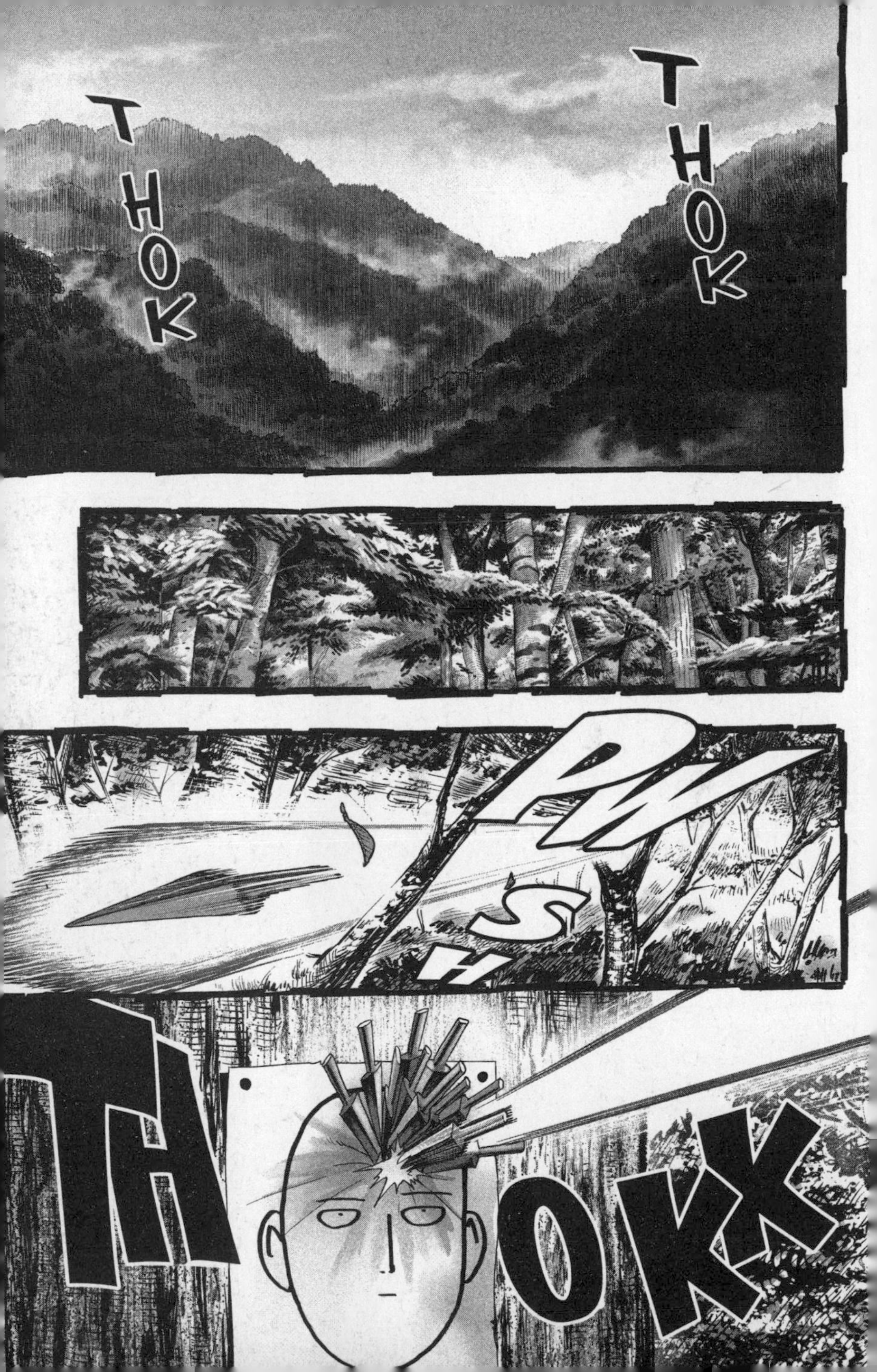
THOK
THOK
PWSH
THOKK

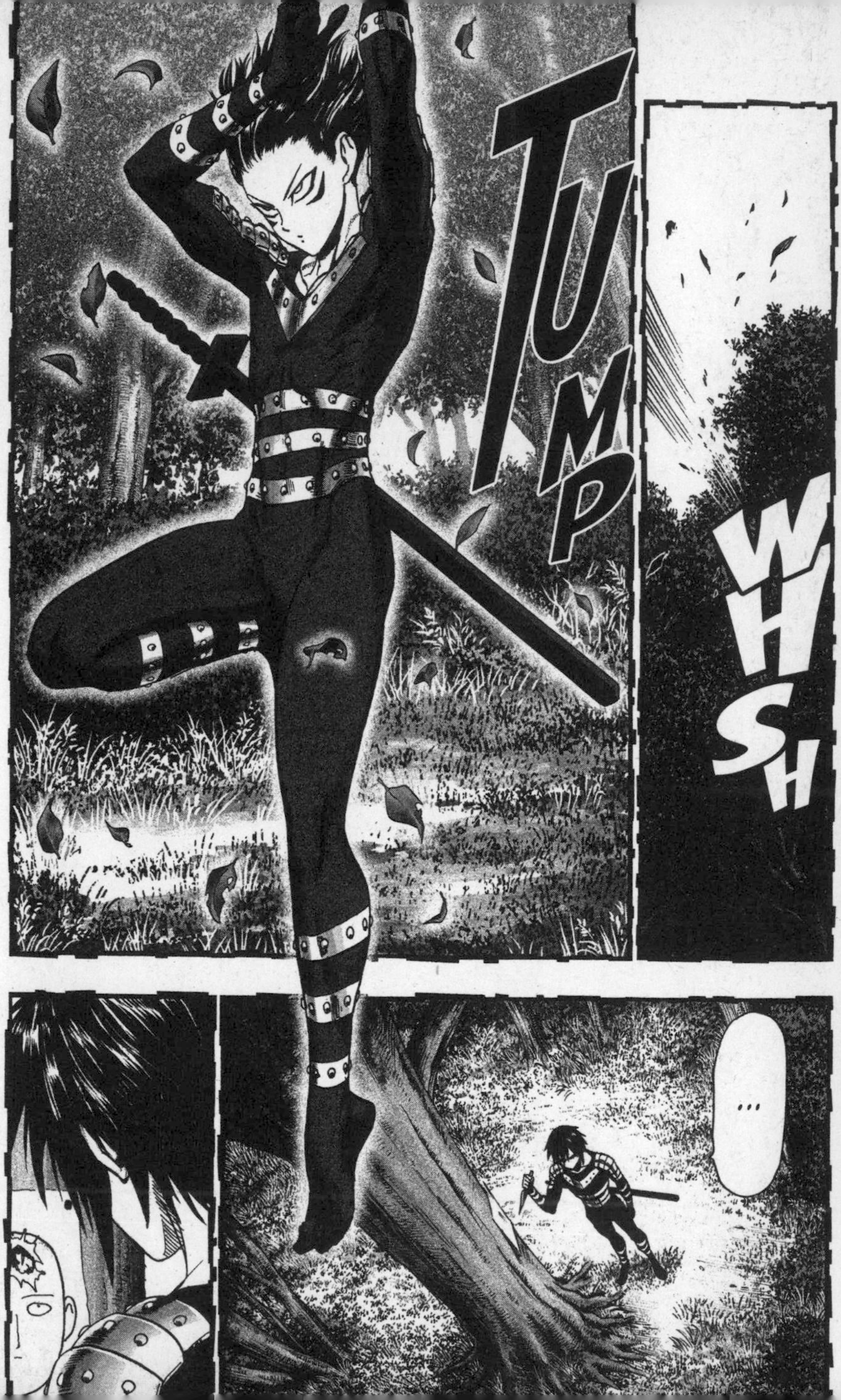
WHSH
TUMP
...

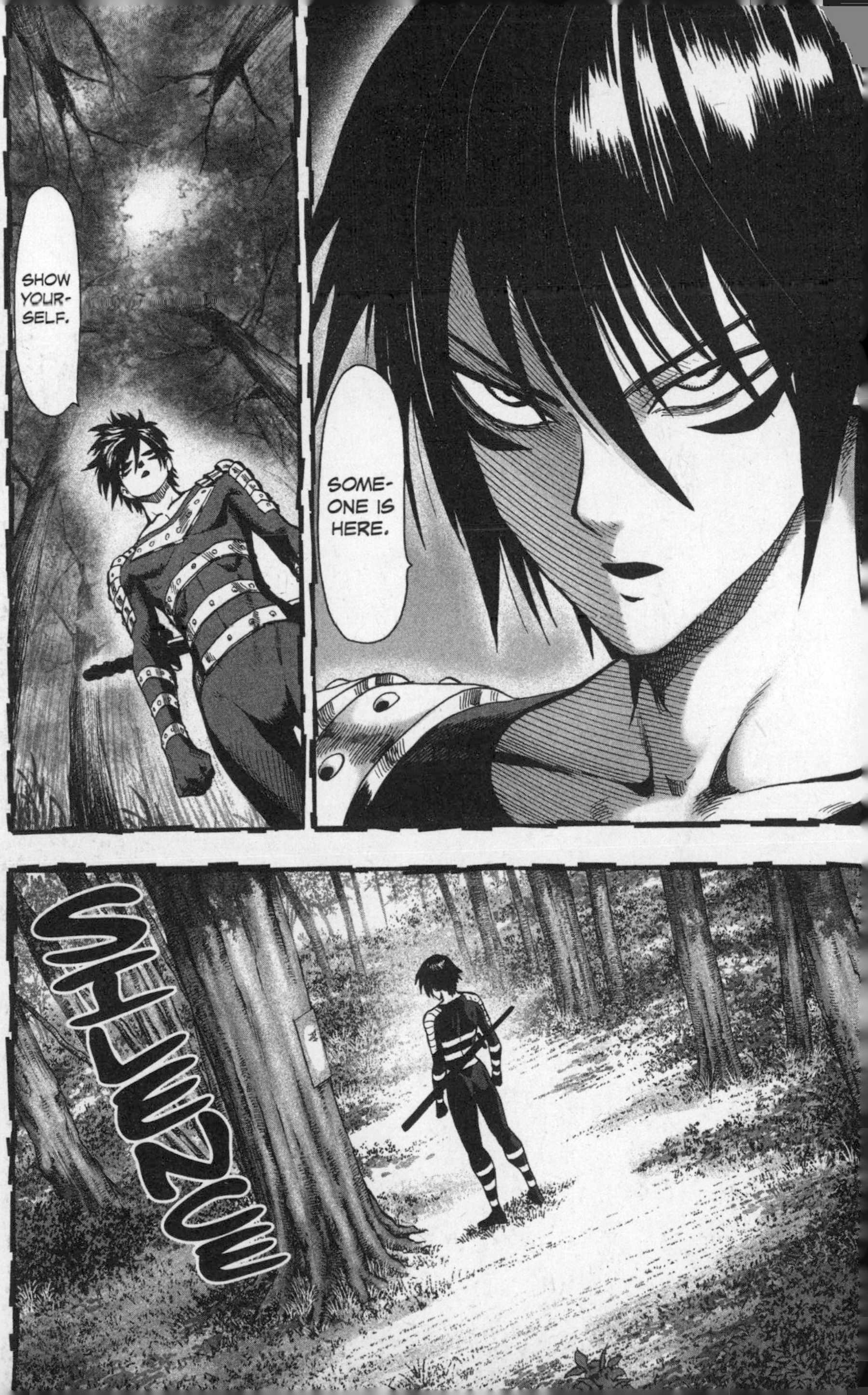
SOME-ONE IS HERE.
SHOW YOUR-SELF.
SILENCE

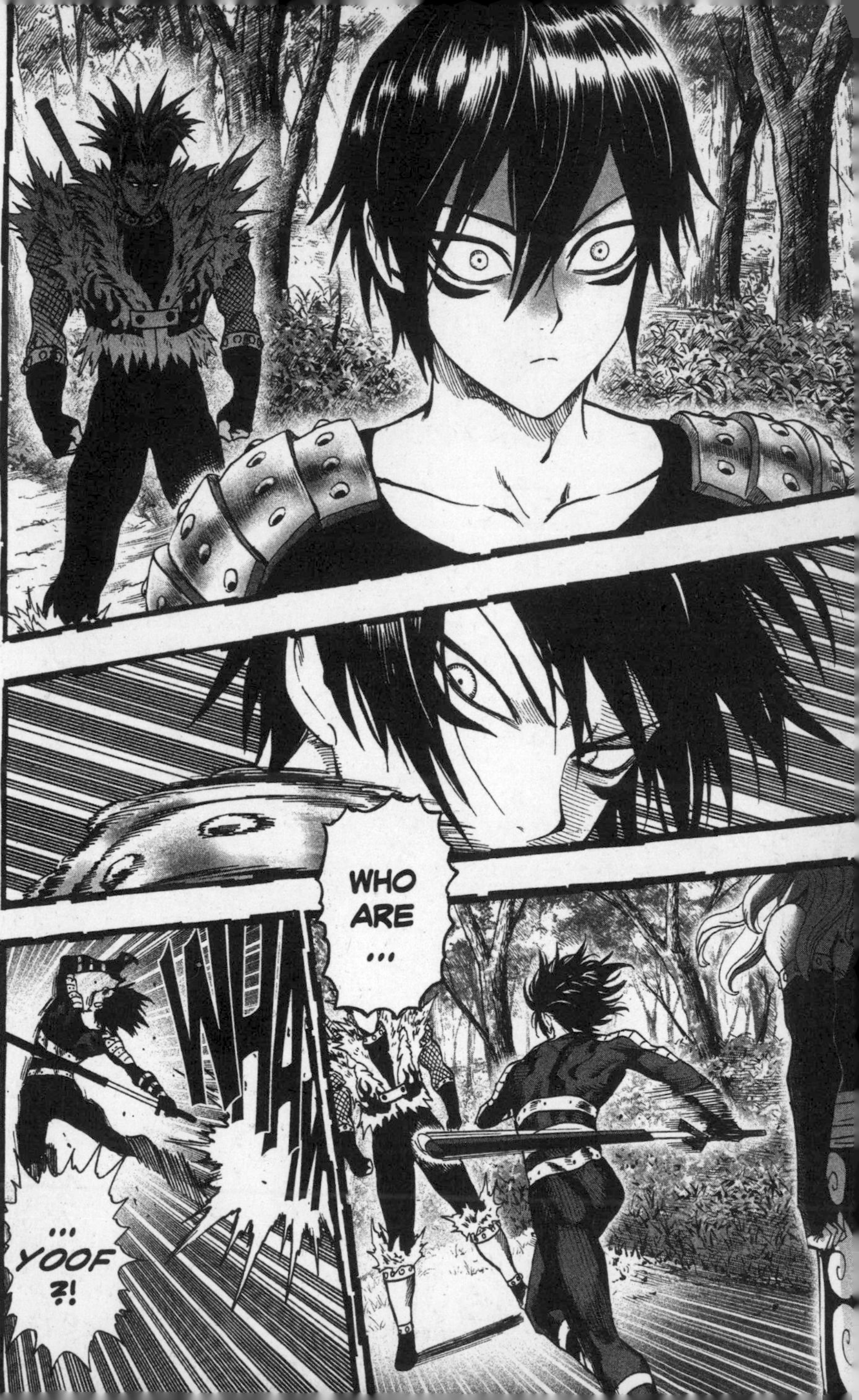
WHO ARE ...
WHA
... YOOF ?!

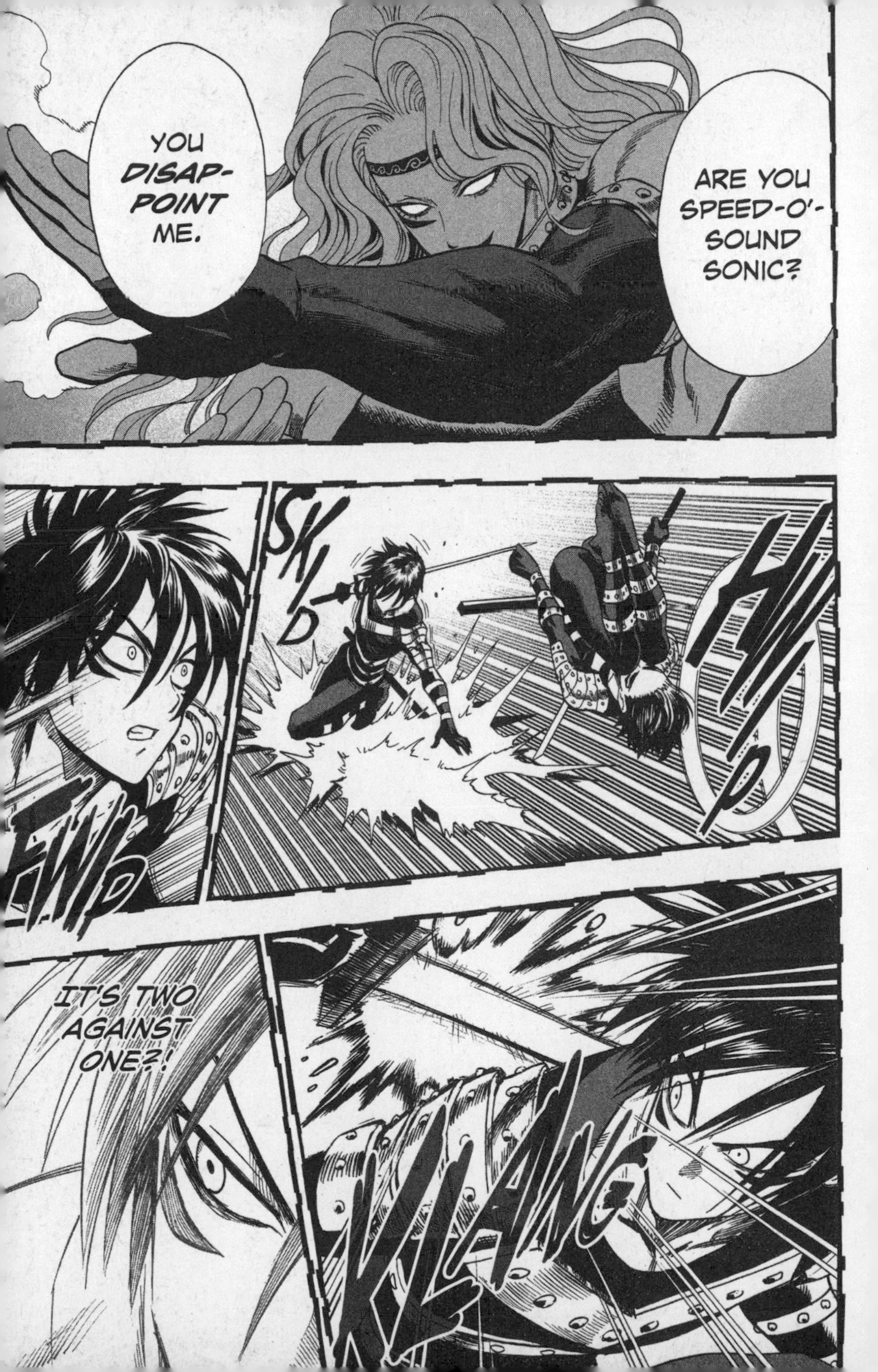
ARE YOU SPEED-O'-SOUND SONIC?
YOU DISAPPOINT ME.
WHIP
SKID
IT'S TWO AGAINST ONE?!

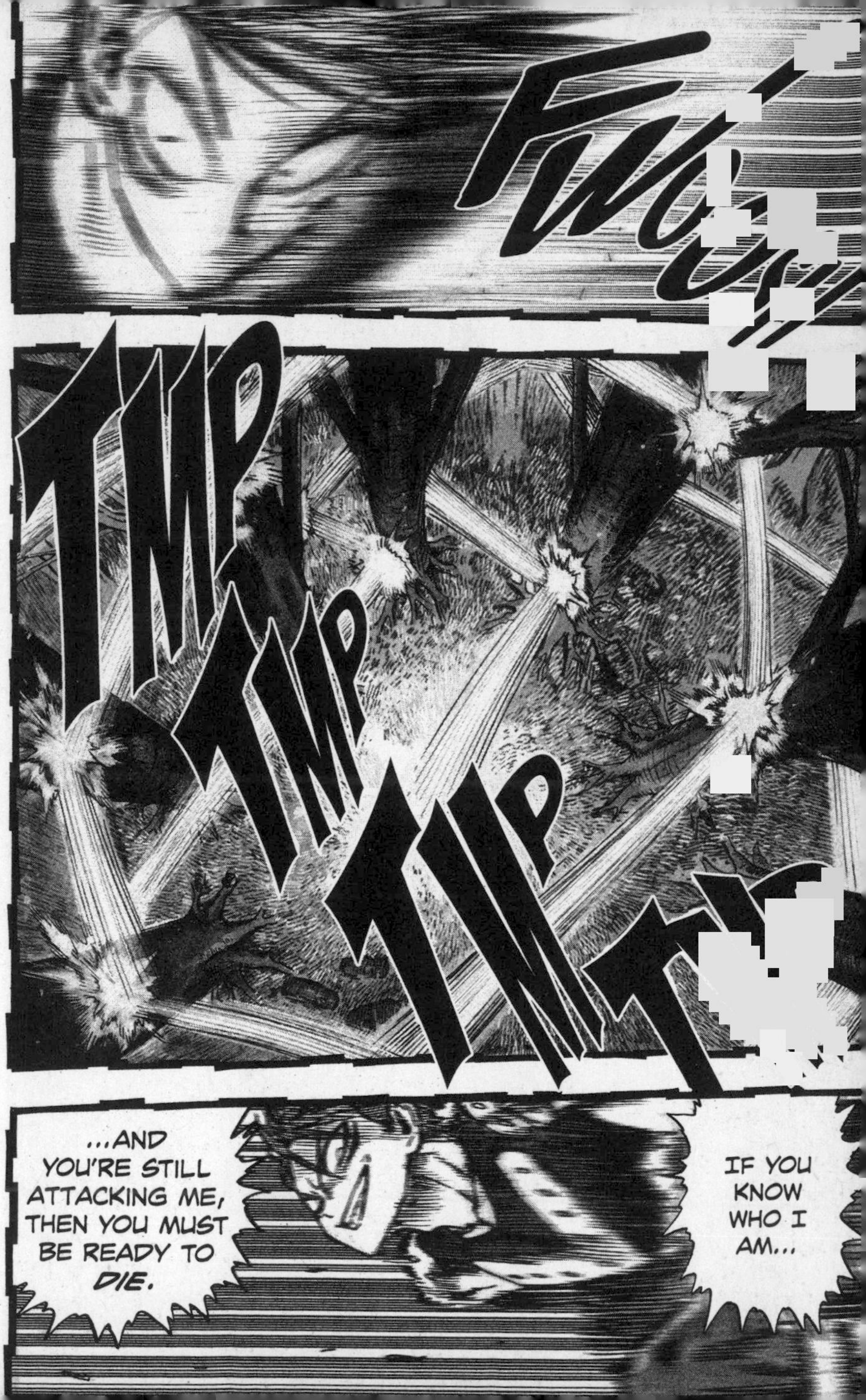
TIMP
TIMP
TIMP
IF YOU KNOW WHO I AM...
...AND YOU'RE STILL ATTACKING ME, THEN YOU MUST BE READY TO *DIE*.

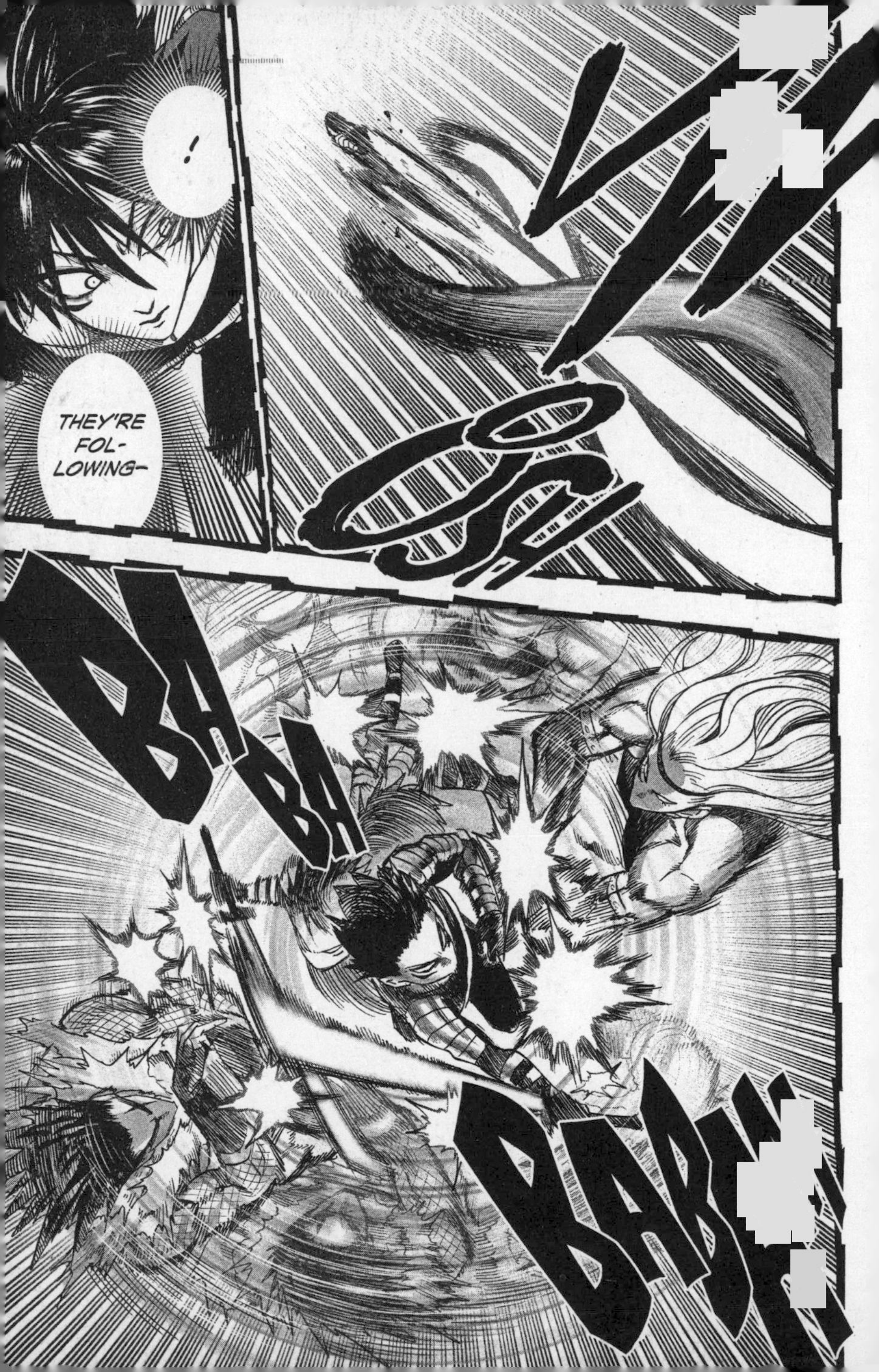
!
THEY'RE FOL-LOWING-
BA BA BA

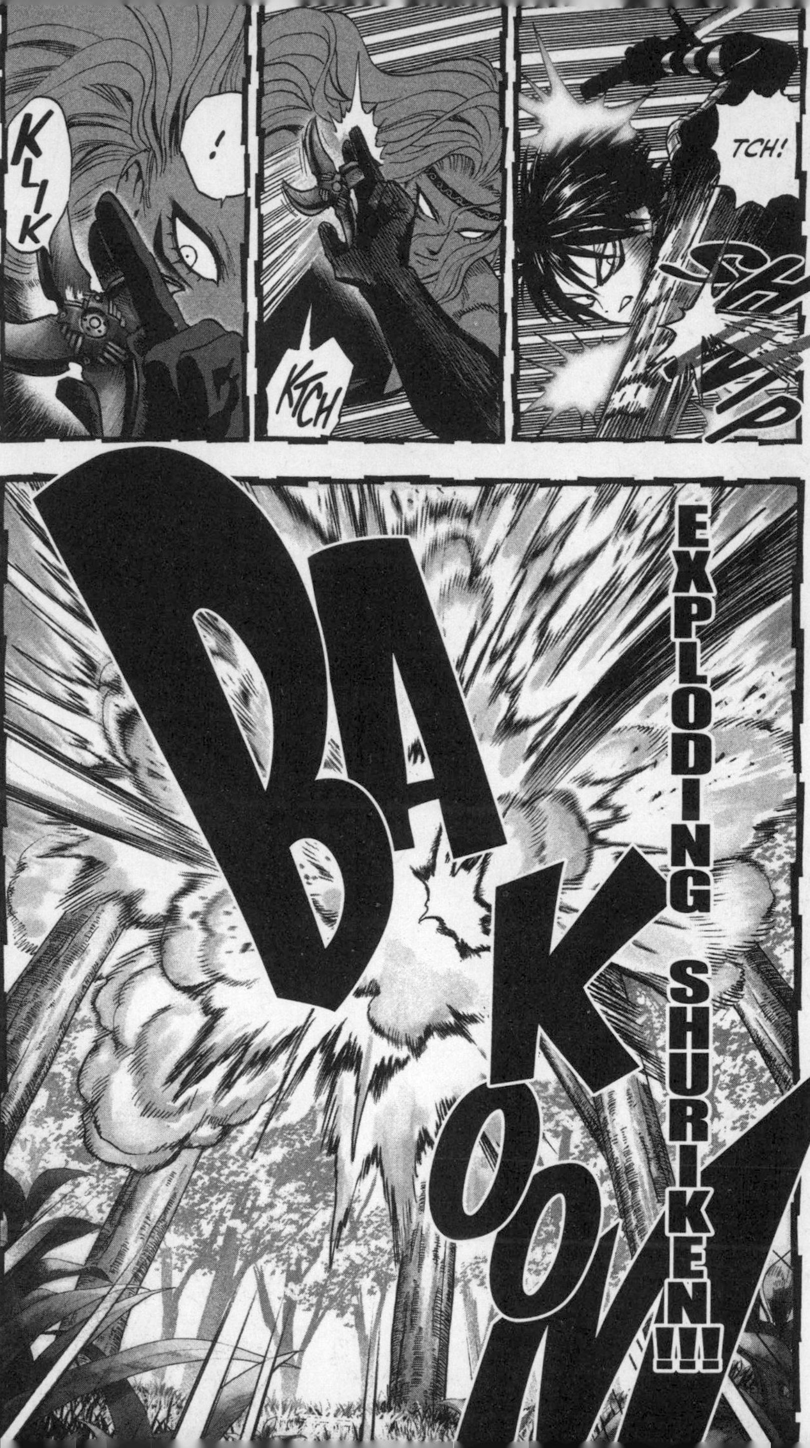
TCH!
SHWIP!
KTCH
KLIK
!
BAKOOM
EXPLODING SHURIKEN!!!

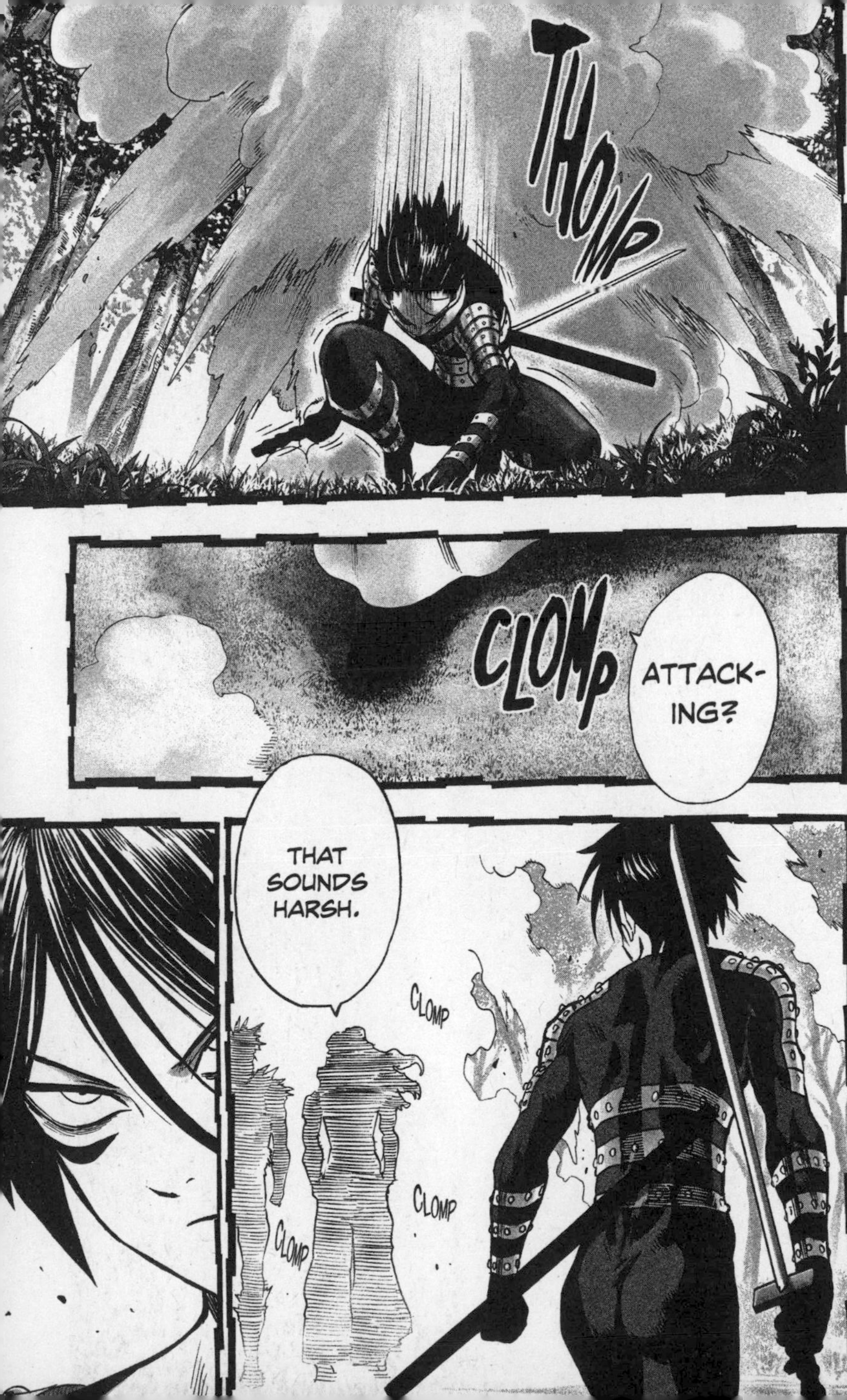
THOMP
CLOMP
ATTACK-ING?
THAT SOUNDS HARSH.
CLOMP
CLOMP
CLOMP

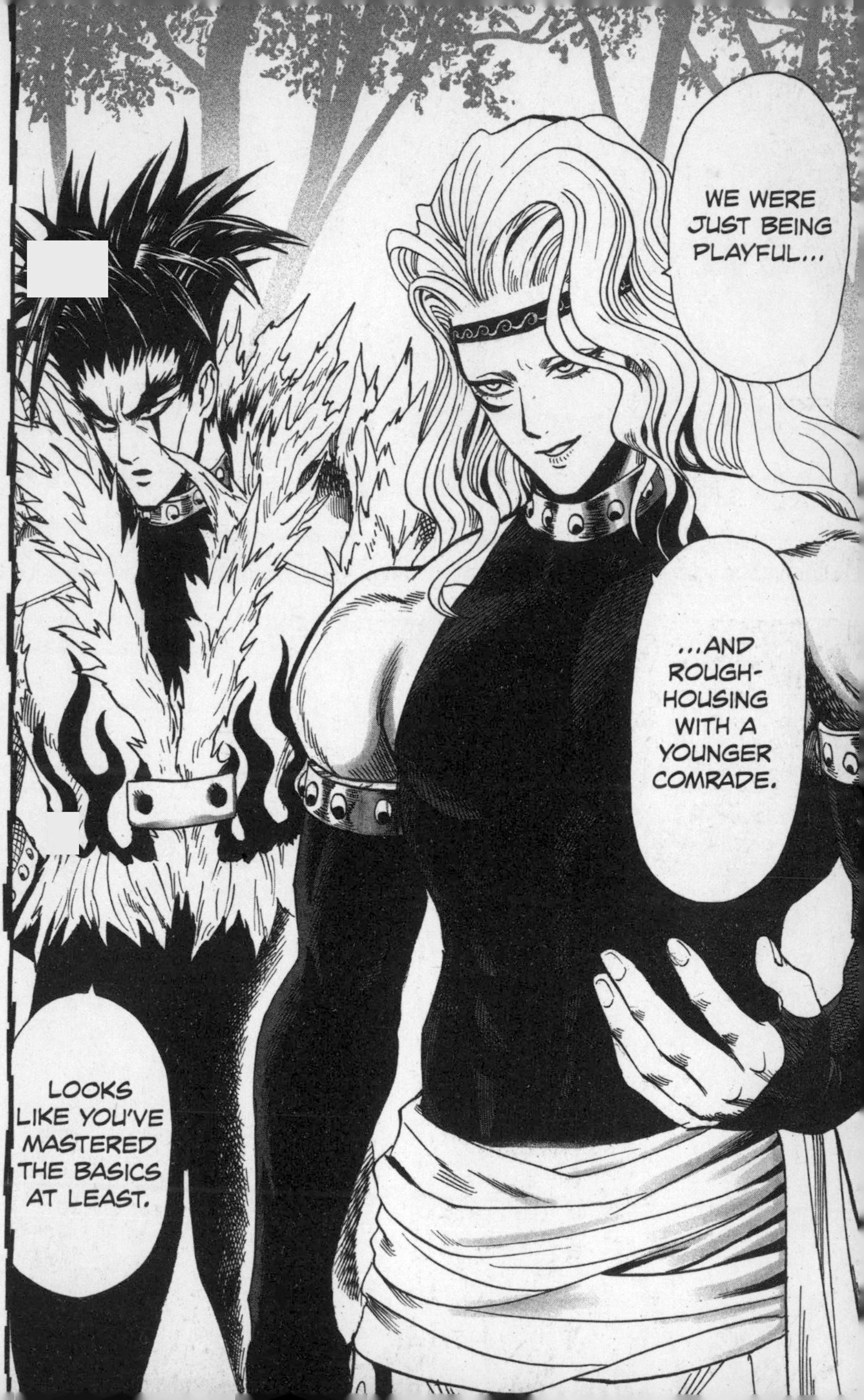
WE WERE JUST BEING PLAYFUL...
...AND ROUGH-HOUSING WITH A YOUNGER COMRADE.
LOOKS LIKE YOU'VE MASTERED THE BASICS AT LEAST.

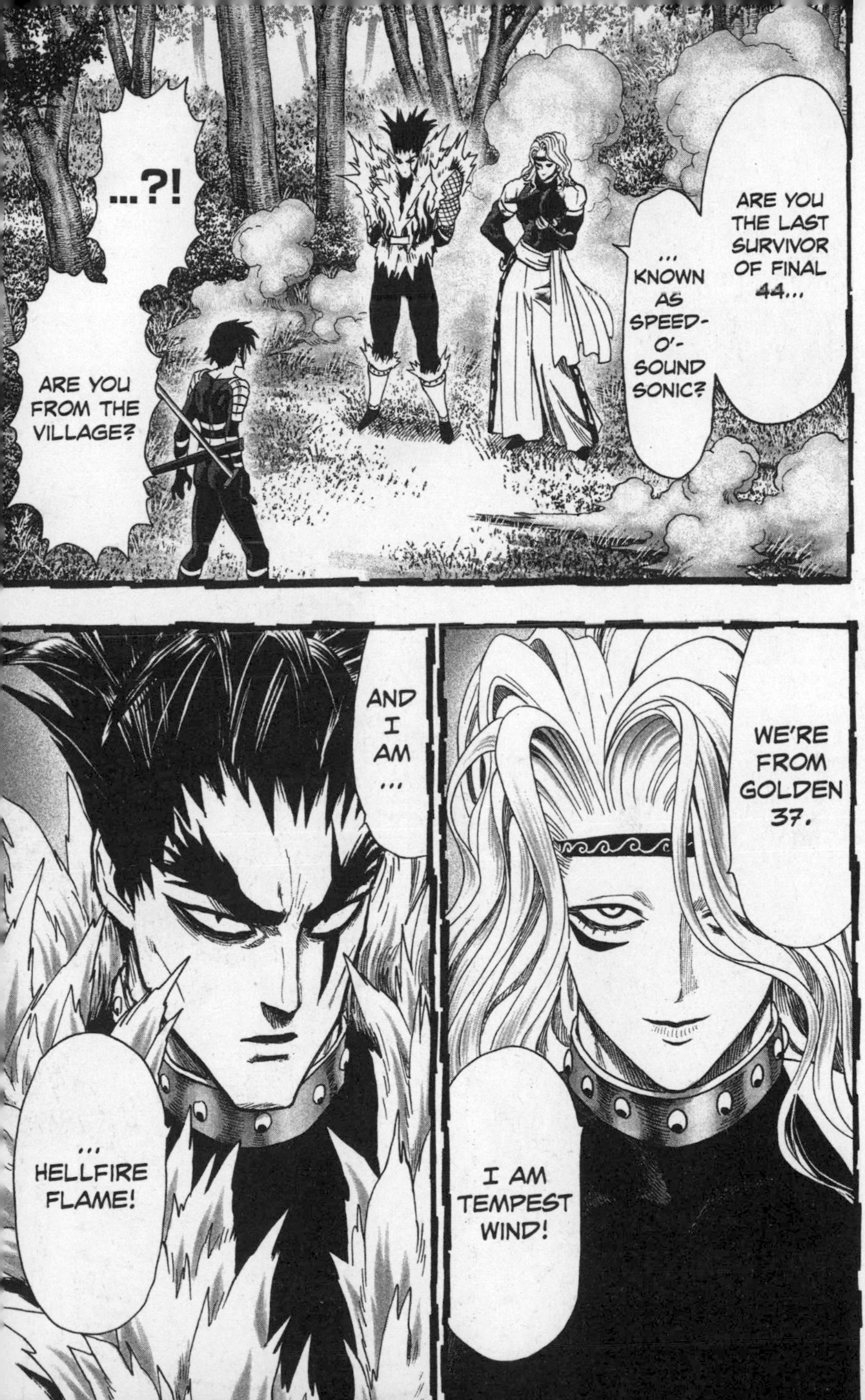
ARE YOU THE LAST SURVIVOR OF FINAL 44...
... KNOWN AS SPEED-O'-SOUND SONIC?
...?!
ARE YOU FROM THE VILLAGE?
WE'RE FROM GOLDEN 37.
I AM TEMPEST WIND!
AND I AM ...
... HELLFIRE FLAME!

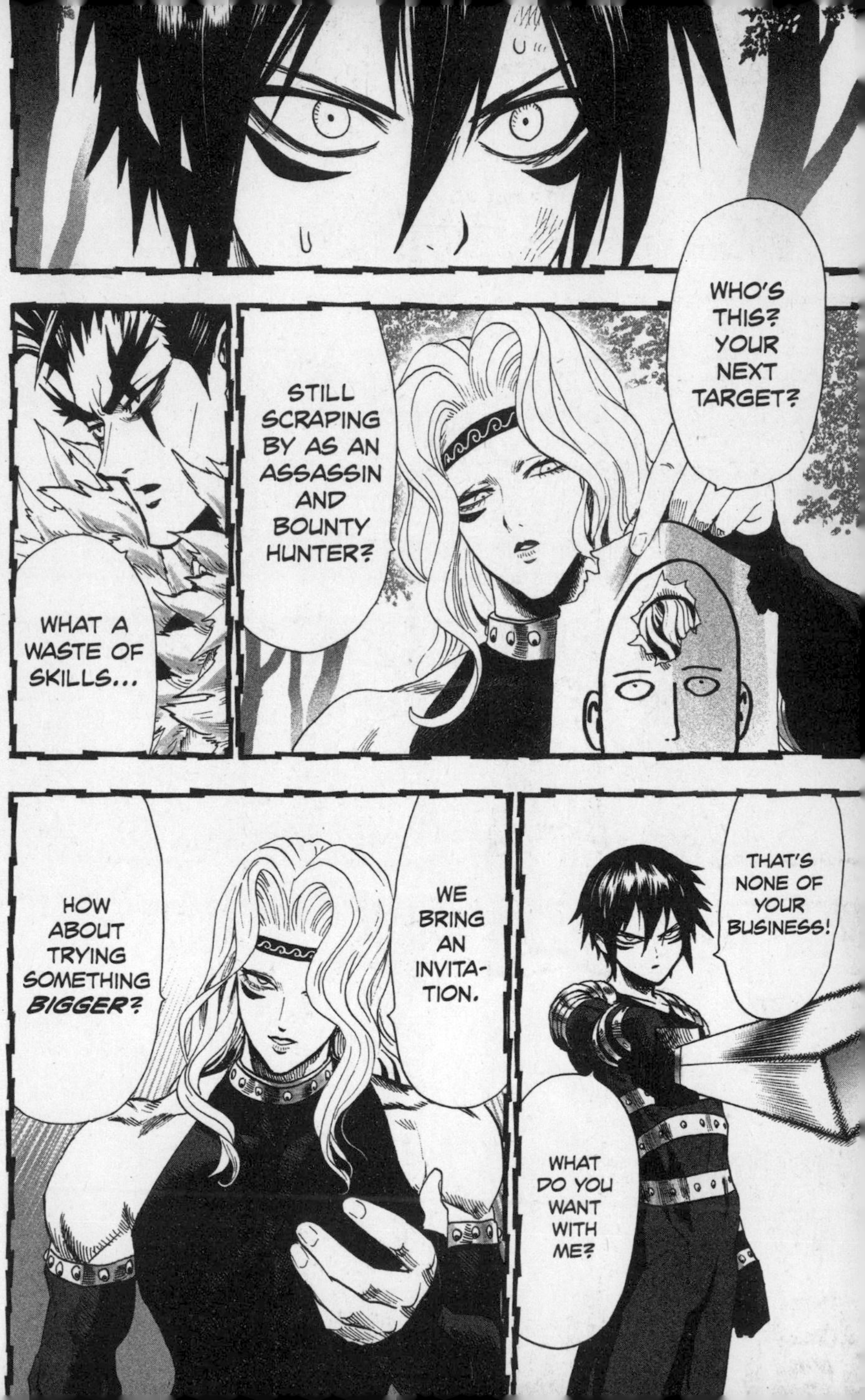
WHO'S THIS? YOUR NEXT TARGET?
STILL SCRAPING BY AS AN ASSASSIN AND BOUNTY HUNTER?
WHAT A WASTE OF SKILLS...
THAT'S NONE OF YOUR BUSINESS!
WHAT DO YOU WANT WITH ME?
WE BRING AN INVITATION.
HOW ABOUT TRYING SOMETHING *BIGGER*?

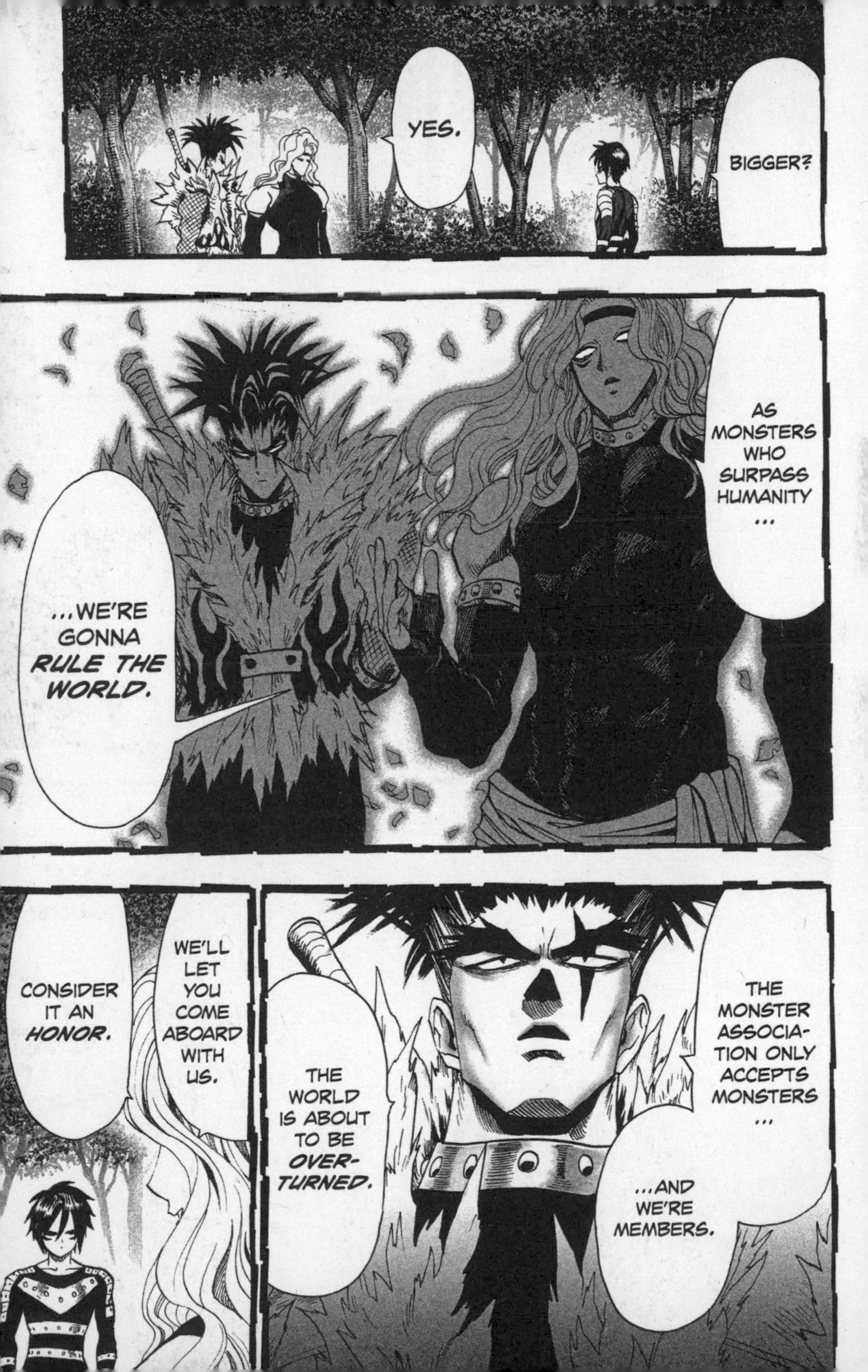
BIGGER?
YES.
AS MONSTERS WHO SURPASS HUMANITY...
...WE'RE GONNA RULE THE WORLD.
THE MONSTER ASSOCIATION ONLY ACCEPTS MONSTERS...
...AND WE'RE MEMBERS.
THE WORLD IS ABOUT TO BE OVERTURNED.
WE'LL LET YOU COME ABOARD WITH US.
CONSIDER IT AN HONOR.

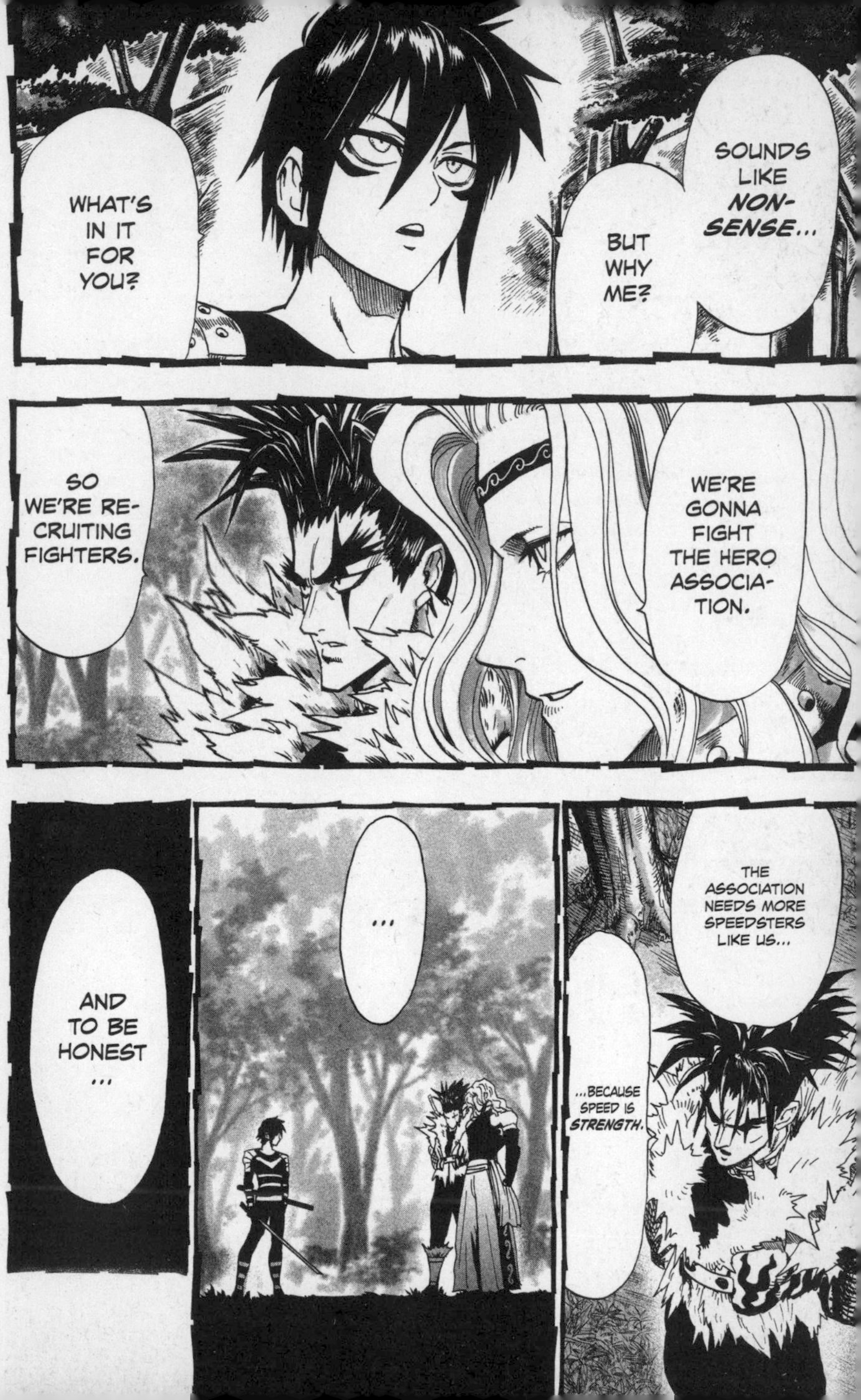
SOUNDS LIKE NON-SENSE...
BUT WHY ME?
WHAT'S IN IT FOR YOU?
WE'RE GONNA FIGHT THE HERO ASSOCIA-TION.
SO WE'RE RE-CRUITING FIGHTERS.
THE ASSOCIATION NEEDS MORE SPEEDSTERS LIKE US...
...BECAUSE SPEED IS STRENGTH.
...
AND TO BE HONEST ...

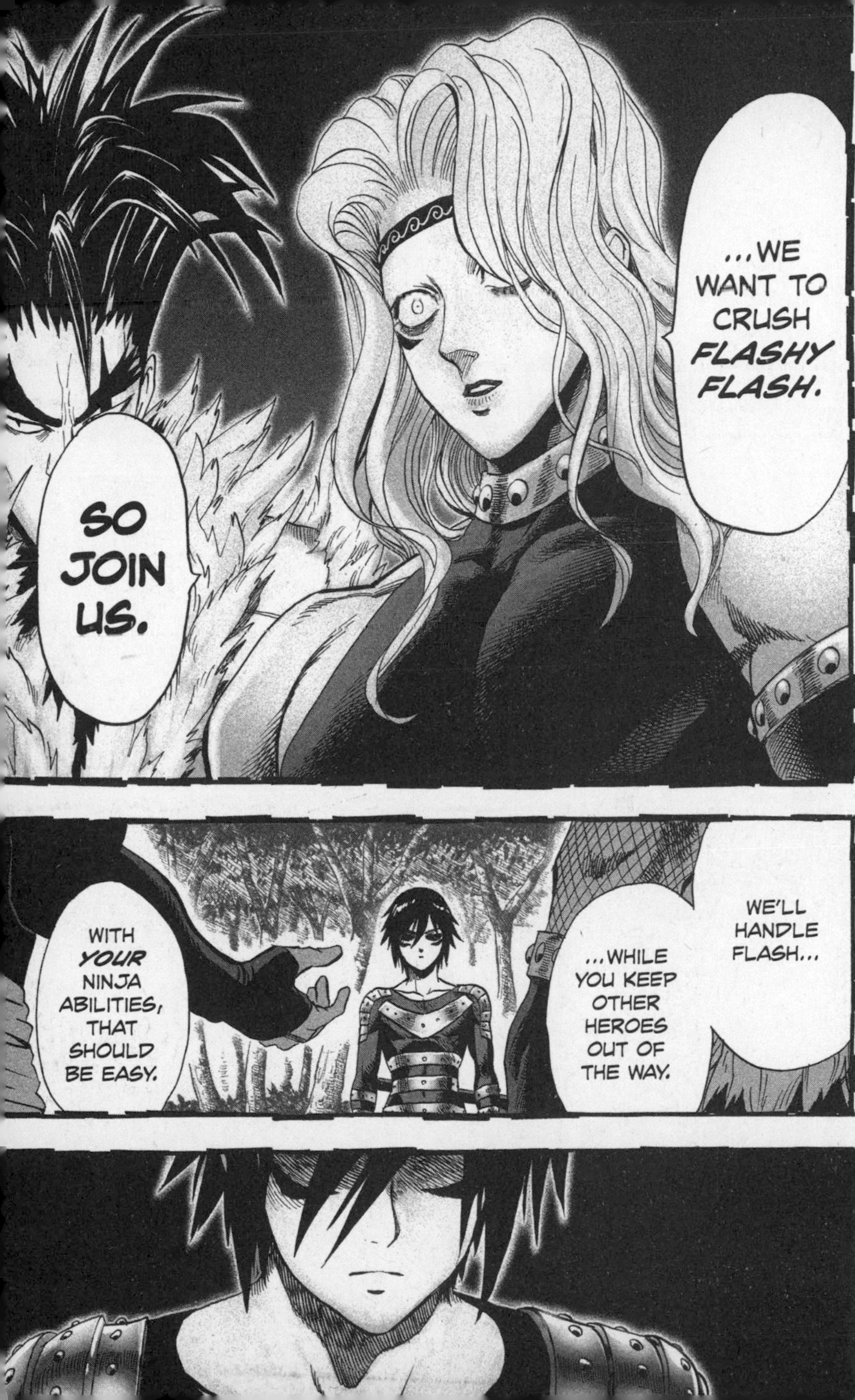
...WE WANT TO CRUSH *FLASHY FLASH*.
SO JOIN US.
WE'LL HANDLE FLASH...
...WHILE YOU KEEP OTHER HEROES OUT OF THE WAY.
WITH *YOUR* NINJA ABILITIES, THAT SHOULD BE EASY.

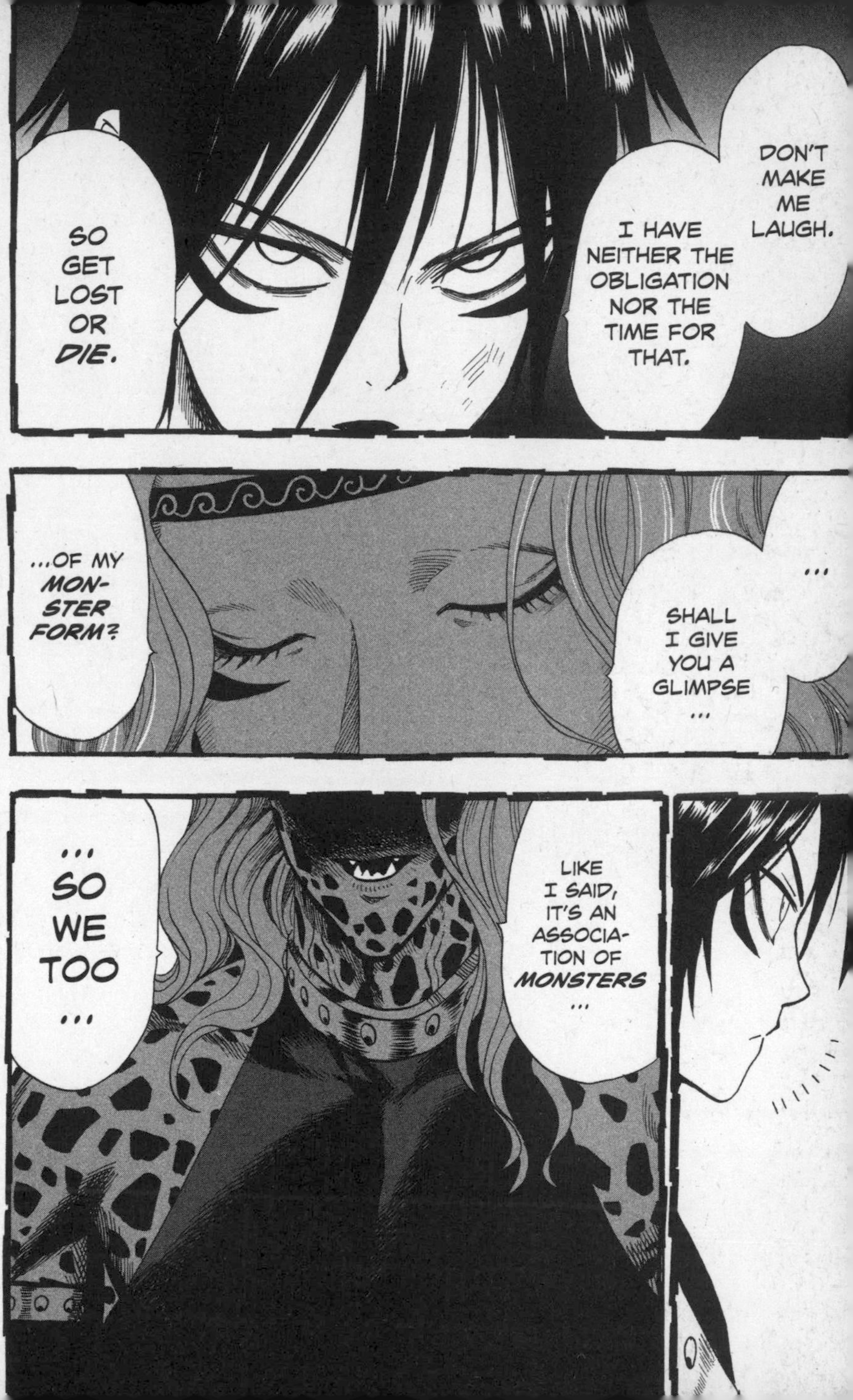
DON'T MAKE ME LAUGH.
I HAVE NEITHER THE OBLIGATION NOR THE TIME FOR THAT.
SO GET LOST OR *DIE*.
...
SHALL I GIVE YOU A GLIMPSE...
...OF MY *MONSTER FORM*?
LIKE I SAID, IT'S AN ASSOCIATION OF *MONSTERS*...
...SO WE TOO...

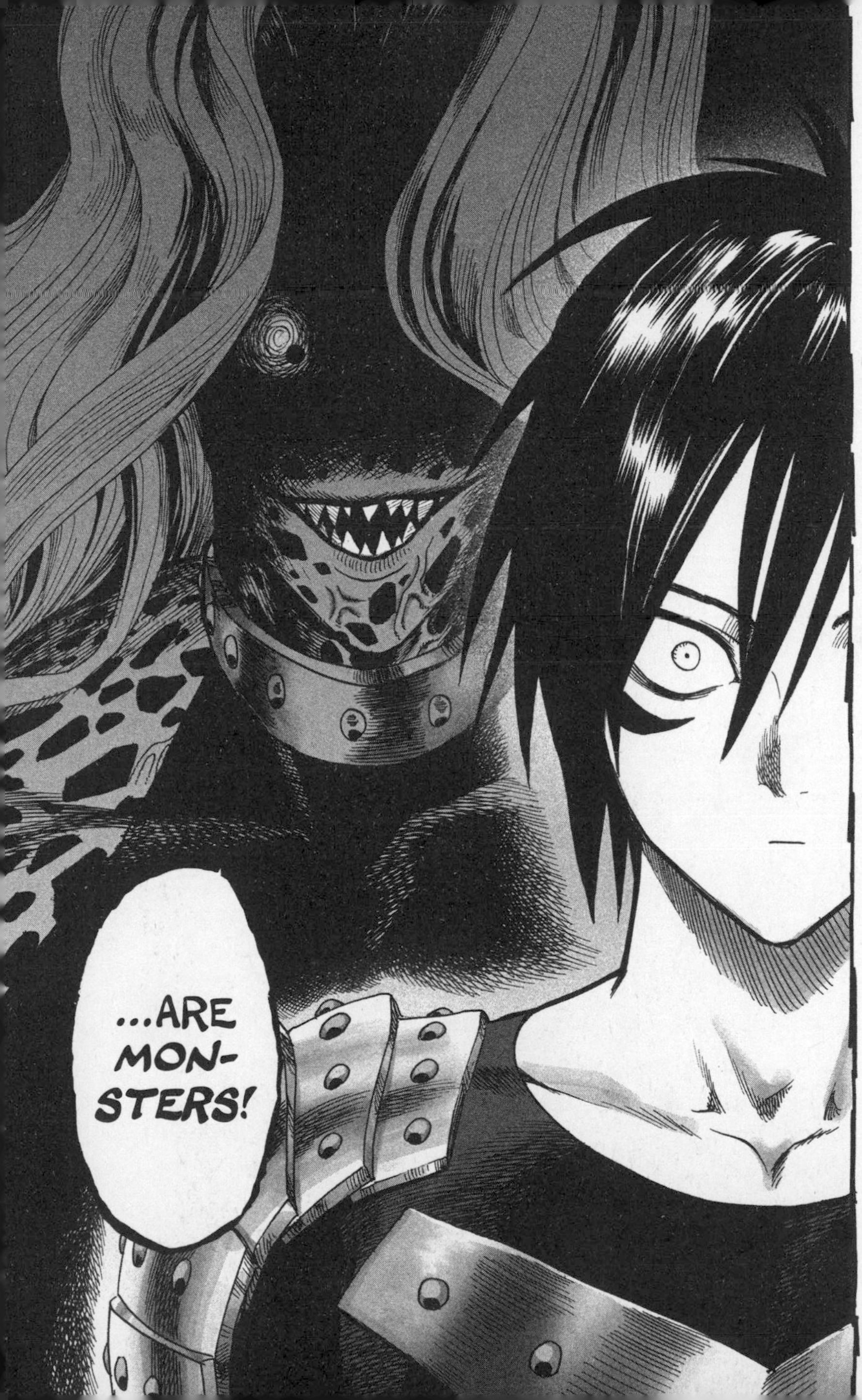
...ARE MON-STERS!

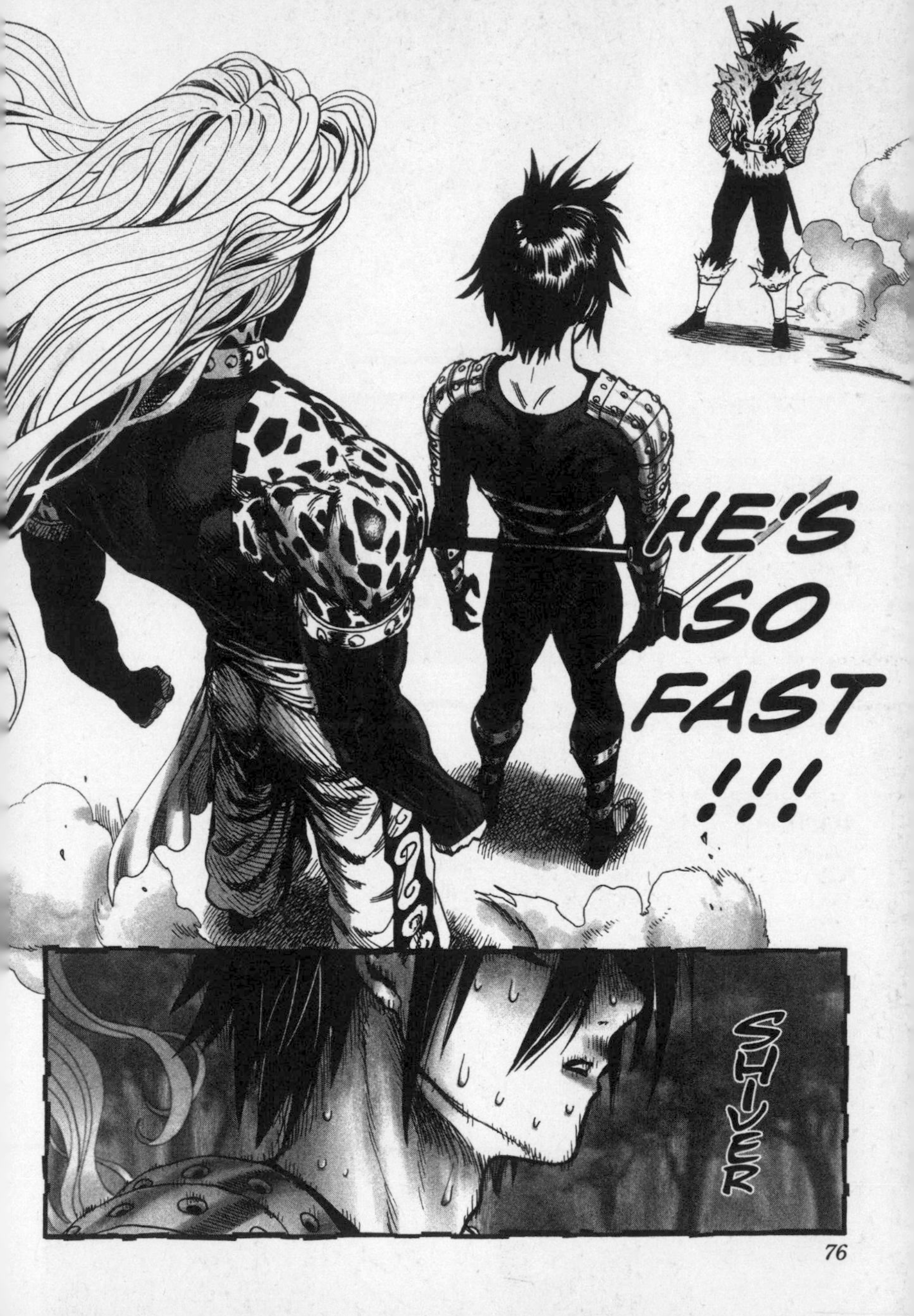
HE'S SO FAST!!!
SHIVER

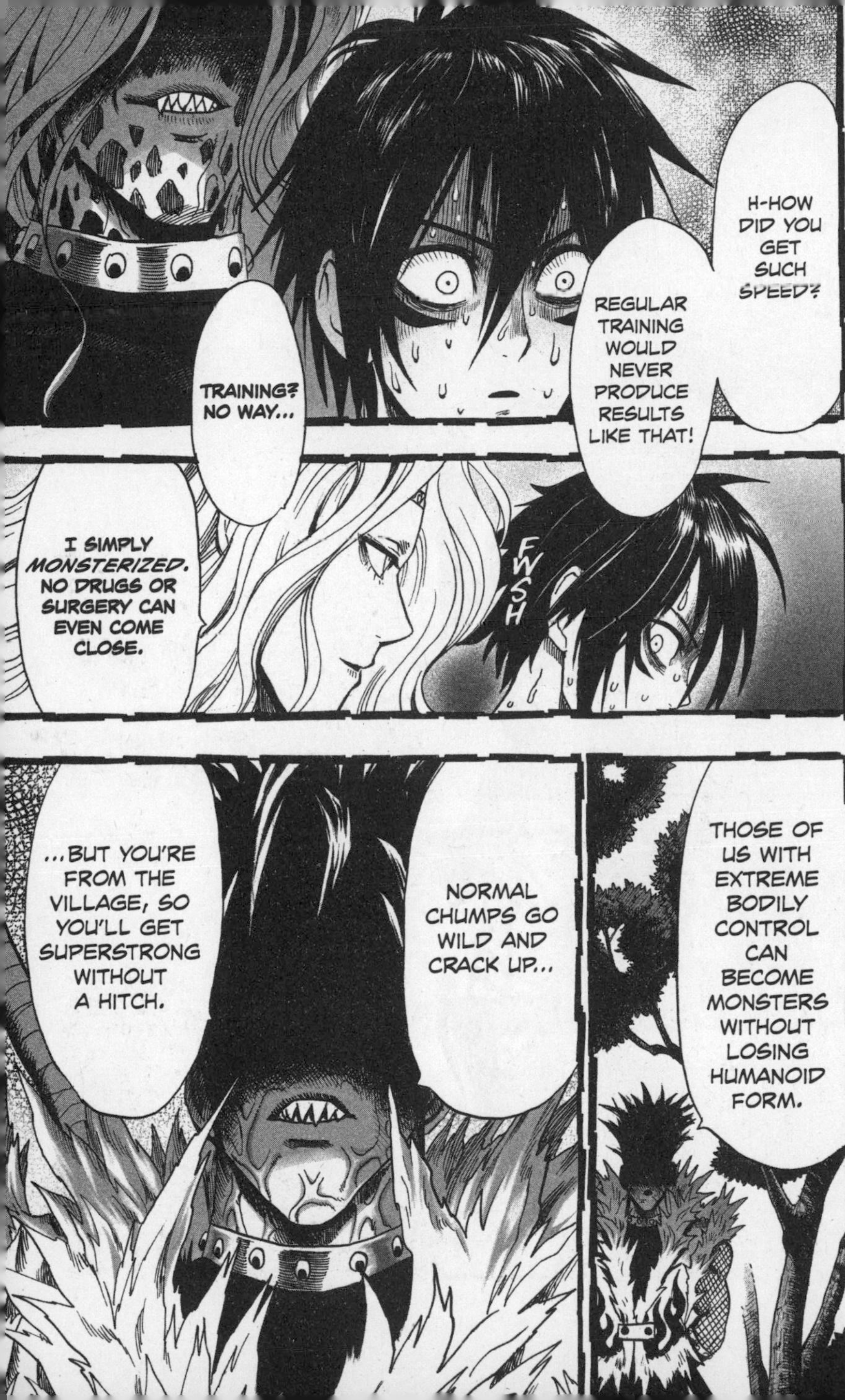
H-HOW DID YOU GET SUCH SPEED?
REGULAR TRAINING WOULD NEVER PRODUCE RESULTS LIKE THAT!
TRAINING? NO WAY...
FWSH
I SIMPLY *MONSTERIZED*. NO DRUGS OR SURGERY CAN EVEN COME CLOSE.
THOSE OF US WITH EXTREME BODILY CONTROL CAN BECOME MONSTERS WITHOUT LOSING HUMANOID FORM.
NORMAL CHUMPS GO WILD AND CRACK UP...
...BUT YOU'RE FROM THE VILLAGE, SO YOU'LL GET SUPERSTRONG WITHOUT A HITCH.

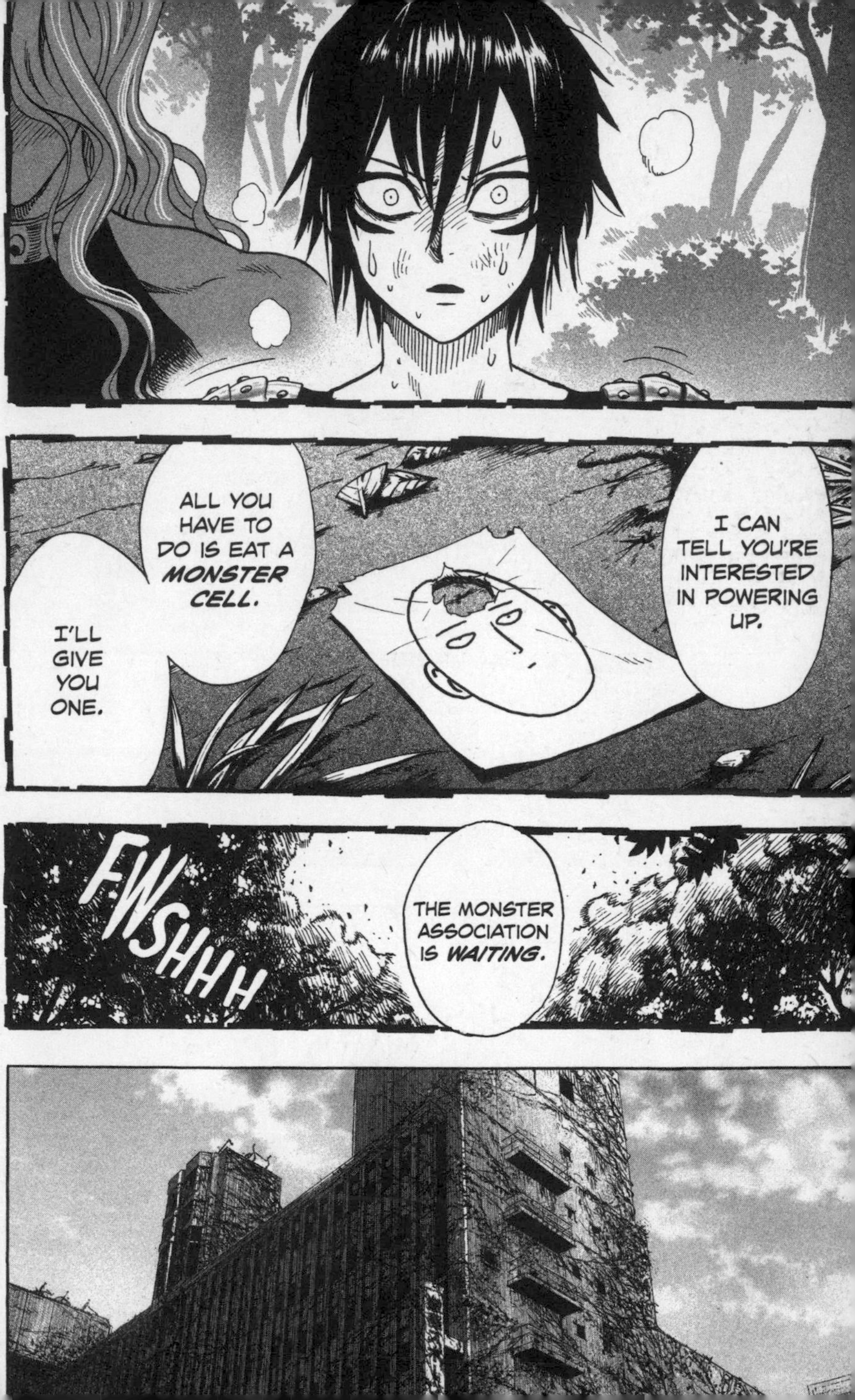
I CAN TELL YOU'RE INTERESTED IN POWERING UP.
ALL YOU HAVE TO DO IS EAT A *MONSTER CELL.*
I'LL GIVE YOU ONE.
THE MONSTER ASSOCIATION IS *WAITING.*
FWSHHH

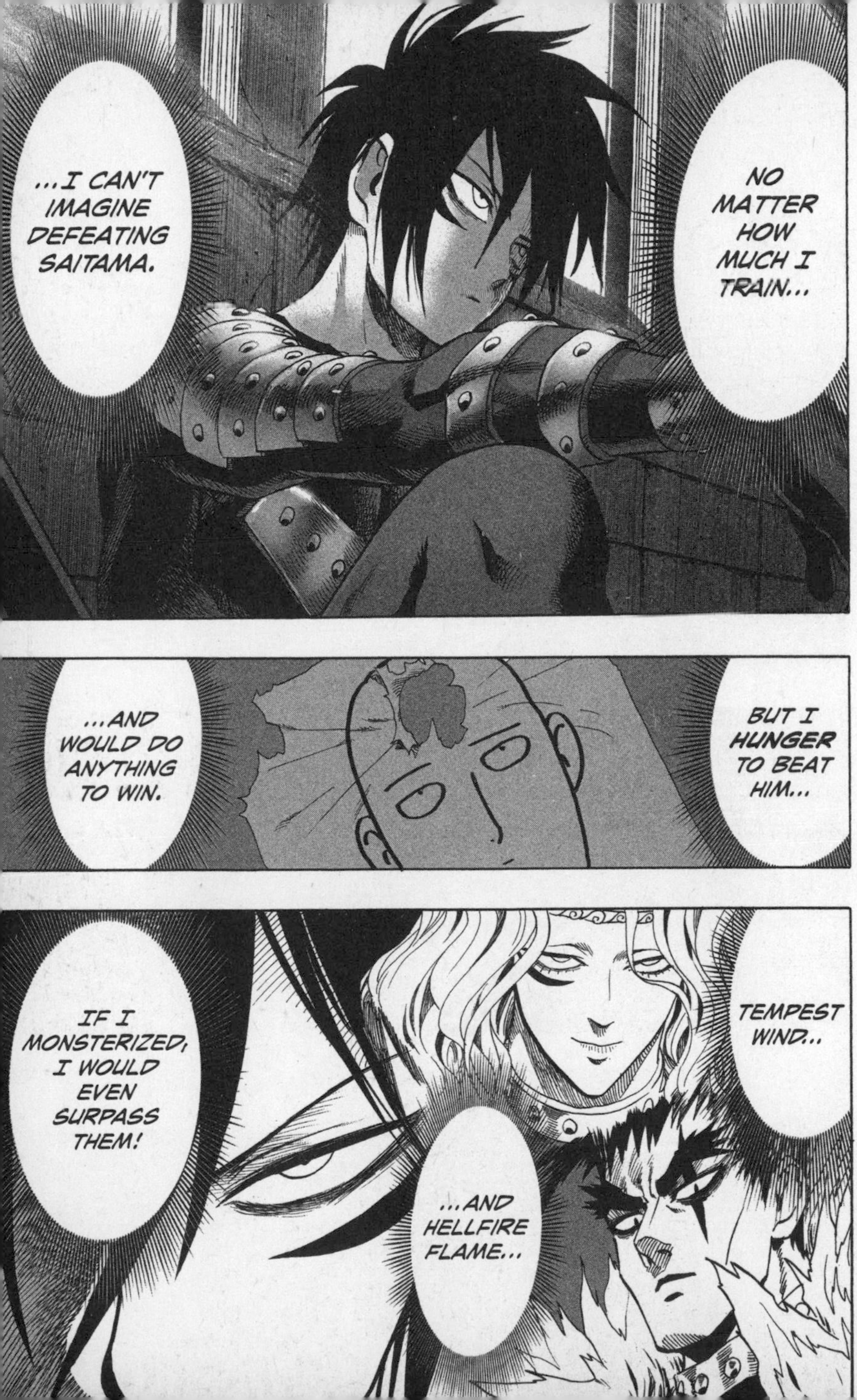
NO MATTER HOW MUCH I TRAIN...
...I CAN'T IMAGINE DEFEATING SAITAMA.
BUT I HUNGER TO BEAT HIM...
...AND WOULD DO ANYTHING TO WIN.
TEMPEST WIND...
...AND HELLFIRE FLAME...
IF I MONSTERIZED, I WOULD EVEN SURPASS THEM!

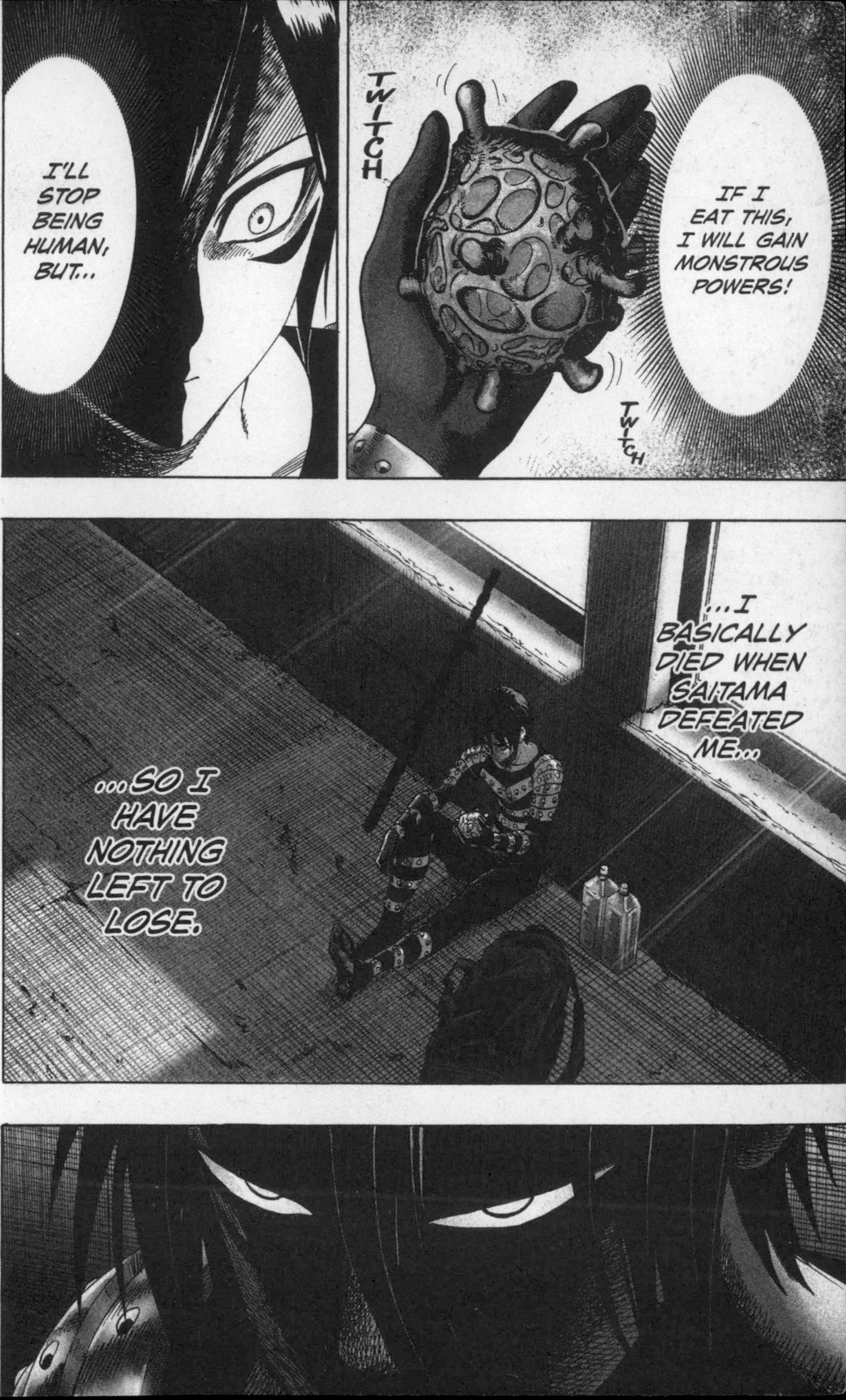
IF I EAT THIS, I WILL GAIN MONSTROUS POWERS!
TWITCH
TWITCH
I'LL STOP BEING HUMAN, BUT...
...I BASICALLY DIED WHEN SAITAMA DEFEATED ME...
...SO I HAVE NOTHING LEFT TO LOSE.

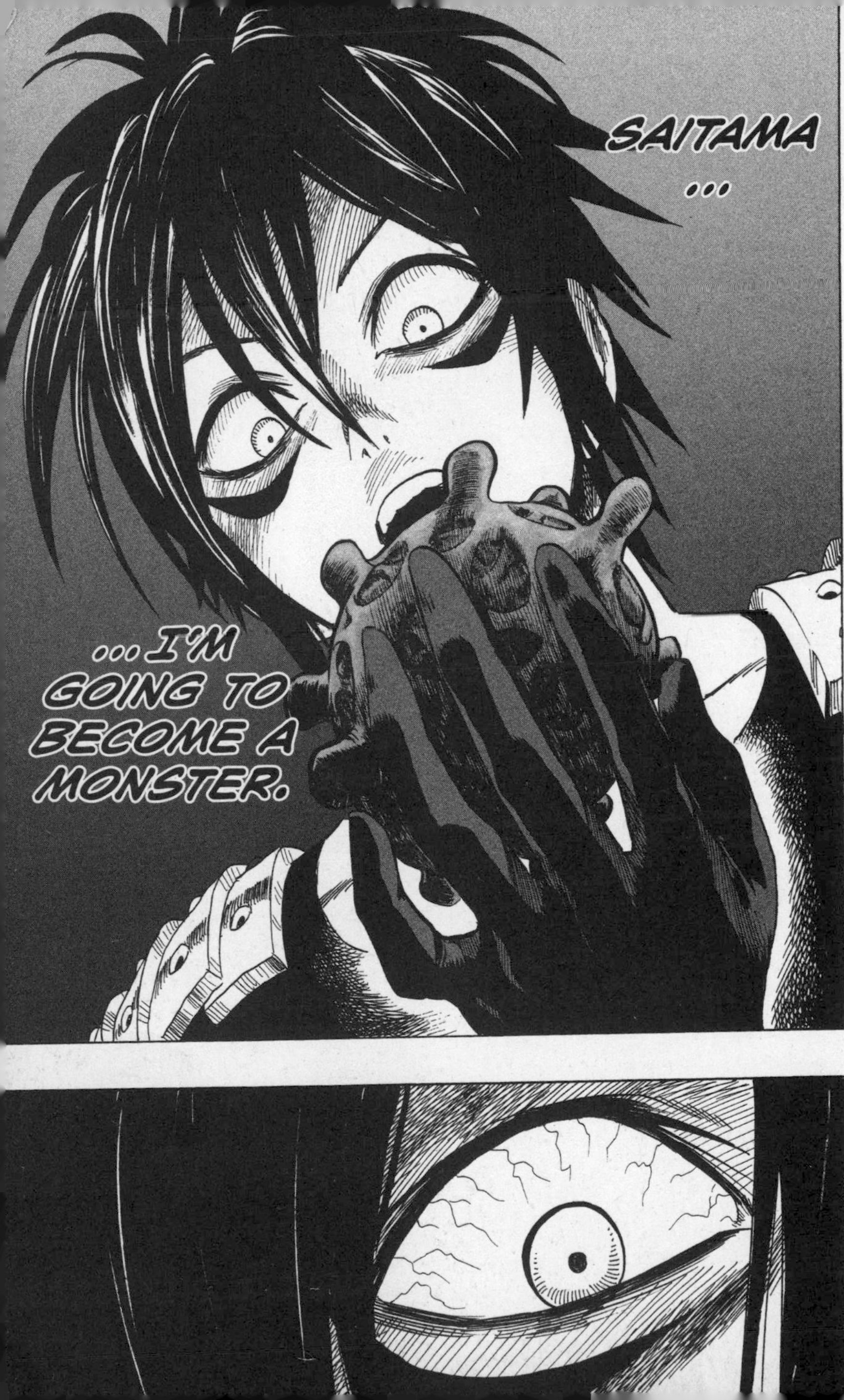
SAITAMA ...
...I'M GOING TO BECOME A MONSTER.

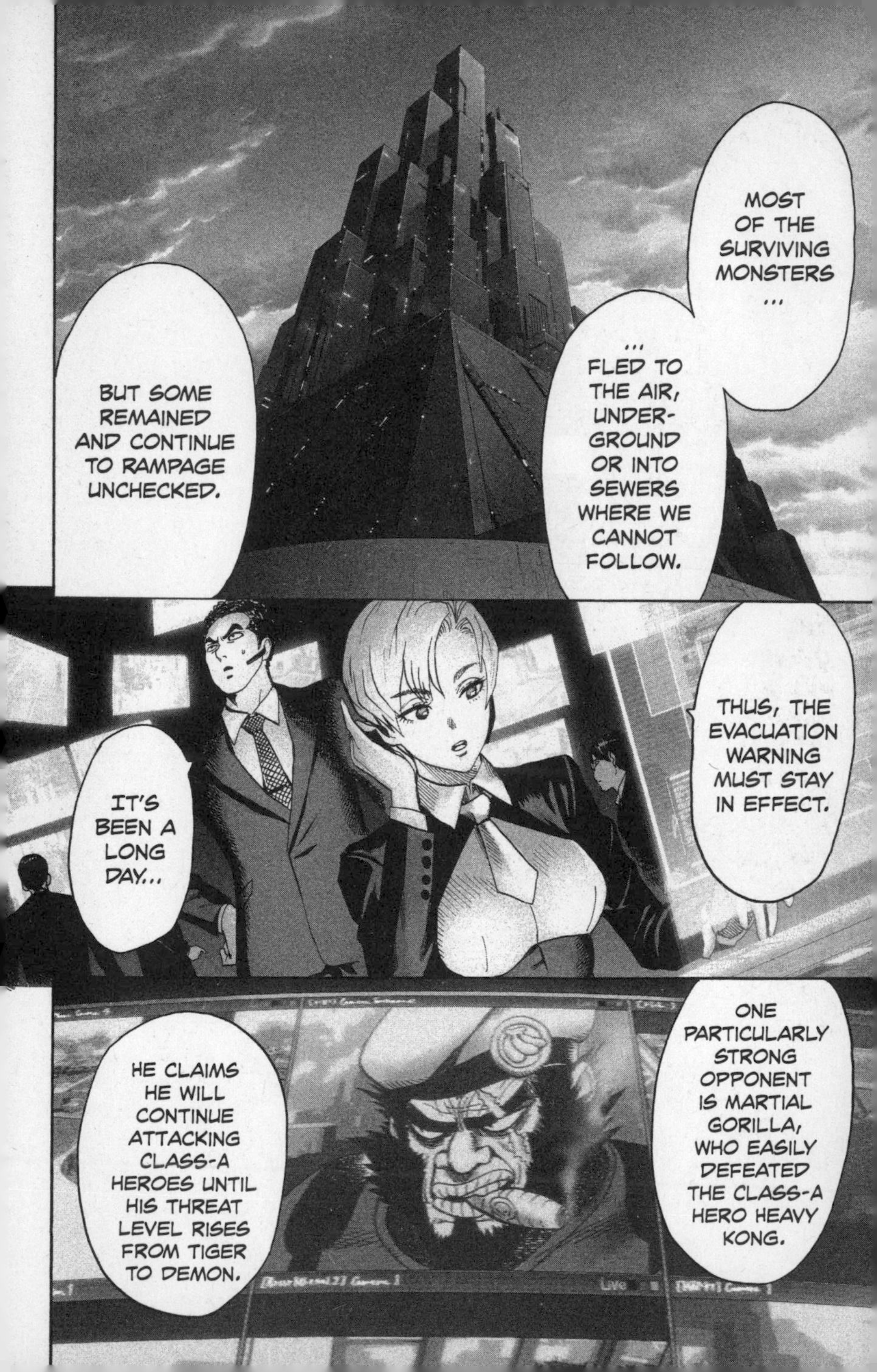
MOST OF THE SURVIVING MONSTERS ...
... FLED TO THE AIR, UNDER-GROUND OR INTO SEWERS WHERE WE CANNOT FOLLOW.
BUT SOME REMAINED AND CONTINUE TO RAMPAGE UNCHECKED.
THUS, THE EVACUATION WARNING MUST STAY IN EFFECT.
IT'S BEEN A LONG DAY...
ONE PARTICULARLY STRONG OPPONENT IS MARTIAL GORILLA, WHO EASILY DEFEATED THE CLASS-A HERO HEAVY KONG.
HE CLAIMS HE WILL CONTINUE ATTACKING CLASS-A HEROES UNTIL HIS THREAT LEVEL RISES FROM TIGER TO DEMON.

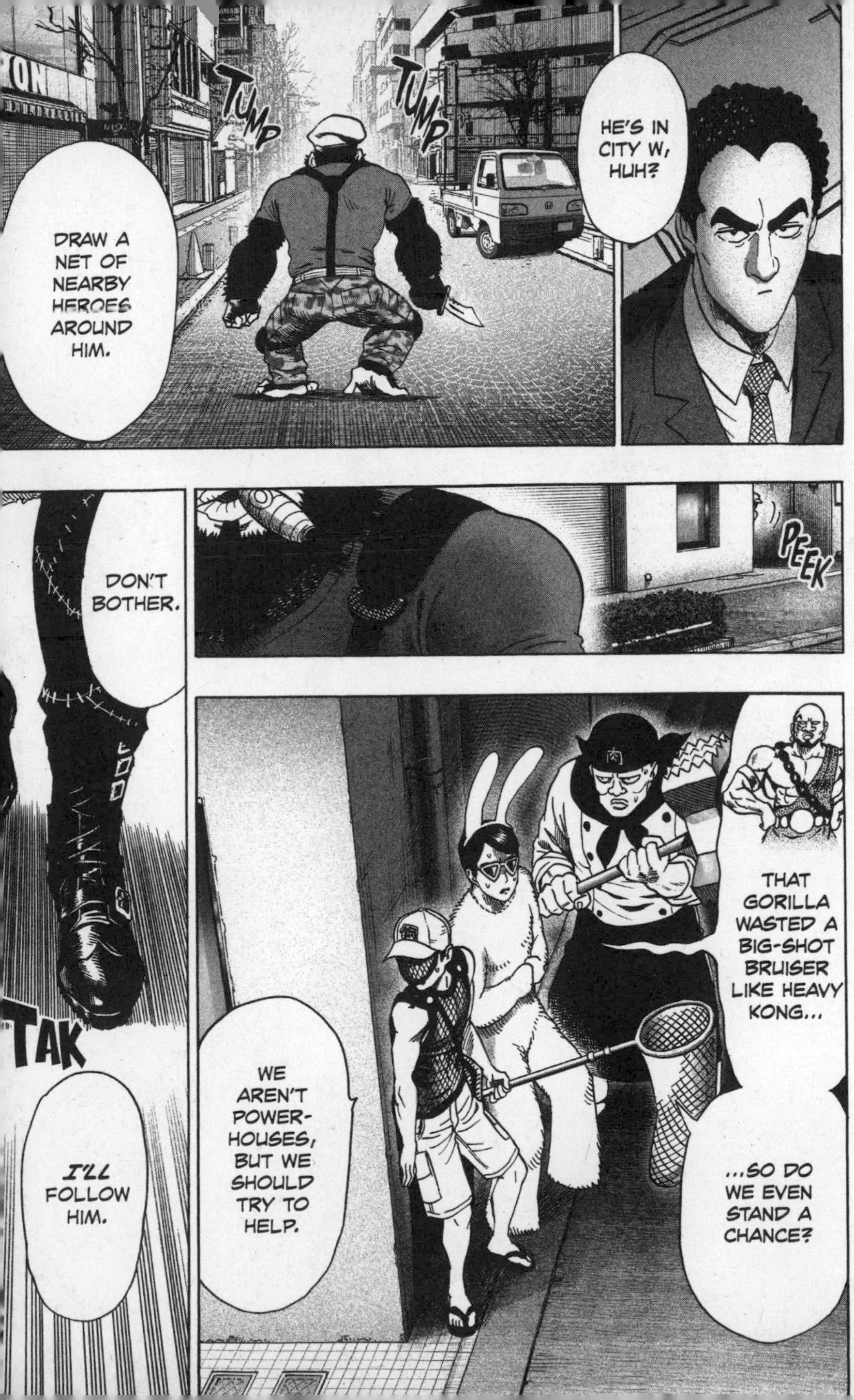
HE'S IN CITY W, HUH?
TUMP
TUMP
DRAW A NET OF NEARBY HEROES AROUND HIM.
PEEK
THAT GORILLA WASTED A BIG-SHOT BRUISER LIKE HEAVY KONG...
...SO DO WE EVEN STAND A CHANCE?
WE AREN'T POWER-HOUSES, BUT WE SHOULD TRY TO HELP.
DON'T BOTHER.
TAK
I'LL FOLLOW HIM.

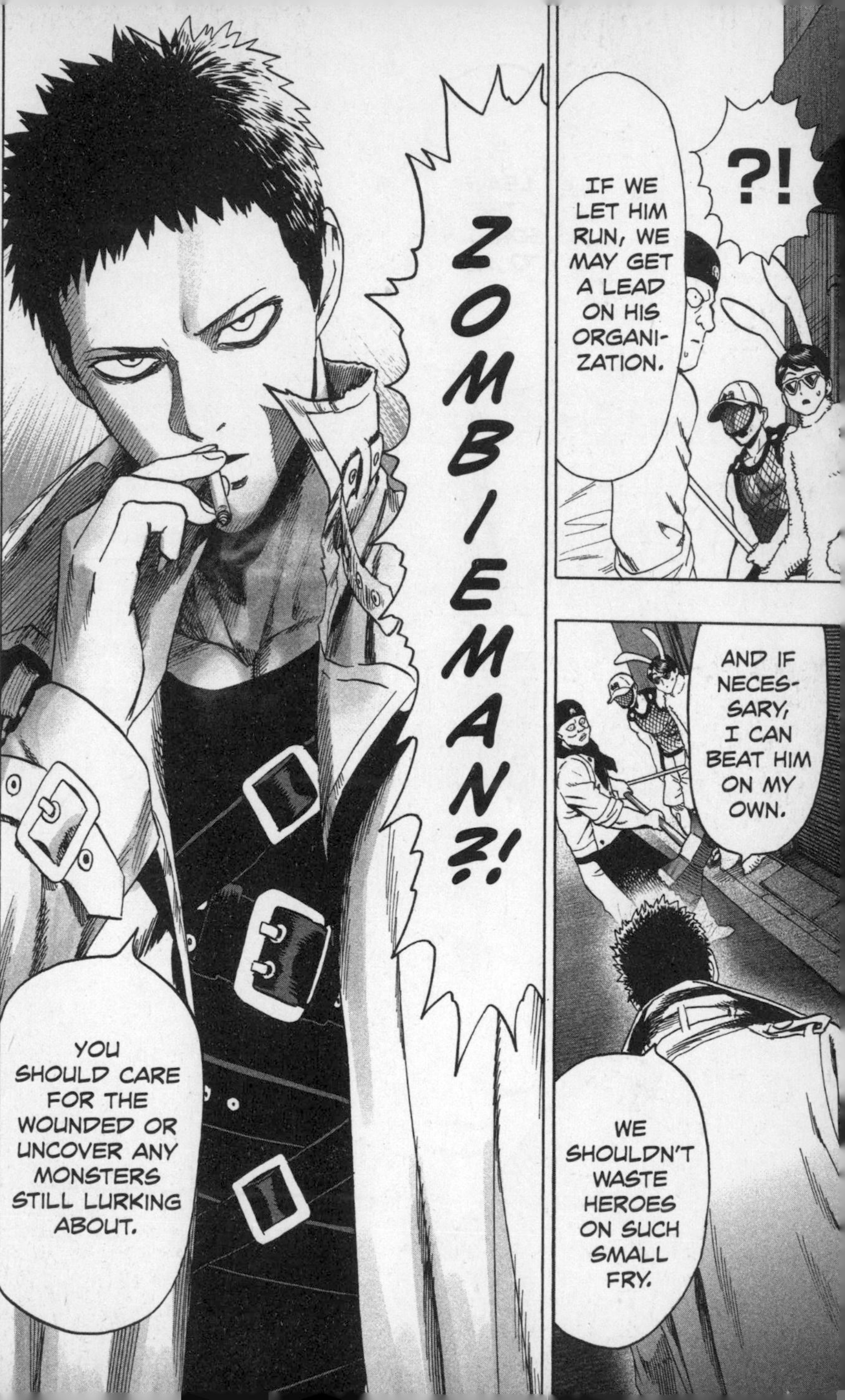
?!
IF WE LET HIM RUN, WE MAY GET A LEAD ON HIS ORGANI-ZATION.
AND IF NECES-SARY, I CAN BEAT HIM ON MY OWN.
WE SHOULDN'T WASTE HEROES ON SUCH SMALL FRY.
ZOMBIEMAN?!
YOU SHOULD CARE FOR THE WOUNDED OR UNCOVER ANY MONSTERS STILL LURKING ABOUT.

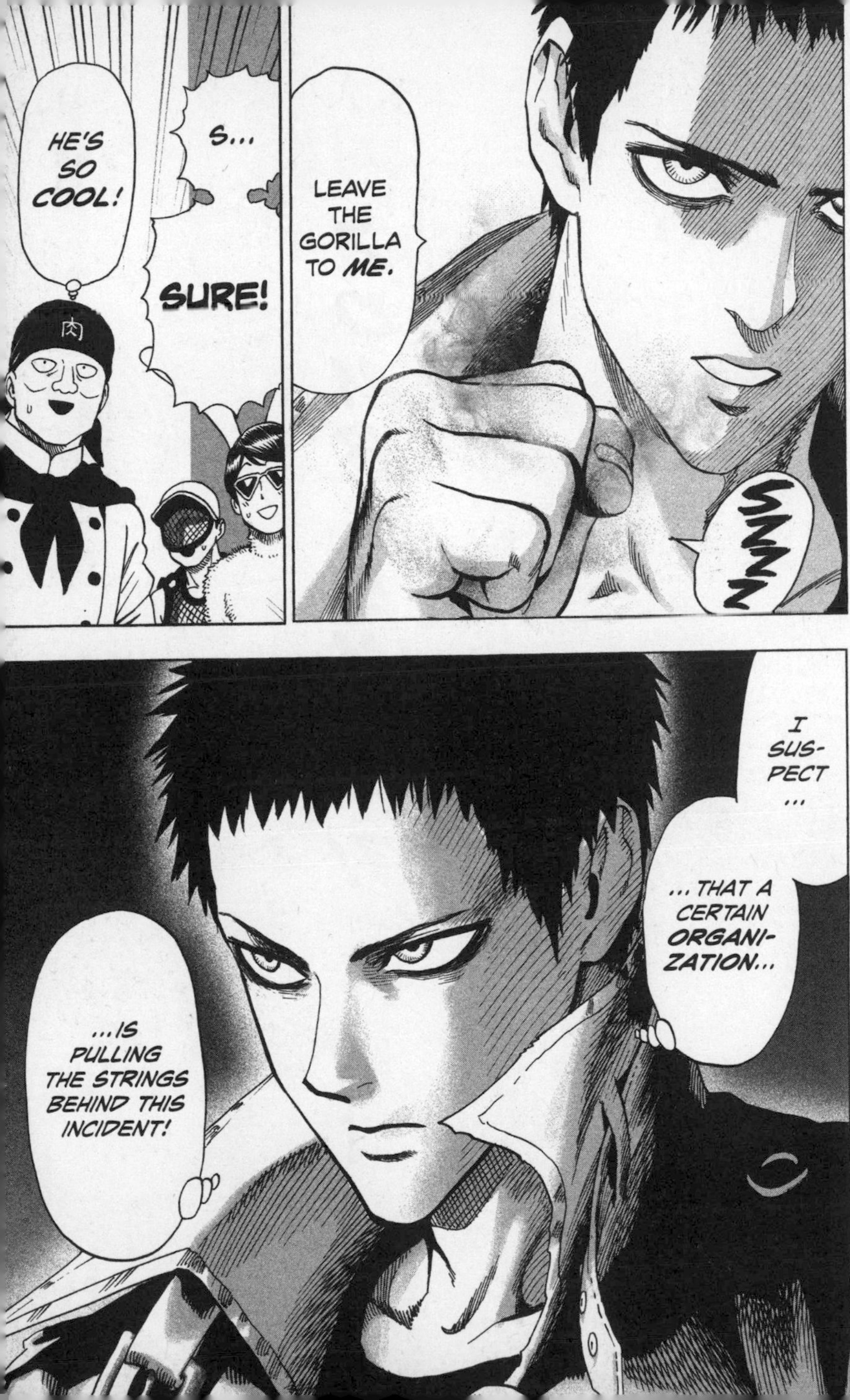
LEAVE THE GORILLA TO ME.
SZZZ
S... SURE!
HE'S SO COOL!
I SUSPECT...
...THAT A CERTAIN ORGANIZATION...
...IS PULLING THE STRINGS BEHIND THIS INCIDENT!

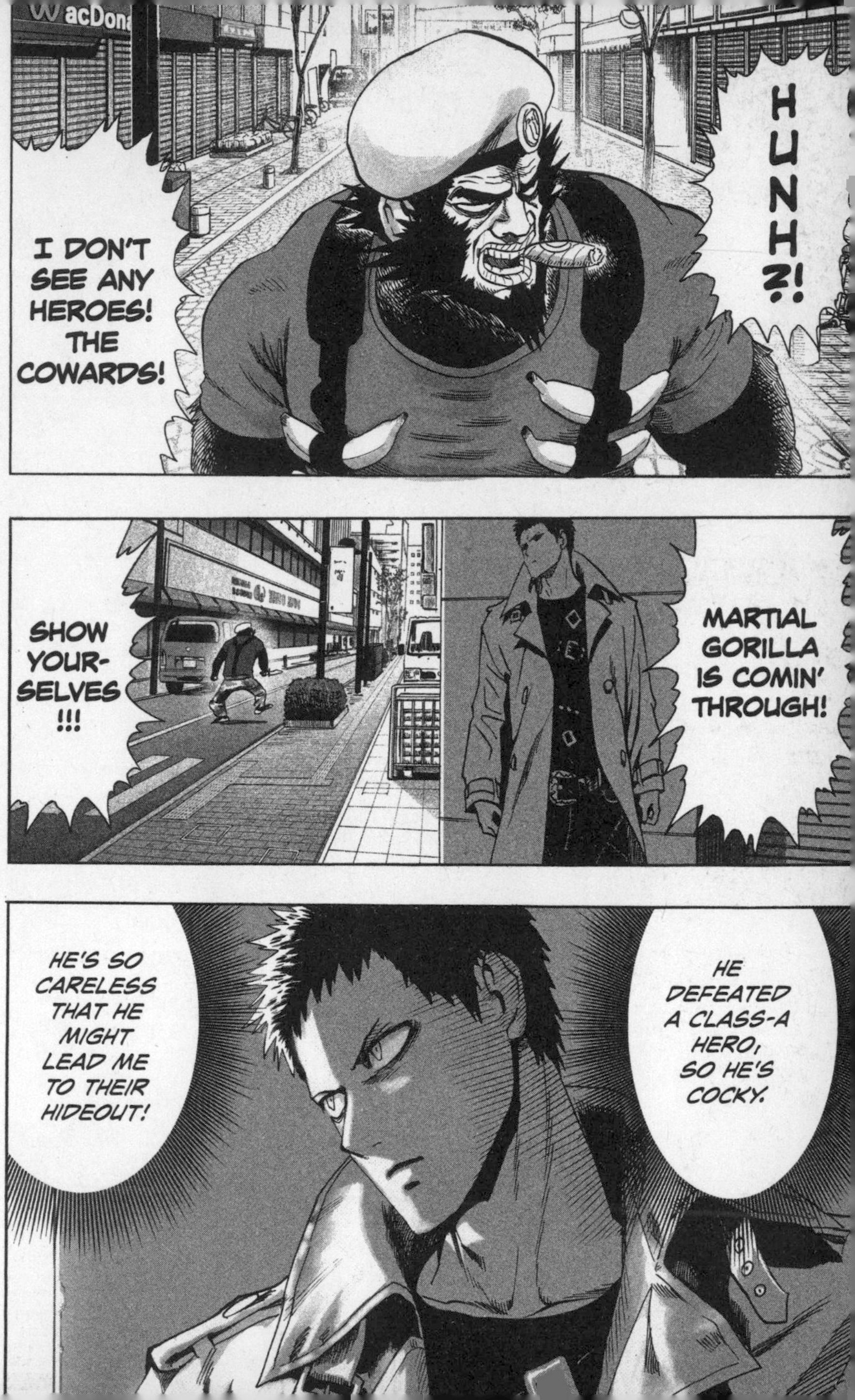
HUNH?!
I DON'T SEE ANY HEROES! THE COWARDS!
MARTIAL GORILLA IS COMIN' THROUGH!
SHOW YOUR-SELVES!!!
HE DEFEATED A CLASS-A HERO, SO HE'S COCKY.
HE'S SO CARELESS THAT HE MIGHT LEAD ME TO THEIR HIDEOUT!

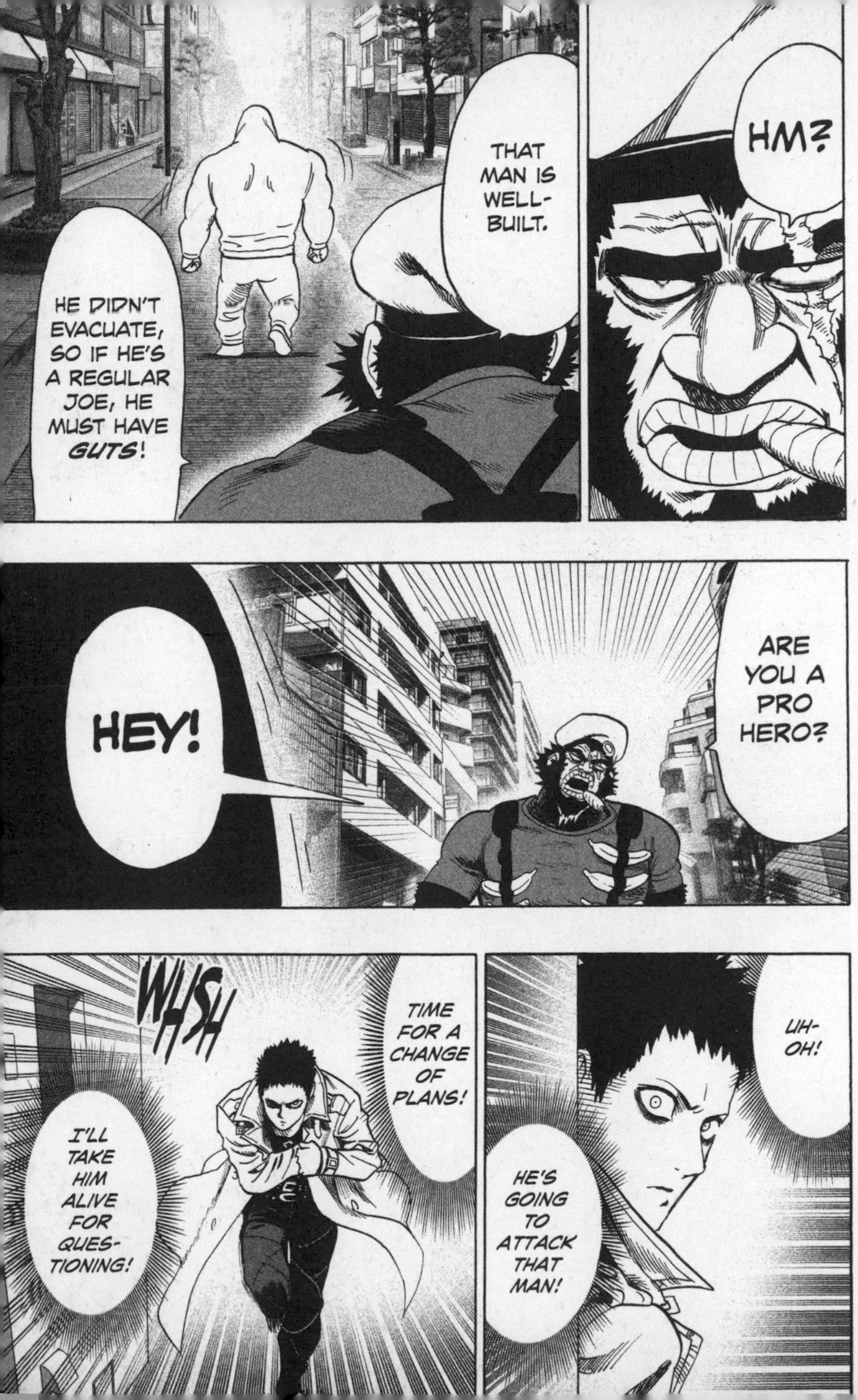
HM?
THAT MAN IS WELL-BUILT.
HE DIDN'T EVACUATE, SO IF HE'S A REGULAR JOE, HE MUST HAVE *GUTS*!
ARE YOU A PRO HERO?
HEY!
UH-OH!
HE'S GOING TO ATTACK THAT MAN!
TIME FOR A CHANGE OF PLANS!
WHSH
I'LL TAKE HIM ALIVE FOR QUES-TIONING!

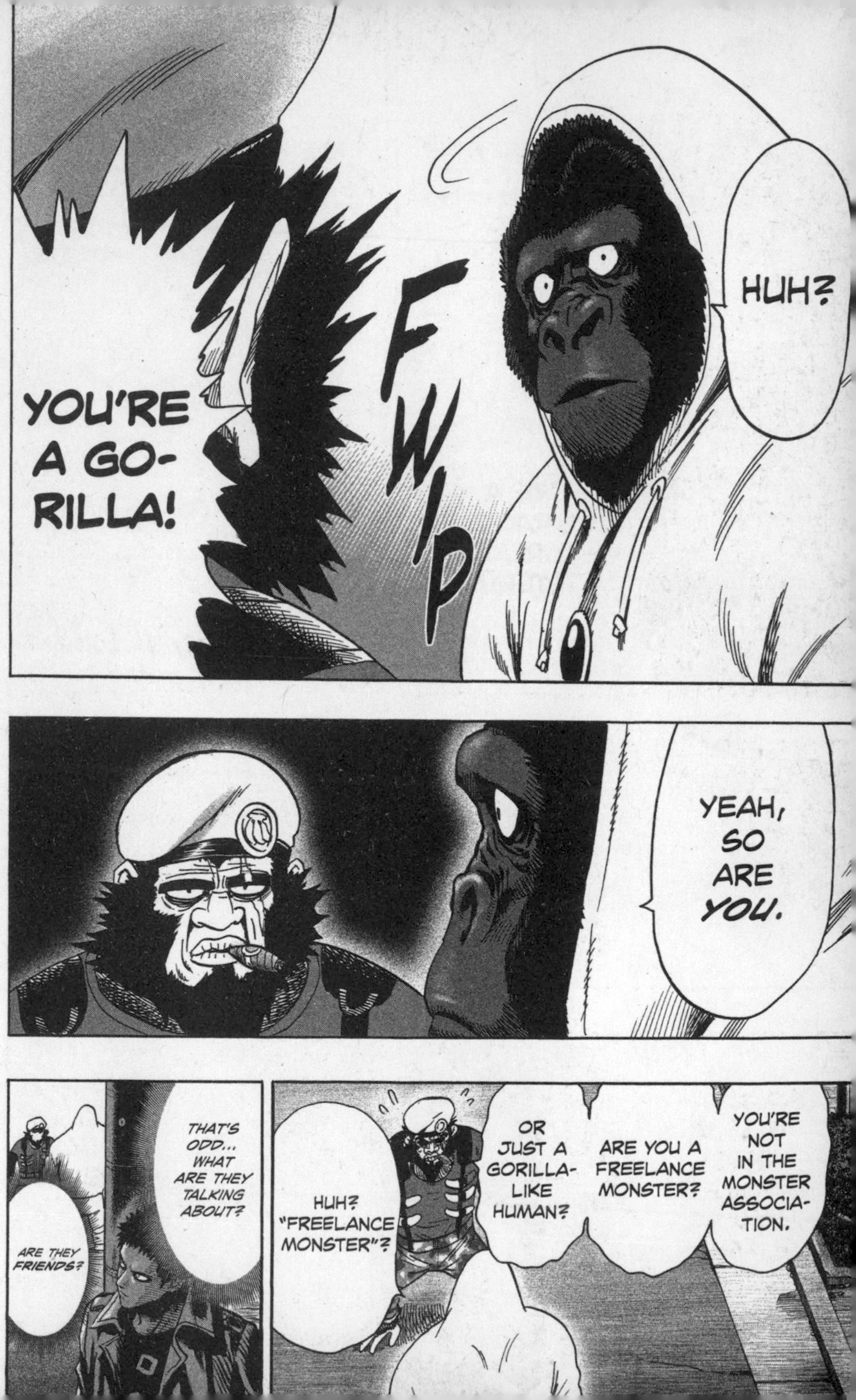
HUH?
FWIP
YOU'RE A GO-RILLA!
YEAH, SO ARE YOU.
YOU'RE NOT IN THE MONSTER ASSOCIATION.
ARE YOU A FREELANCE MONSTER?
OR JUST A GORILLA-LIKE HUMAN?
HUH? "FREELANCE MONSTER"?
THAT'S ODD... WHAT ARE THEY TALKING ABOUT?
ARE THEY FRIENDS?

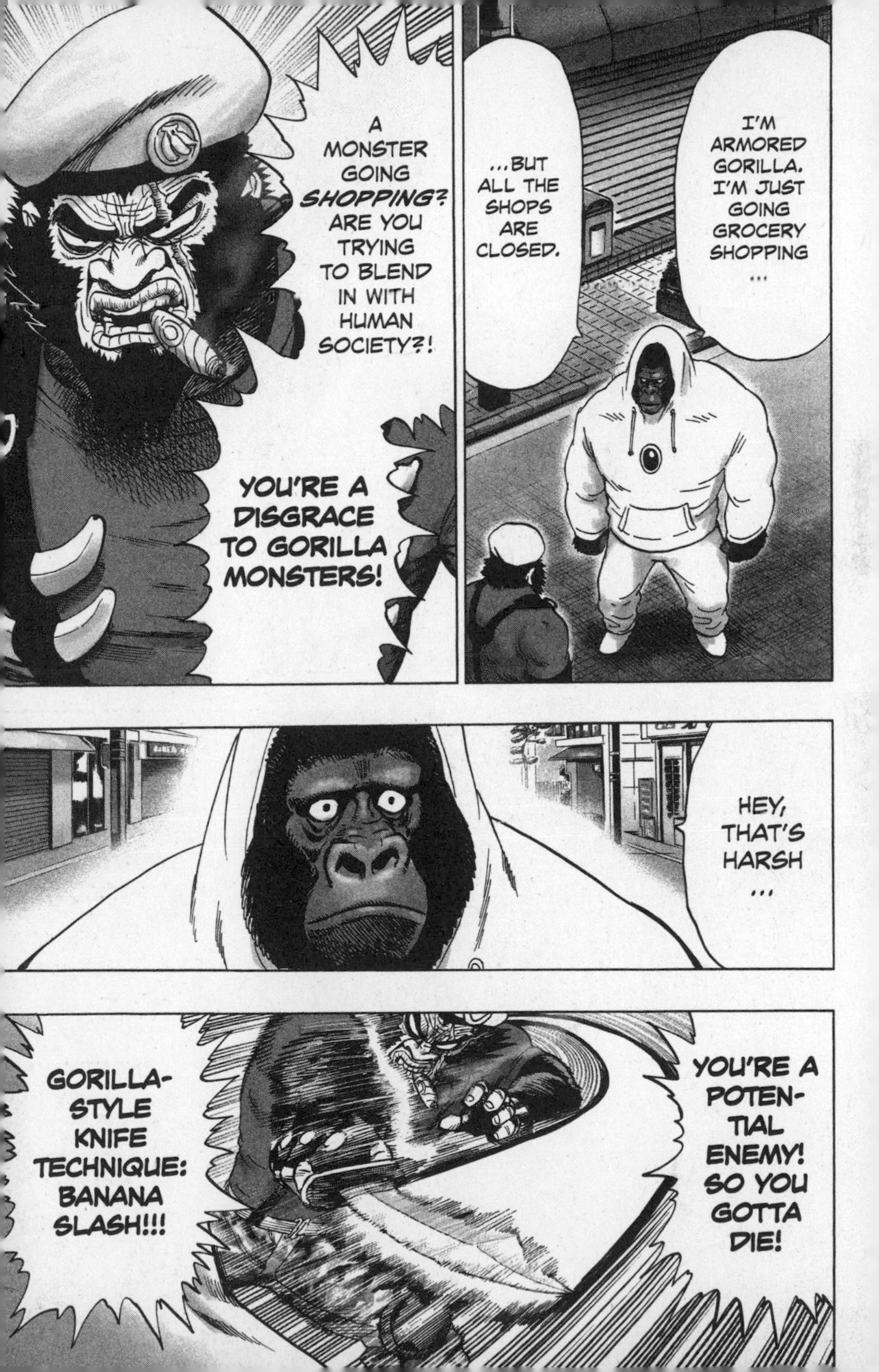

I'M ARMORED GORILLA. I'M JUST GOING GROCERY SHOPPING ...
...BUT ALL THE SHOPS ARE CLOSED.
A MONSTER GOING *SHOPPING*? ARE YOU TRYING TO BLEND IN WITH HUMAN SOCIETY?!
YOU'RE A DISGRACE TO GORILLA MONSTERS!
HEY, THAT'S HARSH ...
YOU'RE A POTEN-TIAL ENEMY! SO YOU GOTTA DIE!
GORILLA-STYLE KNIFE TECHNIQUE: BANANA SLASH!!!

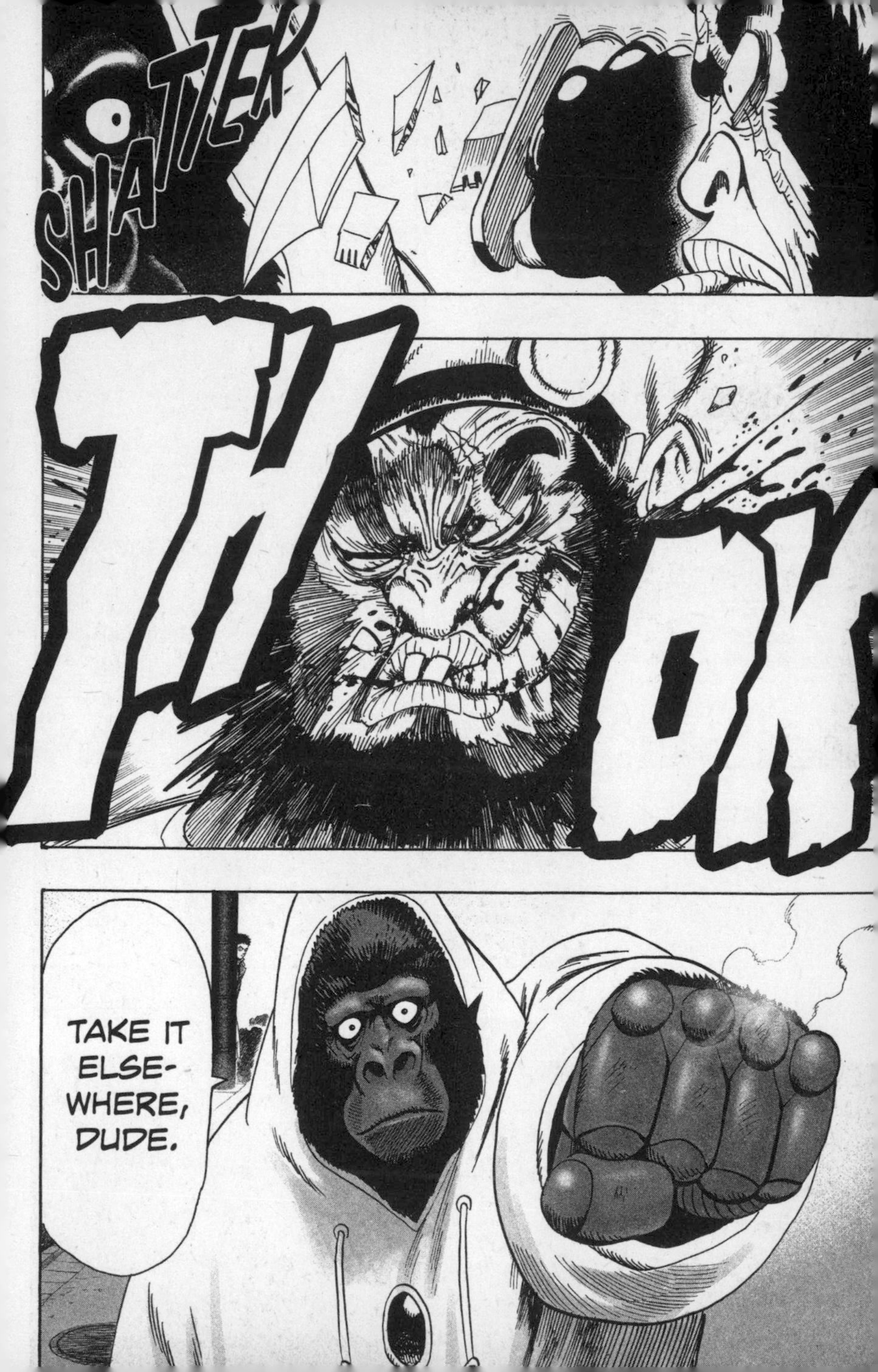
SHATTER
THOK
TAKE IT ELSE-WHERE, DUDE.

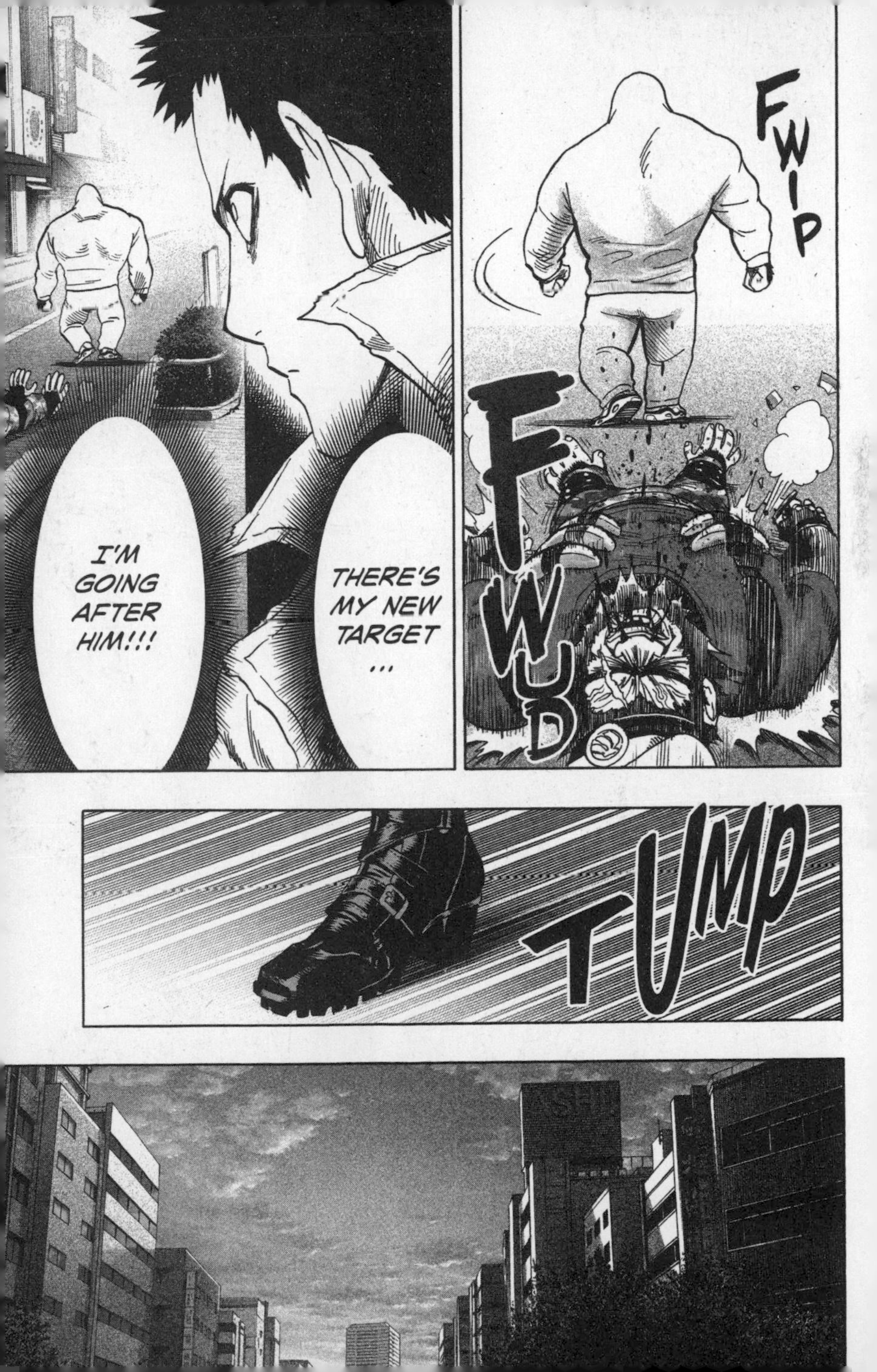
FWIP
FWUD
THERE'S MY NEW TARGET ...
I'M GOING AFTER HIM!!!
TUMP

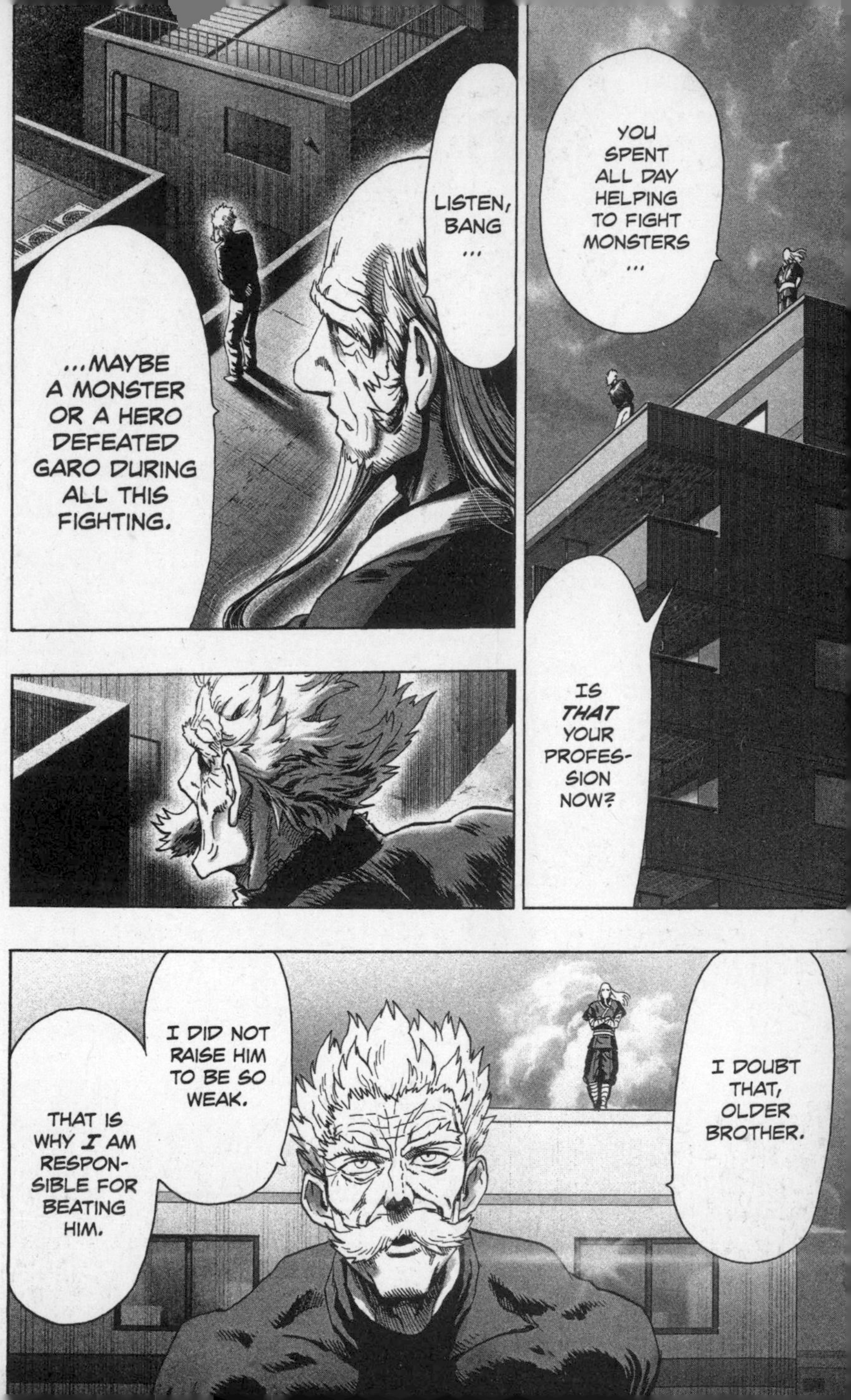
YOU SPENT ALL DAY HELPING TO FIGHT MONSTERS ...
IS *THAT* YOUR PROFES-SION NOW?
LISTEN, BANG ...
...MAYBE A MONSTER OR A HERO DEFEATED GARO DURING ALL THIS FIGHTING.
I DOUBT THAT, OLDER BROTHER.
I DID NOT RAISE HIM TO BE SO WEAK.
THAT IS WHY *I* AM RESPON-SIBLE FOR BEATING HIM.

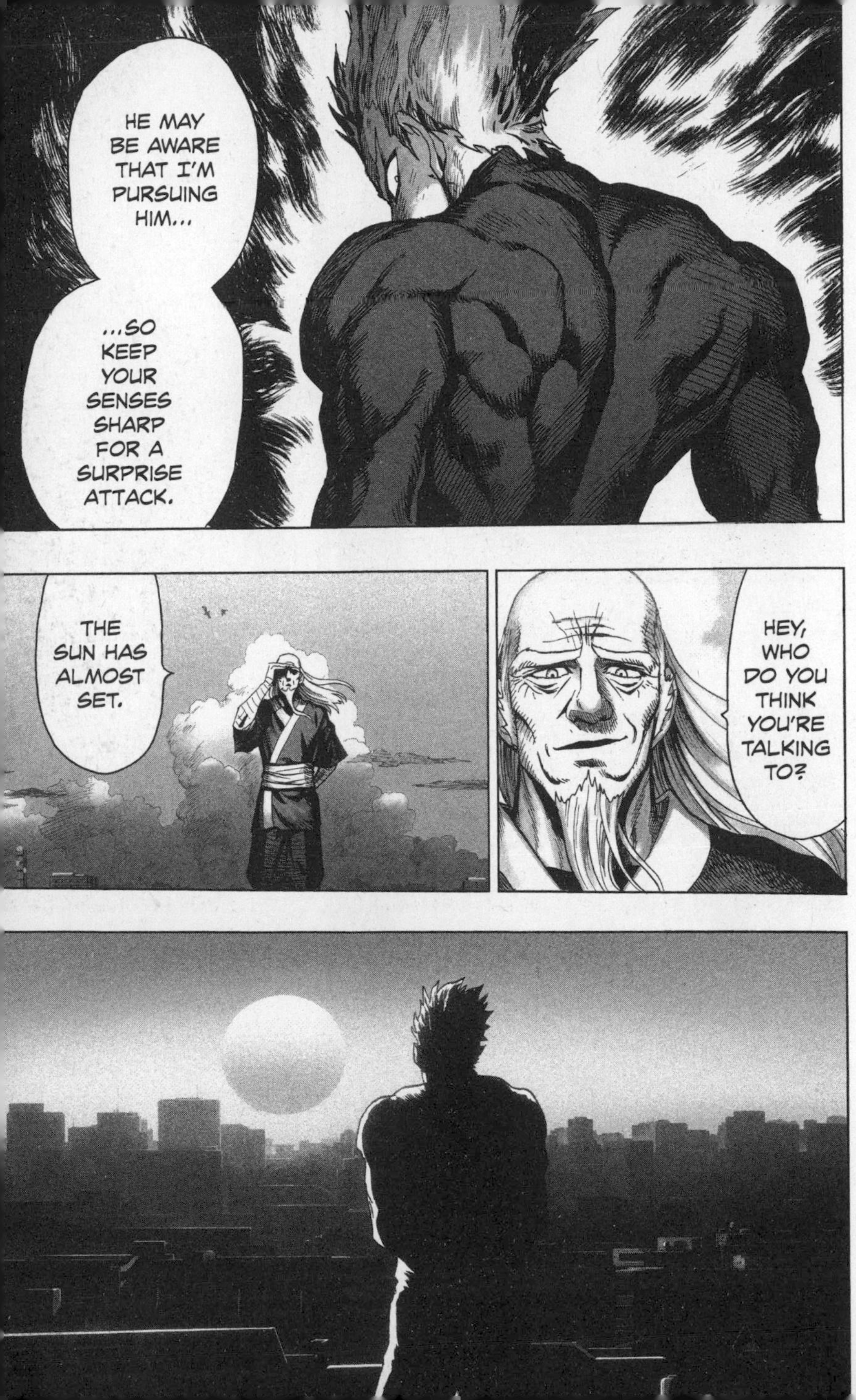
HE MAY BE AWARE THAT I'M PURSUING HIM...
...SO KEEP YOUR SENSES SHARP FOR A SURPRISE ATTACK.
HEY, WHO DO YOU THINK YOU'RE TALKING TO?
THE SUN HAS ALMOST SET.

GARO, DO YOU KNOW WHAT IT MEANS...

...TO BECOME A MONSTER?

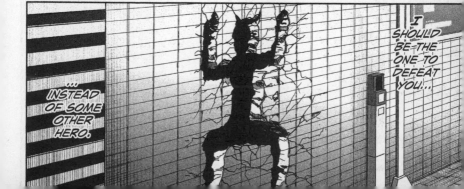

I SHOULD BE THE ONE TO DEFEAT YOU...

...INSTEAD OF SOME OTHER HERO.

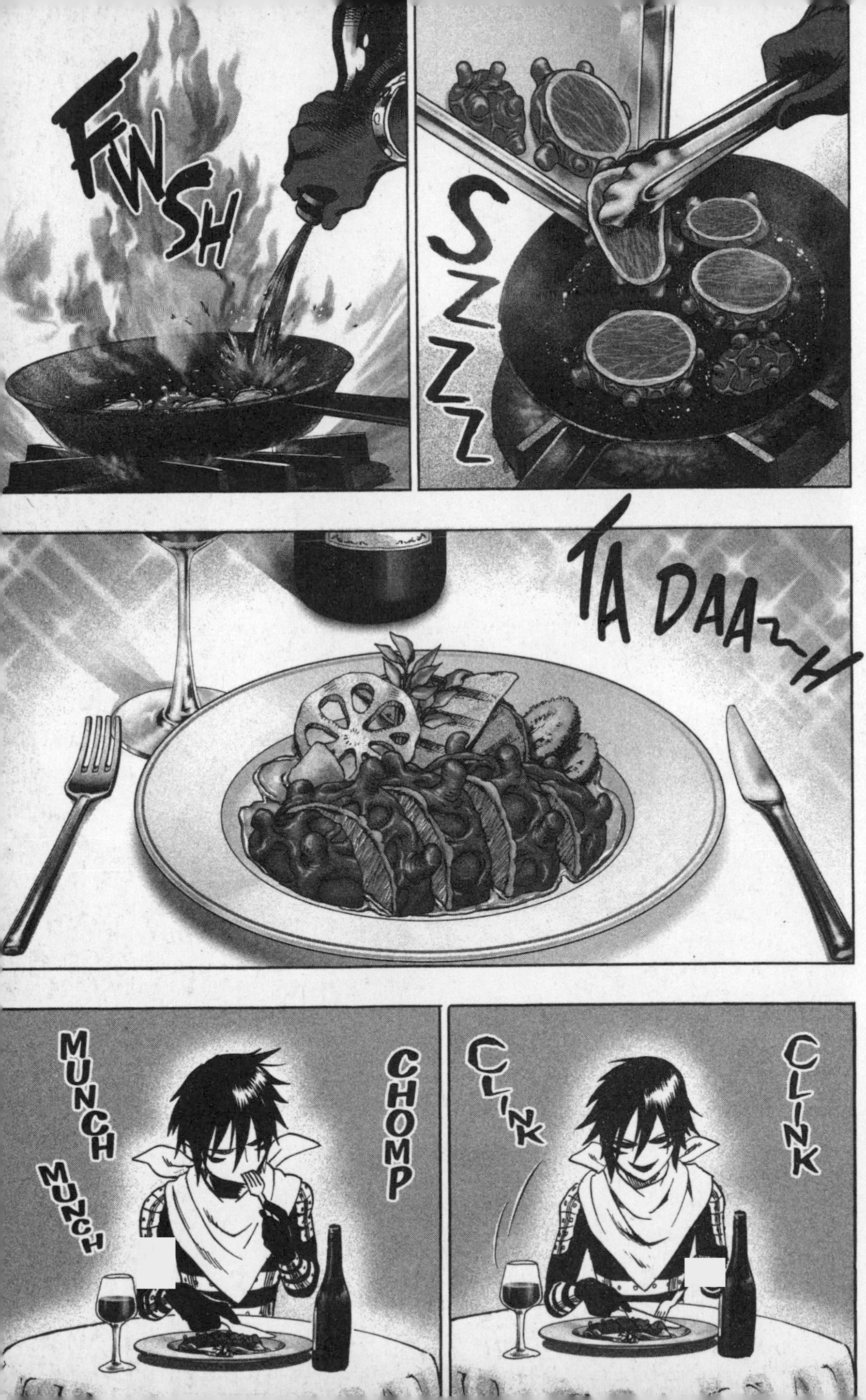
SZZZ
FWSH
TA DAA~H
CLINK
CLINK
CHOMP
MUNCH
MUNCH

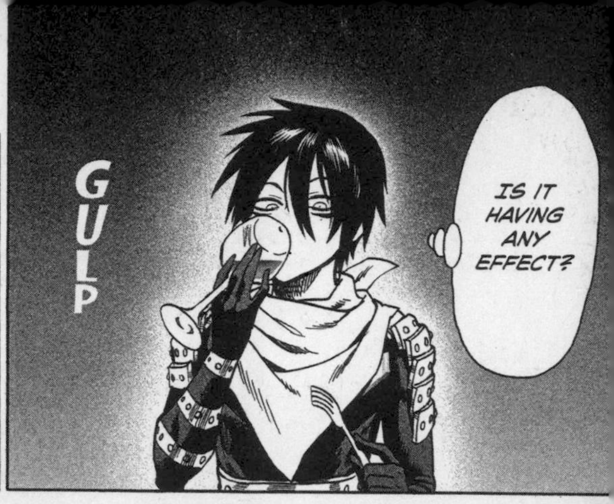
GULP
IS IT HAVING ANY EFFECT?

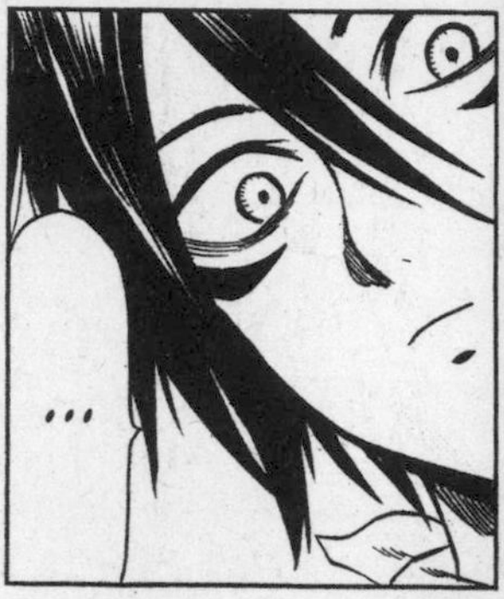
...

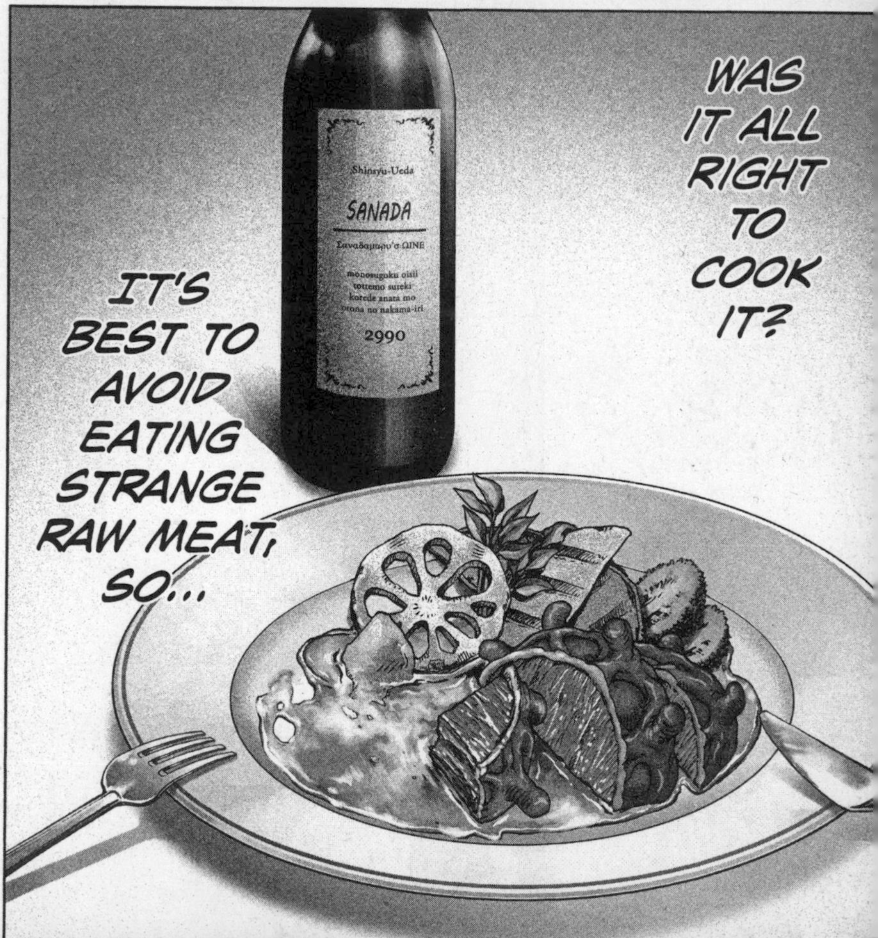
WAS IT ALL RIGHT TO COOK IT?
Shinsyu-Ueda
SANADA
Σαναδαμαρυ'σ ΩINE
monosugoku oisii
tottemo sureki
korede anata mo
otona no nakama-iri
2990
IT'S BEST TO AVOID EATING STRANGE RAW MEAT, SO...

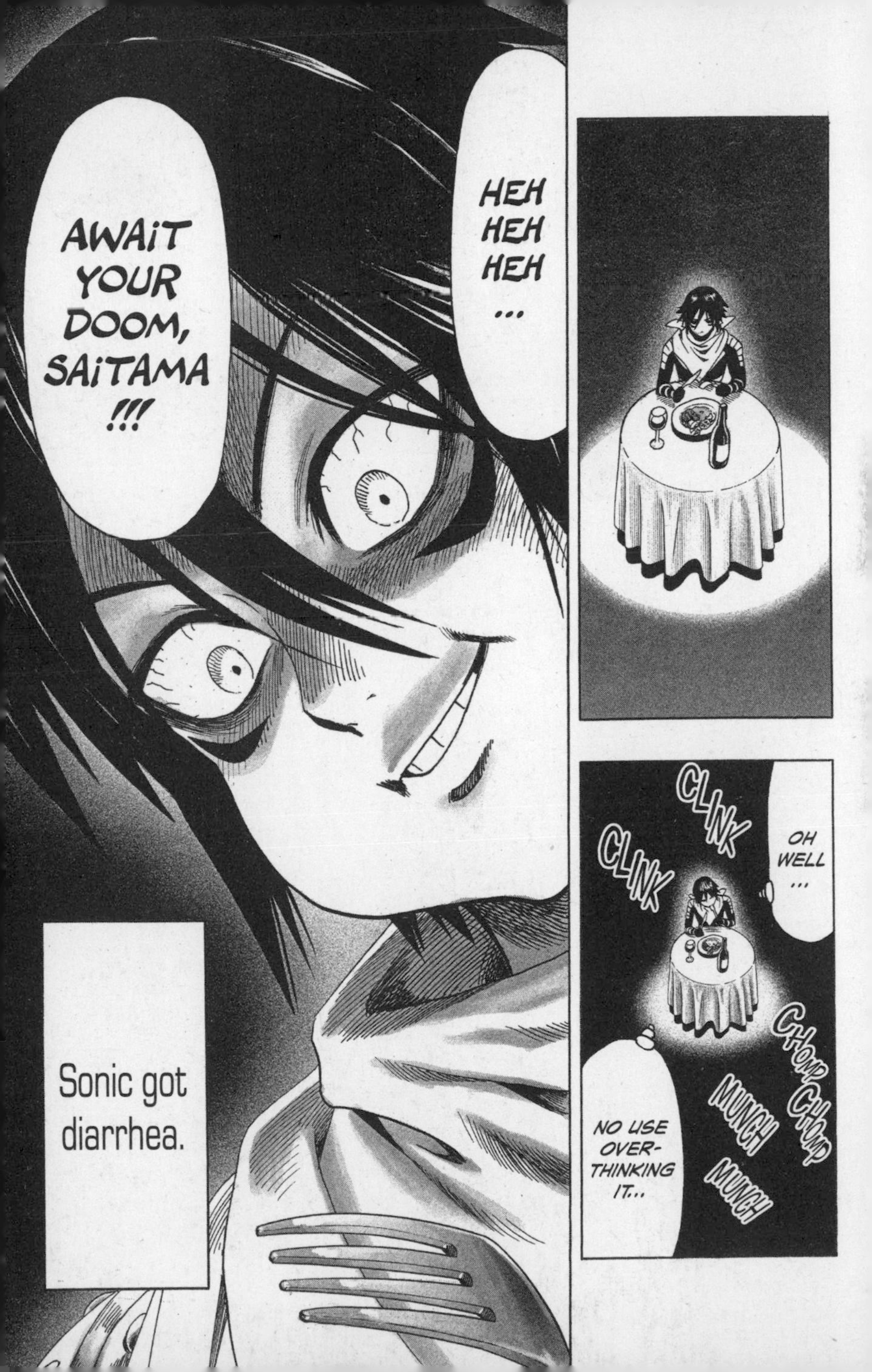
OH WELL ...
CLINK
CLINK
CHOMP CHOMP
MUNCH MUNCH
NO USE OVER-THINKING IT...
HEH HEH HEH ...
AWAIT YOUR DOOM, SAITAMA !!!
Sonic got diarrhea.

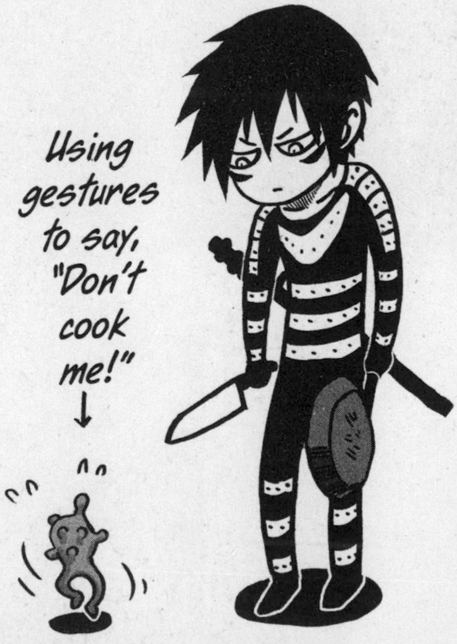
Using gestures to say, "Don't cook me!"

PUNCH 79: CHEAPO TRICK

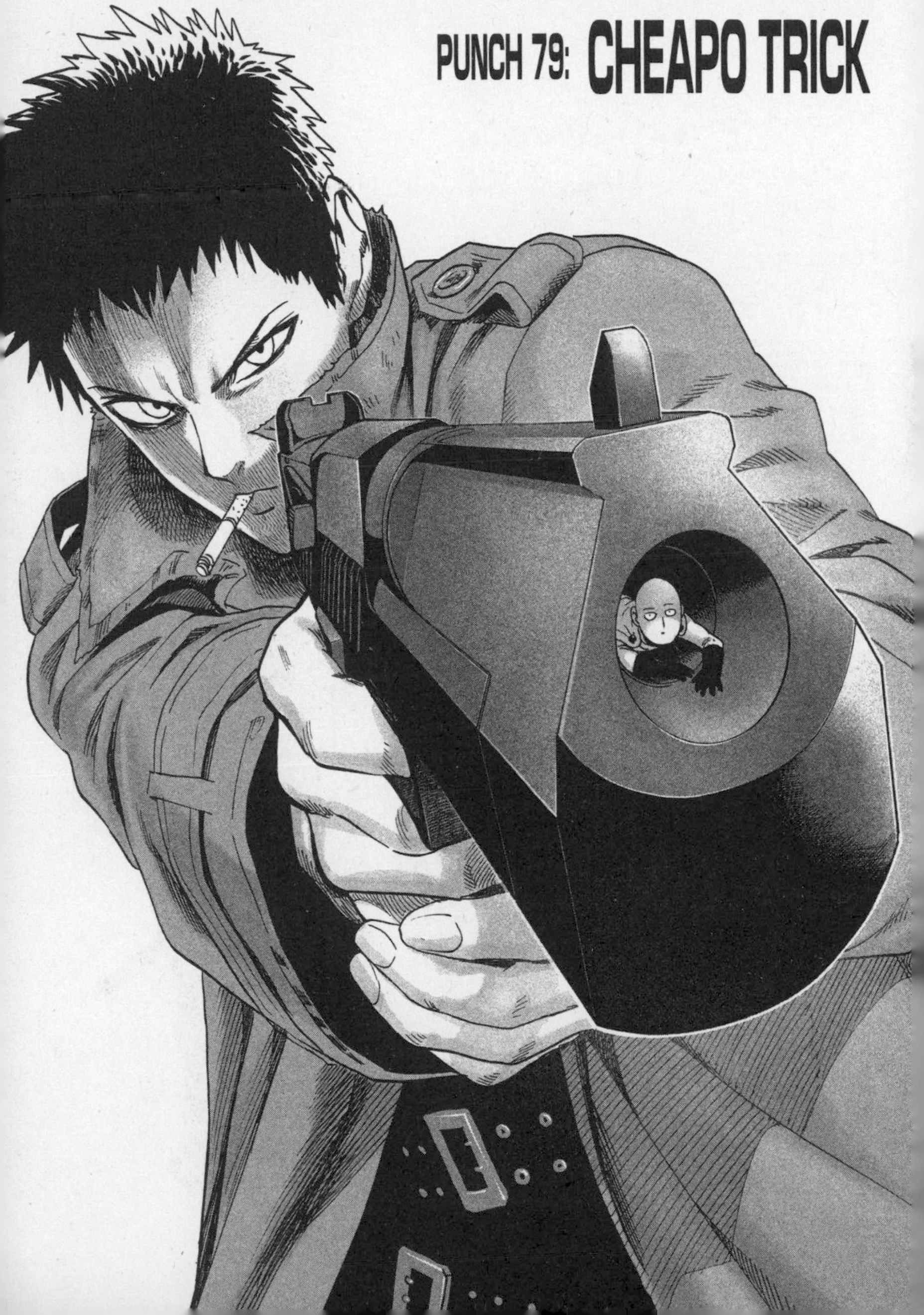

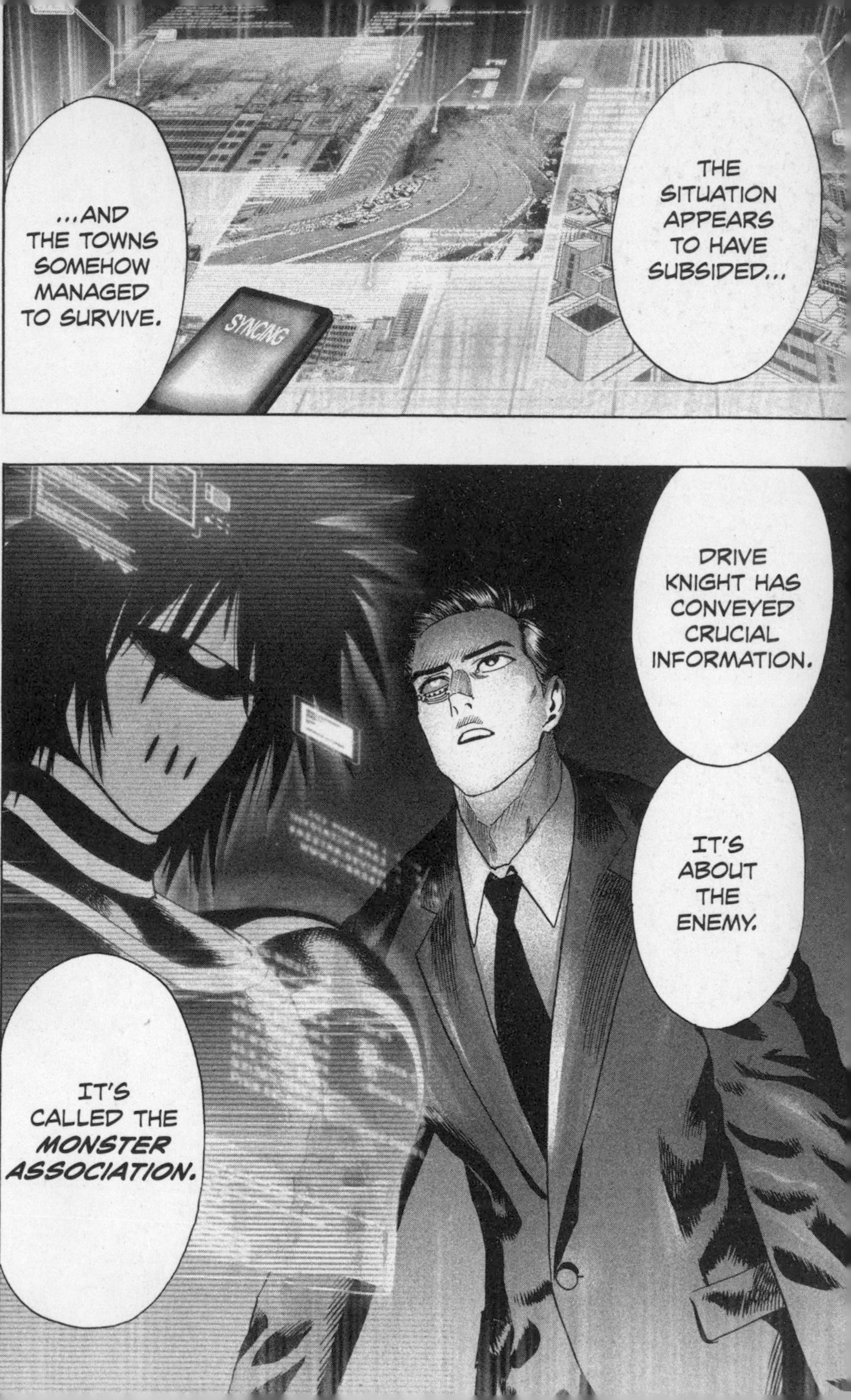
THE SITUATION APPEARS TO HAVE SUBSIDED...
...AND THE TOWNS SOMEHOW MANAGED TO SURVIVE.
SYNCING
DRIVE KNIGHT HAS CONVEYED CRUCIAL INFORMATION.
IT'S ABOUT THE ENEMY.
IT'S CALLED THE *MONSTER ASSOCIATION.*

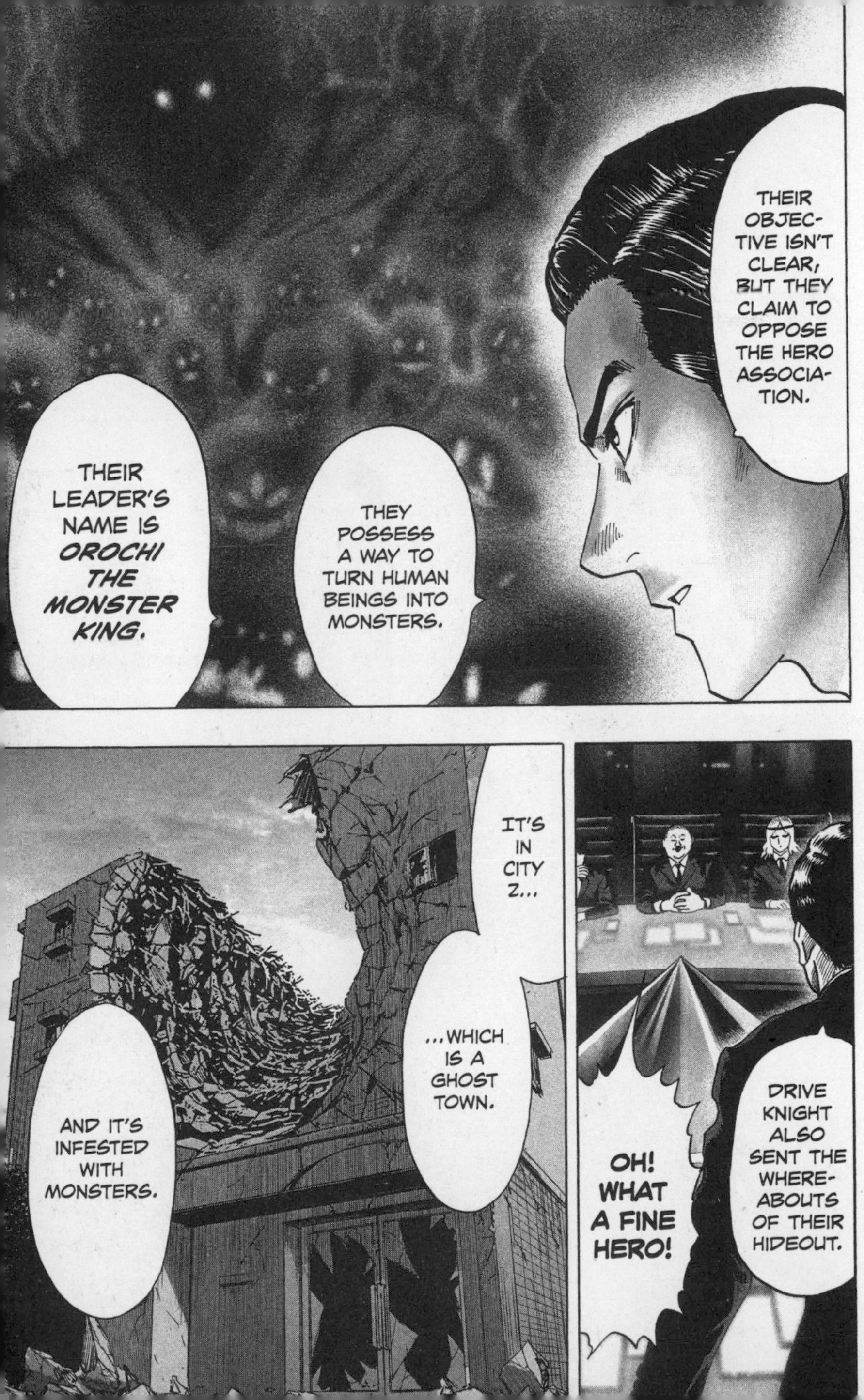
THEIR OBJECTIVE ISN'T CLEAR, BUT THEY CLAIM TO OPPOSE THE HERO ASSOCIATION.
THEY POSSESS A WAY TO TURN HUMAN BEINGS INTO MONSTERS.
THEIR LEADER'S NAME IS *OROCHI THE MONSTER KING*.
DRIVE KNIGHT ALSO SENT THE WHEREABOUTS OF THEIR HIDEOUT.
OH! WHAT A FINE HERO!
IT'S IN CITY Z...
...WHICH IS A GHOST TOWN.
AND IT'S INFESTED WITH MONSTERS.

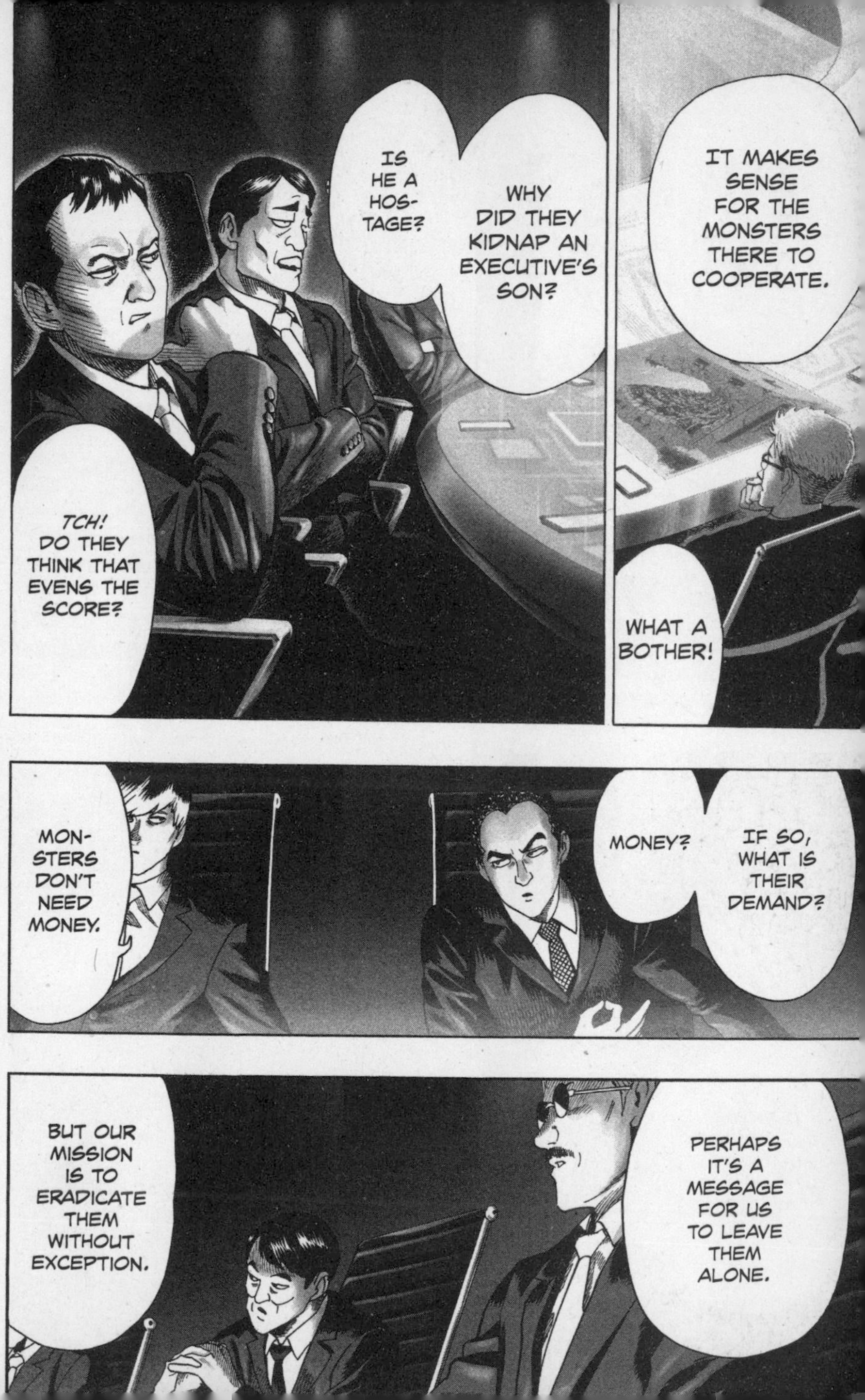
IT MAKES SENSE FOR THE MONSTERS THERE TO COOPERATE.
WHAT A BOTHER!
WHY DID THEY KIDNAP AN EXECUTIVE'S SON?
IS HE A HOS-TAGE?
TCH! DO THEY THINK THAT EVENS THE SCORE?
IF SO, WHAT IS THEIR DEMAND?
MONEY?
MON-STERS DON'T NEED MONEY.
PERHAPS IT'S A MESSAGE FOR US TO LEAVE THEM ALONE.
BUT OUR MISSION IS TO ERADICATE THEM WITHOUT EXCEPTION.

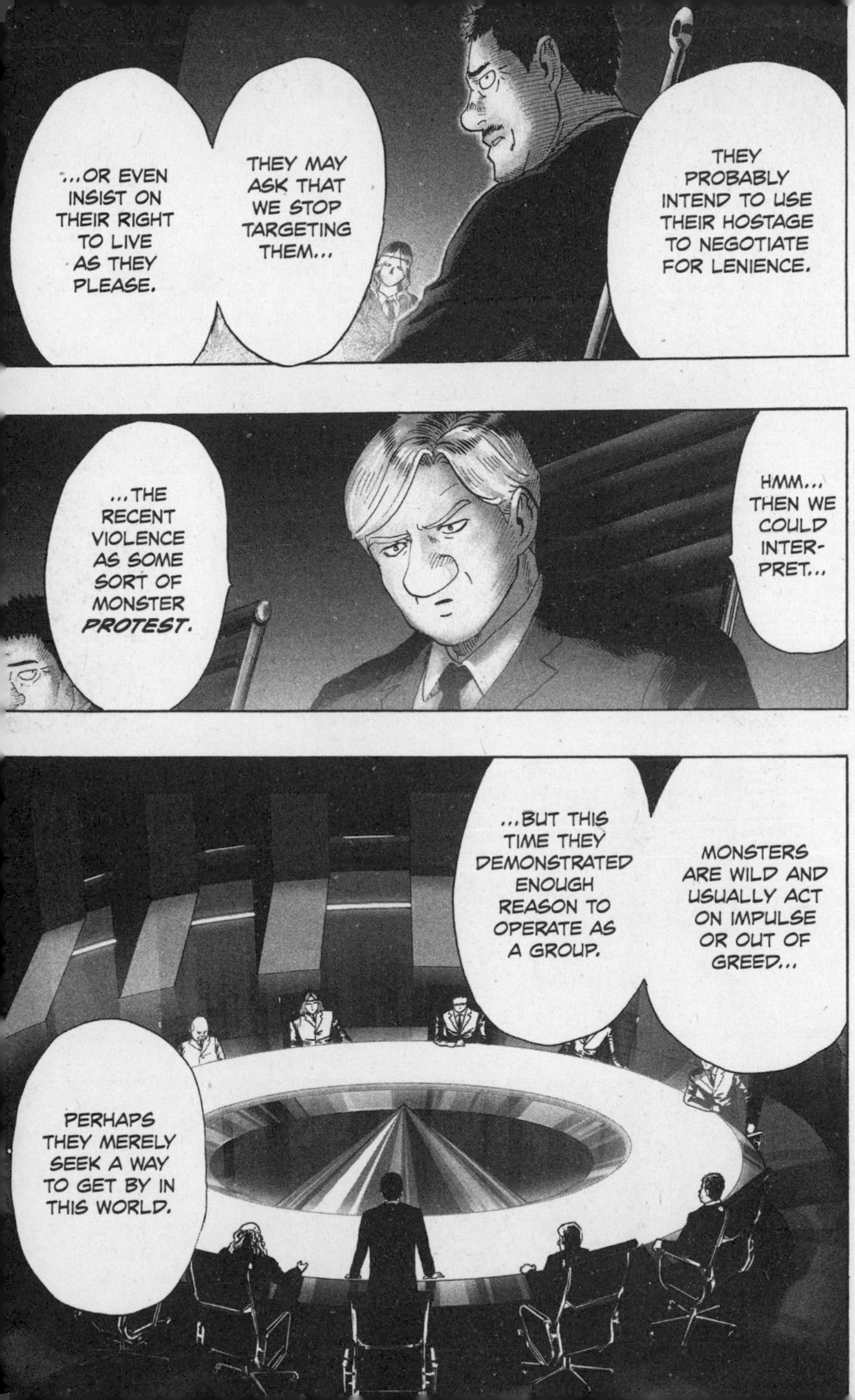
THEY PROBABLY INTEND TO USE THEIR HOSTAGE TO NEGOTIATE FOR LENIENCE.
THEY MAY ASK THAT WE STOP TARGETING THEM...
...OR EVEN INSIST ON THEIR RIGHT TO LIVE AS THEY PLEASE.
HMM... THEN WE COULD INTERPRET...
...THE RECENT VIOLENCE AS SOME SORT OF MONSTER *PROTEST*.
MONSTERS ARE WILD AND USUALLY ACT ON IMPULSE OR OUT OF GREED...
...BUT THIS TIME THEY DEMONSTRATED ENOUGH REASON TO OPERATE AS A GROUP.
PERHAPS THEY MERELY SEEK A WAY TO GET BY IN THIS WORLD.

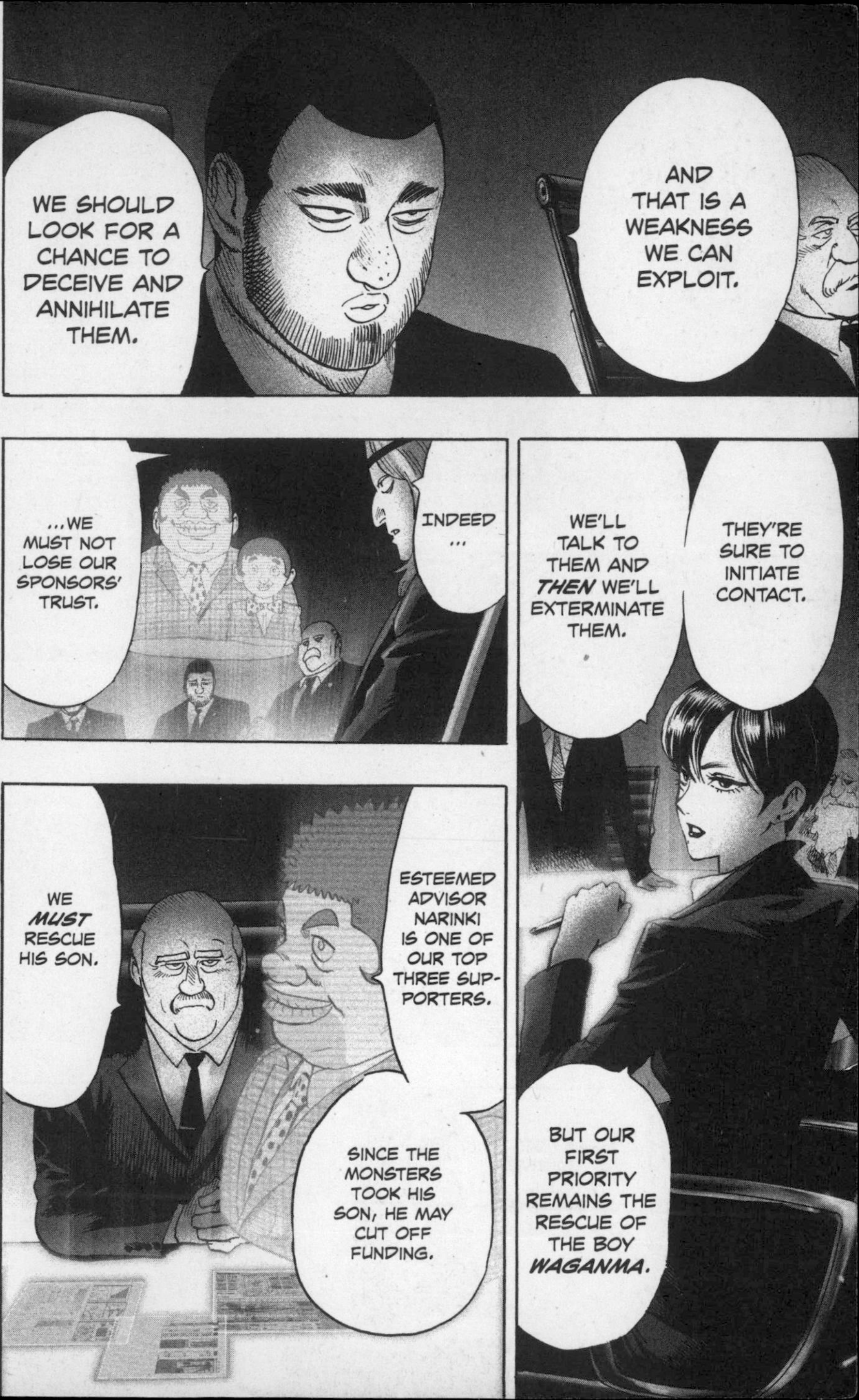
AND THAT IS A WEAKNESS WE CAN EXPLOIT.
WE SHOULD LOOK FOR A CHANCE TO DECEIVE AND ANNIHILATE THEM.
THEY'RE SURE TO INITIATE CONTACT.
WE'LL TALK TO THEM AND *THEN* WE'LL EXTERMINATE THEM.
BUT OUR FIRST PRIORITY REMAINS THE RESCUE OF THE BOY *WAGANMA*.
INDEED...
...WE MUST NOT LOSE OUR SPONSORS' TRUST.
ESTEEMED ADVISOR NARINKI IS ONE OF OUR TOP THREE SUP-PORTERS.
SINCE THE MONSTERS TOOK HIS SON, HE MAY CUT OFF FUNDING.
WE *MUST* RESCUE HIS SON.

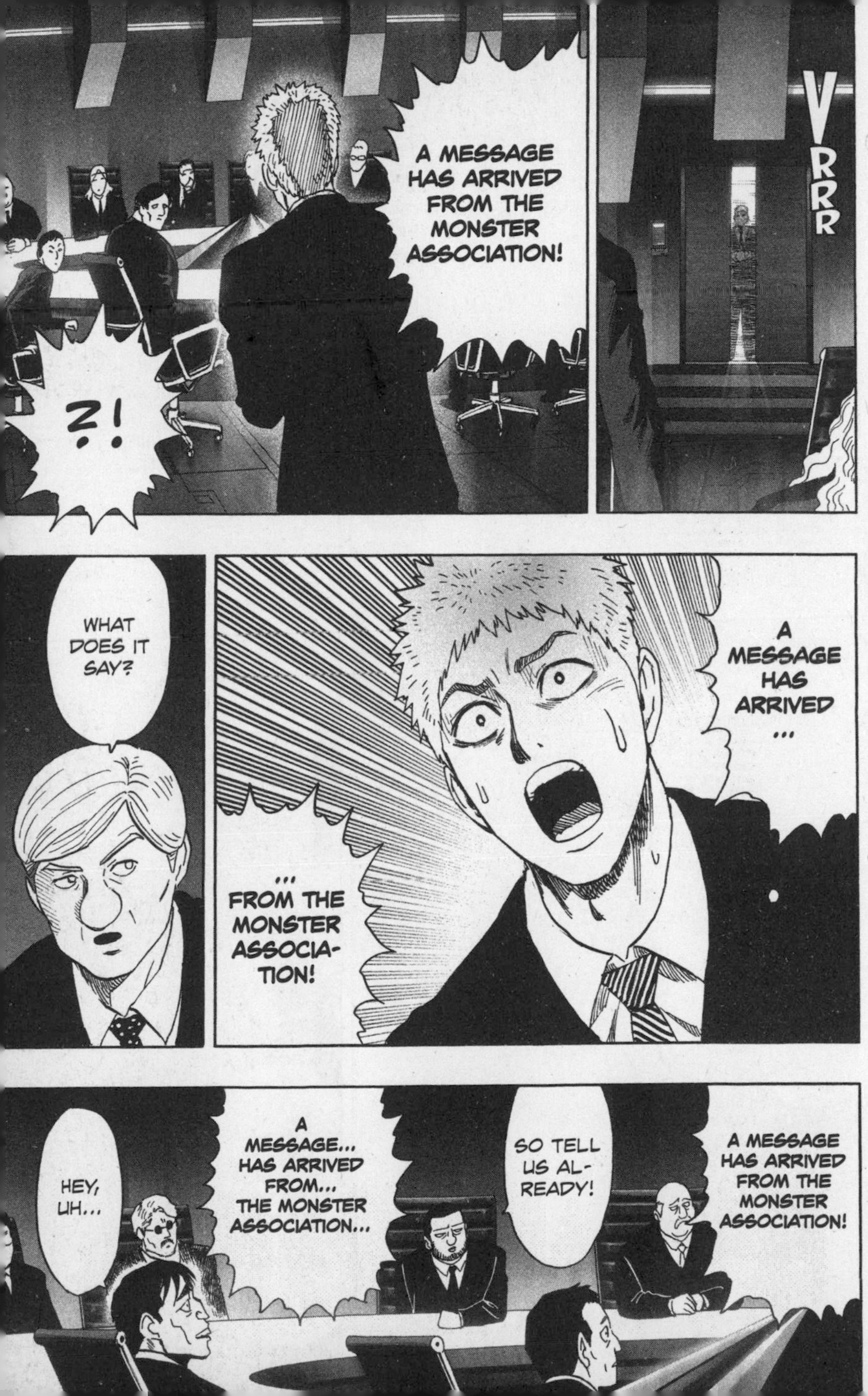
VRRR
A MESSAGE HAS ARRIVED FROM THE MONSTER ASSOCIATION!
?!
A MESSAGE HAS ARRIVED ...
... FROM THE MONSTER ASSOCIA-TION!
WHAT DOES IT SAY?
A MESSAGE HAS ARRIVED FROM THE MONSTER ASSOCIATION!
SO TELL US AL-READY!
A MESSAGE... HAS ARRIVED FROM... THE MONSTER ASSOCIATION...
HEY, UH...

A MESSAGE HAS ARRIVED FROM THE MONSTER ASSOCIATION!

A MESSAGE HAS ARRIVED FROM THE MONSTER ASSOCIATION!

CHAK

...SOME-THING IS WRONG WITH HIM!

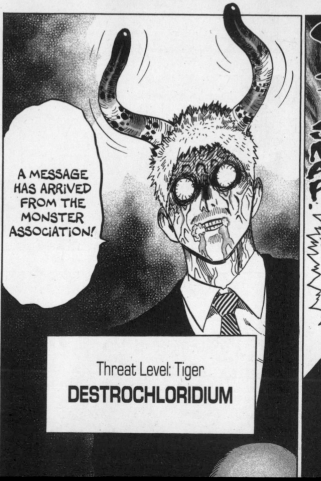

A MESSAGE HAS ARRIVED FROM THE MONSTER ASSOCIATION!

Threat Level: Tiger
DESTROCHLORIDIUM

CRITK SNAP.

AMM...

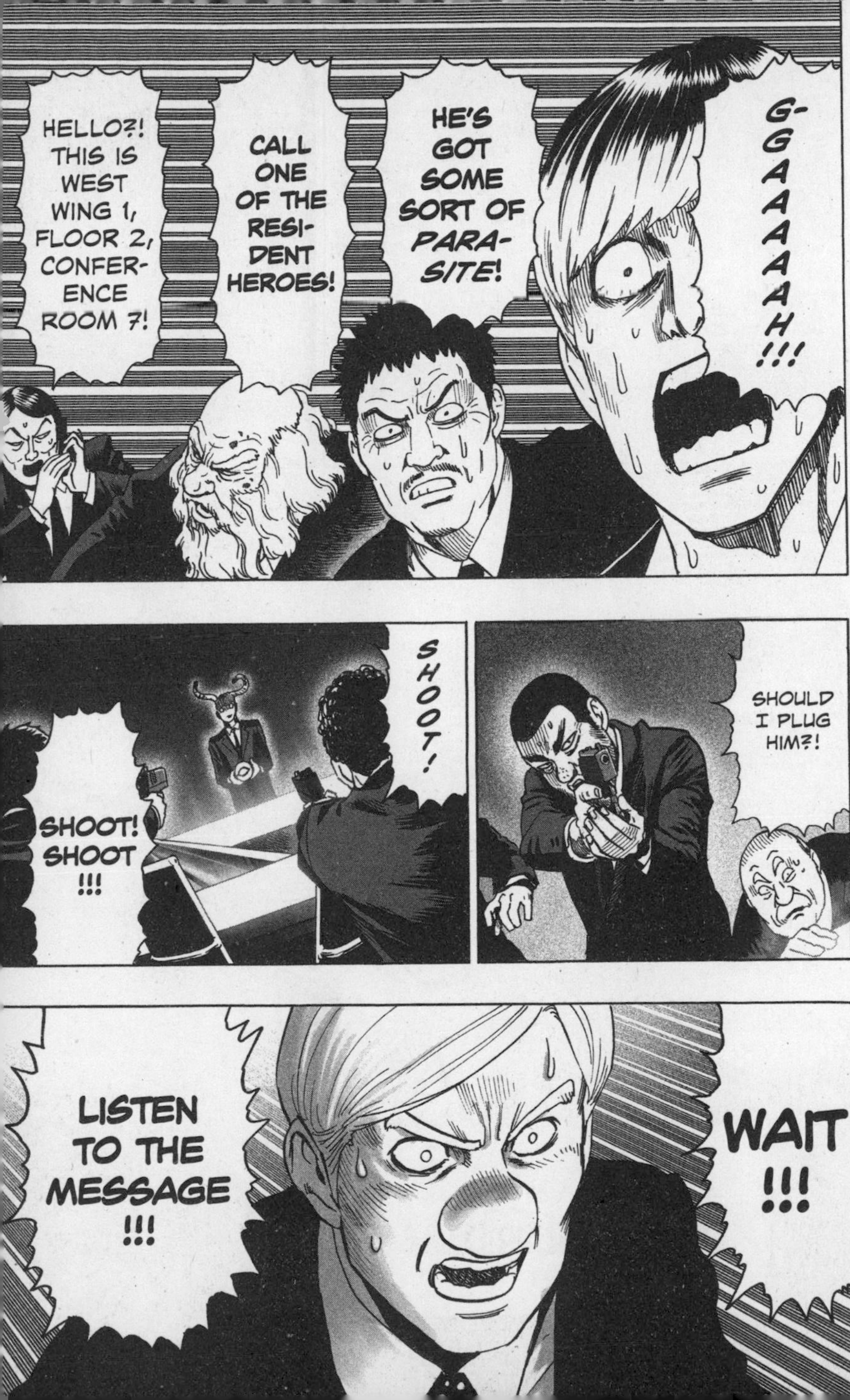
G-GAAAAAH!!!
HE'S GOT SOME SORT OF PARA-SITE!
CALL ONE OF THE RESI-DENT HEROES!
HELLO?! THIS IS WEST WING 1, FLOOR 2, CONFER-ENCE ROOM 7!
SHOULD I PLUG HIM?!
SHOOT!
SHOOT! SHOOT!!!
WAIT!!!
LISTEN TO THE MESSAGE!!!

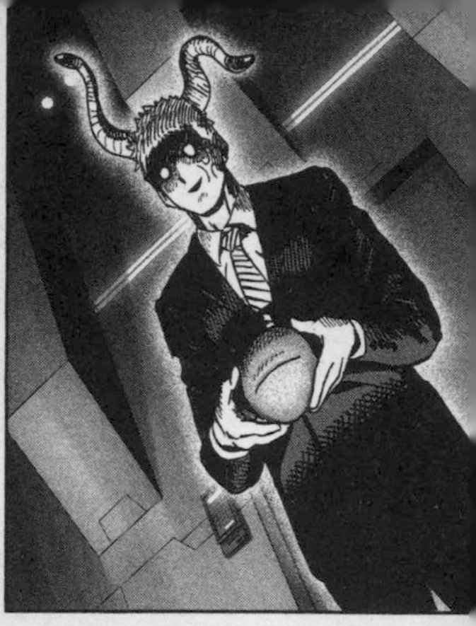

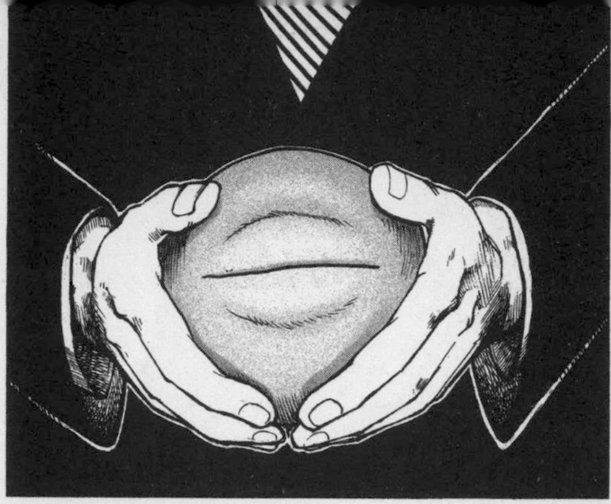

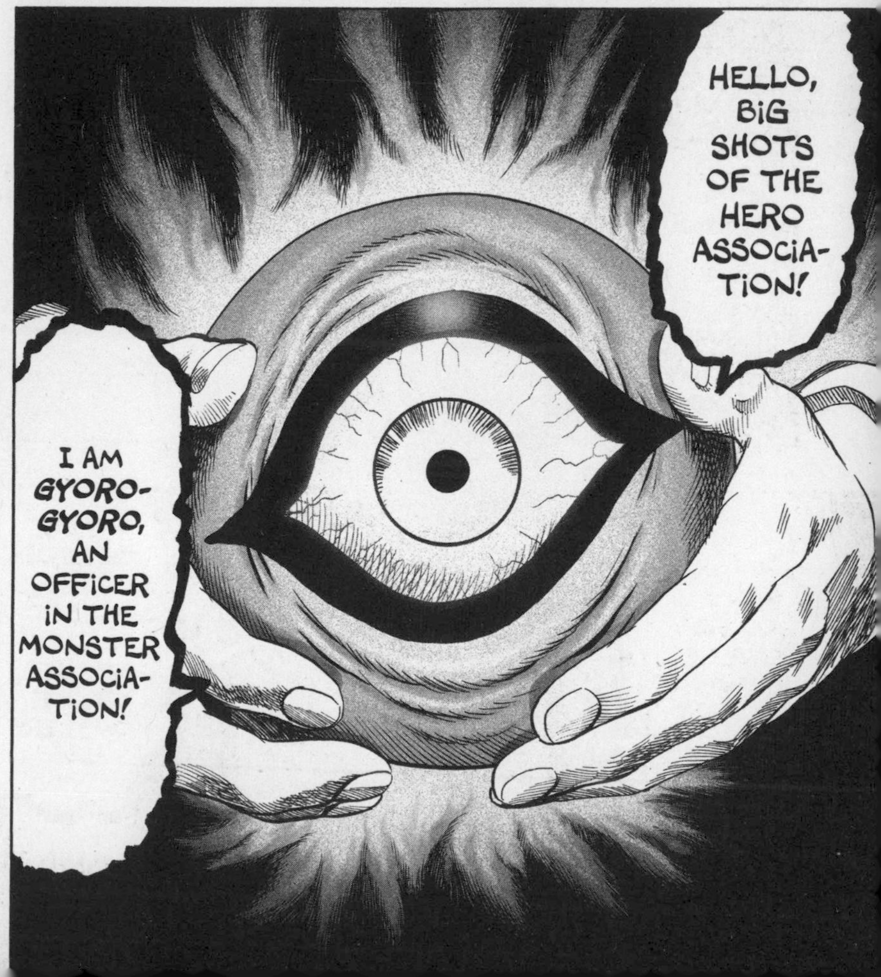
HELLO, BIG SHOTS OF THE HERO ASSOCIATION!
I AM GYORO-GYORO, AN OFFICER IN THE MONSTER ASSOCIATION!

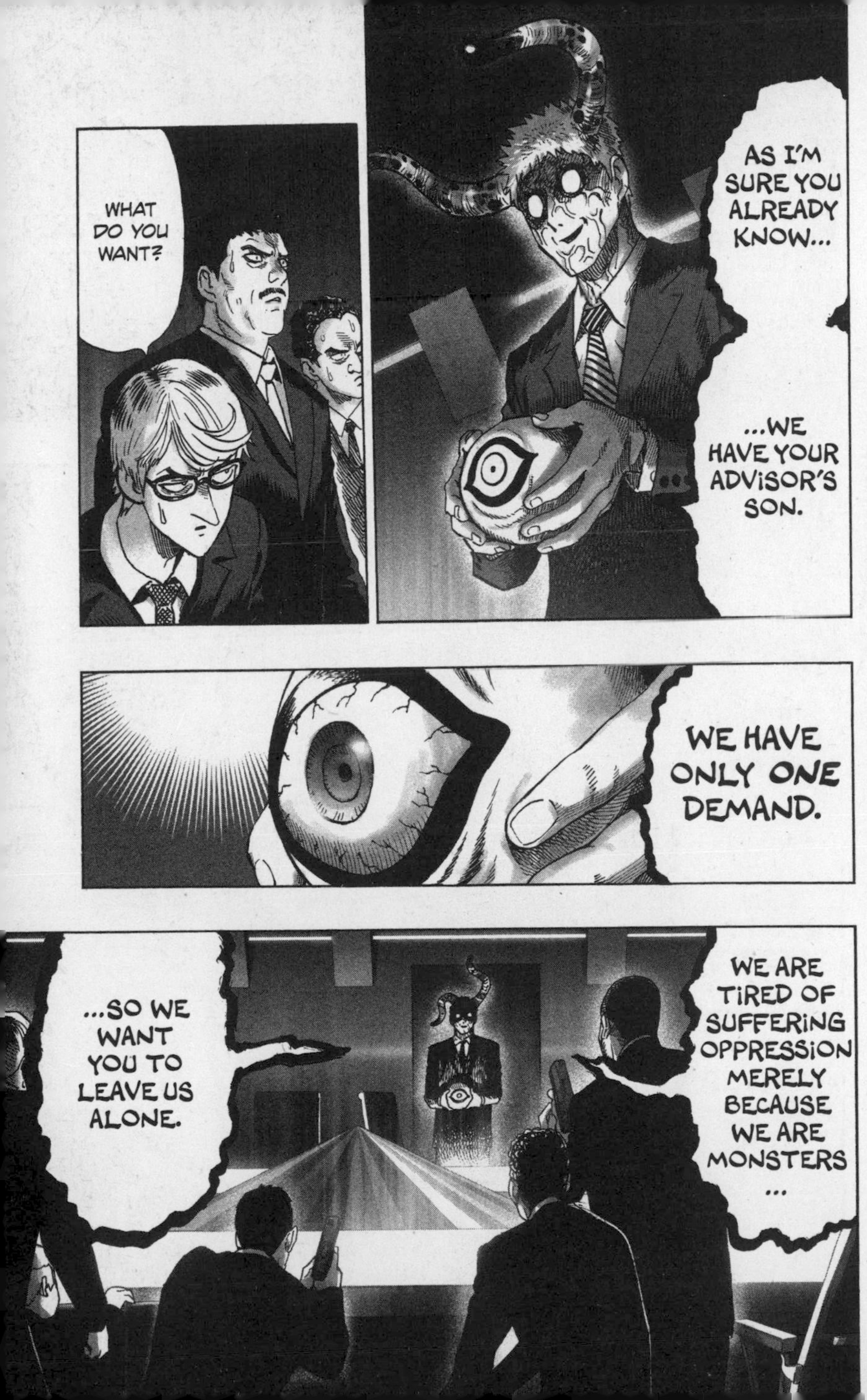
AS I'M SURE YOU ALREADY KNOW...
...WE HAVE YOUR ADVISOR'S SON.
WHAT DO YOU WANT?
WE HAVE ONLY ONE DEMAND.
WE ARE TIRED OF SUFFERING OPPRESSION MERELY BECAUSE WE ARE MONSTERS ...
...SO WE WANT YOU TO LEAVE US ALONE.

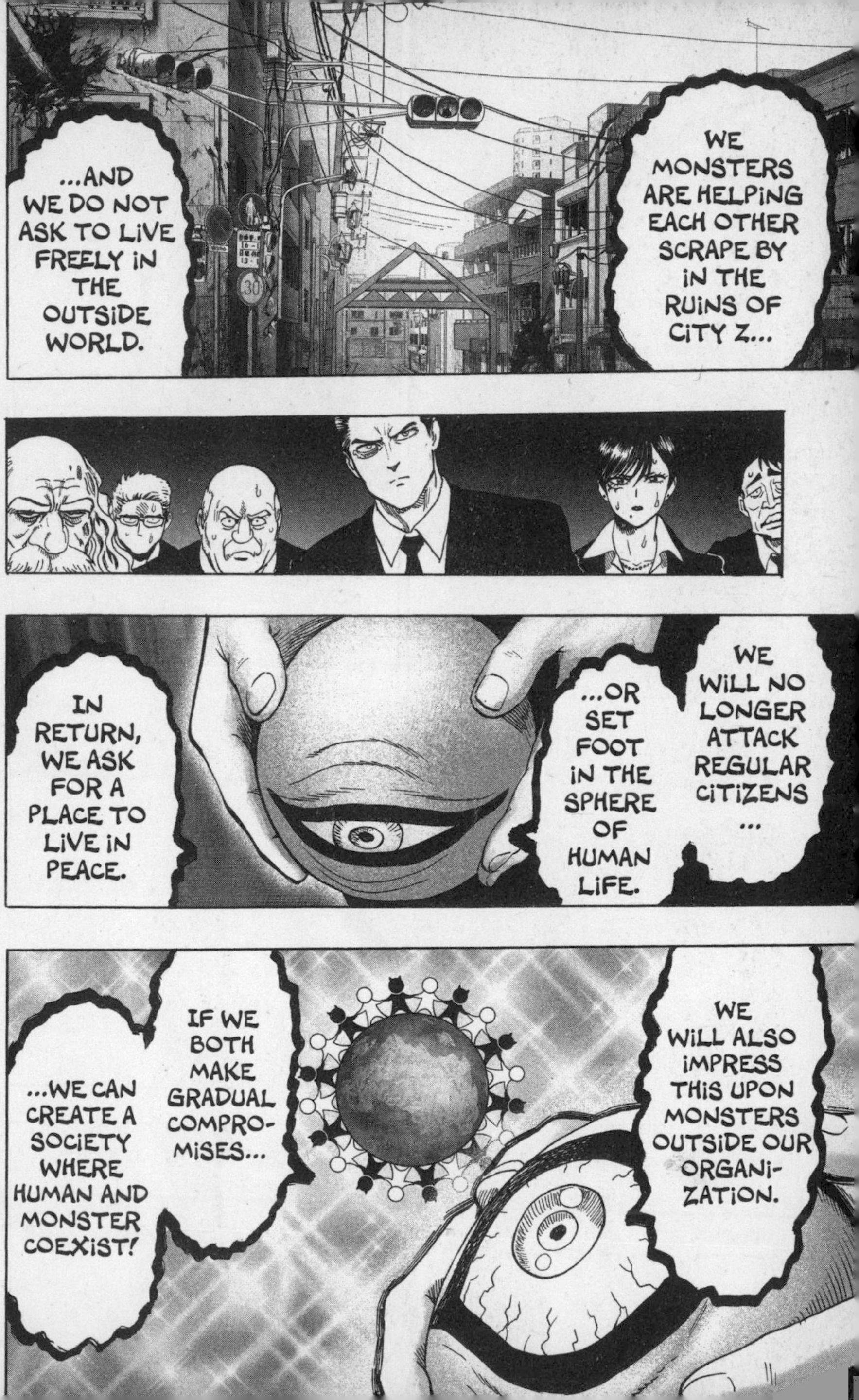
WE MONSTERS ARE HELPING EACH OTHER SCRAPE BY IN THE RUINS OF CITY Z...
...AND WE DO NOT ASK TO LIVE FREELY IN THE OUTSIDE WORLD.
WE WILL NO LONGER ATTACK REGULAR CITIZENS ...
...OR SET FOOT IN THE SPHERE OF HUMAN LIFE.
IN RETURN, WE ASK FOR A PLACE TO LIVE IN PEACE.
WE WILL ALSO IMPRESS THIS UPON MONSTERS OUTSIDE OUR ORGANIZATION.
IF WE BOTH MAKE GRADUAL COMPROMISES...
...WE CAN CREATE A SOCIETY WHERE HUMAN AND MONSTER COEXIST!

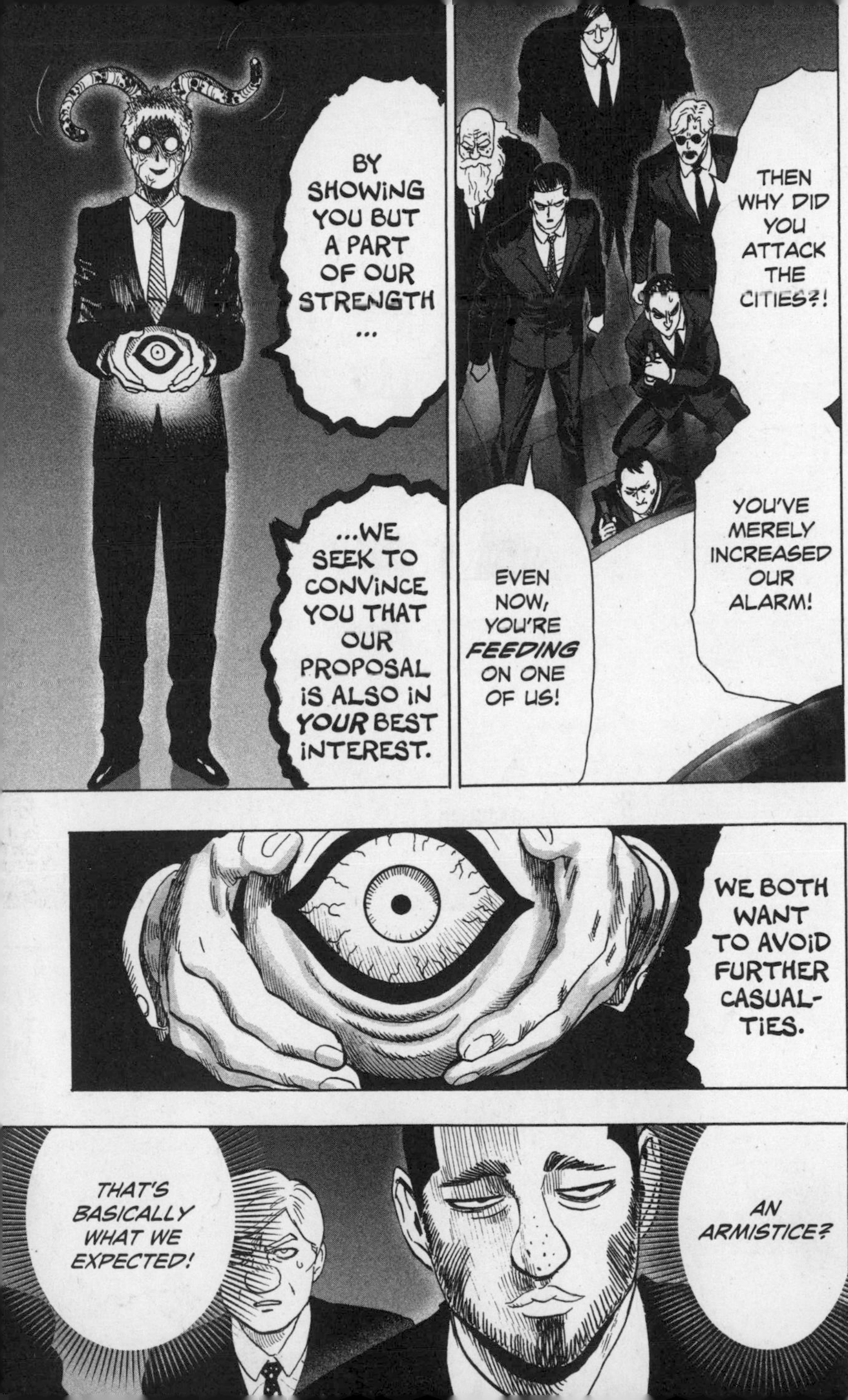
THEN WHY DID YOU ATTACK THE CITIES?!
YOU'VE MERELY INCREASED OUR ALARM!
EVEN NOW, YOU'RE *FEEDING* ON ONE OF US!
BY SHOWING YOU BUT A PART OF OUR STRENGTH ...
...WE SEEK TO CONVINCE YOU THAT OUR PROPOSAL IS ALSO IN *YOUR* BEST INTEREST.
WE BOTH WANT TO AVOID FURTHER CASUAL-TIES.
AN ARMISTICE?
THAT'S BASICALLY WHAT WE EXPECTED!

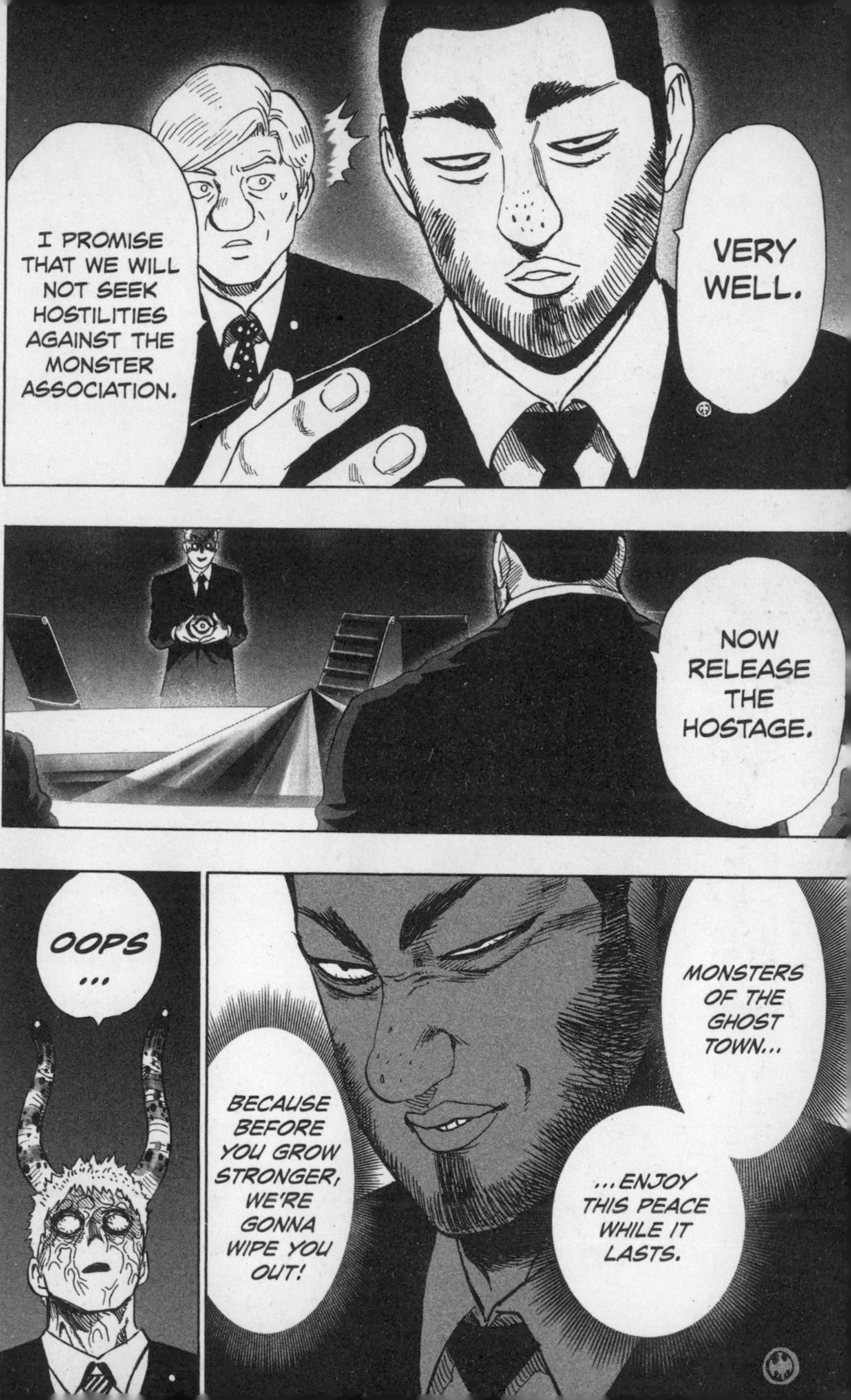
VERY WELL.
I PROMISE THAT WE WILL NOT SEEK HOSTILITIES AGAINST THE MONSTER ASSOCIATION.
NOW RELEASE THE HOSTAGE.
MONSTERS OF THE GHOST TOWN...
...ENJOY THIS PEACE WHILE IT LASTS.
BECAUSE BEFORE YOU GROW STRONGER, WE'RE GONNA WIPE YOU OUT!
OOPS ...

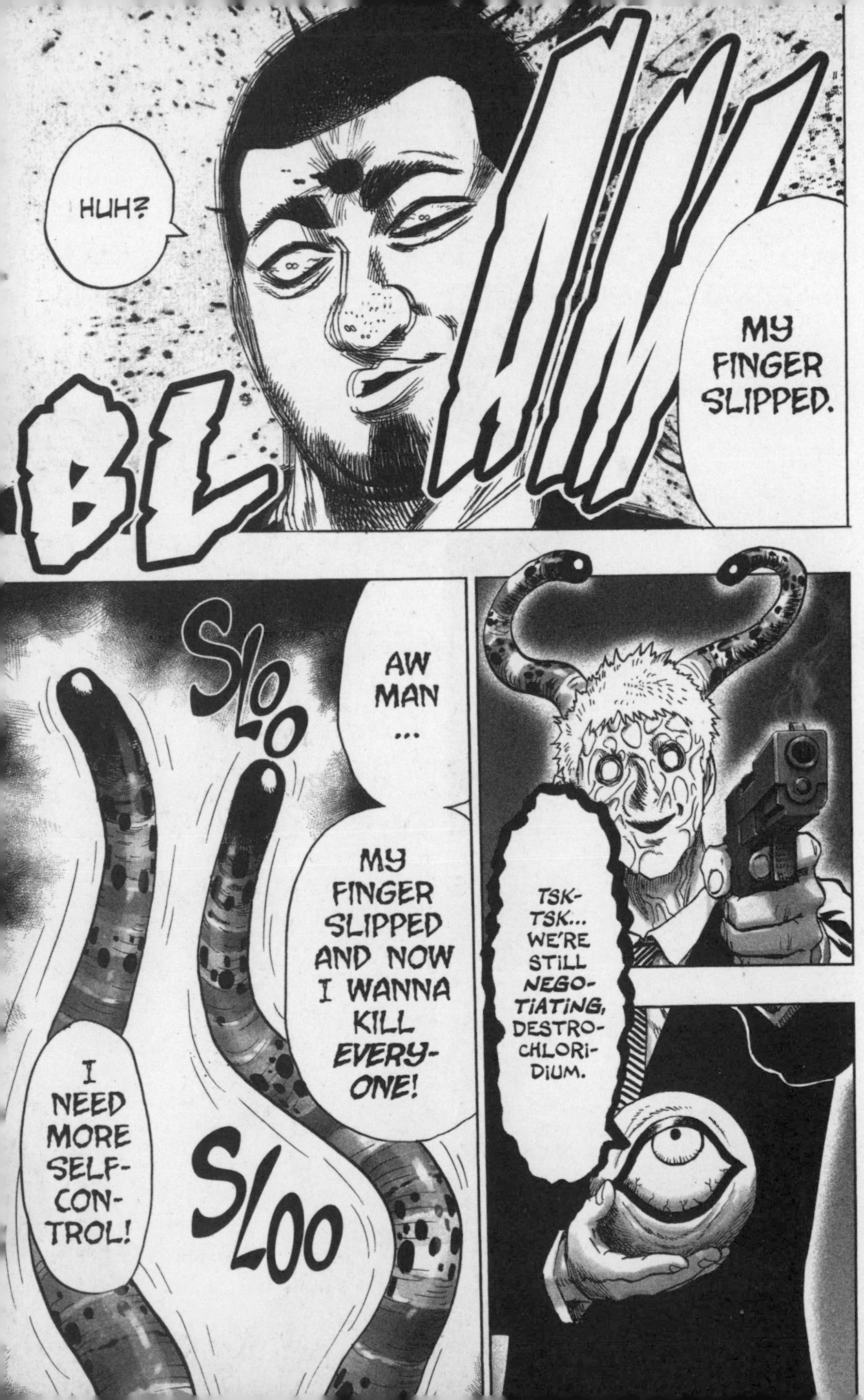
MY FINGER SLIPPED.
HUH?
BLAM
TSK-TSK... WE'RE STILL NEGOTIATING, DESTROCHLORIDIUM.
SLOO
AW MAN...
MY FINGER SLIPPED AND NOW I WANNA KILL EVERYONE!
SLOO
I NEED MORE SELF-CONTROL!

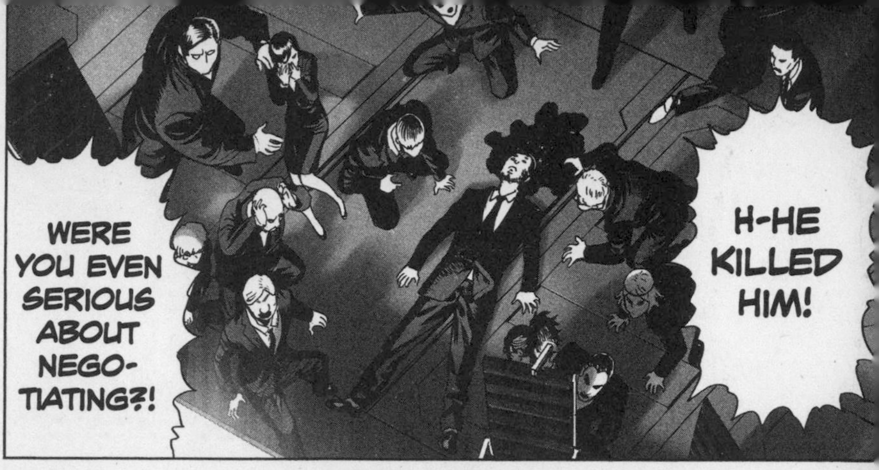
H-HE KILLED HIM!
WERE YOU EVEN SERIOUS ABOUT NEGO-TIATING?!

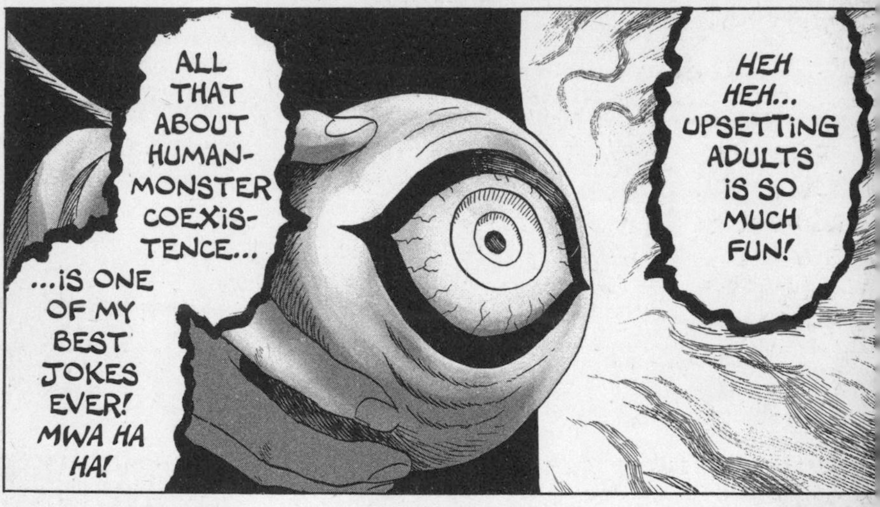
HEH HEH... UPSETTING ADULTS IS SO MUCH FUN!
ALL THAT ABOUT HUMAN-MONSTER COEXIS-TENCE...
...IS ONE OF MY BEST JOKES EVER! MWA HA HA!

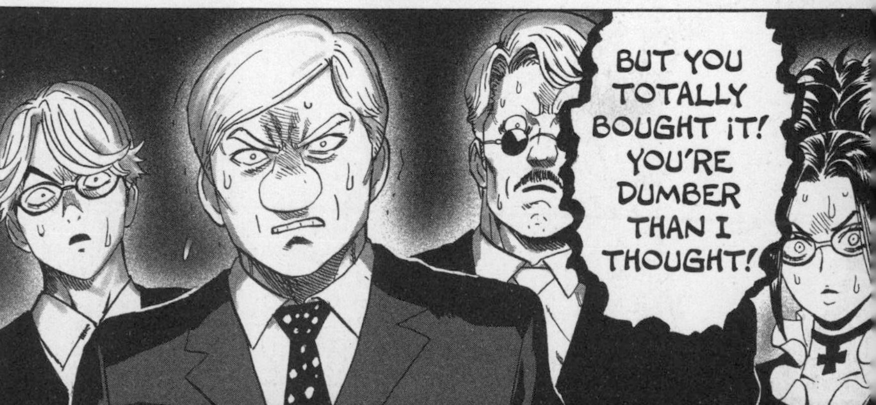
BUT YOU TOTALLY BOUGHT IT! YOU'RE DUMBER THAN I THOUGHT!

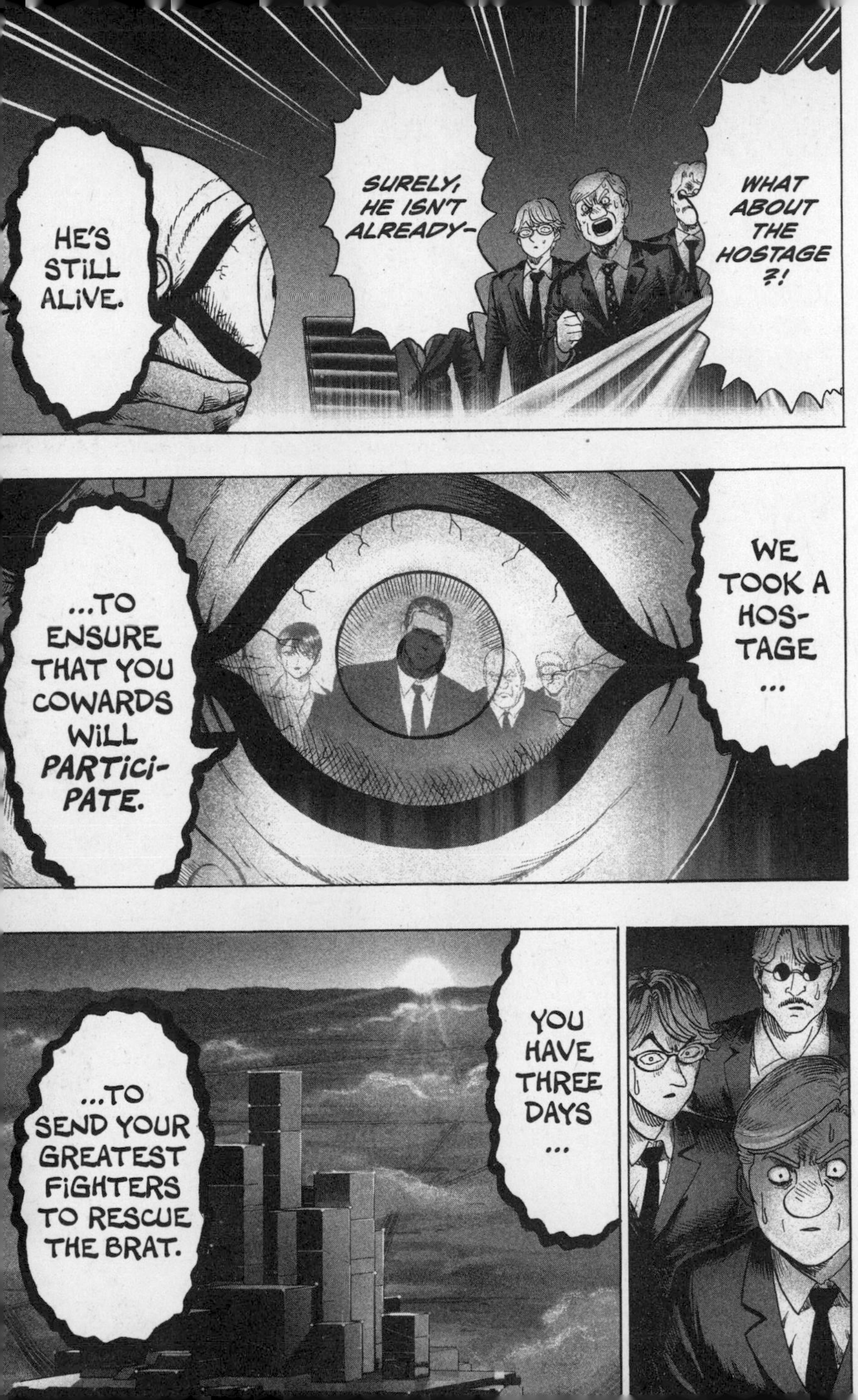
WHAT ABOUT THE HOSTAGE ?!
SURELY, HE ISN'T ALREADY-
HE'S STILL ALIVE.
WE TOOK A HOSTAGE ...
...TO ENSURE THAT YOU COWARDS WILL PARTICIPATE.
YOU HAVE THREE DAYS ...
...TO SEND YOUR GREATEST FIGHTERS TO RESCUE THE BRAT.

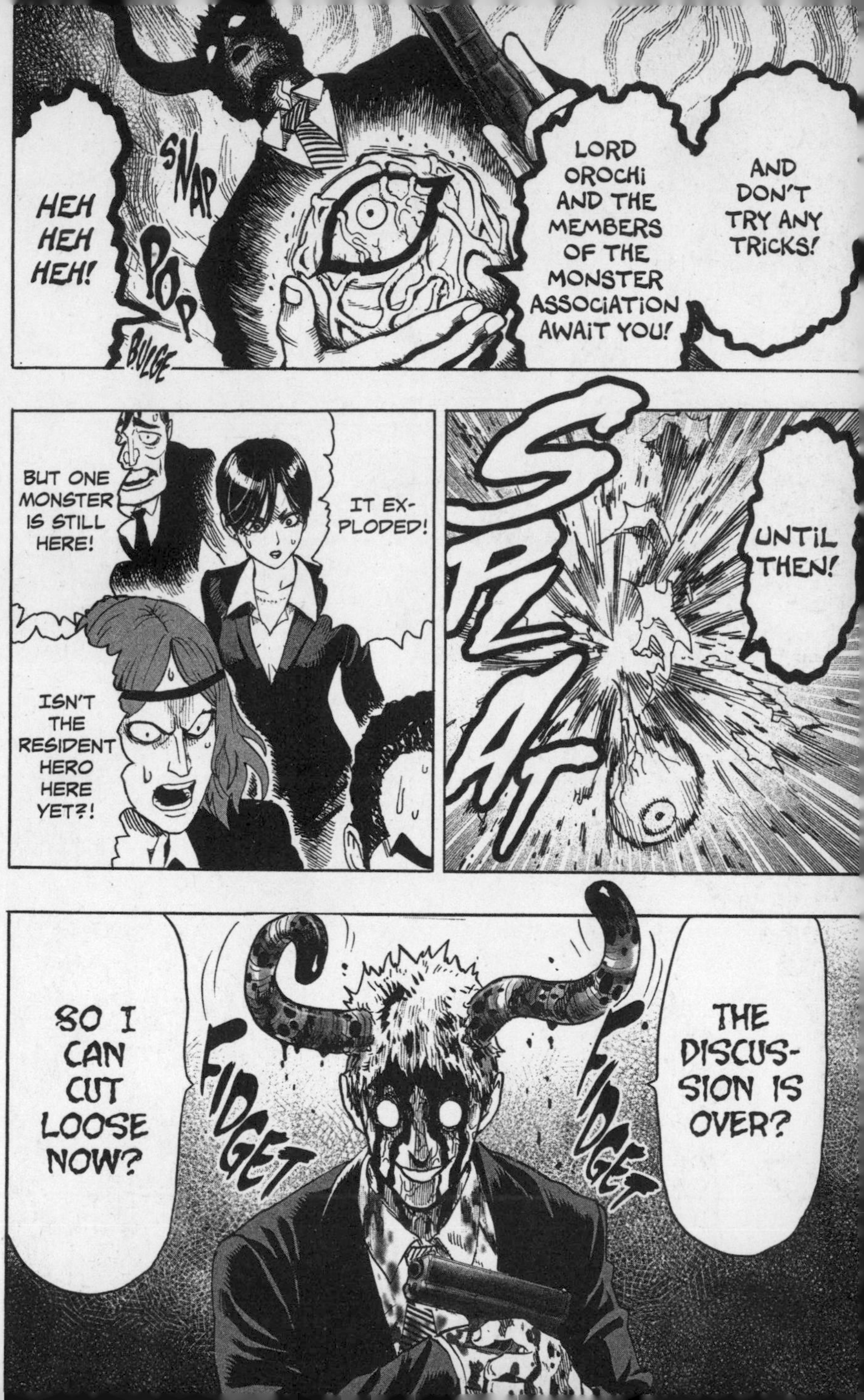
AND DON'T TRY ANY TRICKS!
LORD OROCHI AND THE MEMBERS OF THE MONSTER ASSOCIATION AWAIT YOU!
SNAP
POP
BULGE
HEH HEH HEH!
UNTIL THEN!
SPLAT
IT EX-PLODED!
BUT ONE MONSTER IS STILL HERE!
ISN'T THE RESIDENT HERO HERE YET?!
THE DISCUS-SION IS OVER?
FIDGET
FIDGET
SO I CAN CUT LOOSE NOW?

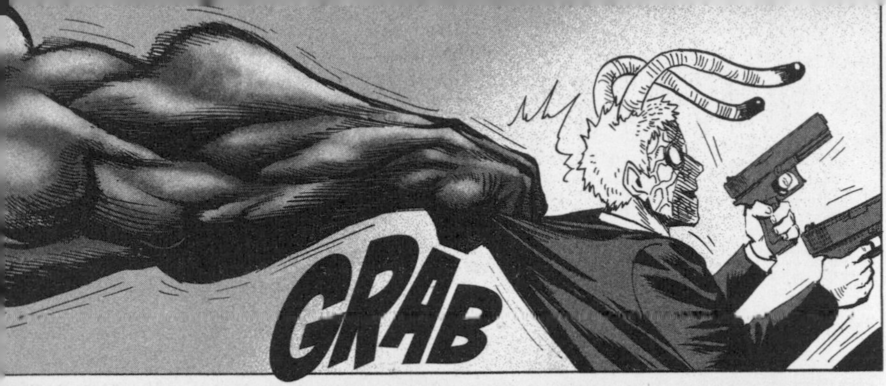
GRAB
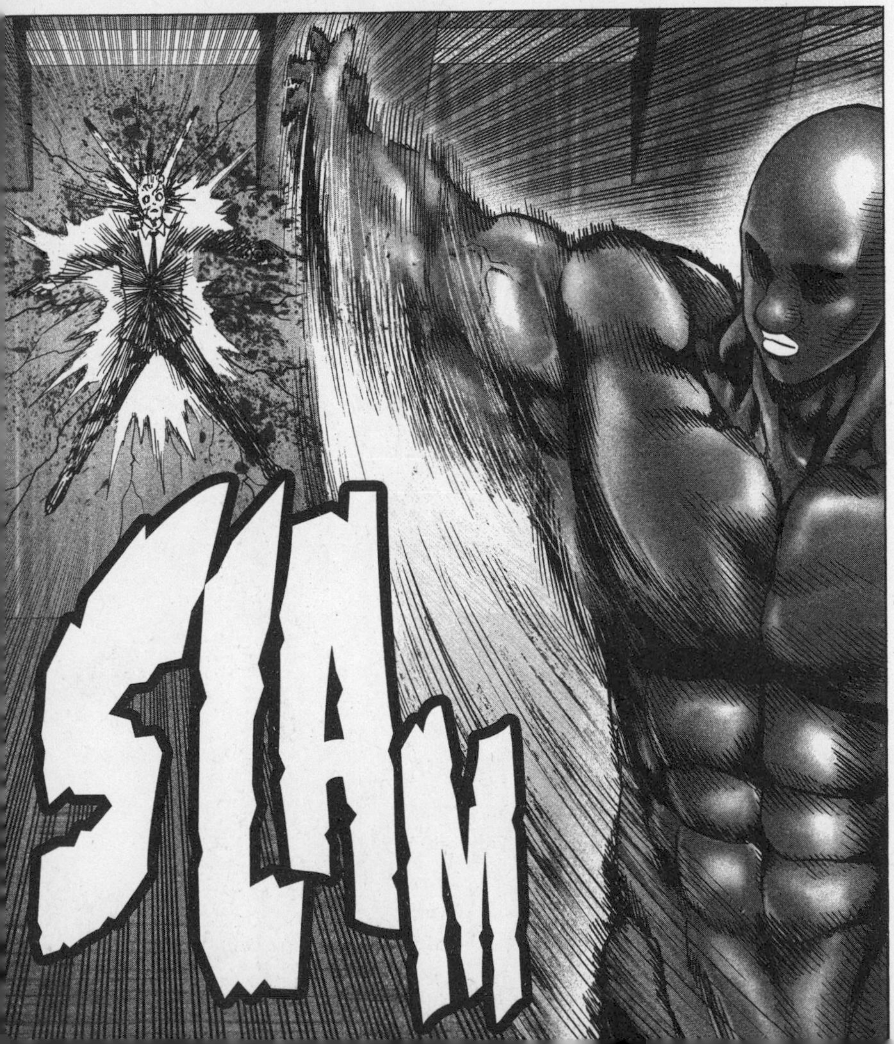
SLAM

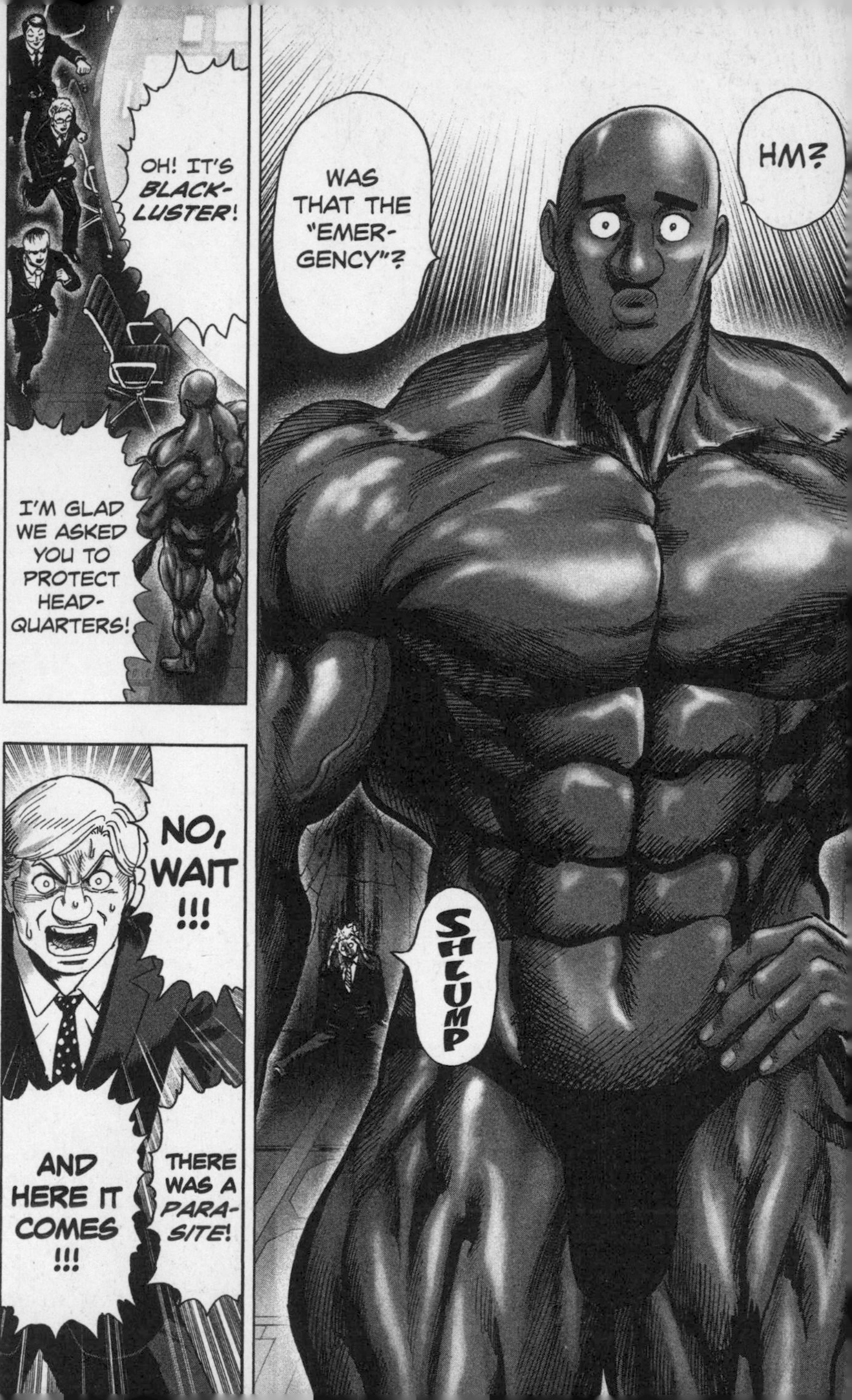
HM?
WAS THAT THE "EMER-GENCY"?
SHLUMP
OH! IT'S BLACK-LUSTER!
I'M GLAD WE ASKED YOU TO PROTECT HEAD-QUARTERS!
NO, WAIT!!!
THERE WAS A PARA-SITE!
AND HERE IT COMES!!!

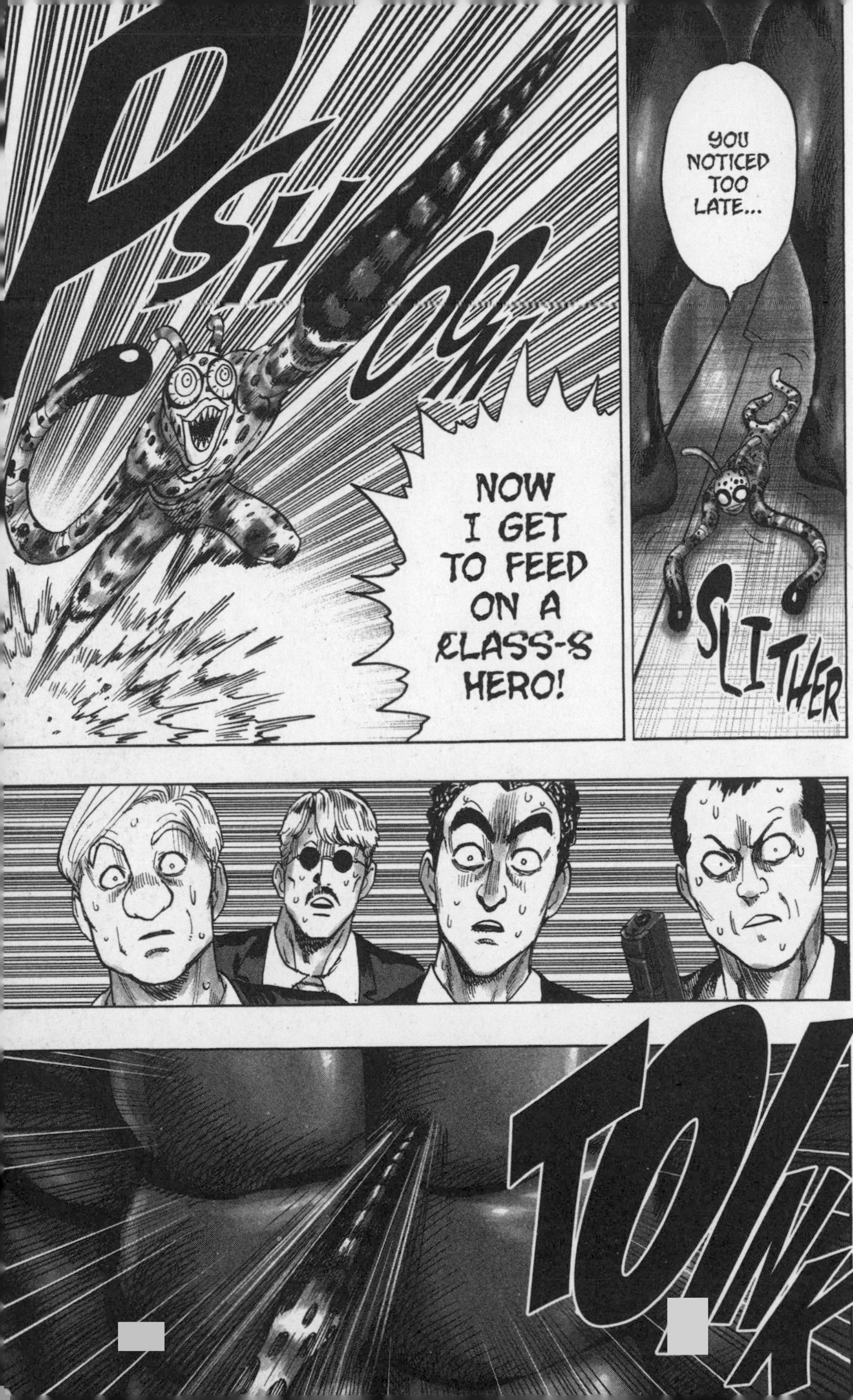
YOU NOTICED TOO LATE...
SLITHER
NOW I GET TO FEED ON A CLASS-S HERO!
TONK

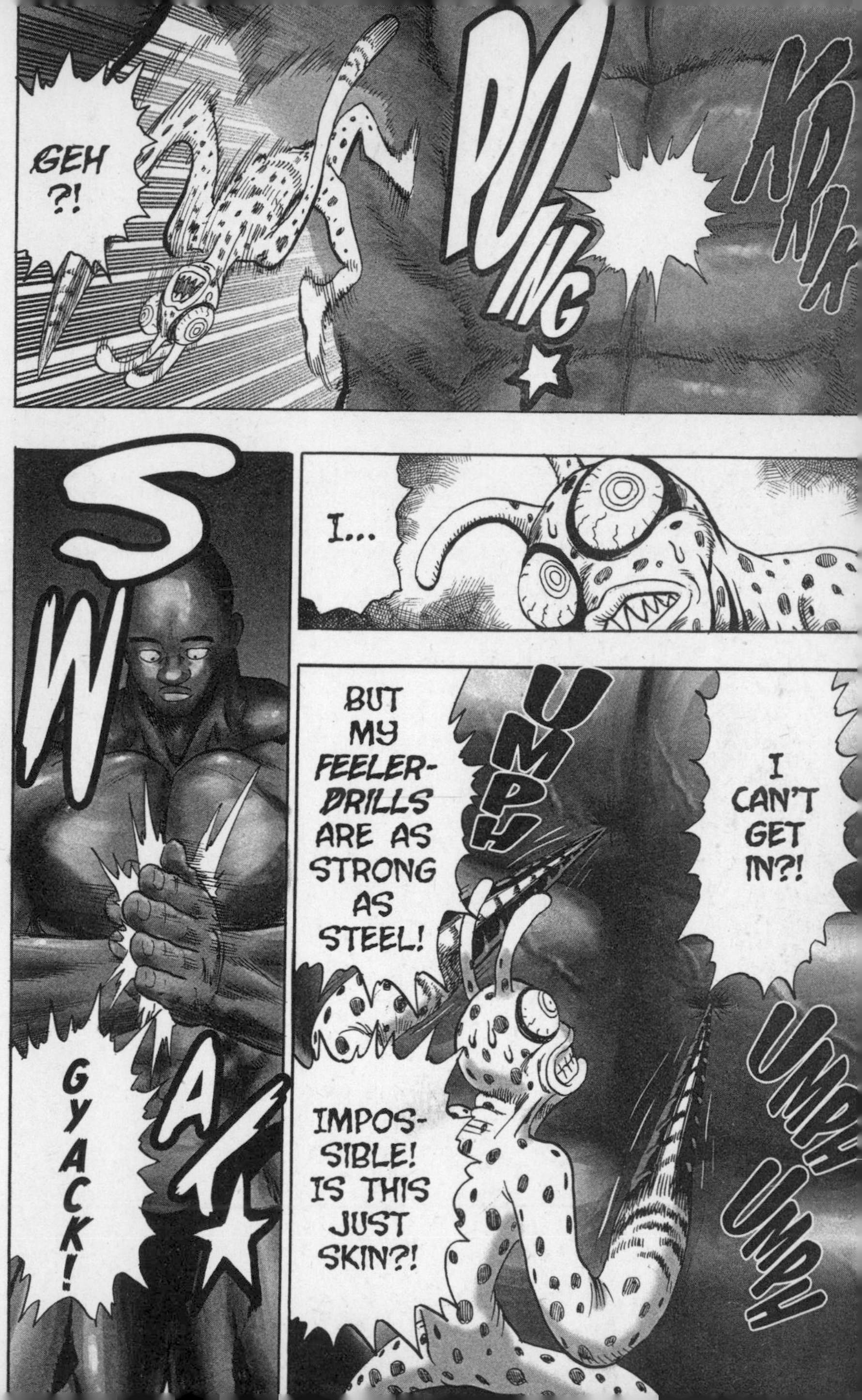
DOING
GEH ?!
I...
I CAN'T GET IN?!
UMPH UMPH
UMPH
BUT MY FEELER-DRILLS ARE AS STRONG AS STEEL!
IMPOSSIBLE! IS THIS JUST SKIN?!
SWA
GYACK!

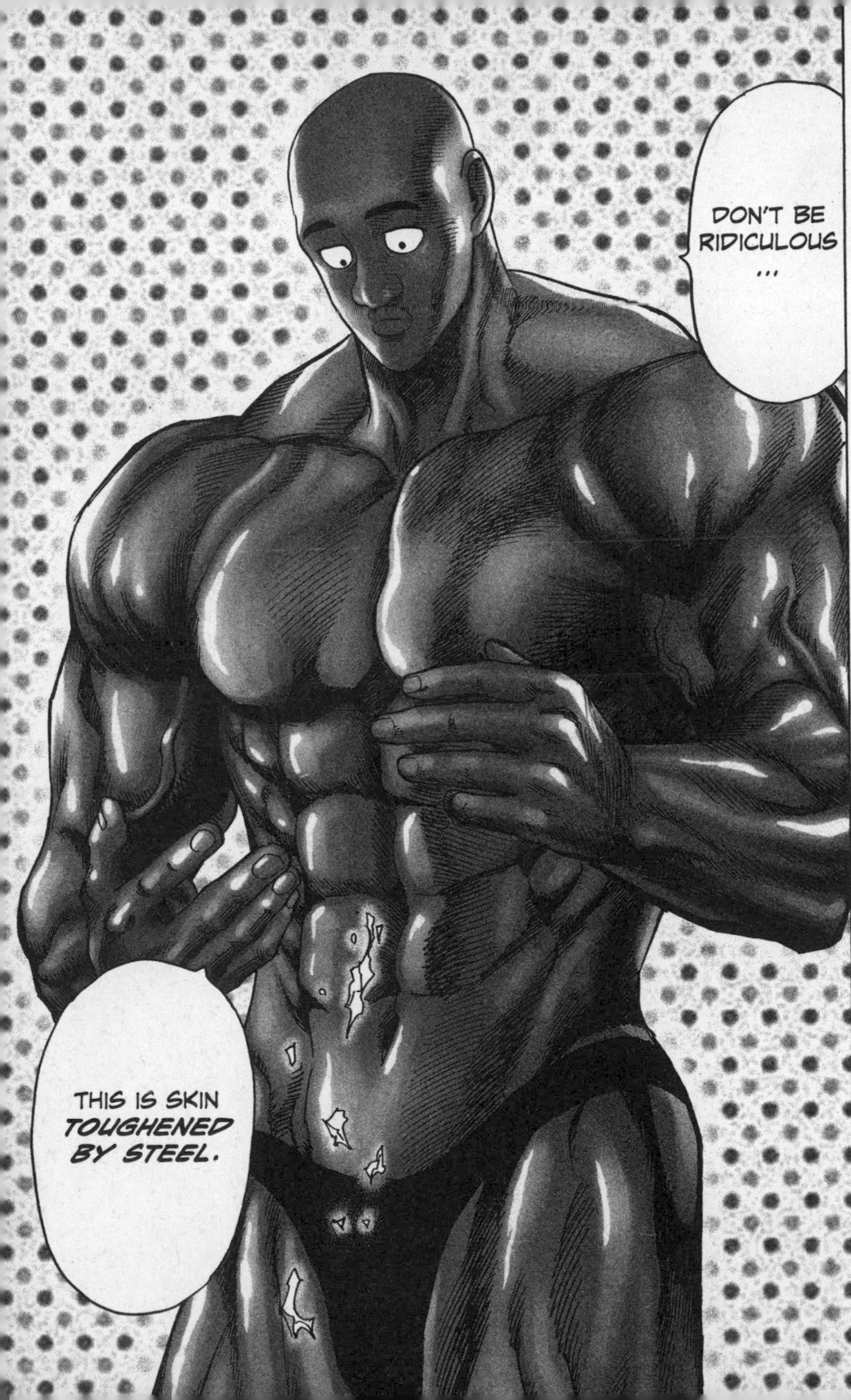
DON'T BE RIDICULOUS ...
THIS IS SKIN *TOUGHENED BY STEEL.*

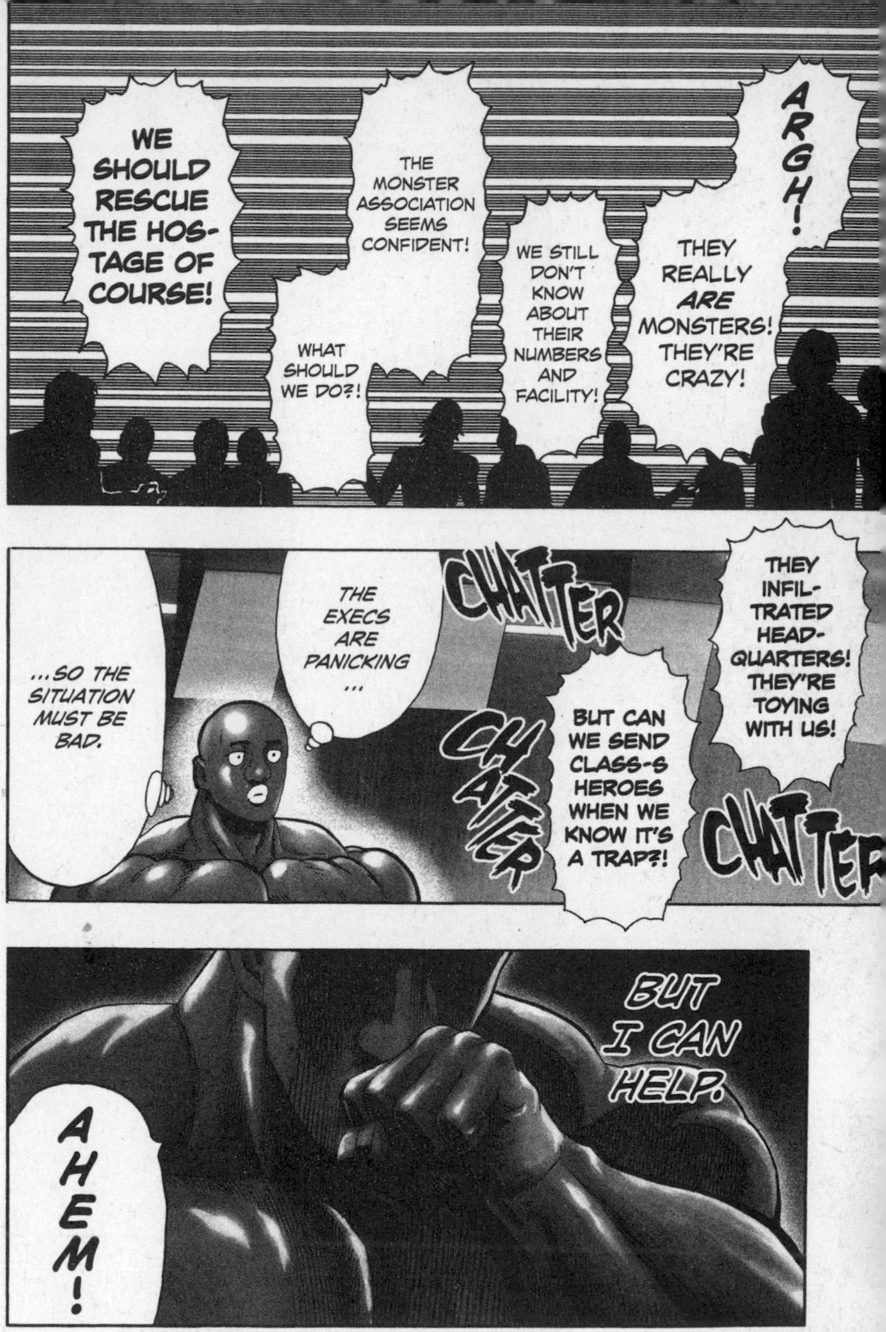
ARGH!
THEY REALLY ARE MONSTERS! THEY'RE CRAZY!
WE STILL DON'T KNOW ABOUT THEIR NUMBERS AND FACILITY!
THE MONSTER ASSOCIATION SEEMS CONFIDENT!
WHAT SHOULD WE DO?!
WE SHOULD RESCUE THE HOS-TAGE OF COURSE!
THEY INFIL-TRATED HEAD-QUARTERS! THEY'RE TOYING WITH US!
CHATTER
BUT CAN WE SEND CLASS-S HEROES WHEN WE KNOW IT'S A TRAP?!
CHATTER
CHATTER
THE EXECS ARE PANICKING ...
...SO THE SITUATION MUST BE BAD.
BUT I CAN HELP.
AHEM!

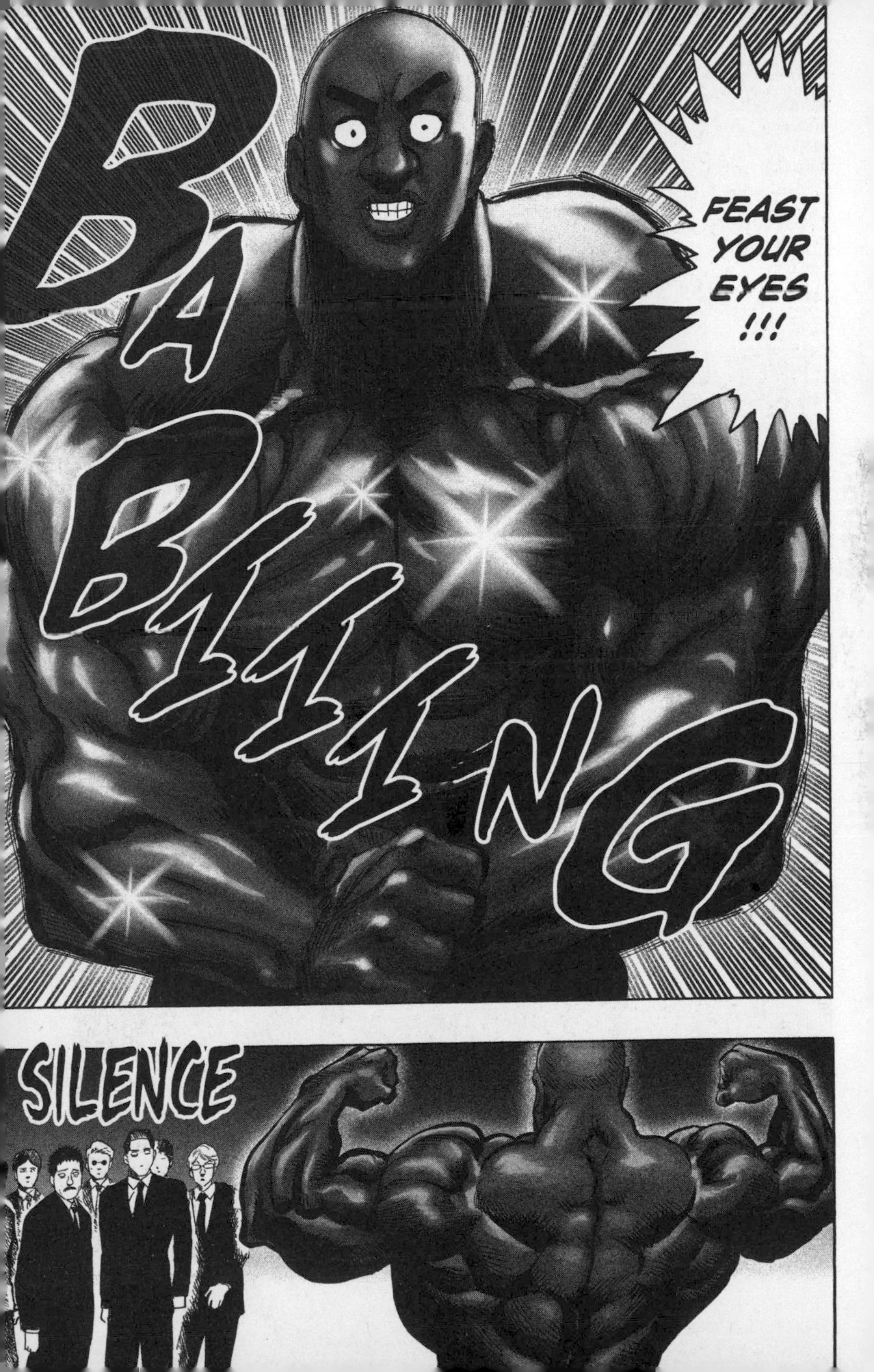
FEAST YOUR EYES!!!
BA
BIIING
SILENCE

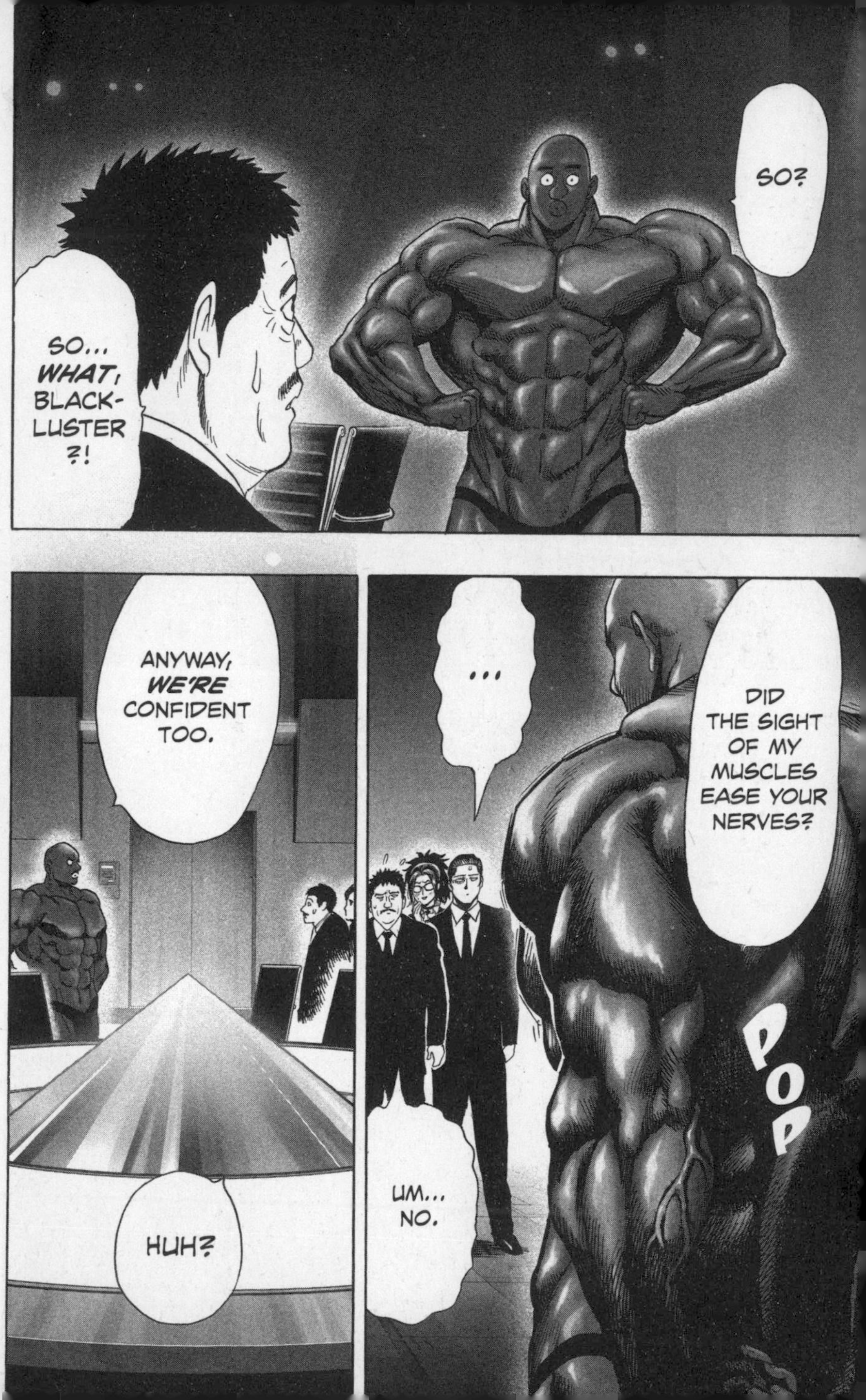
SO?
SO... WHAT, BLACK-LUSTER?!
DID THE SIGHT OF MY MUSCLES EASE YOUR NERVES?
POP
POP
...
UM... NO.
ANYWAY, WE'RE CONFIDENT TOO.
HUH?

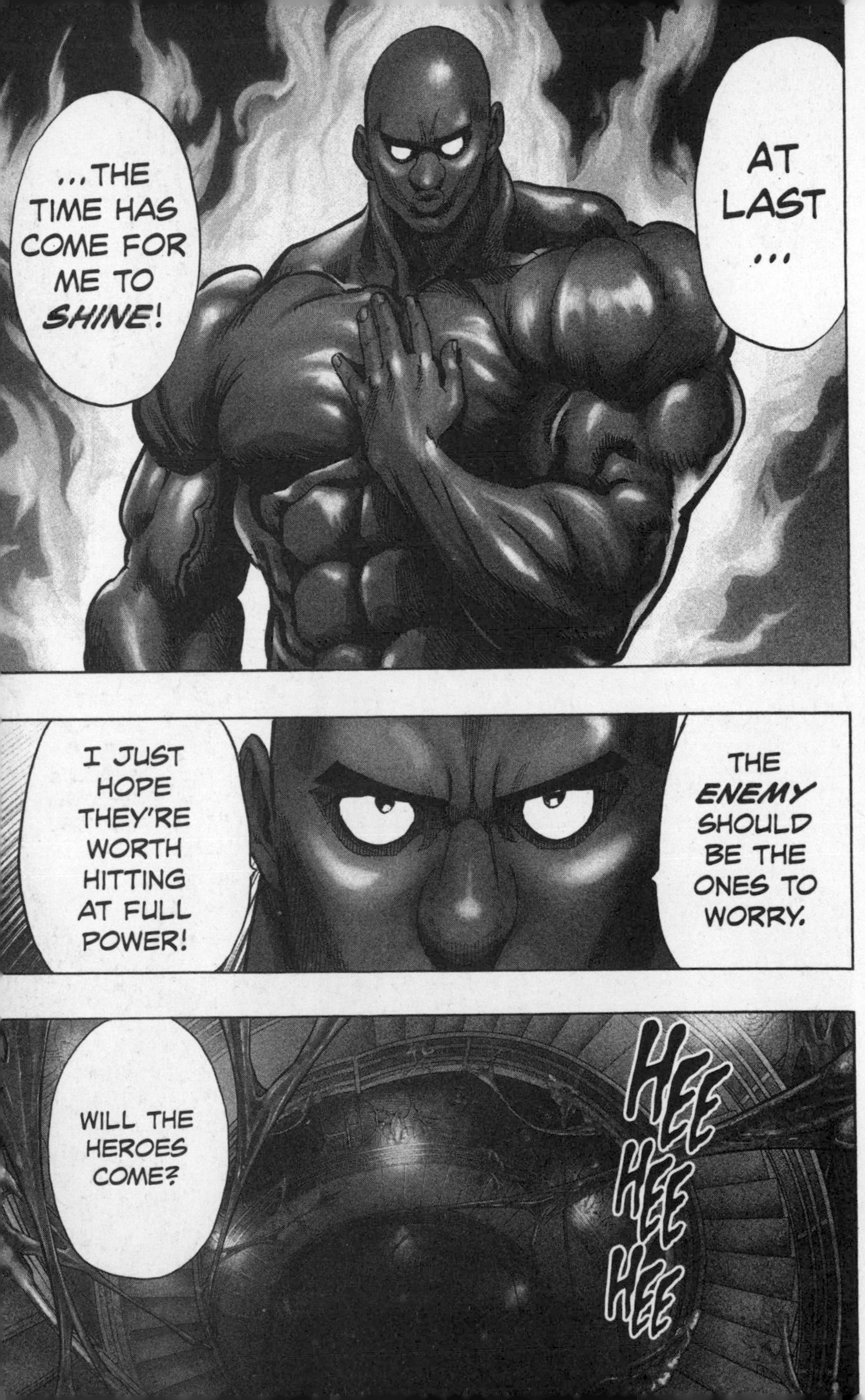
AT LAST...
...THE TIME HAS COME FOR ME TO SHINE!
THE ENEMY SHOULD BE THE ONES TO WORRY.
I JUST HOPE THEY'RE WORTH HITTING AT FULL POWER!
HEE HEE HEE
WILL THE HEROES COME?

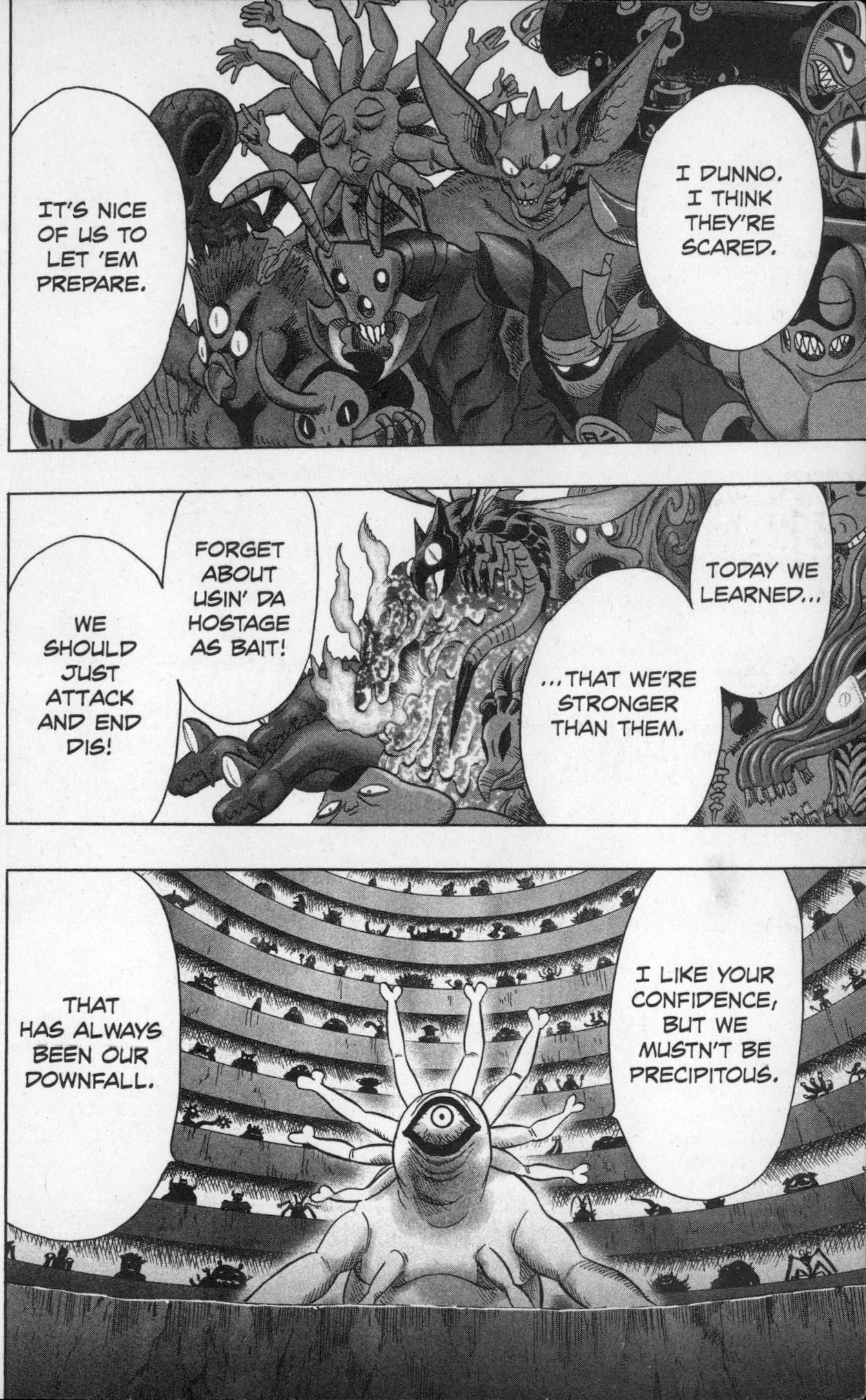
I DUNNO. I THINK THEY'RE SCARED.
IT'S NICE OF US TO LET 'EM PREPARE.
TODAY WE LEARNED...
...THAT WE'RE STRONGER THAN THEM.
FORGET ABOUT USIN' DA HOSTAGE AS BAIT!
WE SHOULD JUST ATTACK AND END DIS!
I LIKE YOUR CONFIDENCE, BUT WE MUSTN'T BE PRECIPITOUS.
THAT HAS ALWAYS BEEN OUR DOWNFALL.

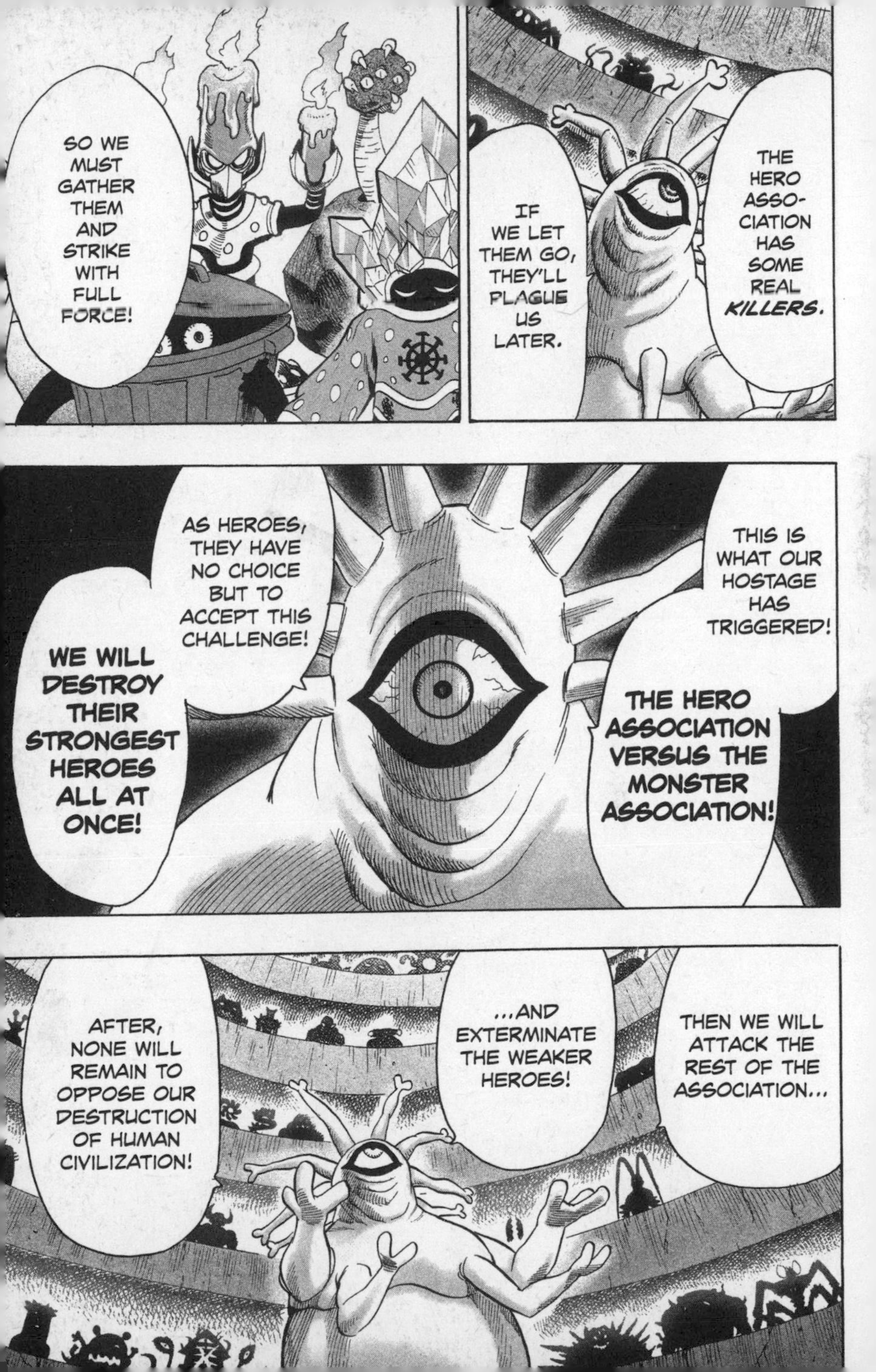
THE HERO ASSOCIATION HAS SOME REAL KILLERS.
IF WE LET THEM GO, THEY'LL PLAGUE US LATER.
SO WE MUST GATHER THEM AND STRIKE WITH FULL FORCE!
THIS IS WHAT OUR HOSTAGE HAS TRIGGERED!
THE HERO ASSOCIATION VERSUS THE MONSTER ASSOCIATION!
AS HEROES, THEY HAVE NO CHOICE BUT TO ACCEPT THIS CHALLENGE!
WE WILL DESTROY THEIR STRONGEST HEROES ALL AT ONCE!
THEN WE WILL ATTACK THE REST OF THE ASSOCIATION...
...AND EXTERMINATE THE WEAKER HEROES!
AFTER, NONE WILL REMAIN TO OPPOSE OUR DESTRUCTION OF HUMAN CIVILIZATION!

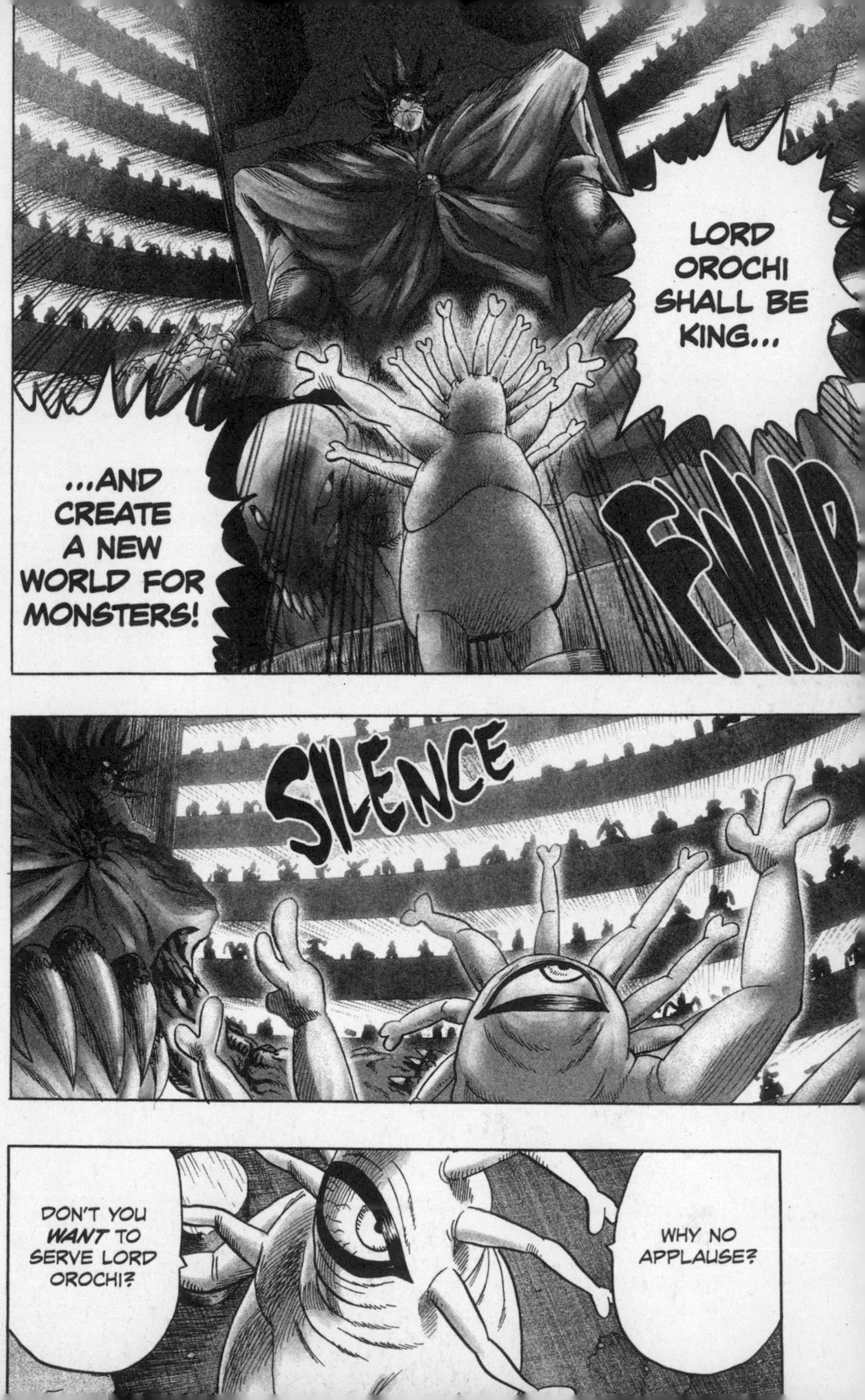
LORD OROCHI SHALL BE KING...
...AND CREATE A NEW WORLD FOR MONSTERS!
SILENCE
WHY NO APPLAUSE?
DON'T YOU *WANT* TO SERVE LORD OROCHI?

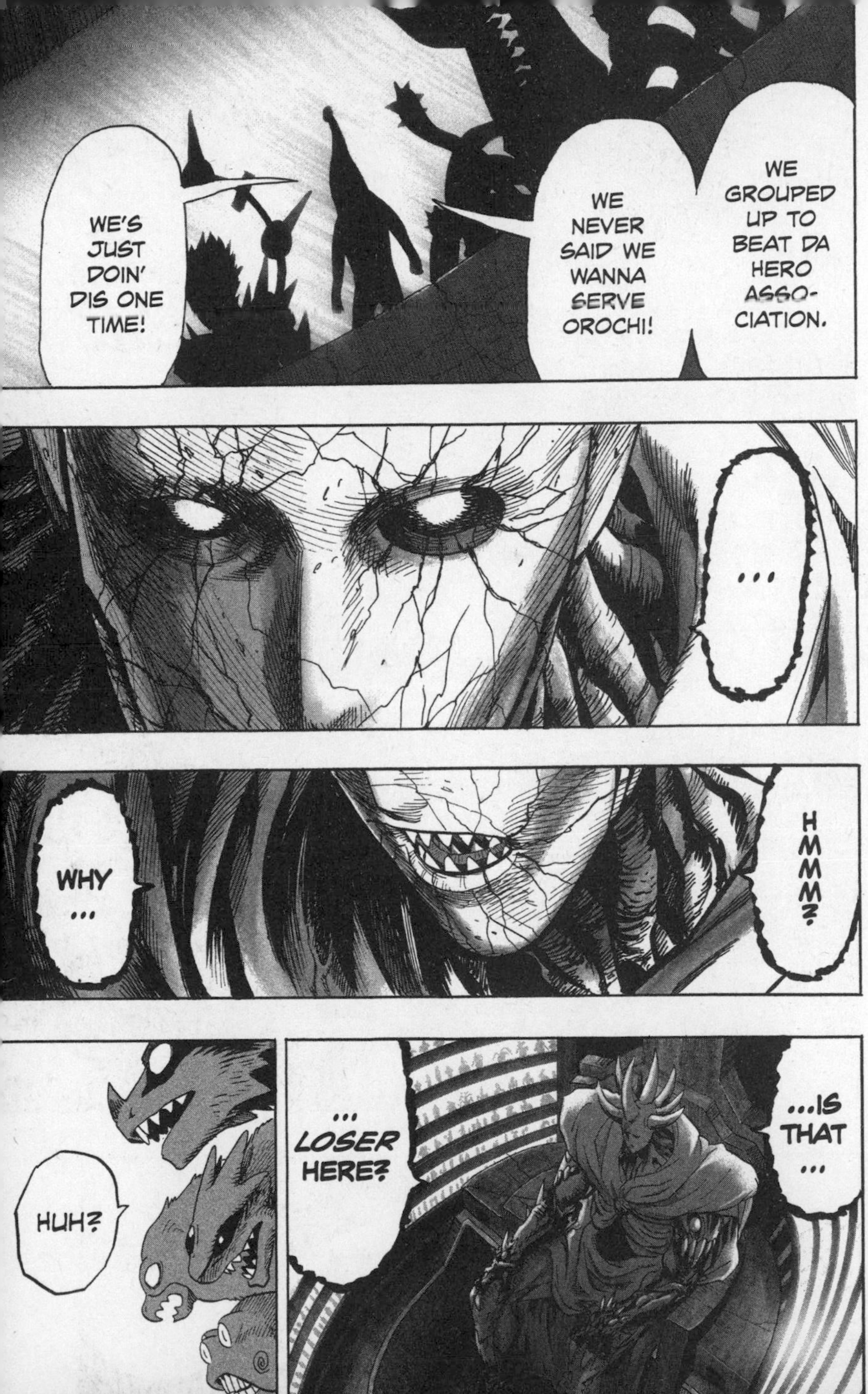
WE GROUPED UP TO BEAT DA HERO ASSO-CIATION.
WE NEVER SAID WE WANNA SERVE OROCHI!
WE'S JUST DOIN' DIS ONE TIME!
...
HMMMM?
WHY ...
...IS THAT ...
... LOSER HERE?
HUH?

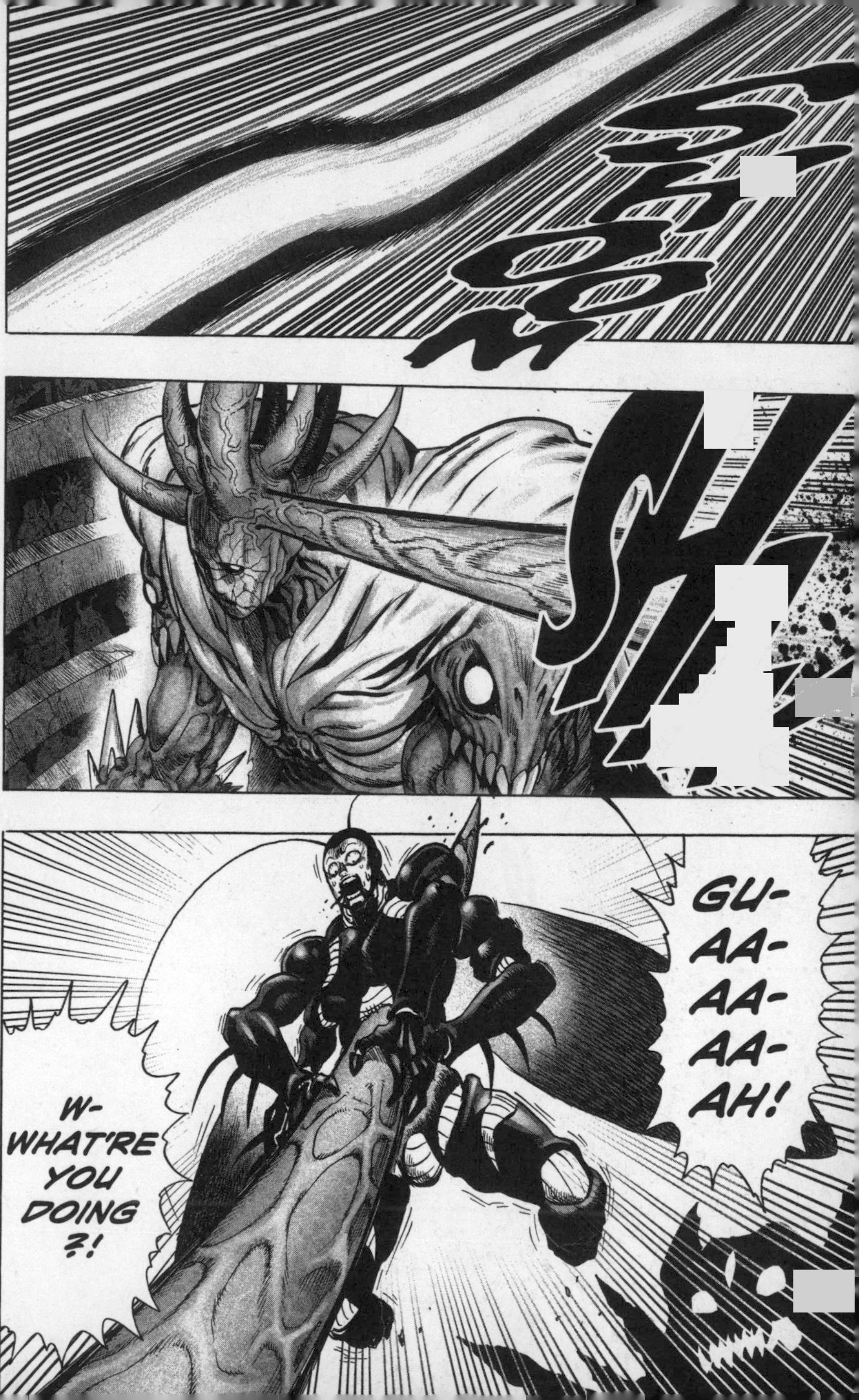
GU-AA-AA-AA-AH!
W-WHAT'RE YOU DOING ?!

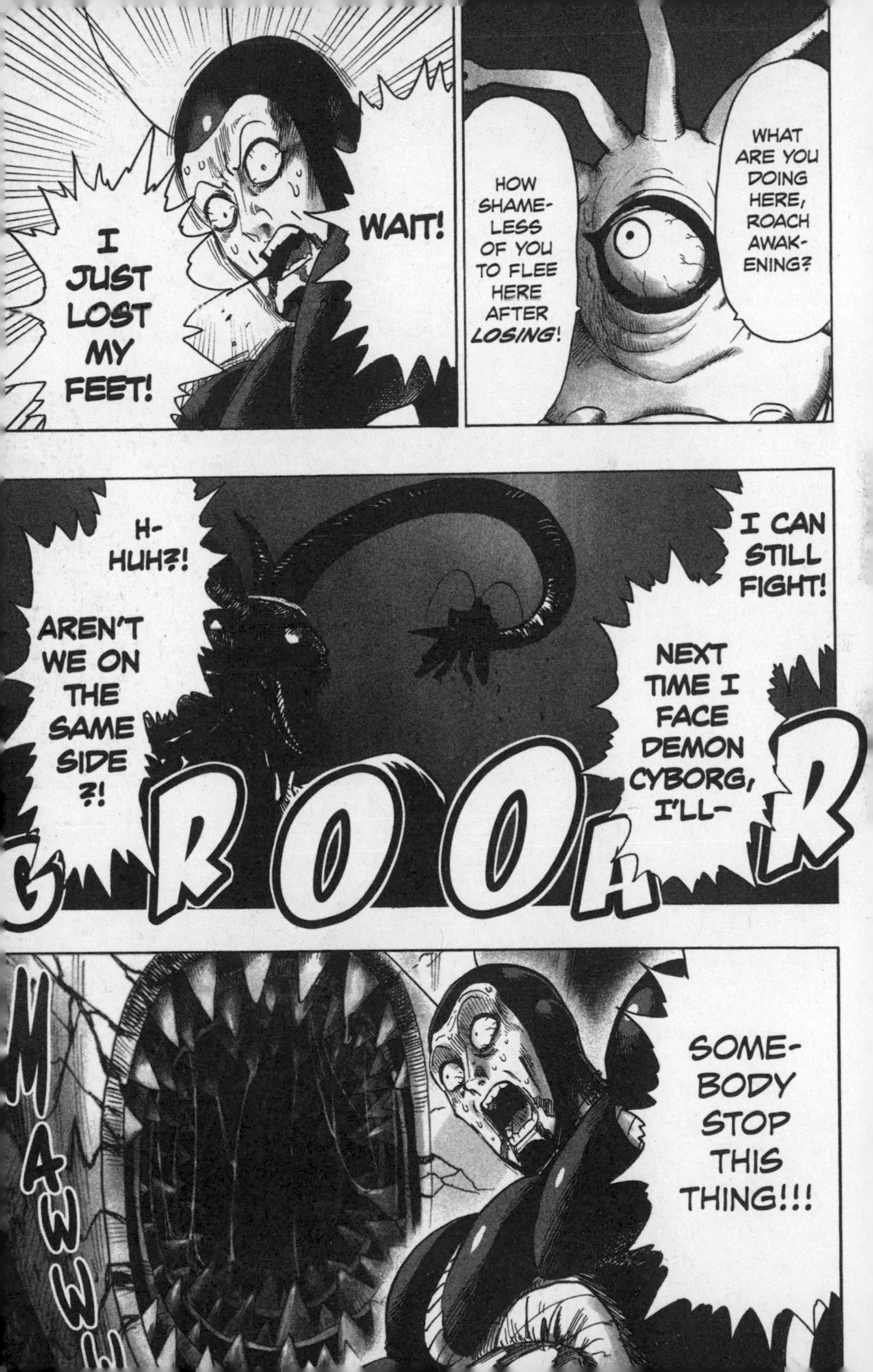
WHAT ARE YOU DOING HERE, ROACH AWAKENING?
HOW SHAMELESS OF YOU TO FLEE HERE AFTER *LOSING*!
WAIT!
I JUST LOST MY FEET!
I CAN STILL FIGHT!
NEXT TIME I FACE DEMON CYBORG, I'LL-
GROOAR
H-HUH?!
AREN'T WE ON THE SAME SIDE?!
SOMEBODY STOP THIS THING!!!
MAWW

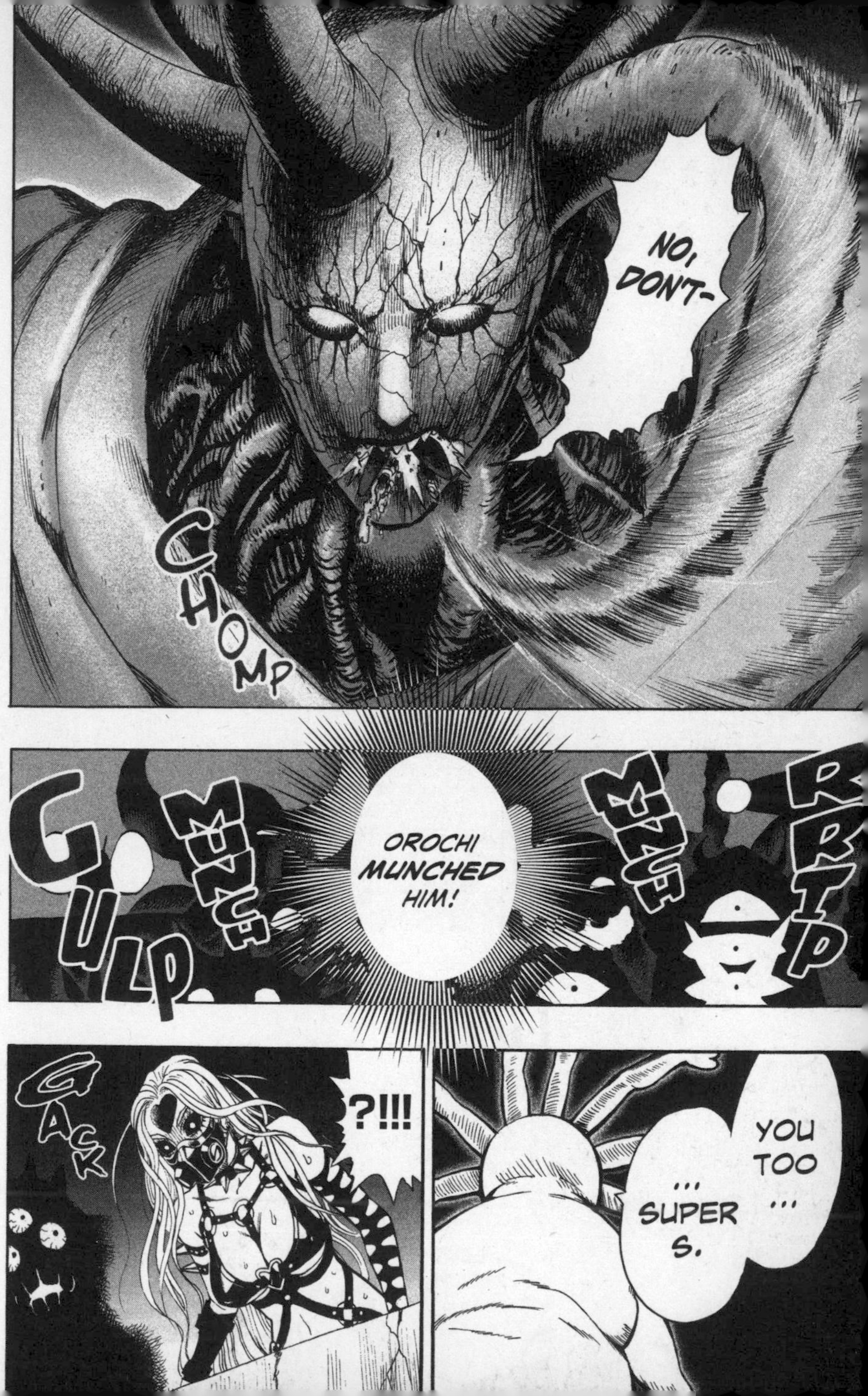
NO, DON'T-
CHOMP
RRIP
MUNCH
OROCHI MUNCHED HIM!
MUNCH
GULP
YOU TOO ...
... SUPER S.
?!!!
GACK

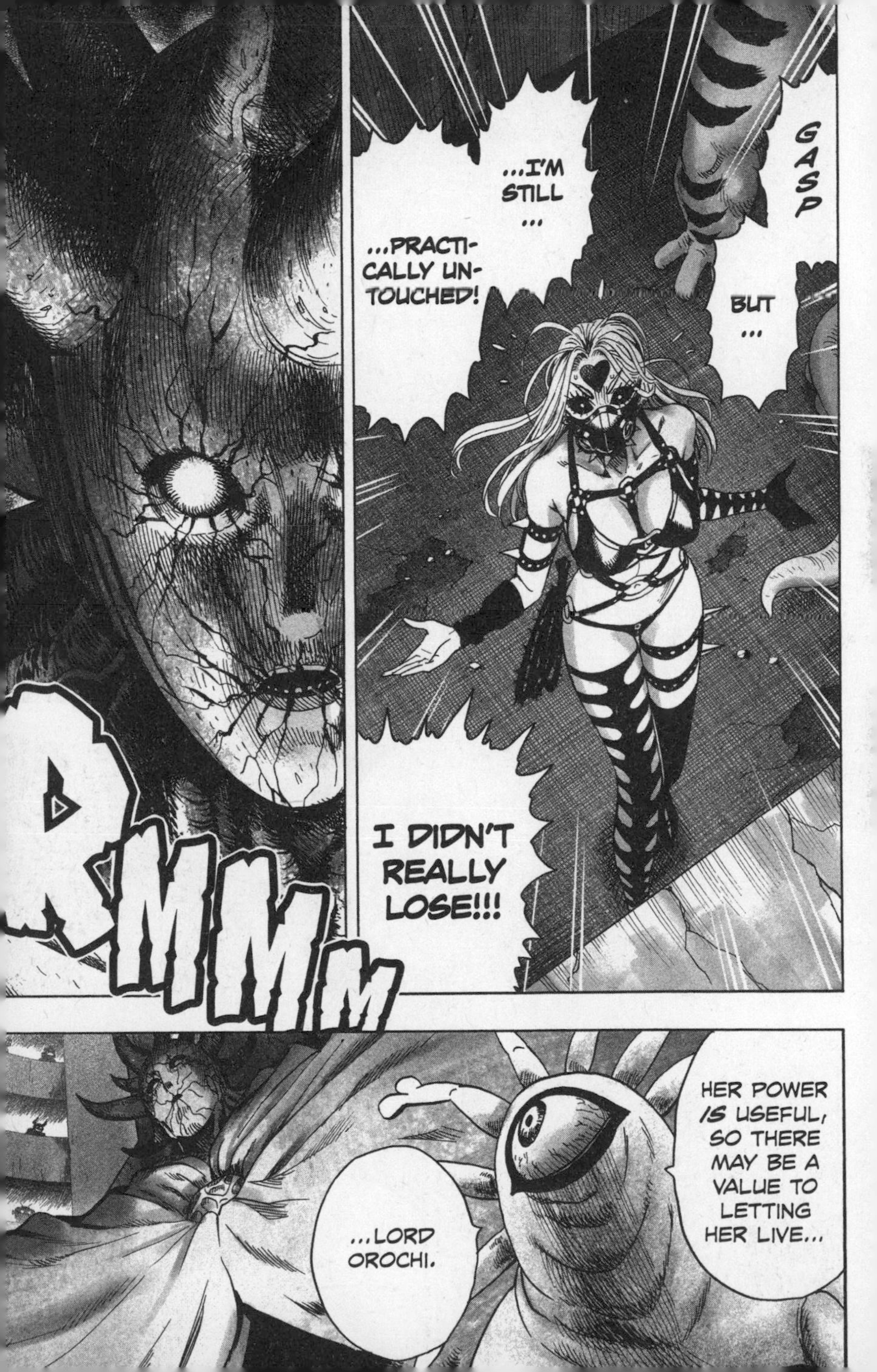
GASP
BUT...
...I'M STILL...
...PRACTI-CALLY UN-TOUCHED!
I DIDN'T REALLY LOSE!!!
MMMM
HER POWER *IS* USEFUL, SO THERE MAY BE A VALUE TO LETTING HER LIVE...
...LORD OROCHI.

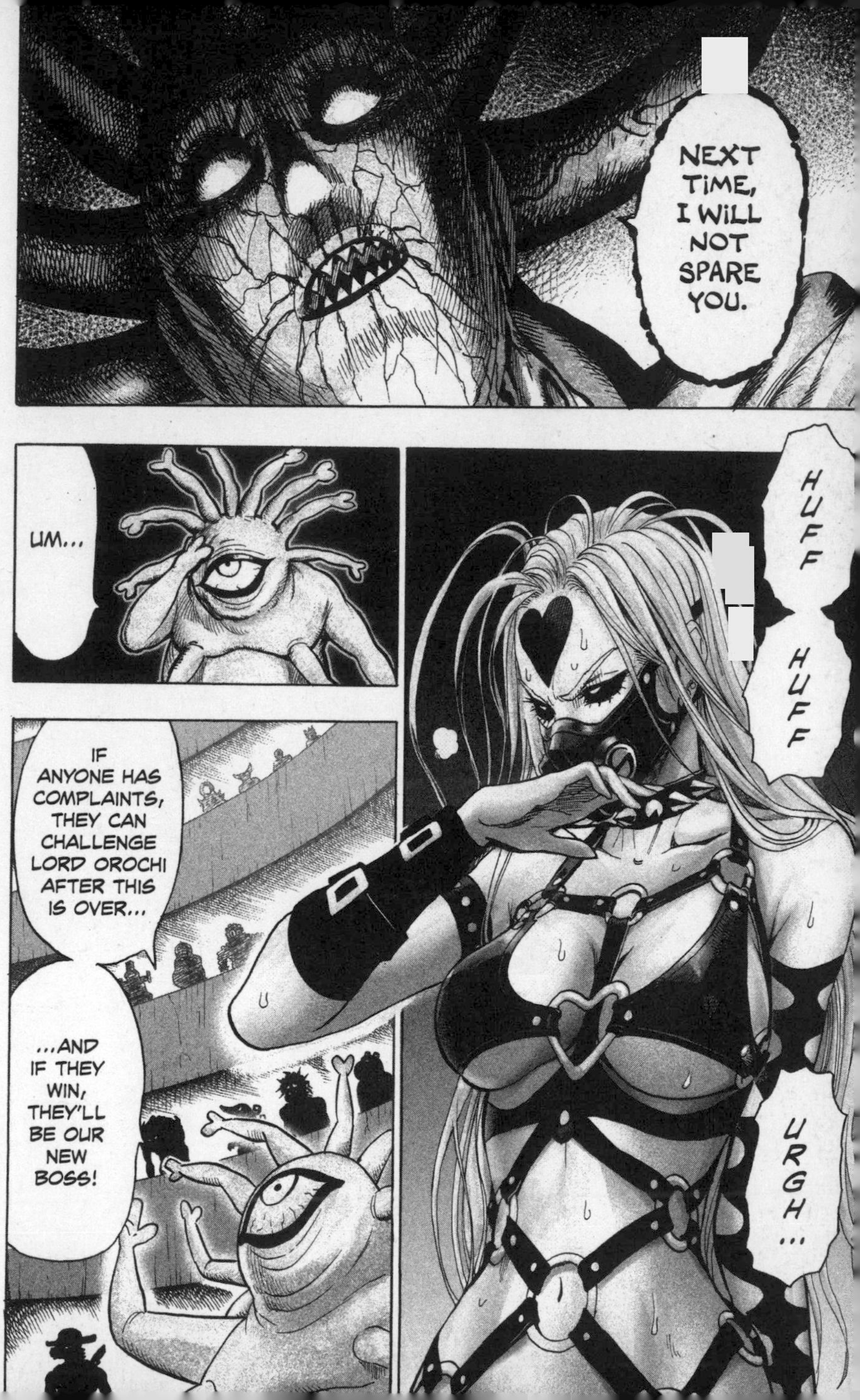
NEXT TIME, I WILL NOT SPARE YOU.
HUFF
HUFF
URGH...
UM...
IF ANYONE HAS COMPLAINTS, THEY CAN CHALLENGE LORD OROCHI AFTER THIS IS OVER...
...AND IF THEY WIN, THEY'LL BE OUR NEW BOSS!

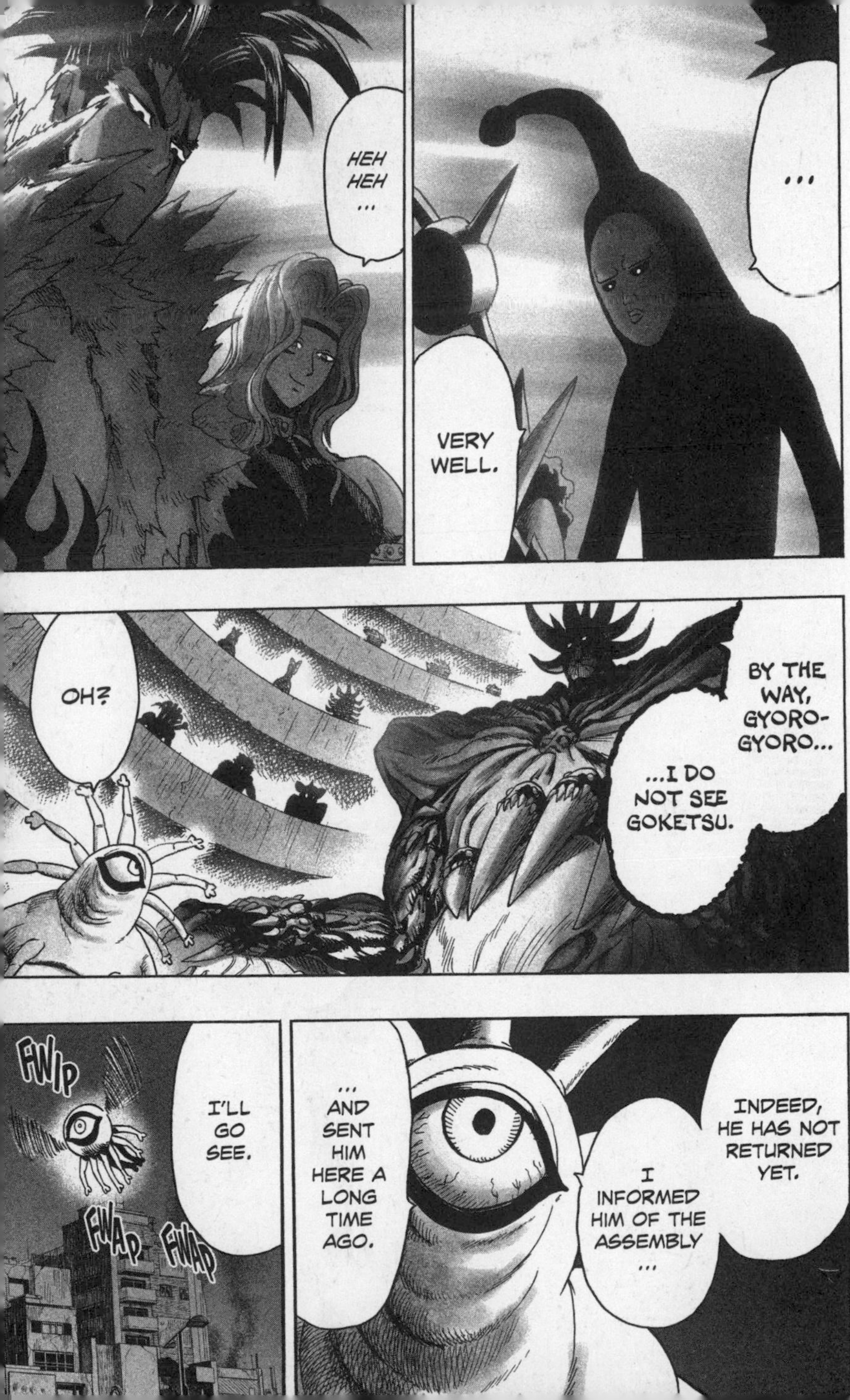
...
VERY WELL.
HEH HEH ...
BY THE WAY, GYORO-GYORO...
...I DO NOT SEE GOKETSU.
OH?
INDEED, HE HAS NOT RETURNED YET.
I INFORMED HIM OF THE ASSEMBLY ...
... AND SENT HIM HERE A LONG TIME AGO.
I'LL GO SEE.
FWIP
FWAP
FWAP

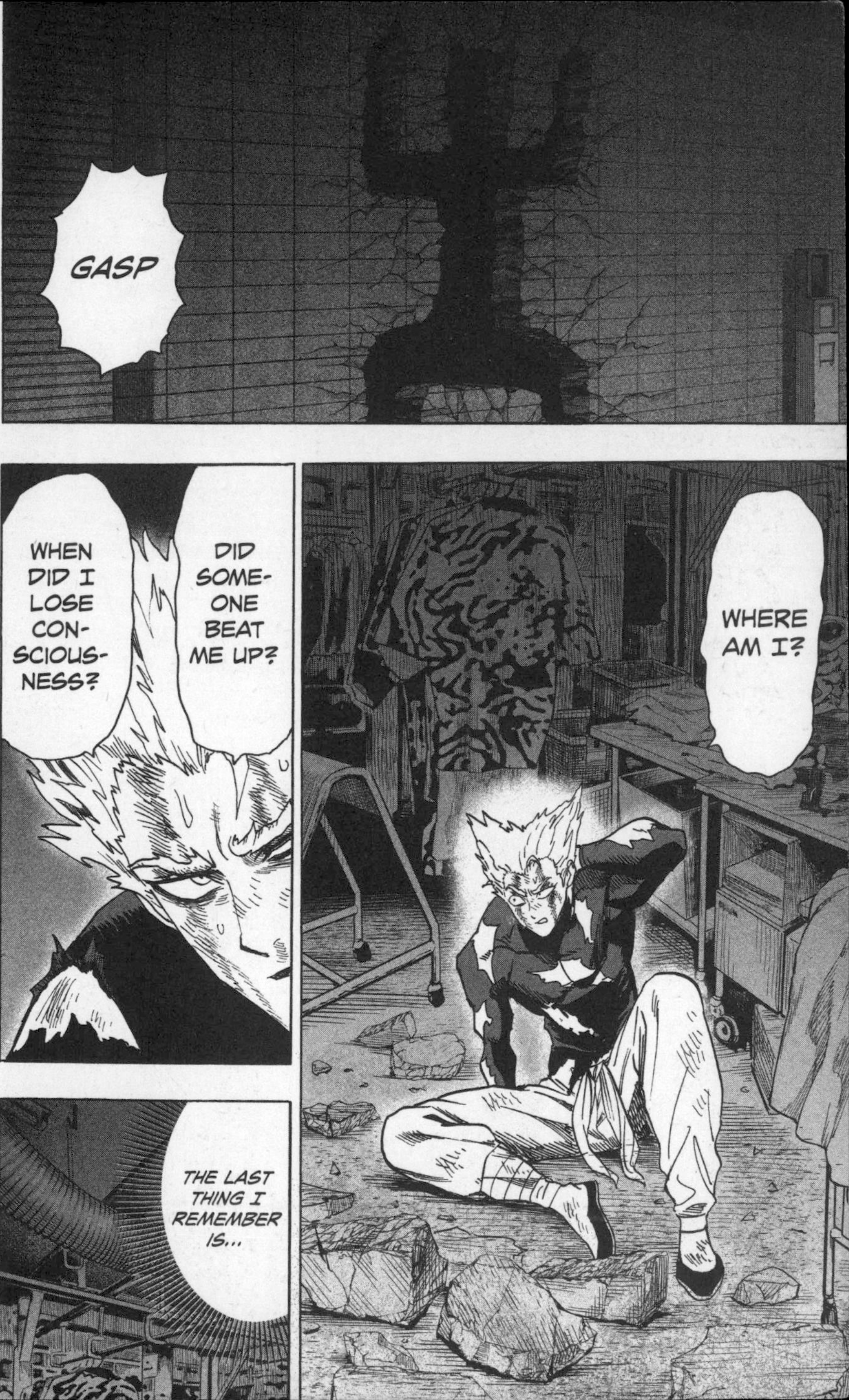
GASP
WHERE AM I?
DID SOME-ONE BEAT ME UP?
WHEN DID I LOSE CON-SCIOUS-NESS?
THE LAST THING I REMEMBER IS...

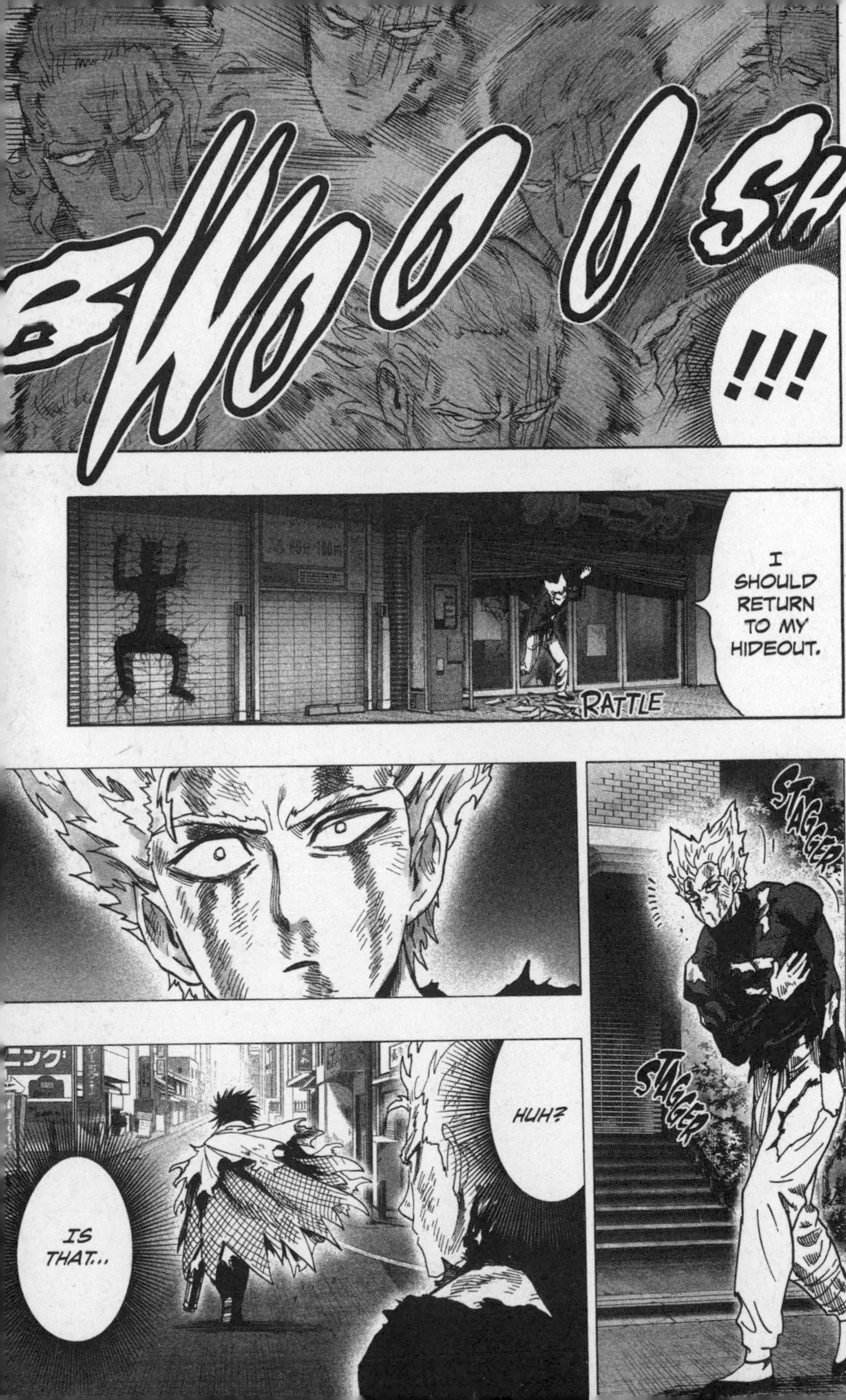
WHOOOSH
!!!
I SHOULD RETURN TO MY HIDEOUT.
RATTLE
STAGGER
STAGGER
HUH?
IS THAT...

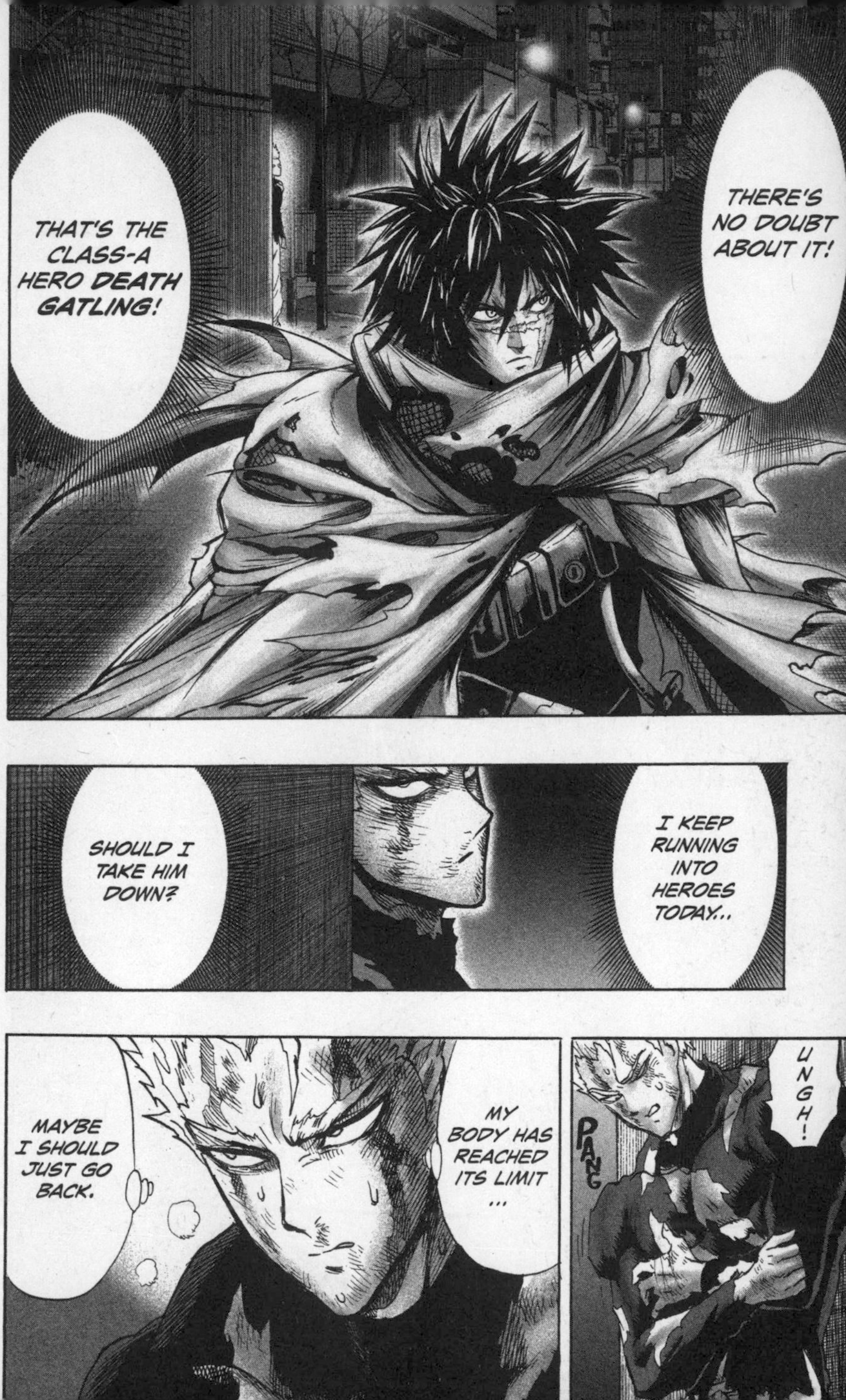
THERE'S NO DOUBT ABOUT IT!
THAT'S THE CLASS-A HERO DEATH GATLING!
I KEEP RUNNING INTO HEROES TODAY...
SHOULD I TAKE HIM DOWN?
UNGH!
PANG
MY BODY HAS REACHED ITS LIMIT ...
MAYBE I SHOULD JUST GO BACK.

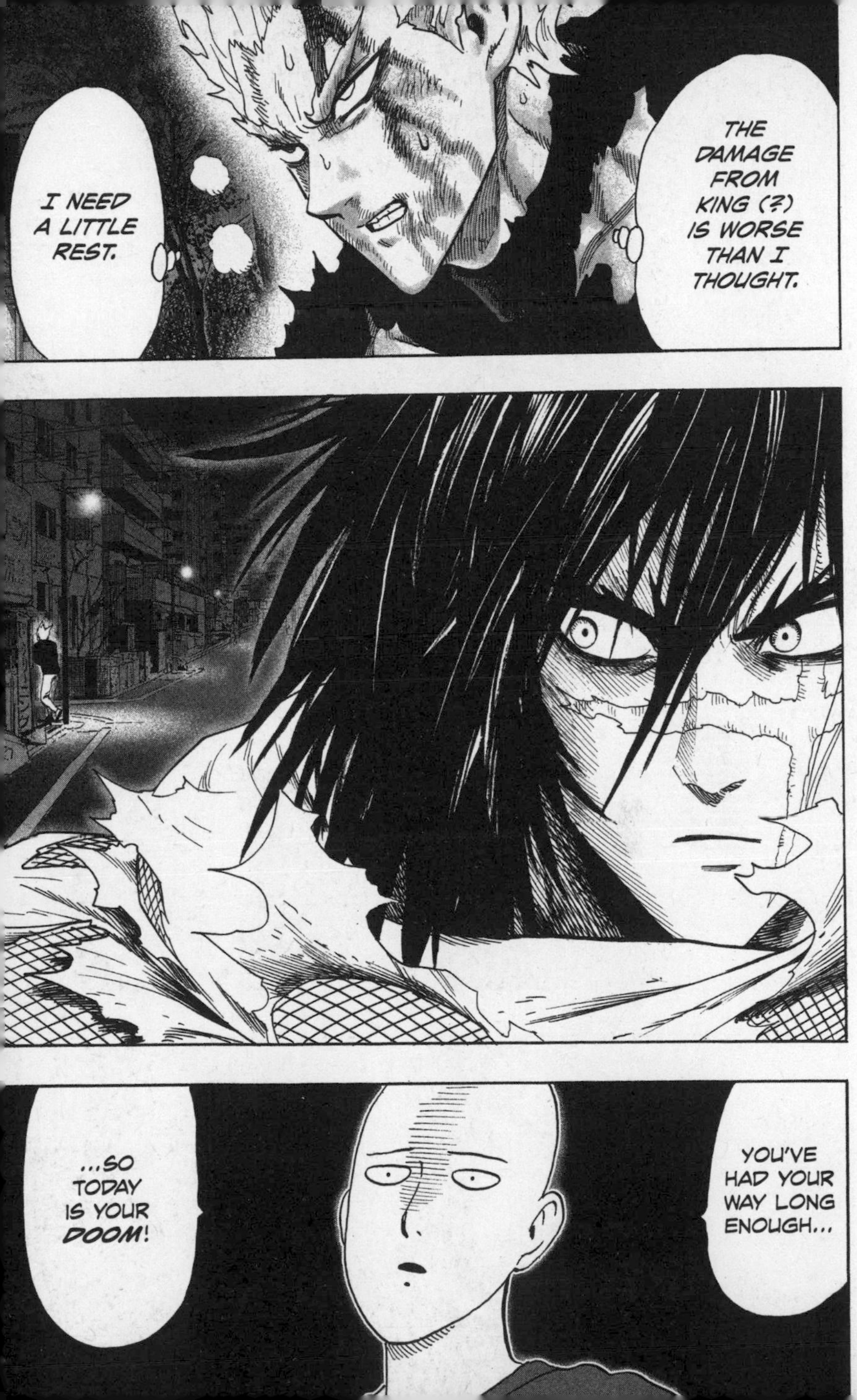
THE DAMAGE FROM KING (?) IS WORSE THAN I THOUGHT.
I NEED A LITTLE REST.
YOU'VE HAD YOUR WAY LONG ENOUGH...
...SO TODAY IS YOUR DOOM!

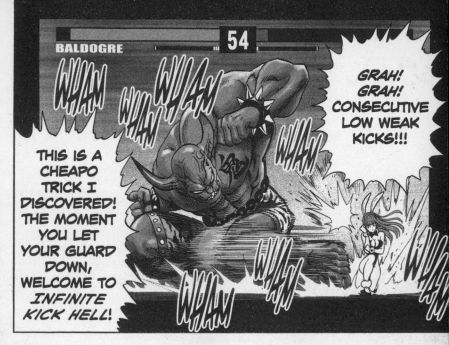

BALDOGRE

54

WHAM WHAM WHAM WHAM WHAM WHAM WHAM WHAM WHAM

GRAH! GRAH! CONSECUTIVE LOW WEAK KICKS!!!

THIS IS A CHEAPO TRICK I DISCOVERED! THE MOMENT YOU LET YOUR GUARD DOWN, WELCOME TO *INFINITE KICK HELL!*

RmMM

YOU DO NOT EVEN KNOW ...

...WHAT CHEAPO MEANS!

SIGH ...OH DEAR.

GRAHGRAHGRAHGRAHGRAHGRAH!

TAP TAP TAP

TAP TAP

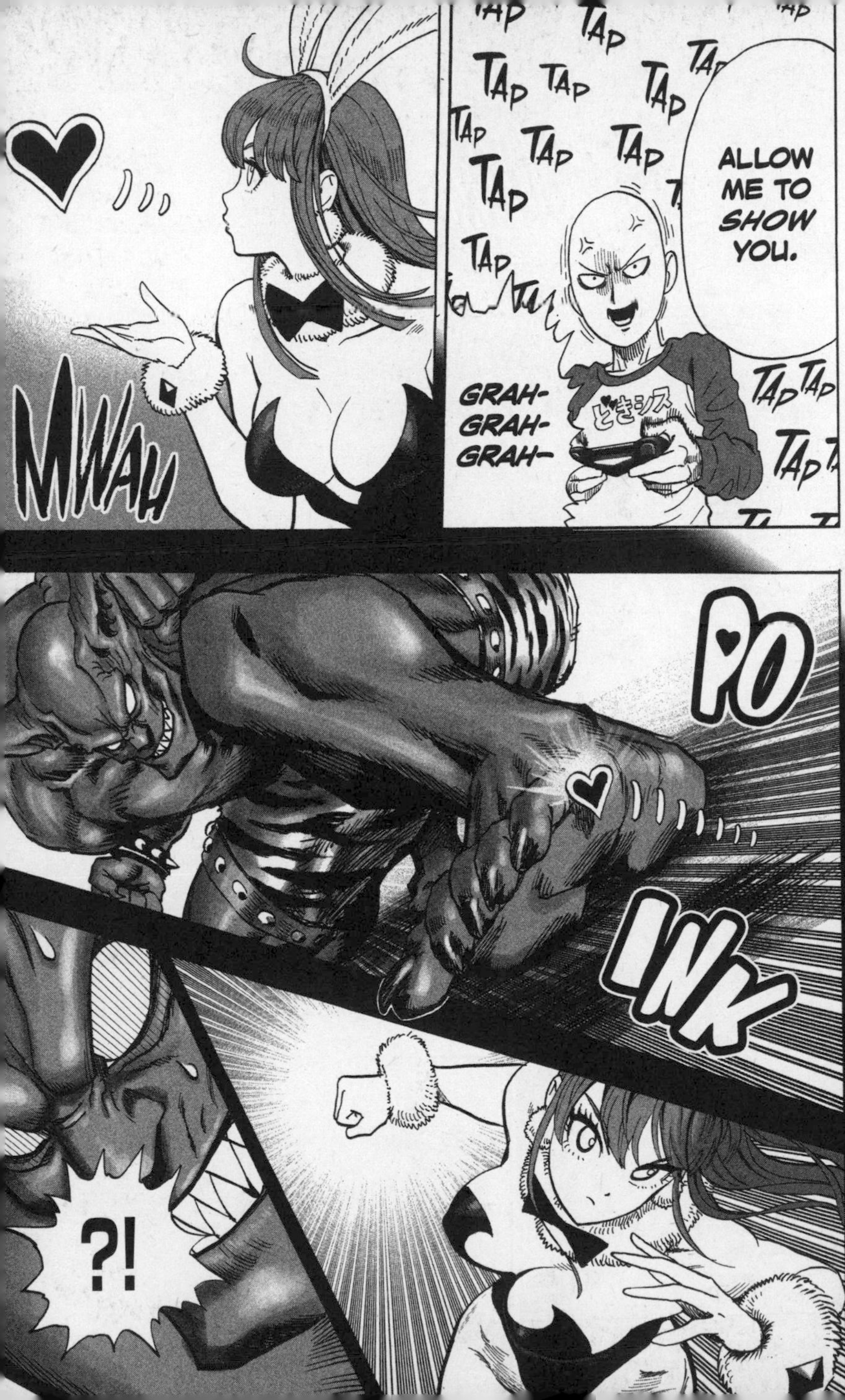
TAP TAP TAP TAP TAP TAP TAP TAP TAP TAP
ALLOW ME TO SHOW YOU.
GRAH-GRAH-GRAH-
ときシス
TAP TAP TAP
MWAH
PO
INK
?!

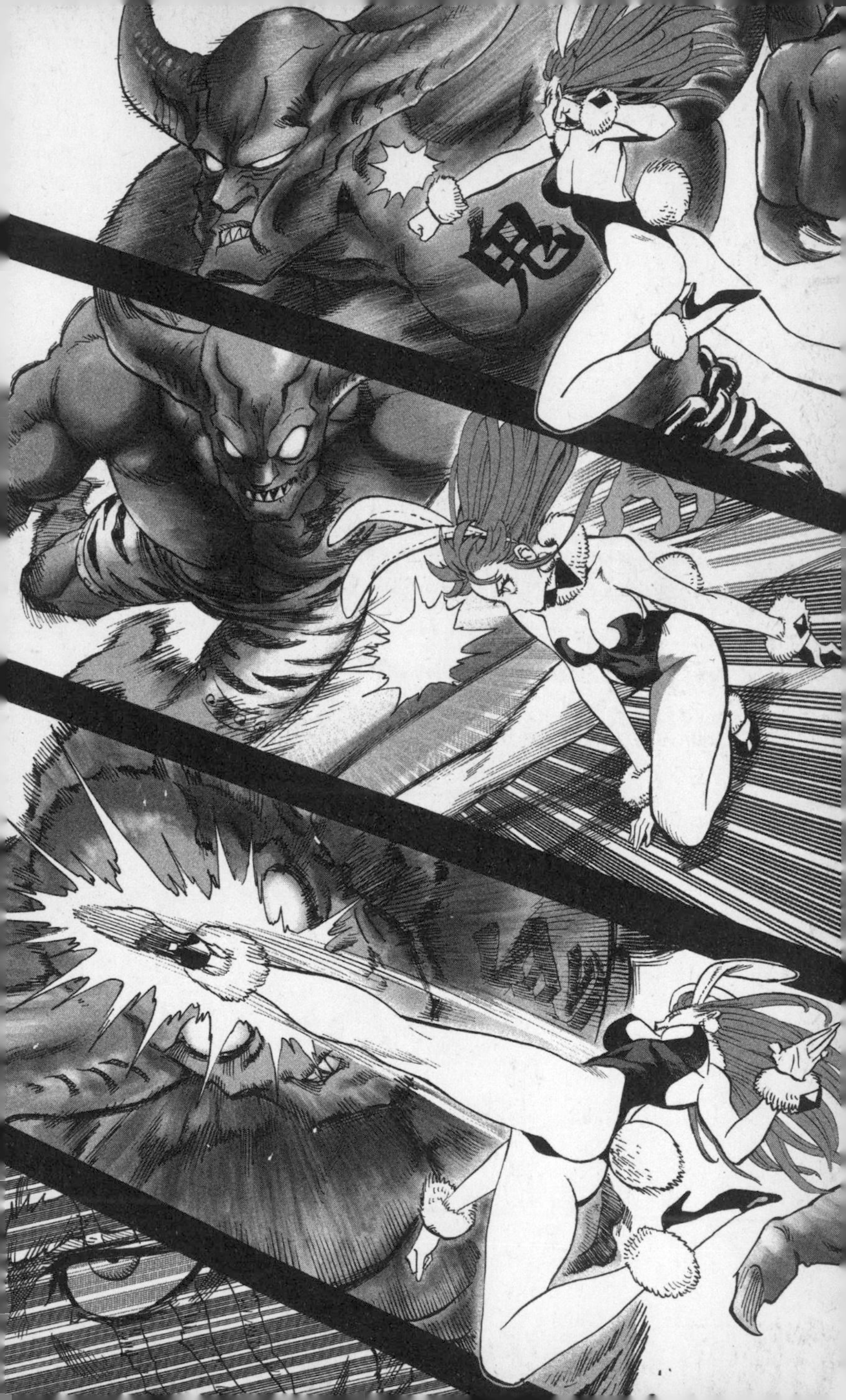
鬼

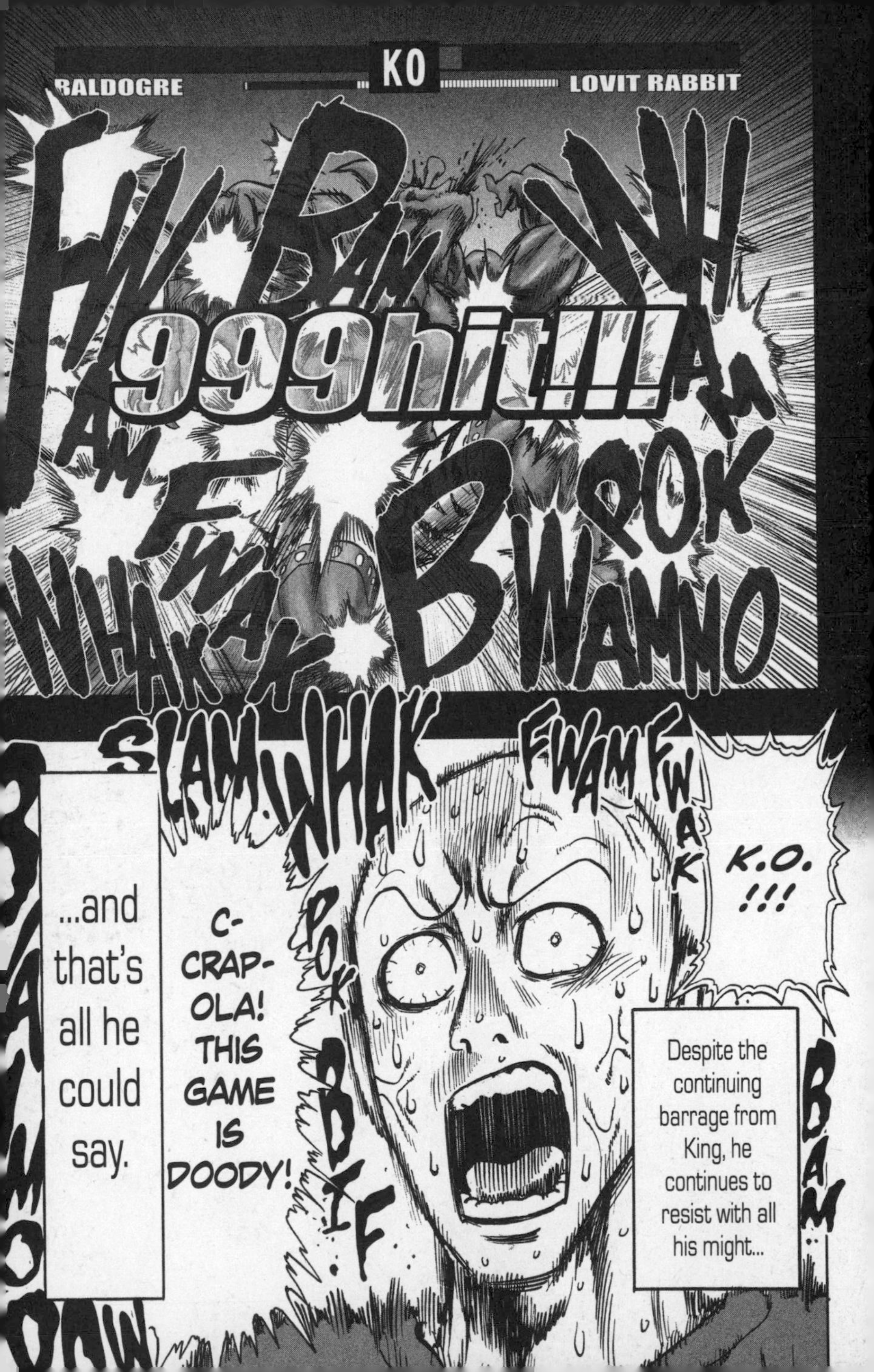
KO
BALDOGRE
LOVIT RABBIT
WHAM
BAM
FWAM
999hit!!!
BAM
POK
BWANNO
FWAK
WHAK
SLAM!!
WHAK
FWAM
FWAK
K.O. !!!
Despite the continuing barrage from King, he continues to resist with all his might...
BAM
POK
BDIF
C-CRAPOLA! THIS GAME IS DOODY!
...and that's all he could say.

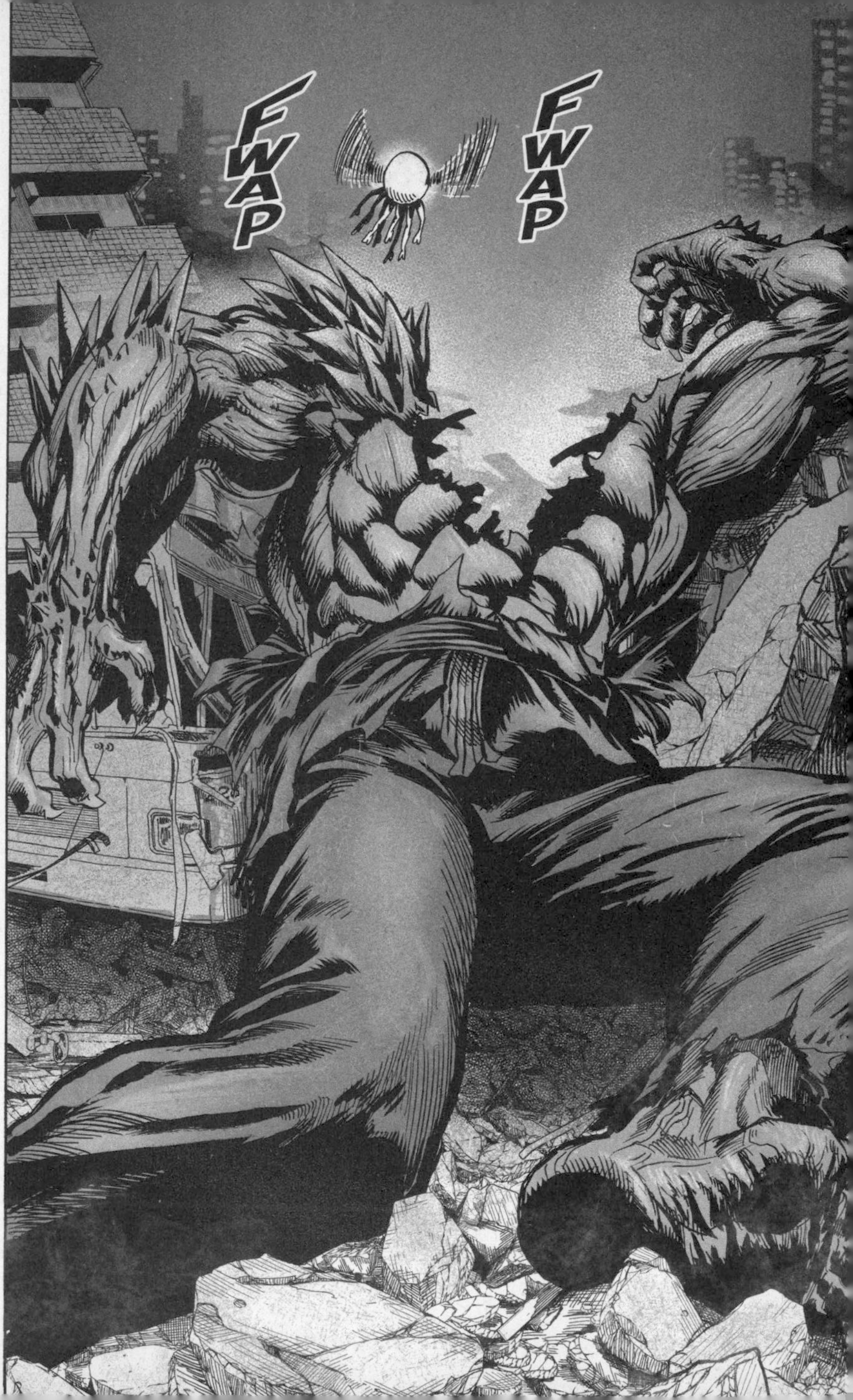
FWAP
FWAP

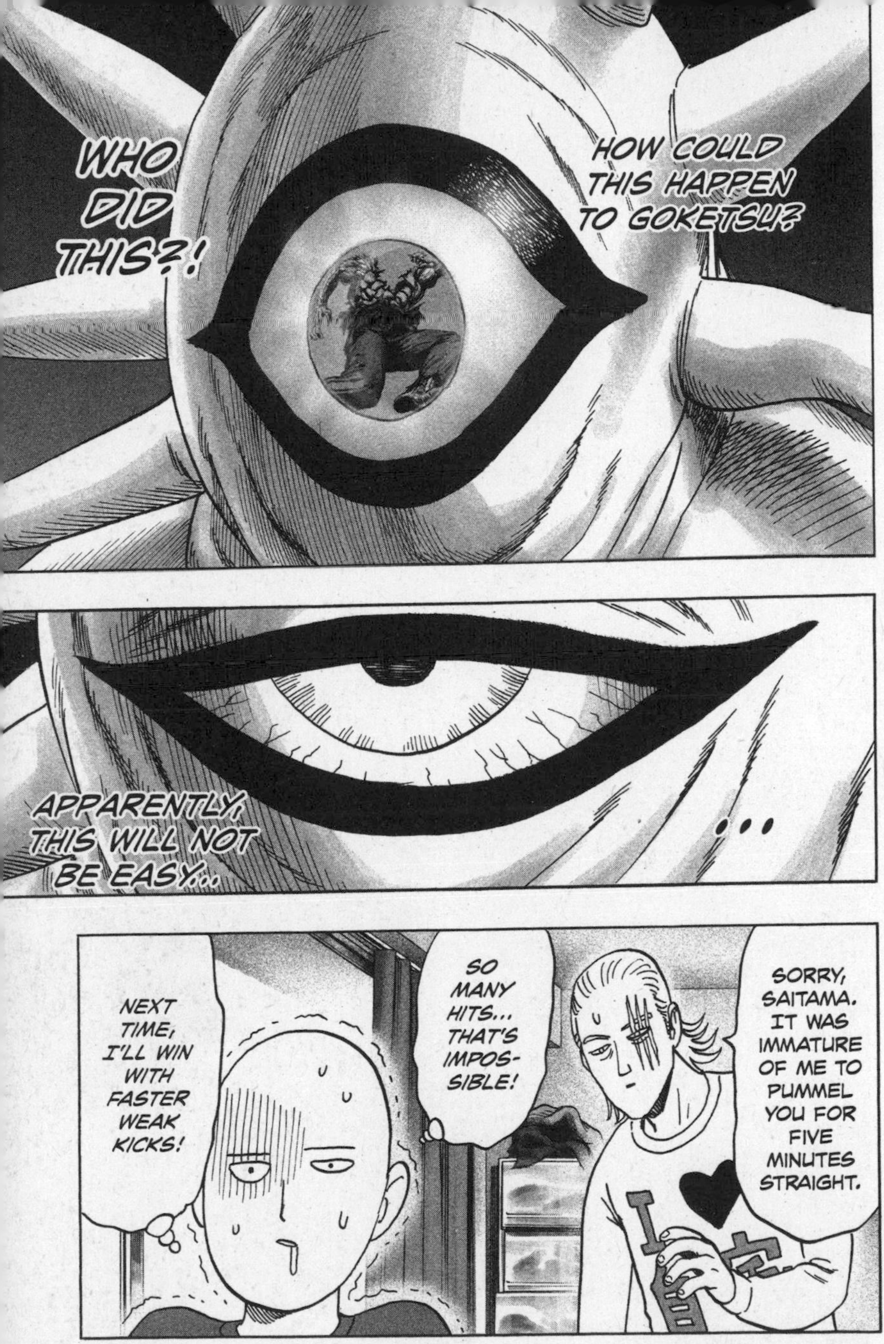
HOW COULD THIS HAPPEN TO GOKETSU?
WHO DID THIS?!
...
APPARENTLY, THIS WILL NOT BE EASY...
SORRY, SAITAMA. IT WAS IMMATURE OF ME TO PUMMEL YOU FOR FIVE MINUTES STRAIGHT.
SO MANY HITS... THAT'S IMPOSSIBLE!
NEXT TIME, I'LL WIN WITH FASTER WEAK KICKS!

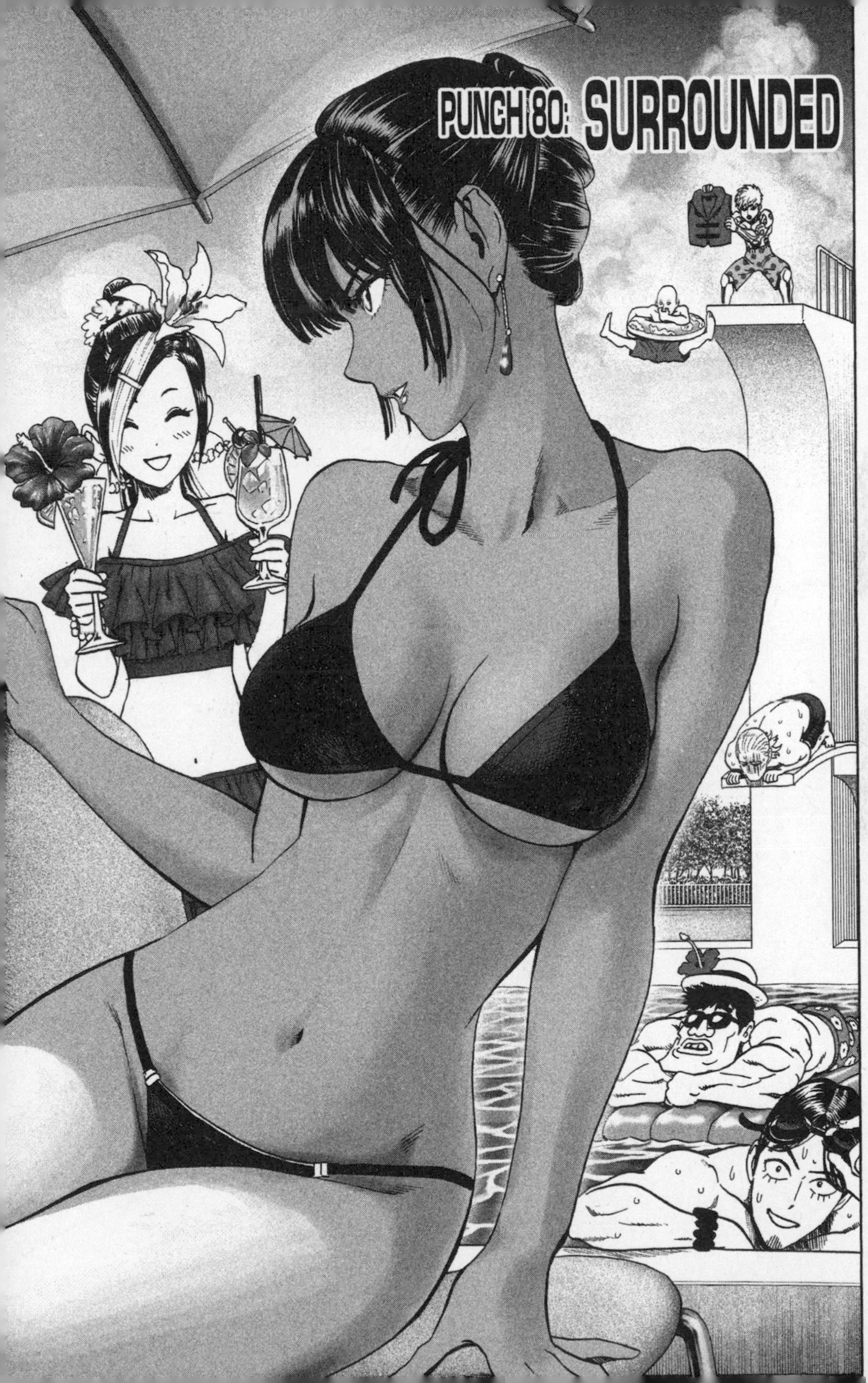
PUNCH 80: SURROUNDED

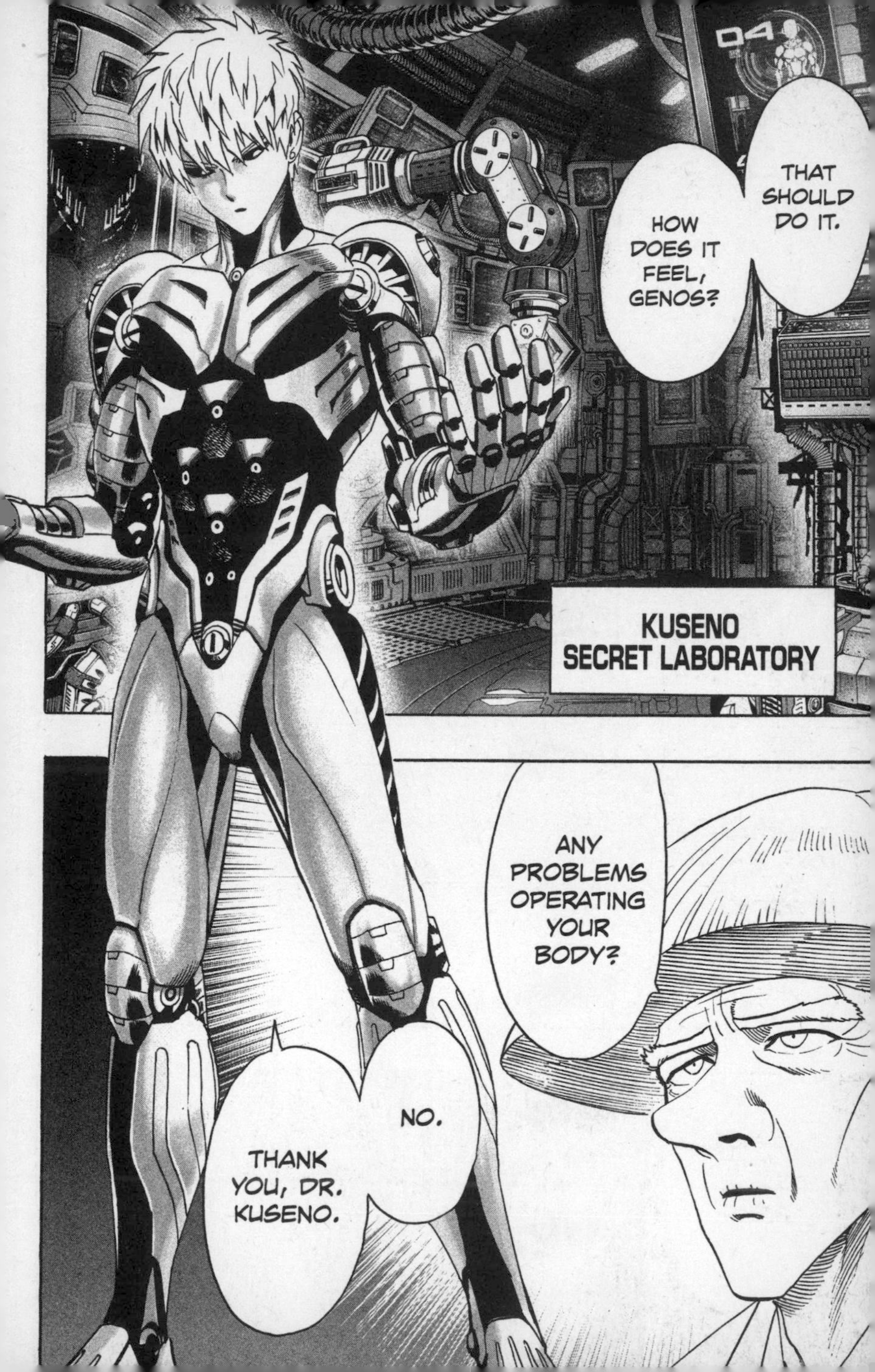
THAT SHOULD DO IT.
HOW DOES IT FEEL, GENOS?
KUSENO SECRET LABORATORY
ANY PROBLEMS OPERATING YOUR BODY?
NO.
THANK YOU, DR. KUSENO.

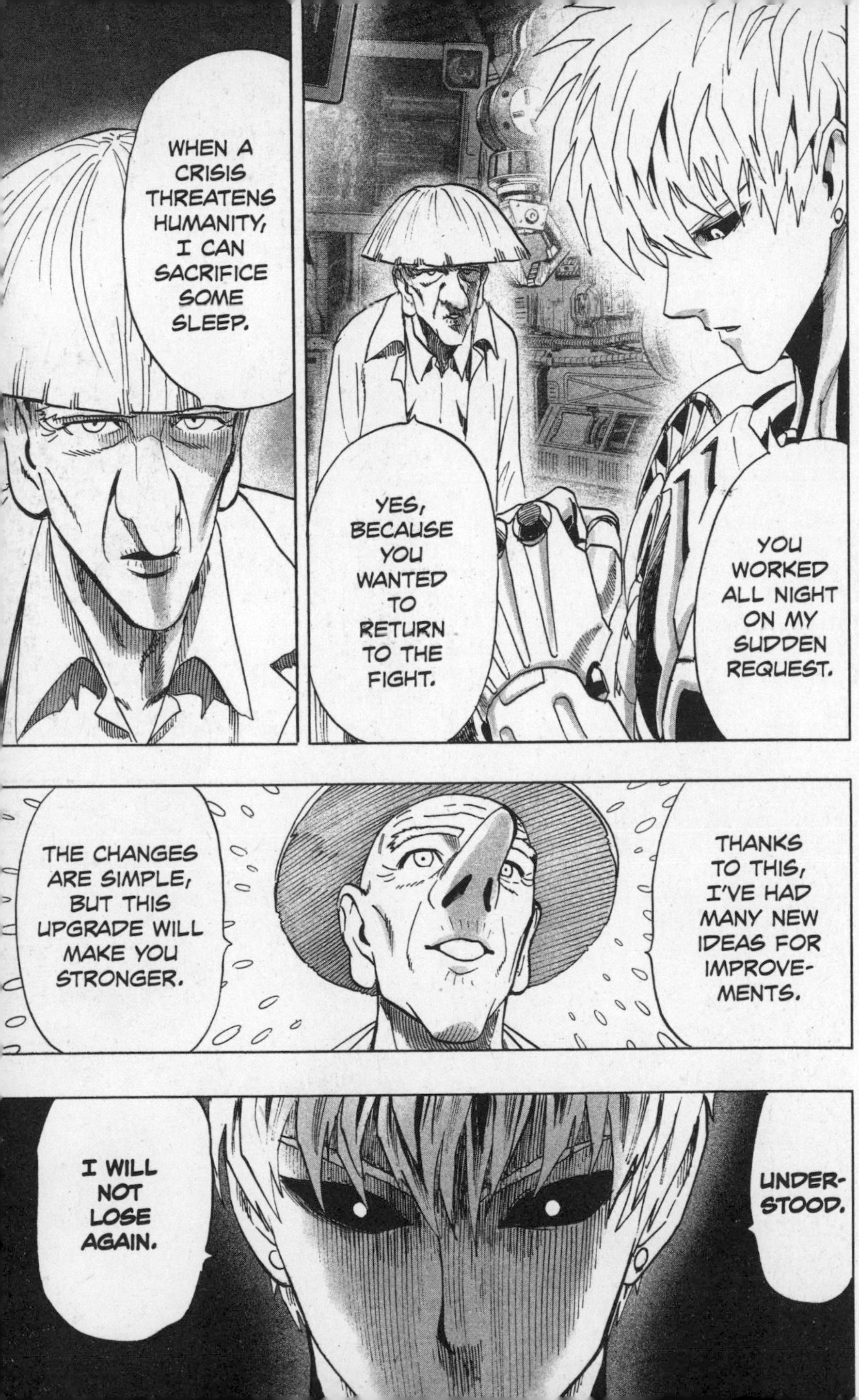
YOU WORKED ALL NIGHT ON MY SUDDEN REQUEST.
YES, BECAUSE YOU WANTED TO RETURN TO THE FIGHT.
WHEN A CRISIS THREATENS HUMANITY, I CAN SACRIFICE SOME SLEEP.
THANKS TO THIS, I'VE HAD MANY NEW IDEAS FOR IMPROVE-MENTS.
THE CHANGES ARE SIMPLE, BUT THIS UPGRADE WILL MAKE YOU STRONGER.
UNDER-STOOD.
I WILL NOT LOSE AGAIN.

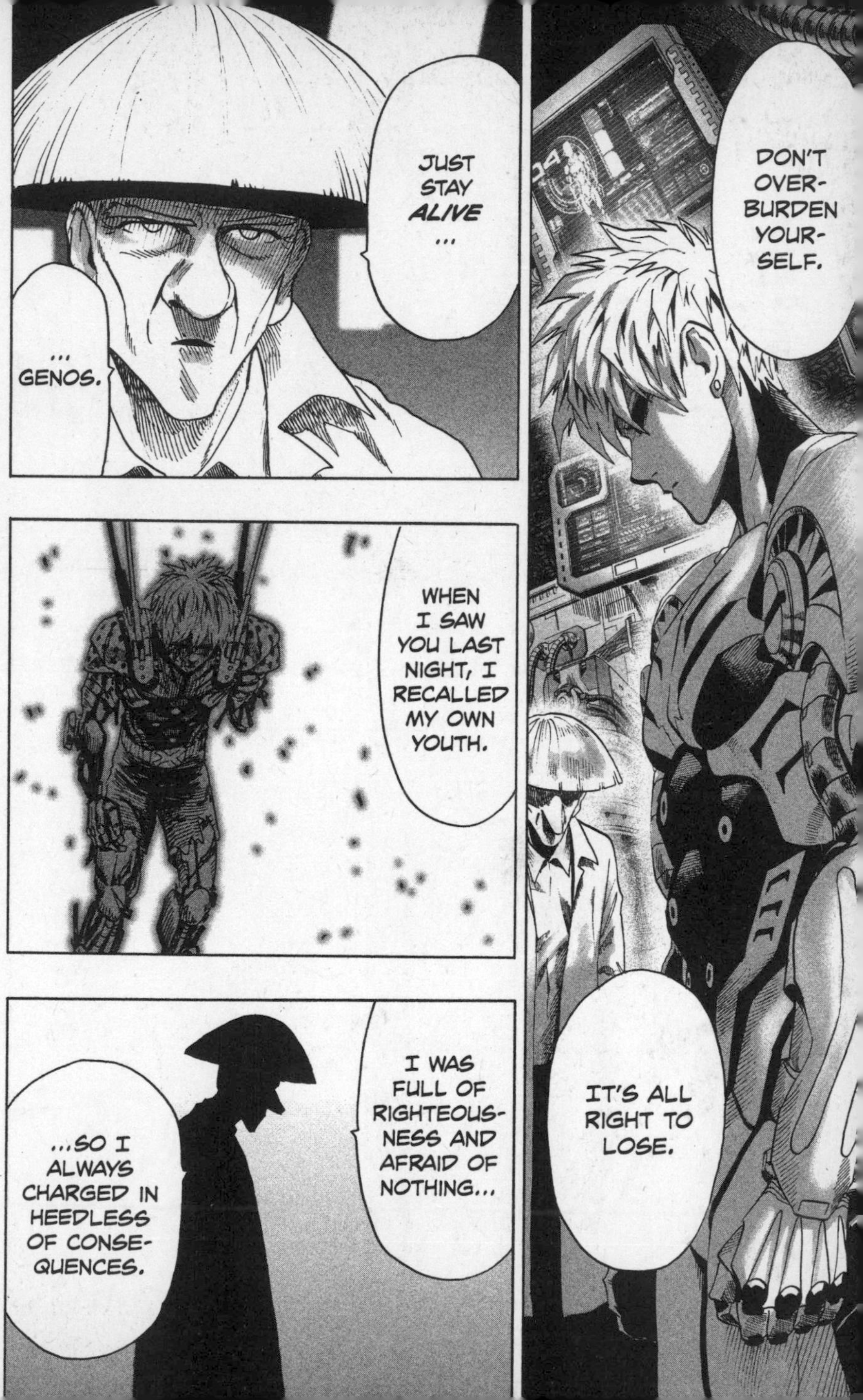
DON'T OVER-BURDEN YOUR-SELF.
IT'S ALL RIGHT TO LOSE.
JUST STAY *ALIVE* ...
... GENOS.
WHEN I SAW YOU LAST NIGHT, I RECALLED MY OWN YOUTH.
I WAS FULL OF RIGHTEOUS-NESS AND AFRAID OF NOTHING...
...SO I ALWAYS CHARGED IN HEEDLESS OF CONSE-QUENCES.

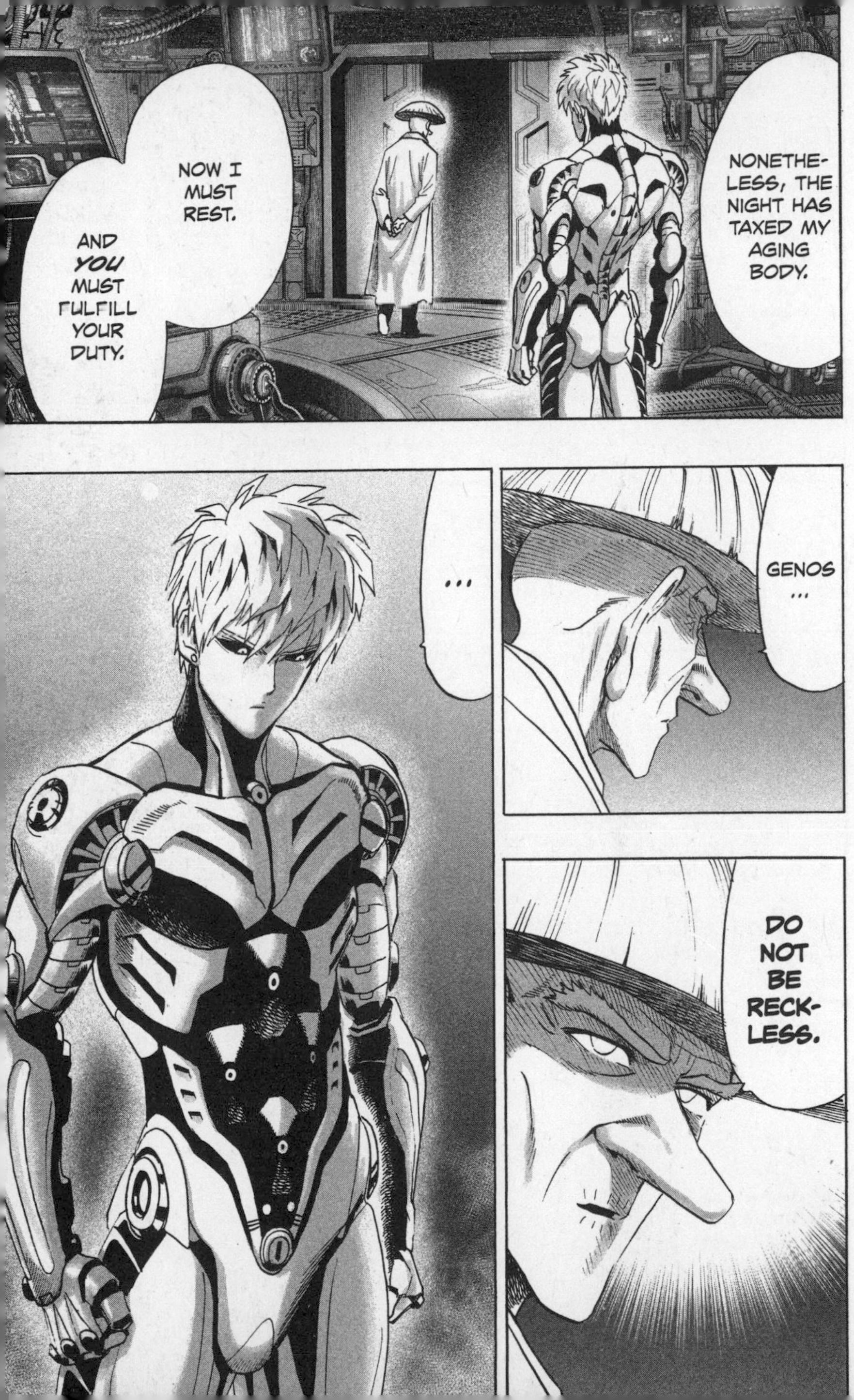
NONETHELESS, THE NIGHT HAS TAXED MY AGING BODY.
NOW I MUST REST.
AND *YOU* MUST FULFILL YOUR DUTY.
GENOS ...
DO NOT BE RECKLESS.
...

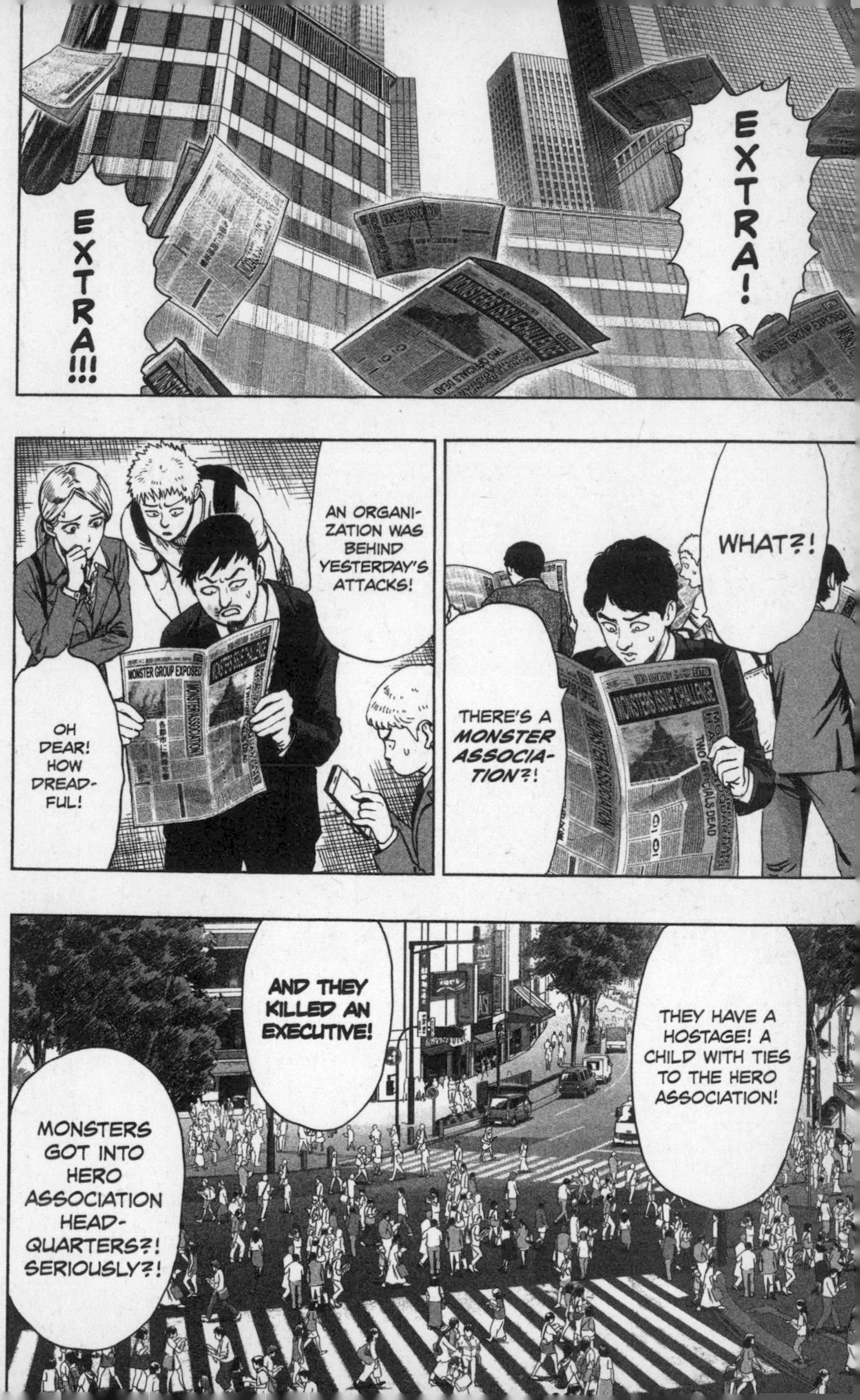
EXTRA!
EXTRA!!!
MONSTER GROUP EXPOSED
MONSTERS ISSUE CHALLENGE
TWO OFFICIALS DEAD
WHAT?!
THERE'S A *MONSTER ASSOCIATION*?!
MONSTERS ISSUE CHALLENGE
MONSTER ASSOCIATION
TWO OFFICIALS DEAD
AN ORGANIZATION WAS BEHIND YESTERDAY'S ATTACKS!
MONSTER GROUP EXPOSED
MONSTER ASSOCIATION
OH DEAR! HOW DREADFUL!
THEY HAVE A HOSTAGE! A CHILD WITH TIES TO THE HERO ASSOCIATION!
AND THEY KILLED AN EXECUTIVE!
MONSTERS GOT INTO HERO ASSOCIATION HEADQUARTERS?! SERIOUSLY?!

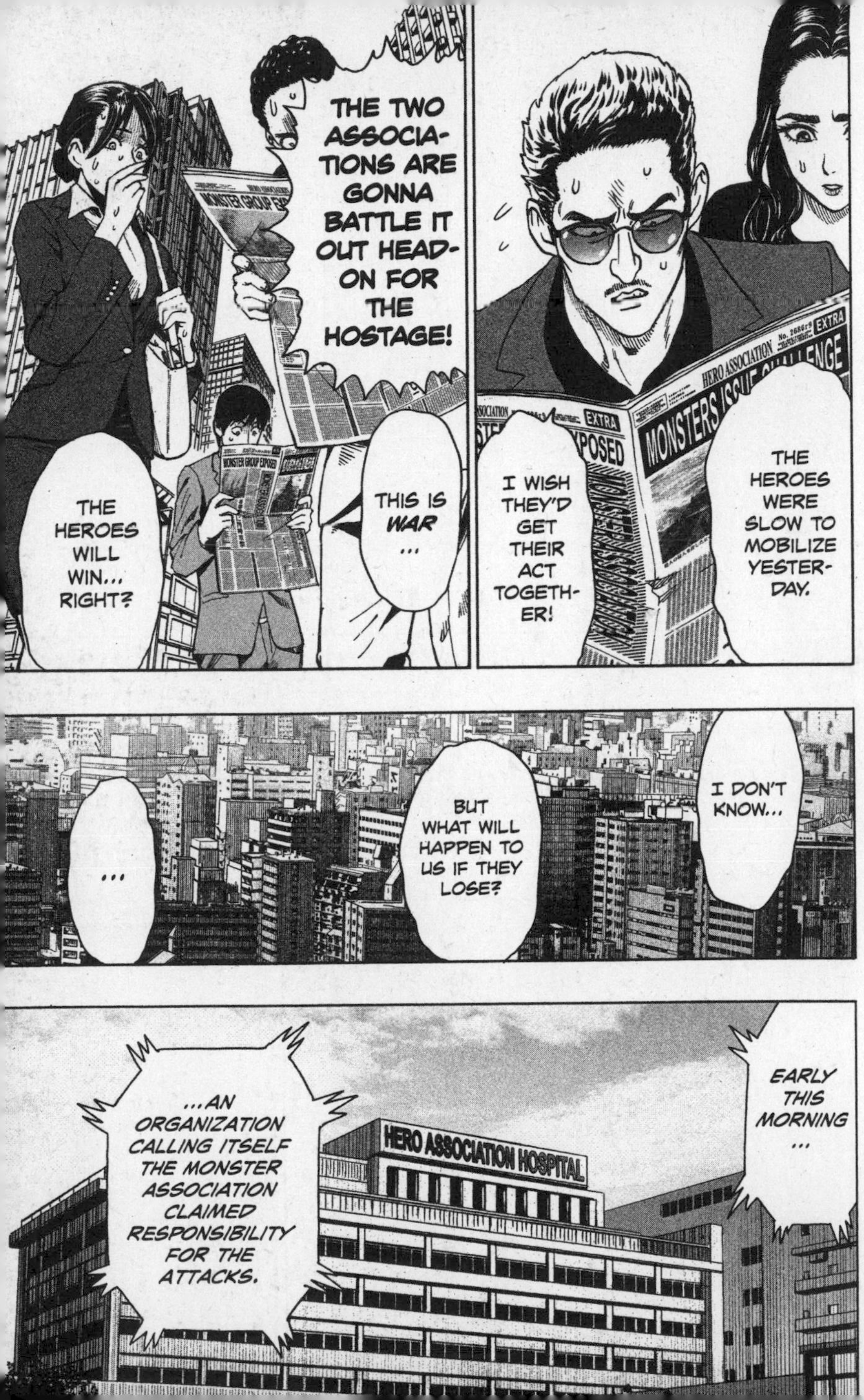
EXTRA
HERO ASSOCIATION
THE HEROES WERE SLOW TO MOBILIZE YESTERDAY.
I WISH THEY'D GET THEIR ACT TOGETHER!
THE TWO ASSOCIATIONS ARE GONNA BATTLE IT OUT HEAD-ON FOR THE HOSTAGE!
THIS IS *WAR* ...
MONSTER GROUP EXPOSED
THE HEROES WILL WIN... RIGHT?
I DON'T KNOW...
BUT WHAT WILL HAPPEN TO US IF THEY LOSE?
...
EARLY THIS MORNING ...
HERO ASSOCIATION HOSPITAL
...AN ORGANIZATION CALLING ITSELF THE MONSTER ASSOCIATION CLAIMED RESPONSIBILITY FOR THE ATTACKS.

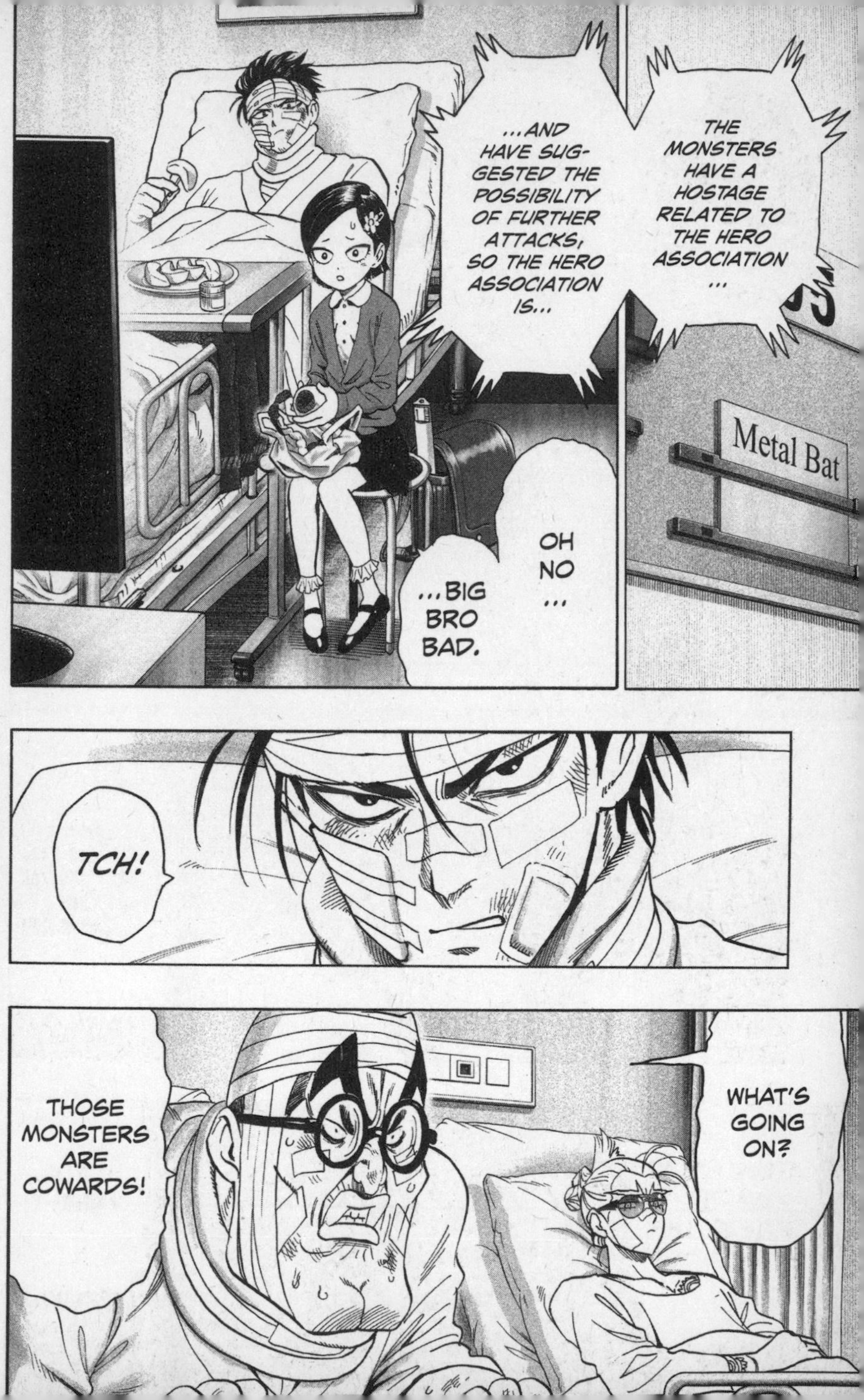
THE MONSTERS HAVE A HOSTAGE RELATED TO THE HERO ASSOCIATION ...
...AND HAVE SUG-GESTED THE POSSIBILITY OF FURTHER ATTACKS, SO THE HERO ASSOCIATION IS...
Metal Bat
OH NO ...
...BIG BRO BAD.
TCH!
WHAT'S GOING ON?
THOSE MONSTERS ARE COWARDS!

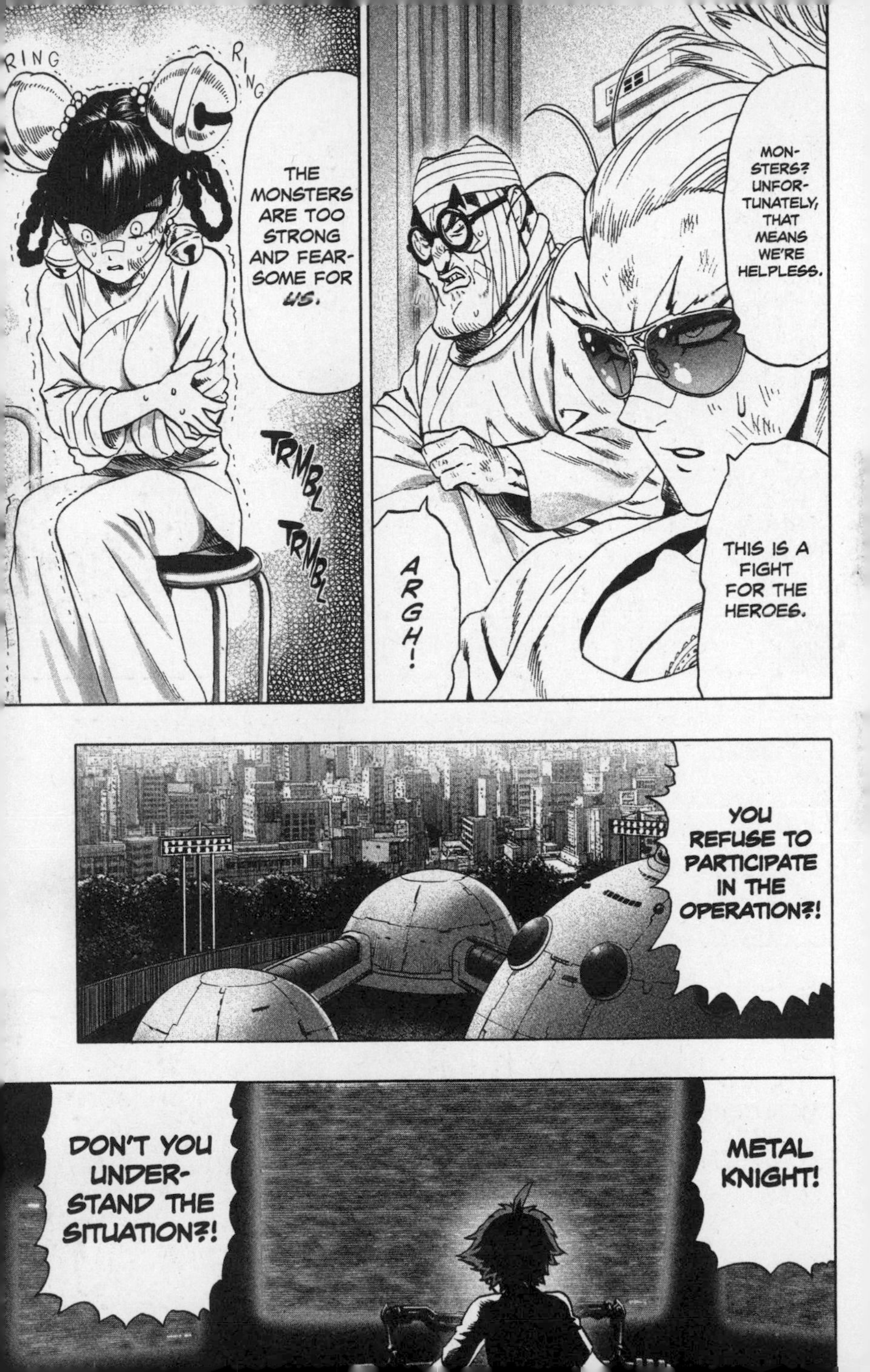
MON-STERS? UNFOR-TUNATELY, THAT MEANS WE'RE HELPLESS.
THIS IS A FIGHT FOR THE HEROES.
ARGH!
RING
RING
THE MONSTERS ARE TOO STRONG AND FEAR-SOME FOR US.
TRMBL
TRMBL
YOU REFUSE TO PARTICIPATE IN THE OPERATION?!
METAL KNIGHT!
DON'T YOU UNDER-STAND THE SITUATION?!

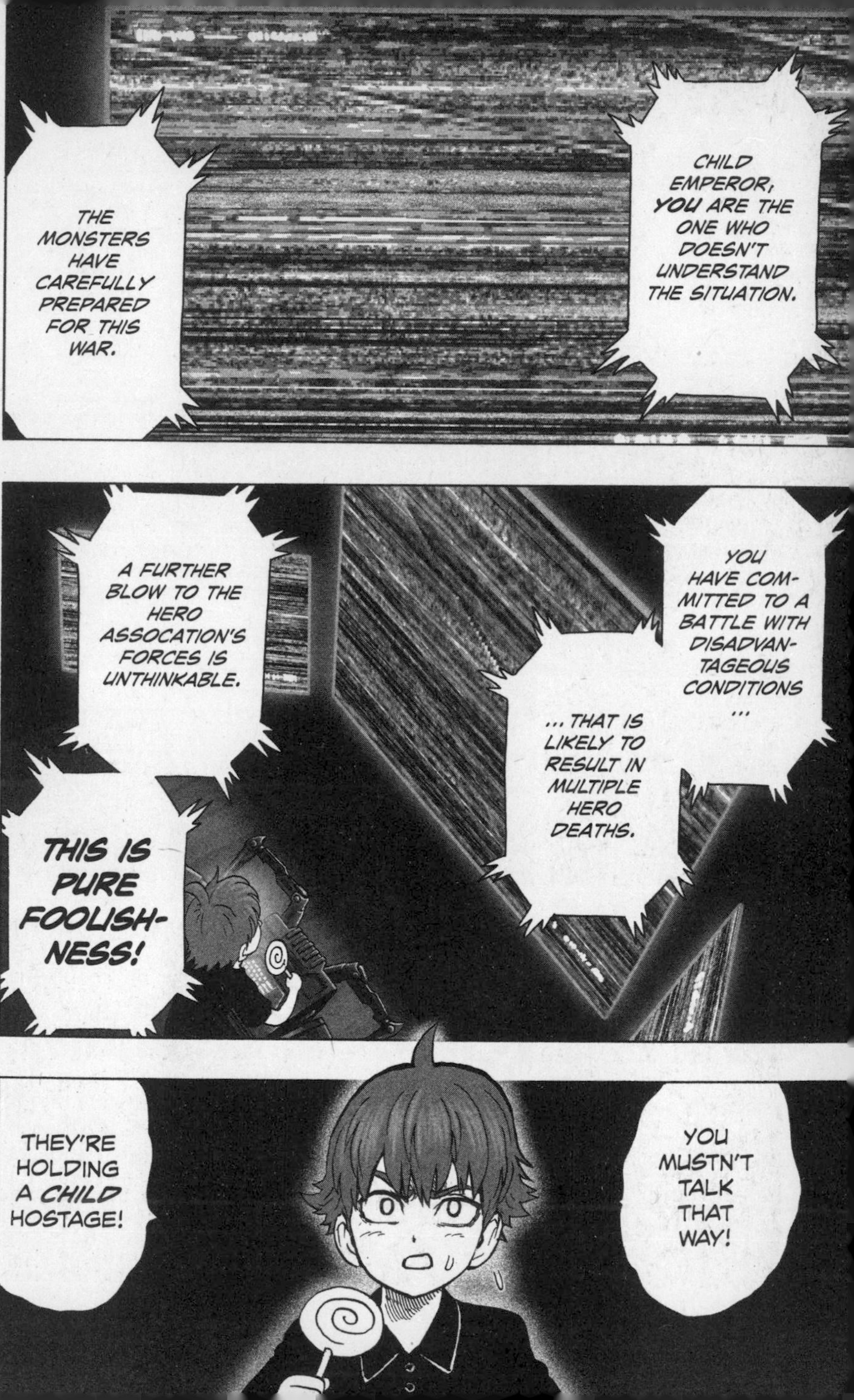
CHILD EMPEROR, YOU ARE THE ONE WHO DOESN'T UNDERSTAND THE SITUATION.
THE MONSTERS HAVE CAREFULLY PREPARED FOR THIS WAR.
YOU HAVE COMMITTED TO A BATTLE WITH DISADVANTAGEOUS CONDITIONS...
...THAT IS LIKELY TO RESULT IN MULTIPLE HERO DEATHS.
A FURTHER BLOW TO THE HERO ASSOCATION'S FORCES IS UNTHINKABLE.
THIS IS PURE FOOLISHNESS!
YOU MUSTN'T TALK THAT WAY!
THEY'RE HOLDING A CHILD HOSTAGE!

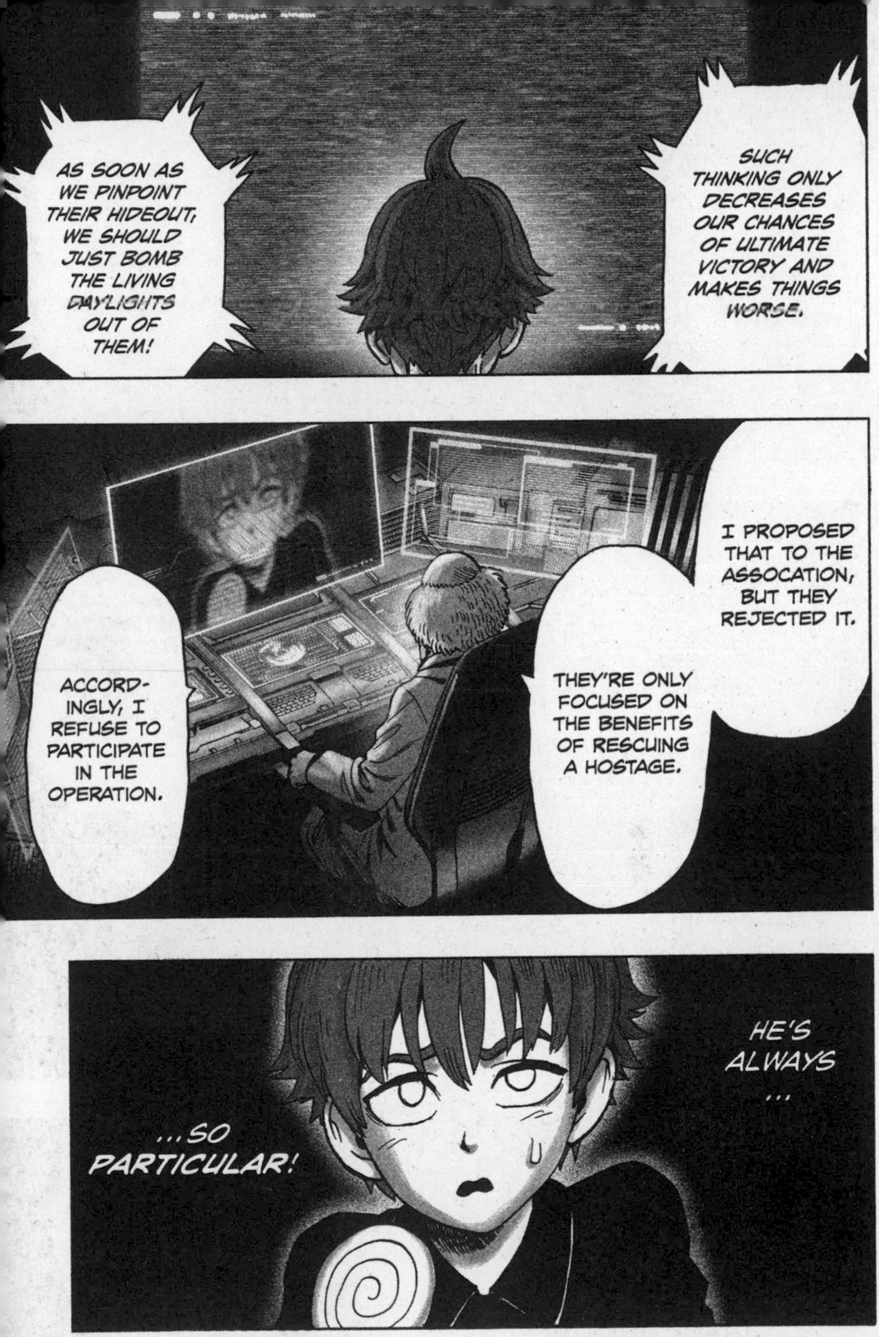
SUCH THINKING ONLY DECREASES OUR CHANCES OF ULTIMATE VICTORY AND MAKES THINGS WORSE.
AS SOON AS WE PINPOINT THEIR HIDEOUT, WE SHOULD JUST BOMB THE LIVING DAYLIGHTS OUT OF THEM!
I PROPOSED THAT TO THE ASSOCATION, BUT THEY REJECTED IT.
THEY'RE ONLY FOCUSED ON THE BENEFITS OF RESCUING A HOSTAGE.
ACCORD-INGLY, I REFUSE TO PARTICIPATE IN THE OPERATION.
HE'S ALWAYS ...
...SO PARTICULAR!

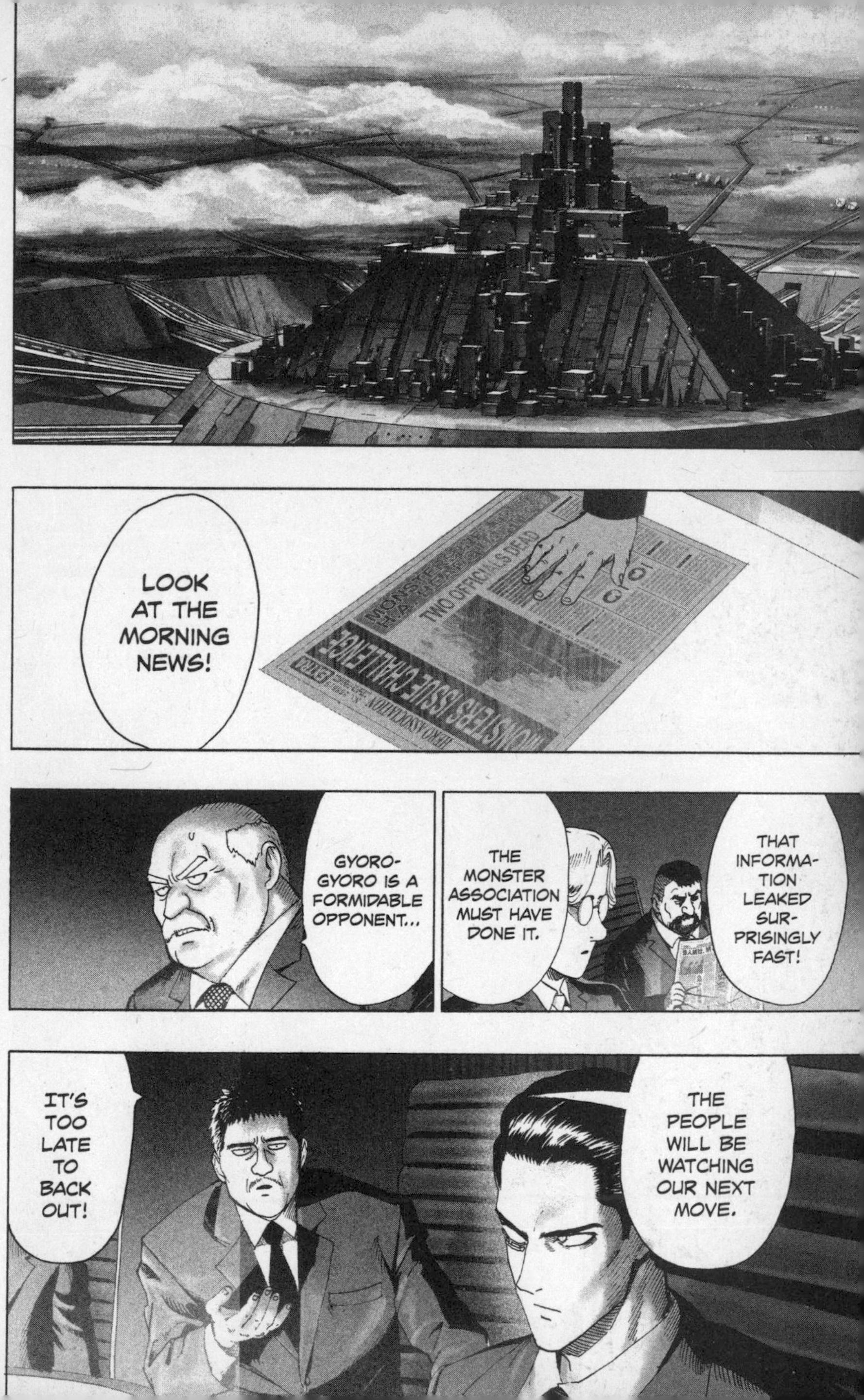
TWO OFFICIALS DEAD
MONSTERS ISSUE CHALLENGE
LOOK AT THE MORNING NEWS!
THAT INFORMATION LEAKED SURPRISINGLY FAST!
THE MONSTER ASSOCIATION MUST HAVE DONE IT.
GYORO-GYORO IS A FORMIDABLE OPPONENT...
THE PEOPLE WILL BE WATCHING OUR NEXT MOVE.
IT'S TOO LATE TO BACK OUT!

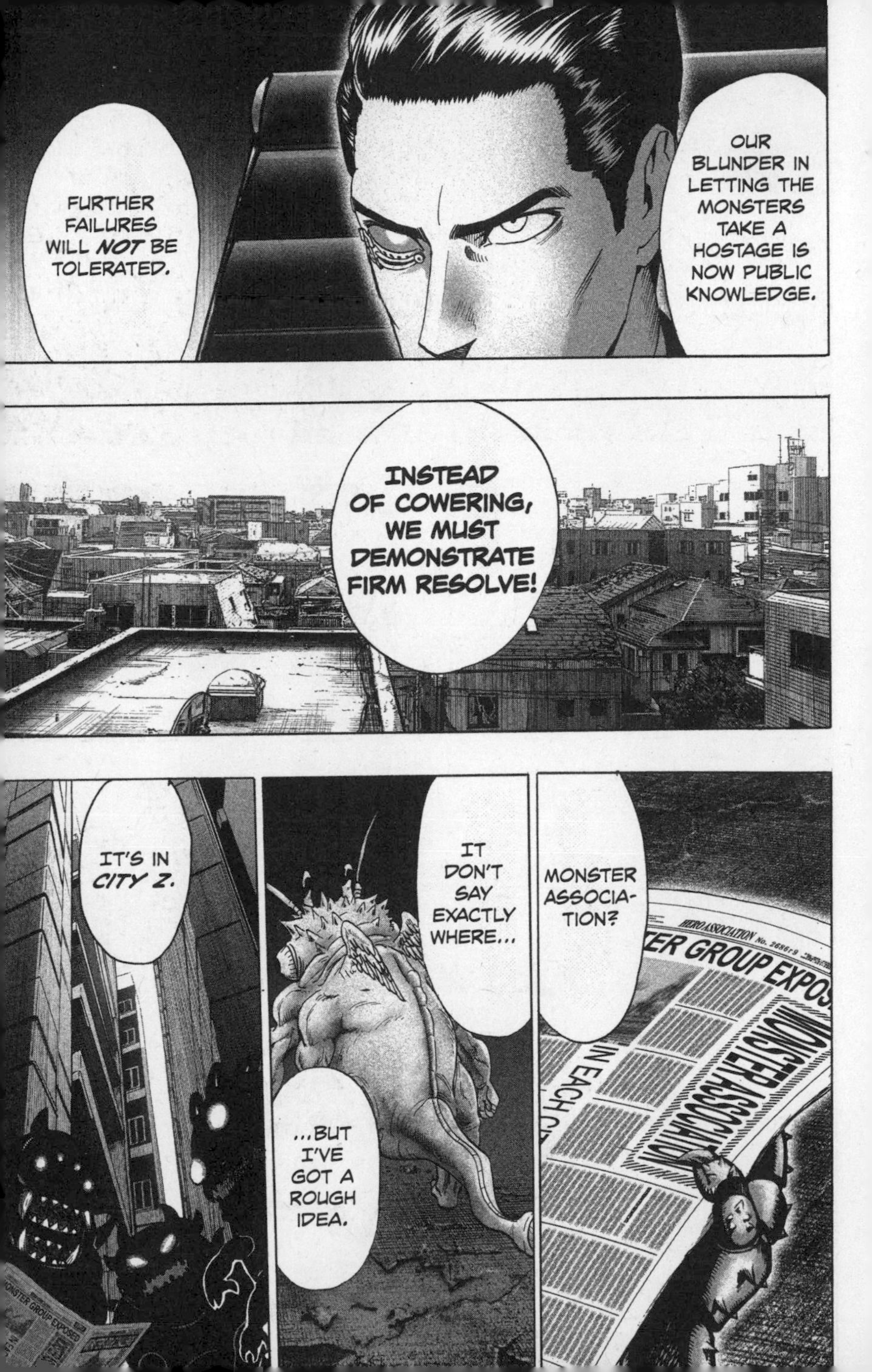
OUR BLUNDER IN LETTING THE MONSTERS TAKE A HOSTAGE IS NOW PUBLIC KNOWLEDGE.
FURTHER FAILURES WILL *NOT* BE TOLERATED.
INSTEAD OF COWERING, WE MUST DEMONSTRATE FIRM RESOLVE!
MONSTER ASSOCIA-TION?
MONSTER ASSOCIATION
IT DON'T SAY EXACTLY WHERE...
...BUT I'VE GOT A ROUGH IDEA.
IT'S IN *CITY Z.*
MONSTER GROUP EXPOSED

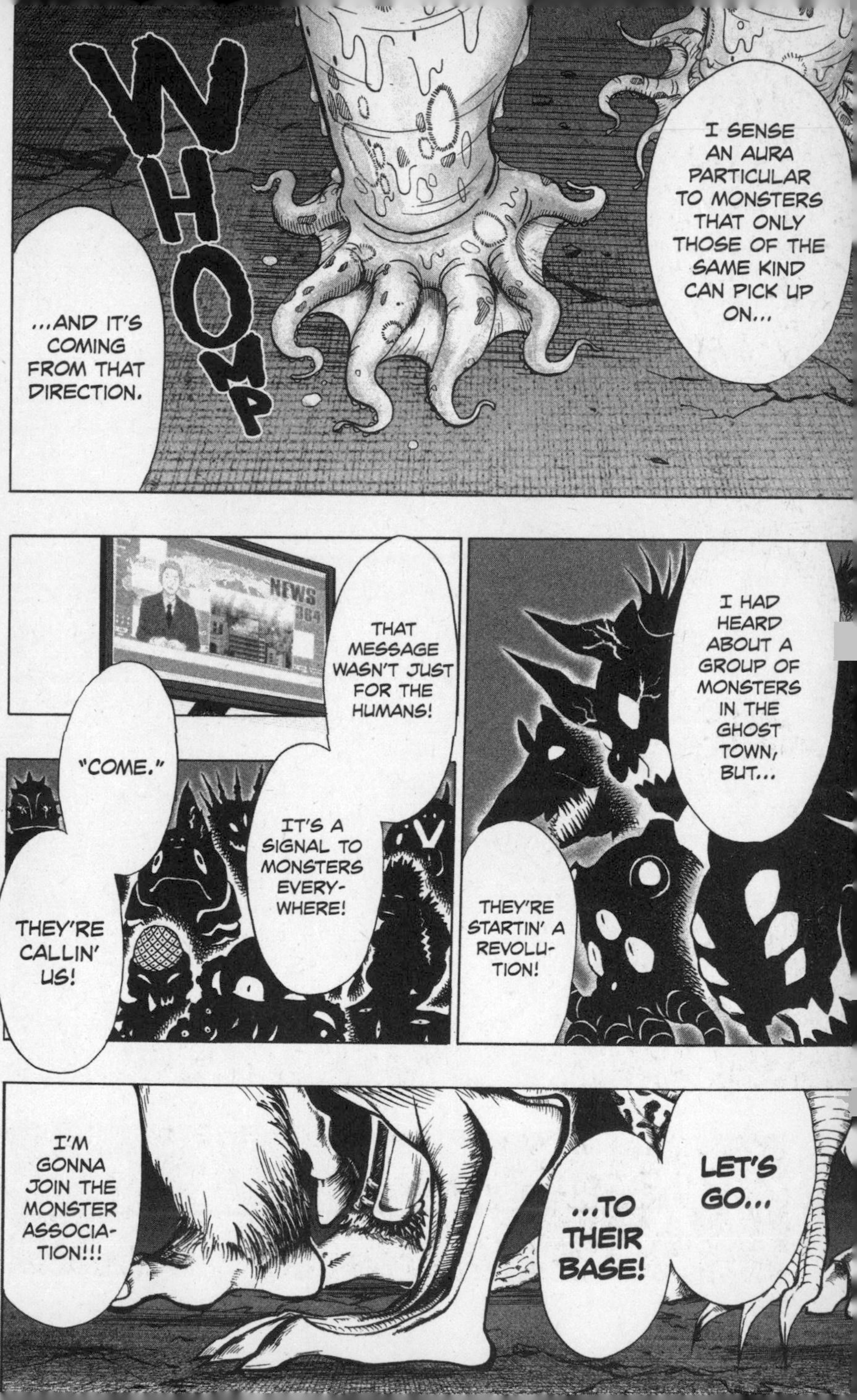
I SENSE AN AURA PARTICULAR TO MONSTERS THAT ONLY THOSE OF THE SAME KIND CAN PICK UP ON...
WHOMP
...AND IT'S COMING FROM THAT DIRECTION.
I HAD HEARD ABOUT A GROUP OF MONSTERS IN THE GHOST TOWN, BUT...
THEY'RE STARTIN' A REVOLUTION!
NEWS
THAT MESSAGE WASN'T JUST FOR THE HUMANS!
"COME."
IT'S A SIGNAL TO MONSTERS EVERY-WHERE!
THEY'RE CALLIN' US!
LET'S GO...
...TO THEIR BASE!
I'M GONNA JOIN THE MONSTER ASSOCIA-TION!!!

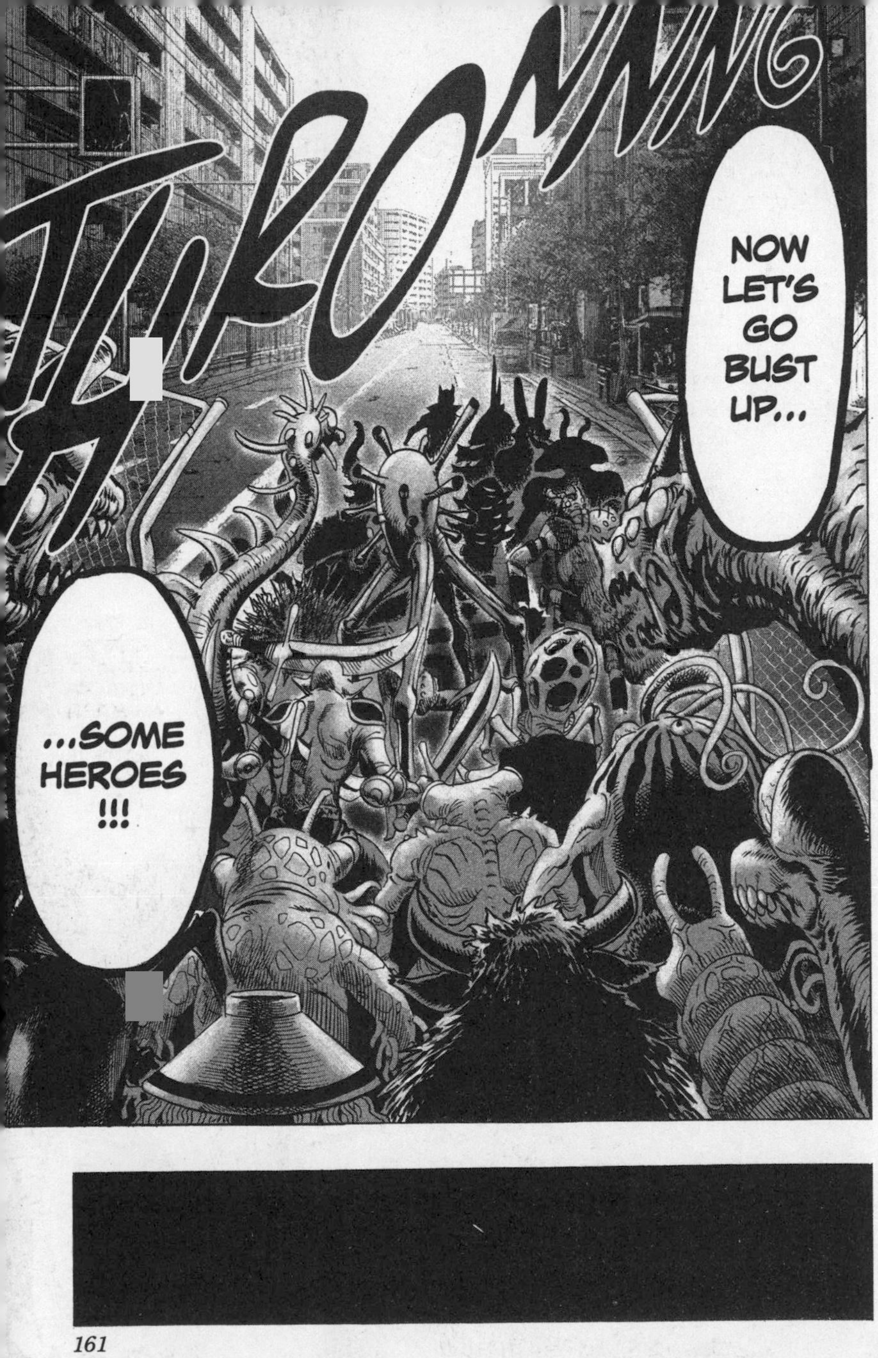
NOW LET'S GO BUST UP...
...SOME HEROES !!!

[redacted]

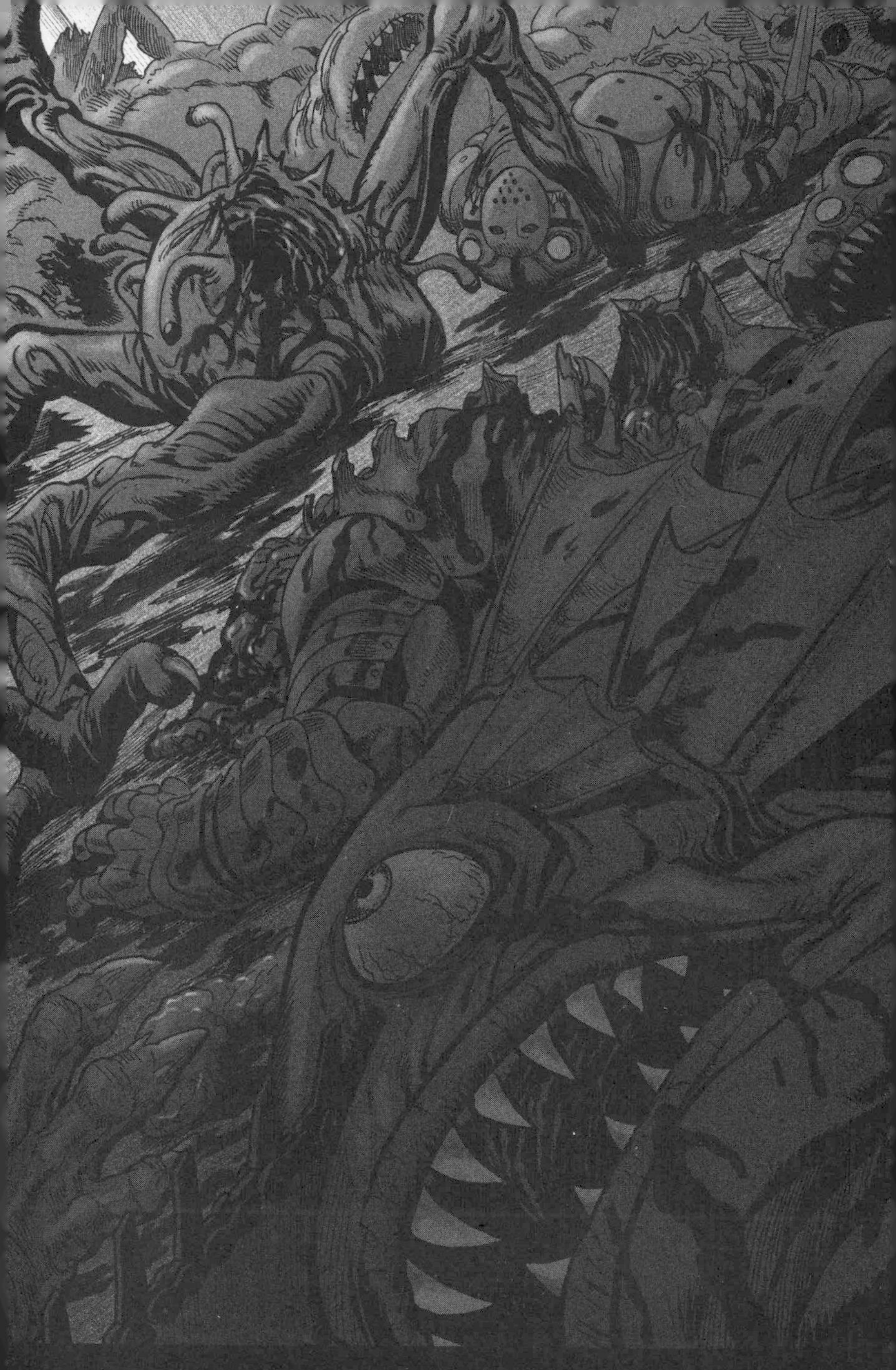

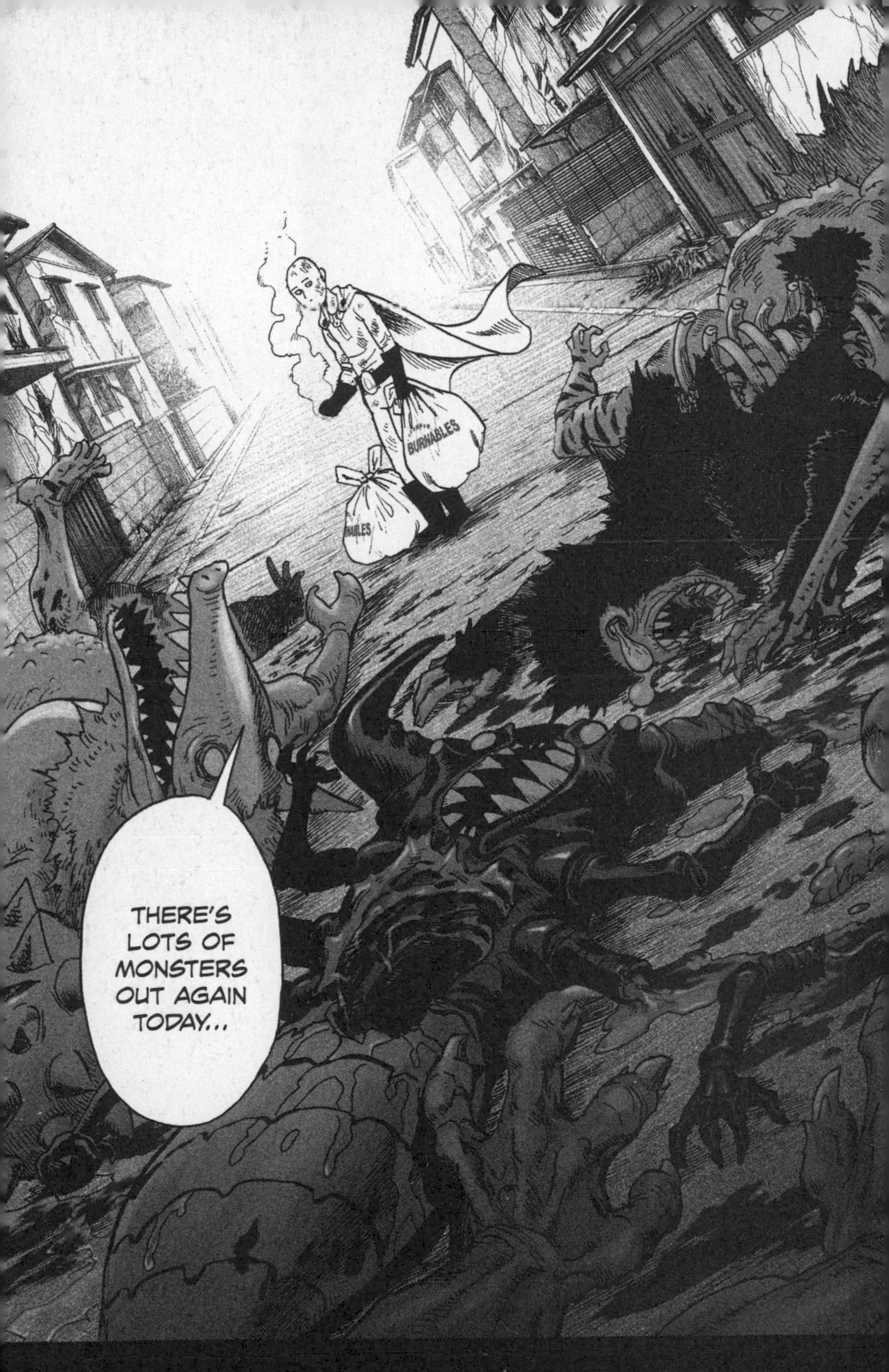
BURNABLES
THERE'S LOTS OF MONSTERS OUT AGAIN TODAY...

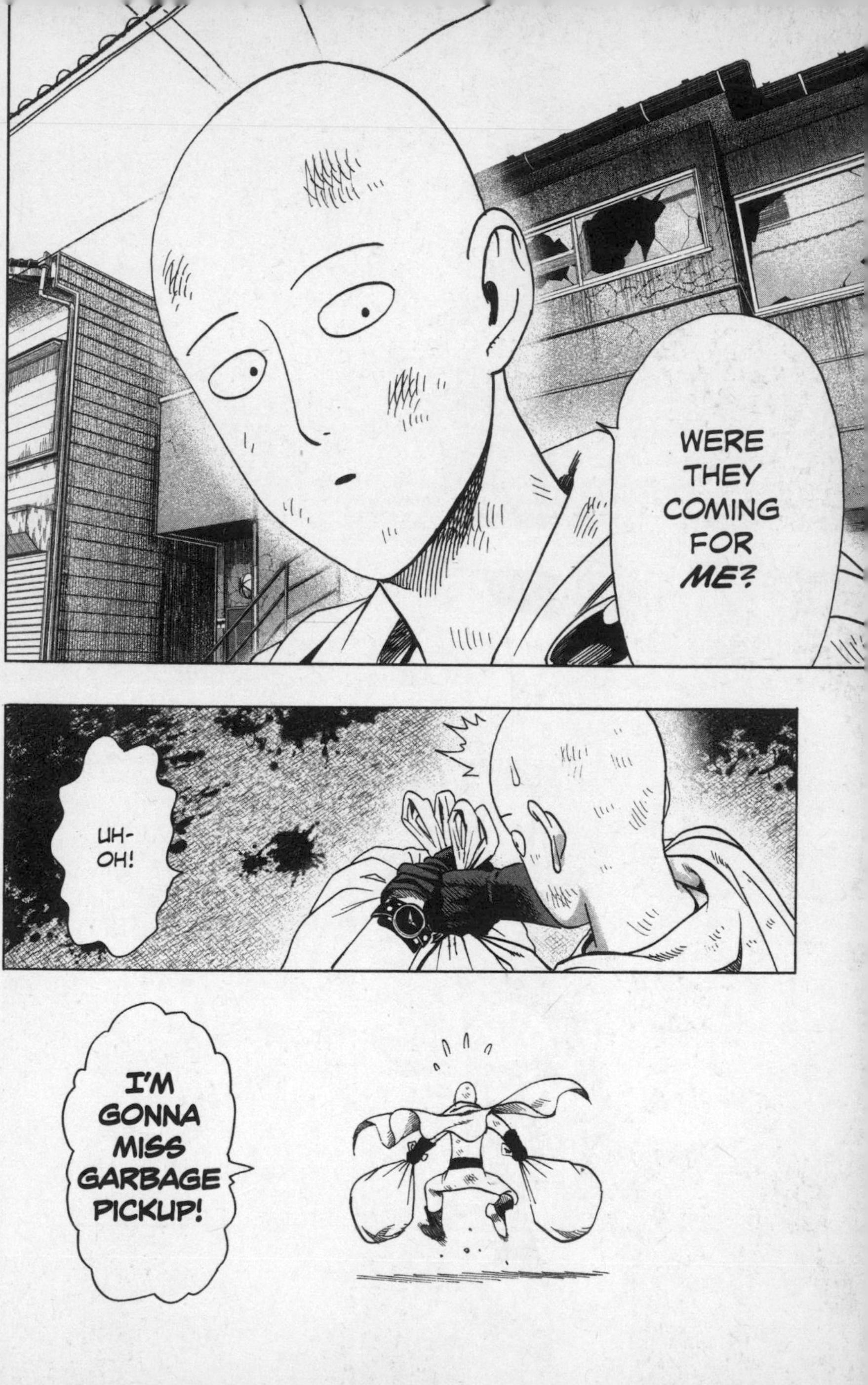
WERE THEY COMING FOR ME?
UH-OH!
I'M GONNA MISS GARBAGE PICKUP!

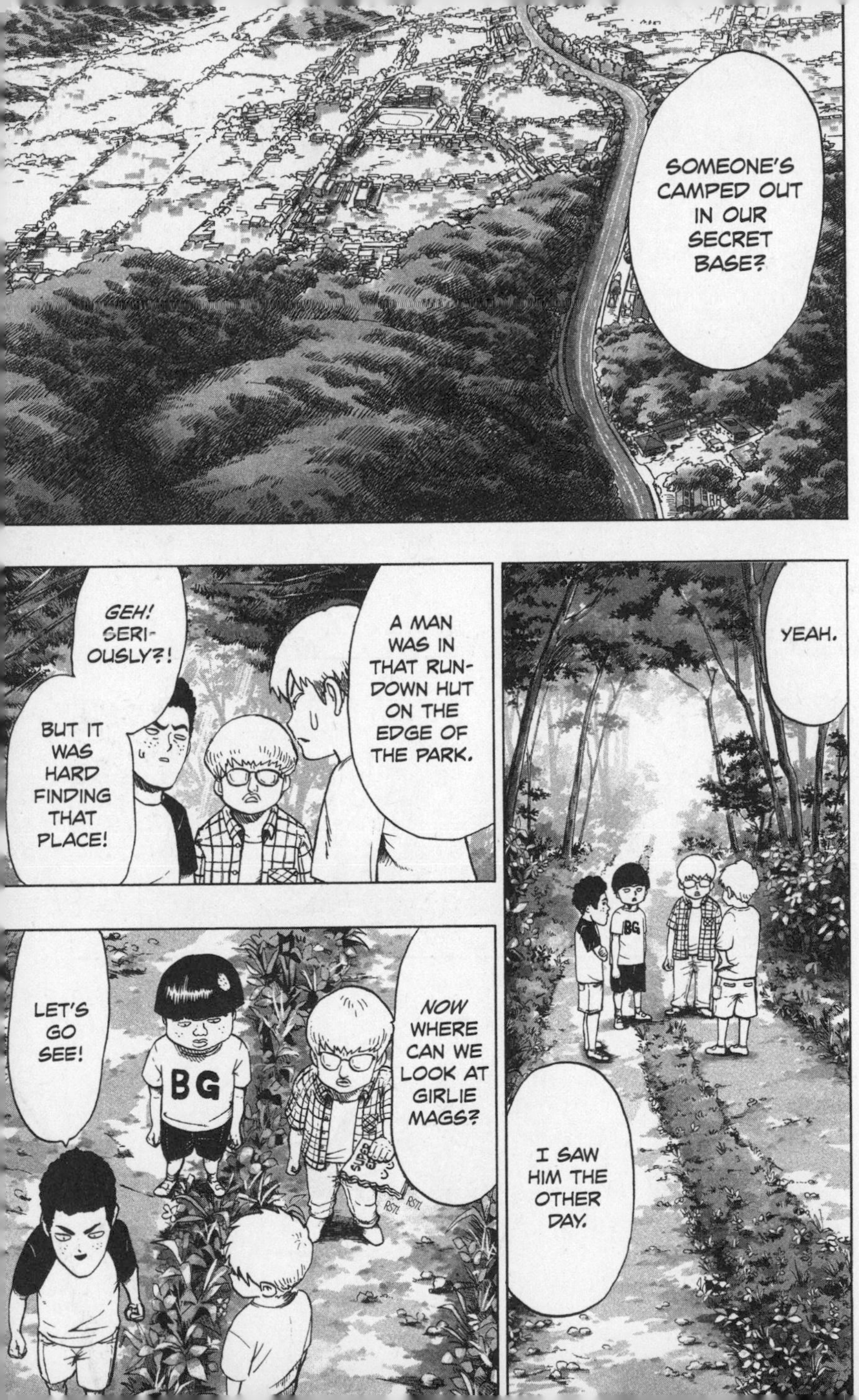
SOMEONE'S CAMPED OUT IN OUR SECRET BASE?
YEAH.
I SAW HIM THE OTHER DAY.
A MAN WAS IN THAT RUN-DOWN HUT ON THE EDGE OF THE PARK.
GEH! SERIOUSLY?!
BUT IT WAS HARD FINDING THAT PLACE!
NOW WHERE CAN WE LOOK AT GIRLIE MAGS?
SUPER
RSTL RSTL
LET'S GO SEE!

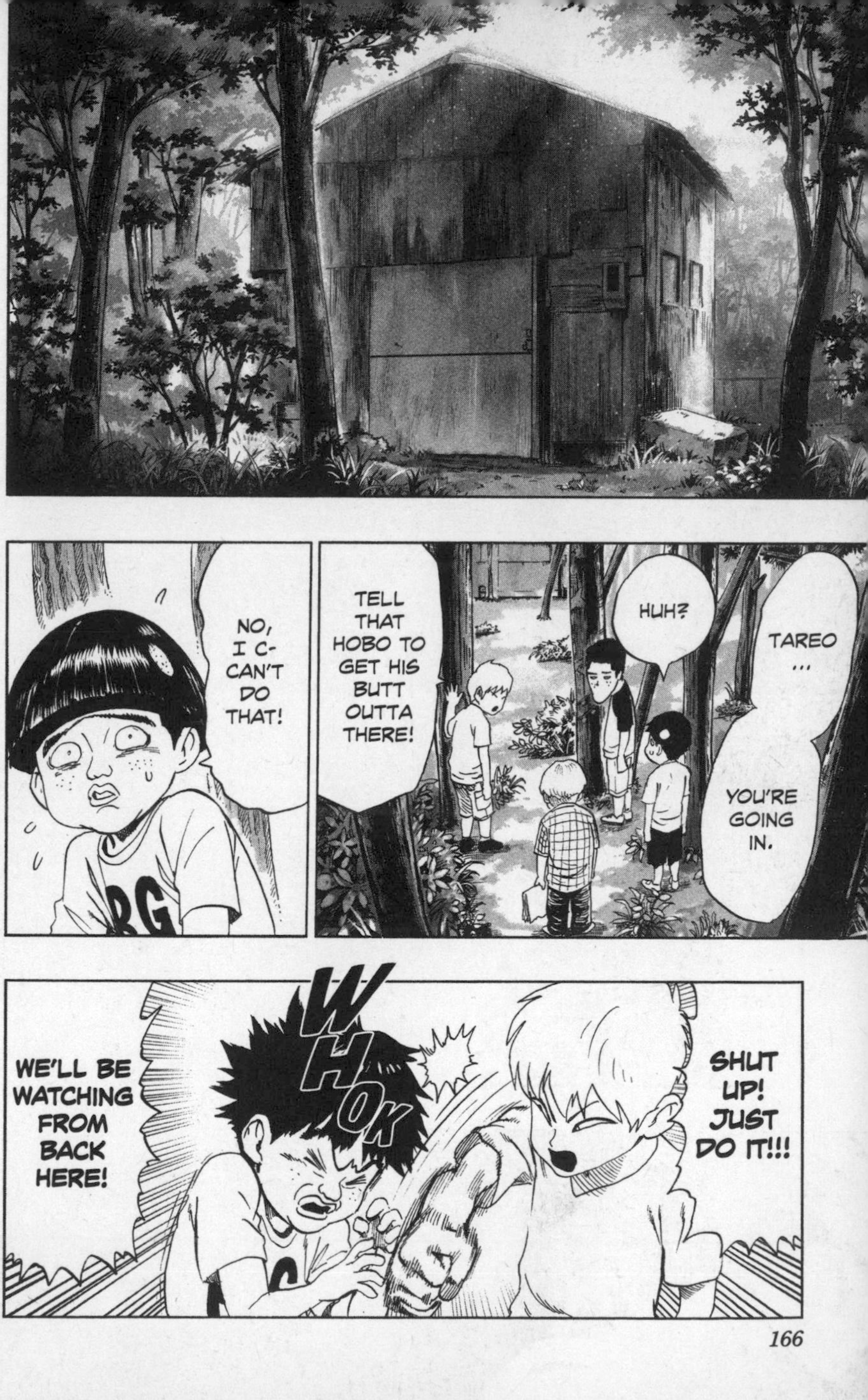
TAREO ...
YOU'RE GOING IN.
HUH?
TELL THAT HOBO TO GET HIS BUTT OUTTA THERE!
NO, I C-CAN'T DO THAT!
SHUT UP! JUST DO IT!!!
WHOK
WE'LL BE WATCHING FROM BACK HERE!

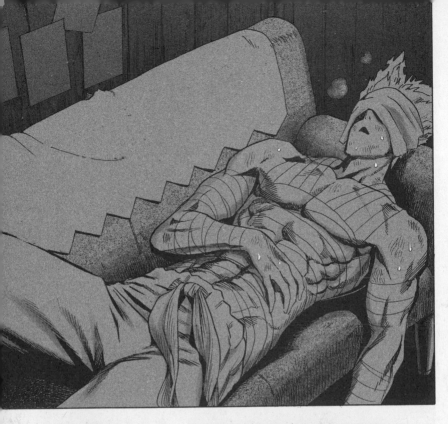

SIGH
...

CHAK

MY FEVER ISN'T GOING DOWN ...

I MAY BE IM-MOBILE FOR TWO OR THREE DAYS!

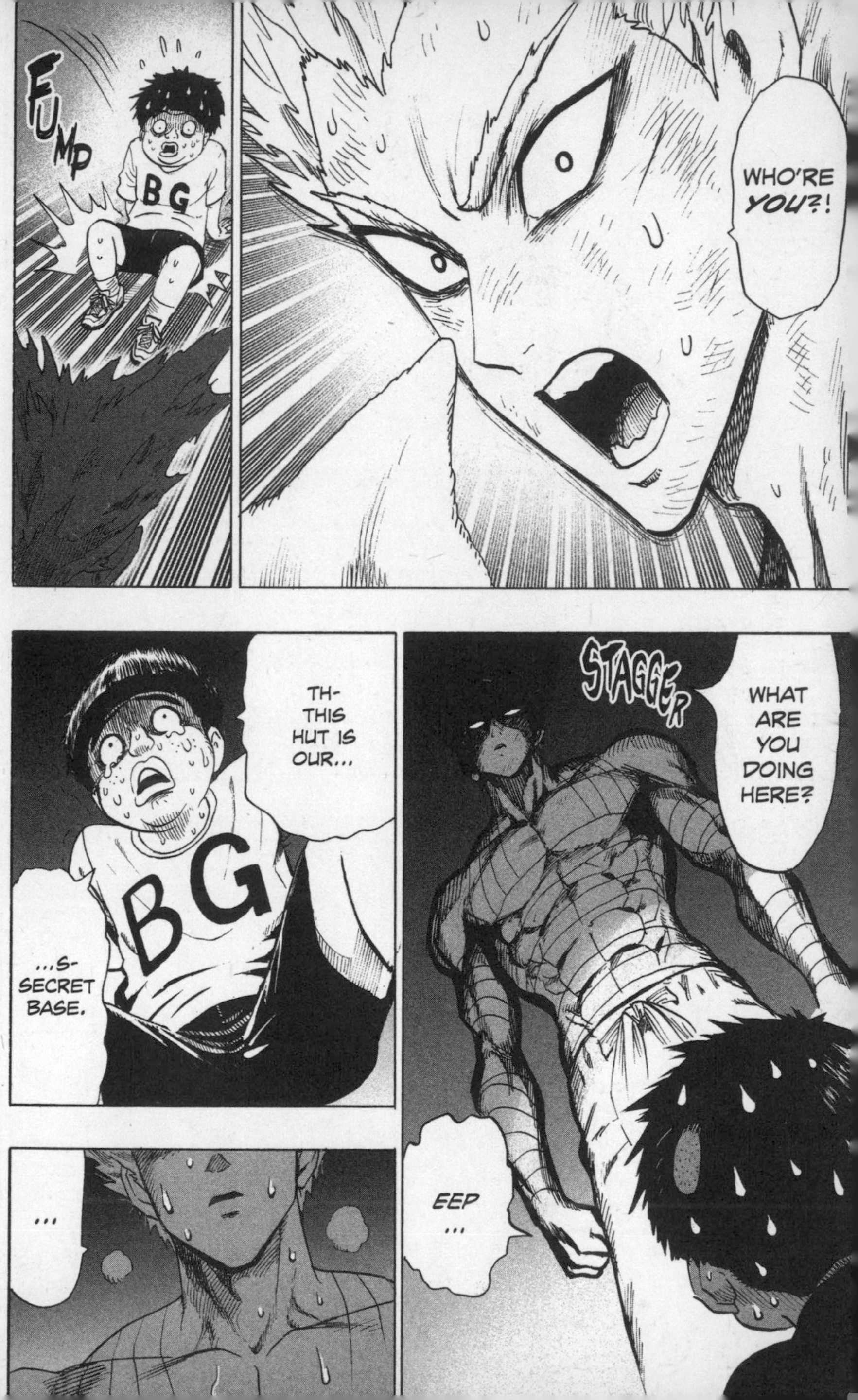
WHO'RE YOU?!
FUMP
STAGGER
WHAT ARE YOU DOING HERE?
EEP ...
TH- THIS HUT IS OUR...
...S- SECRET BASE.
...

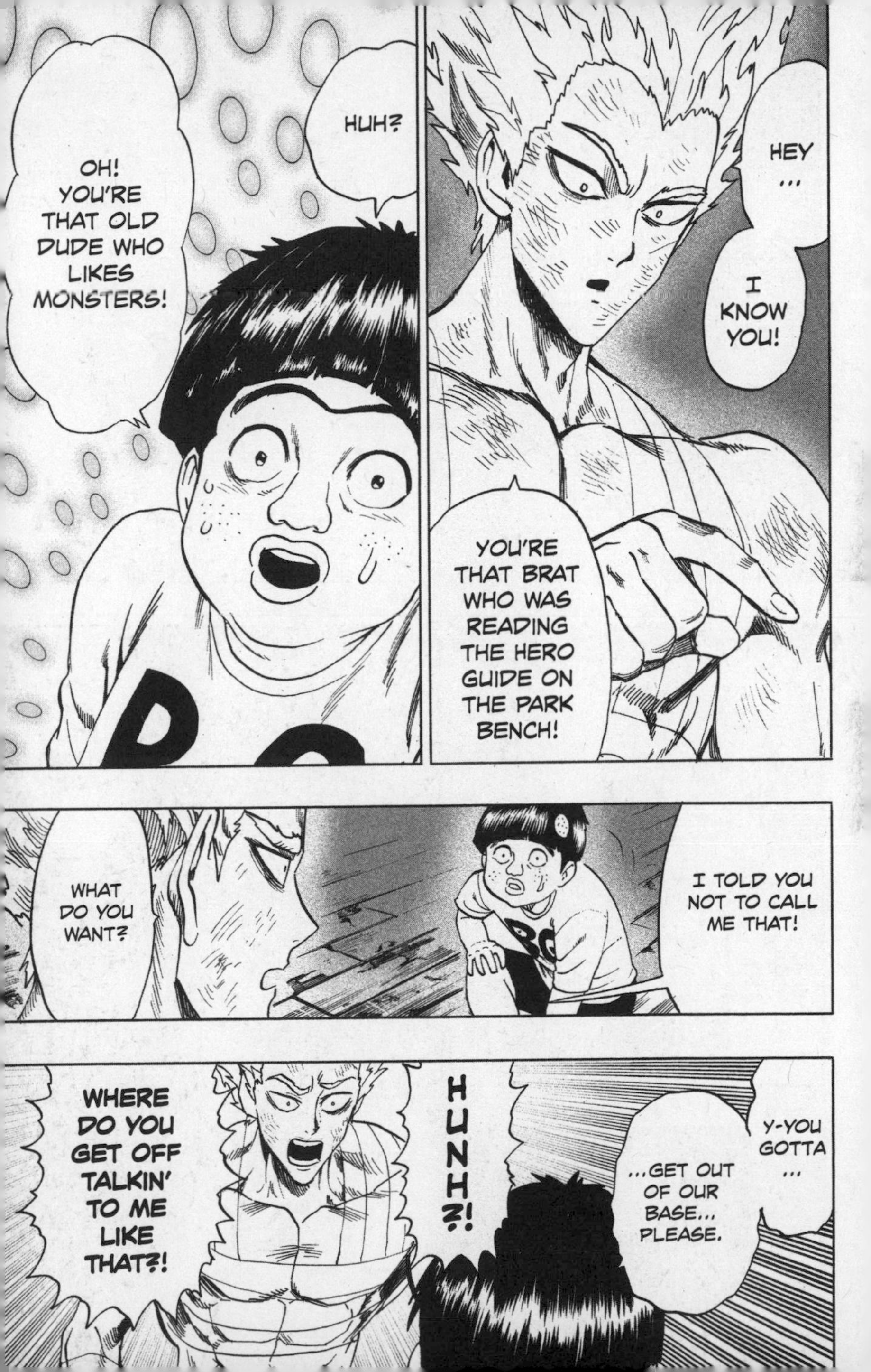
HEY ...
I KNOW YOU!
YOU'RE THAT BRAT WHO WAS READING THE HERO GUIDE ON THE PARK BENCH!
HUH?
OH! YOU'RE THAT OLD DUDE WHO LIKES MONSTERS!
I TOLD YOU NOT TO CALL ME THAT!
WHAT DO YOU WANT?
Y-YOU GOTTA ...
...GET OUT OF OUR BASE... PLEASE.
HUNH?!
WHERE DO YOU GET OFF TALKIN' TO ME LIKE THAT?!

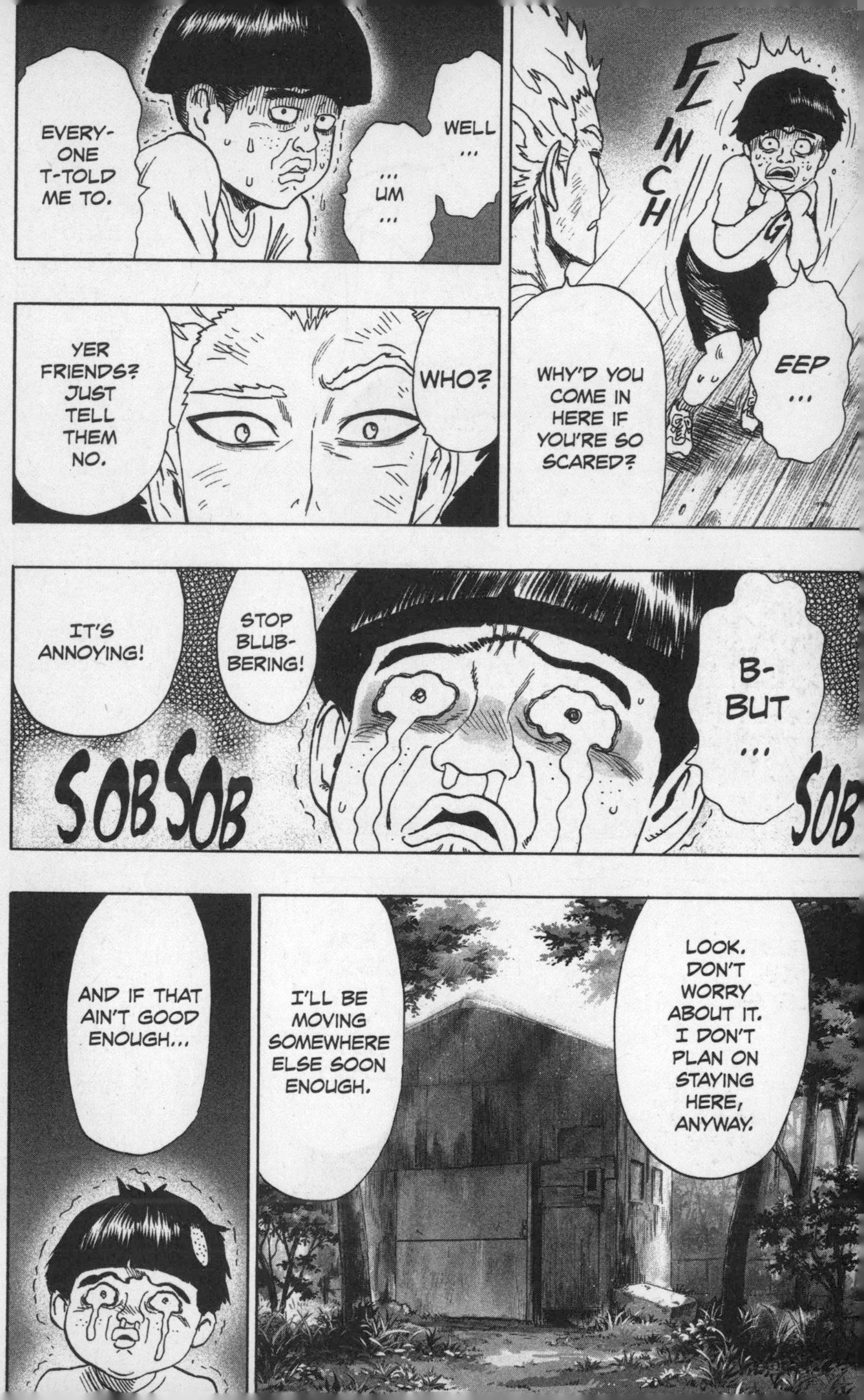
FLINCH
EEP ...
WHY'D YOU COME IN HERE IF YOU'RE SO SCARED?
WELL ...
... UM ...
EVERY-ONE T-TOLD ME TO.
WHO?
YER FRIENDS? JUST TELL THEM NO.
B-BUT ...
SOB
STOP BLUB-BERING!
IT'S ANNOYING!
SOB SOB
LOOK. DON'T WORRY ABOUT IT. I DON'T PLAN ON STAYING HERE, ANYWAY.
I'LL BE MOVING SOMEWHERE ELSE SOON ENOUGH.
AND IF THAT AIN'T GOOD ENOUGH...

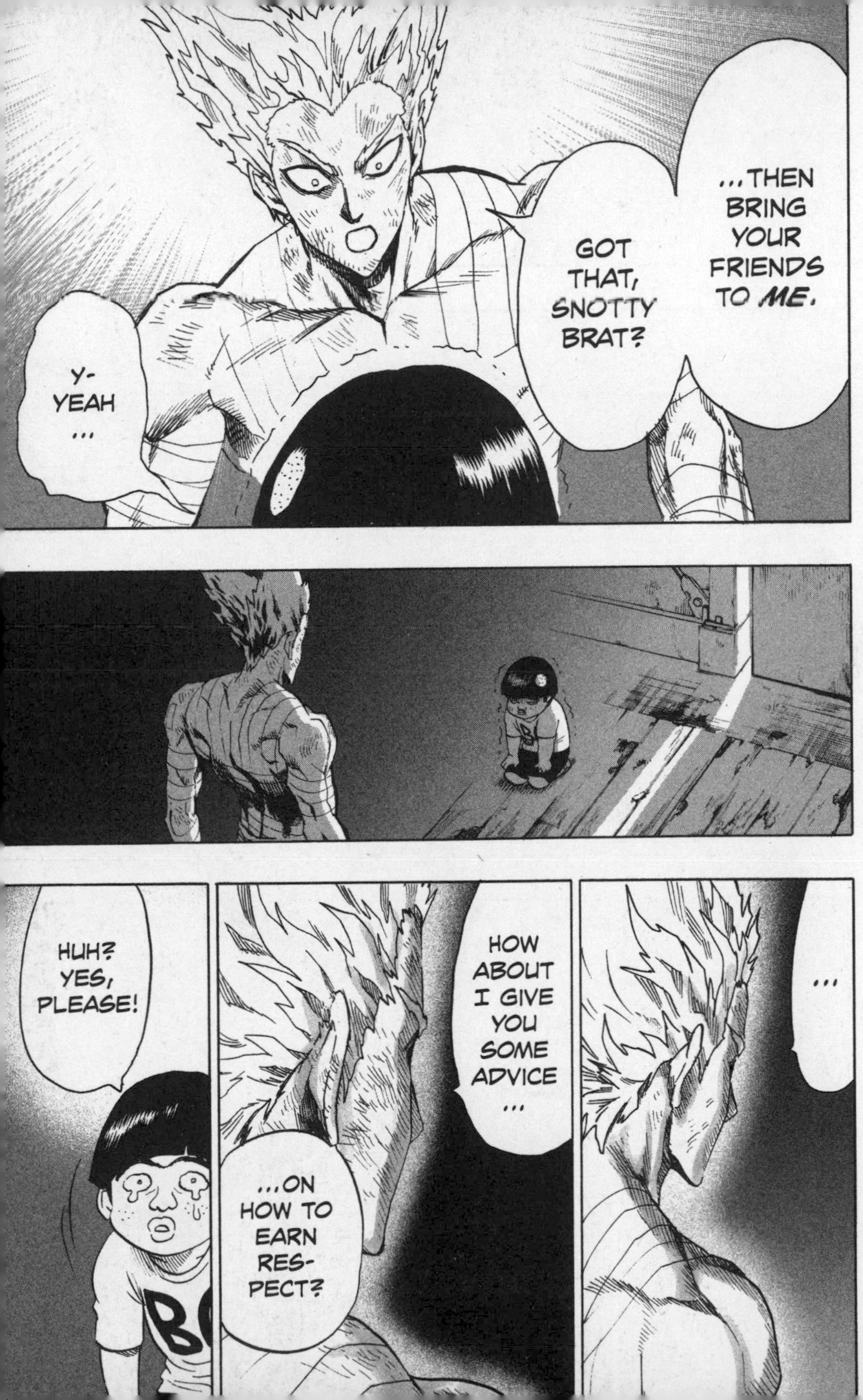
...THEN BRING YOUR FRIENDS TO *ME*.
GOT THAT, SNOTTY BRAT?
Y-YEAH ...
...
HOW ABOUT I GIVE YOU SOME ADVICE ...
...ON HOW TO EARN RES-PECT?
HUH? YES, PLEASE!

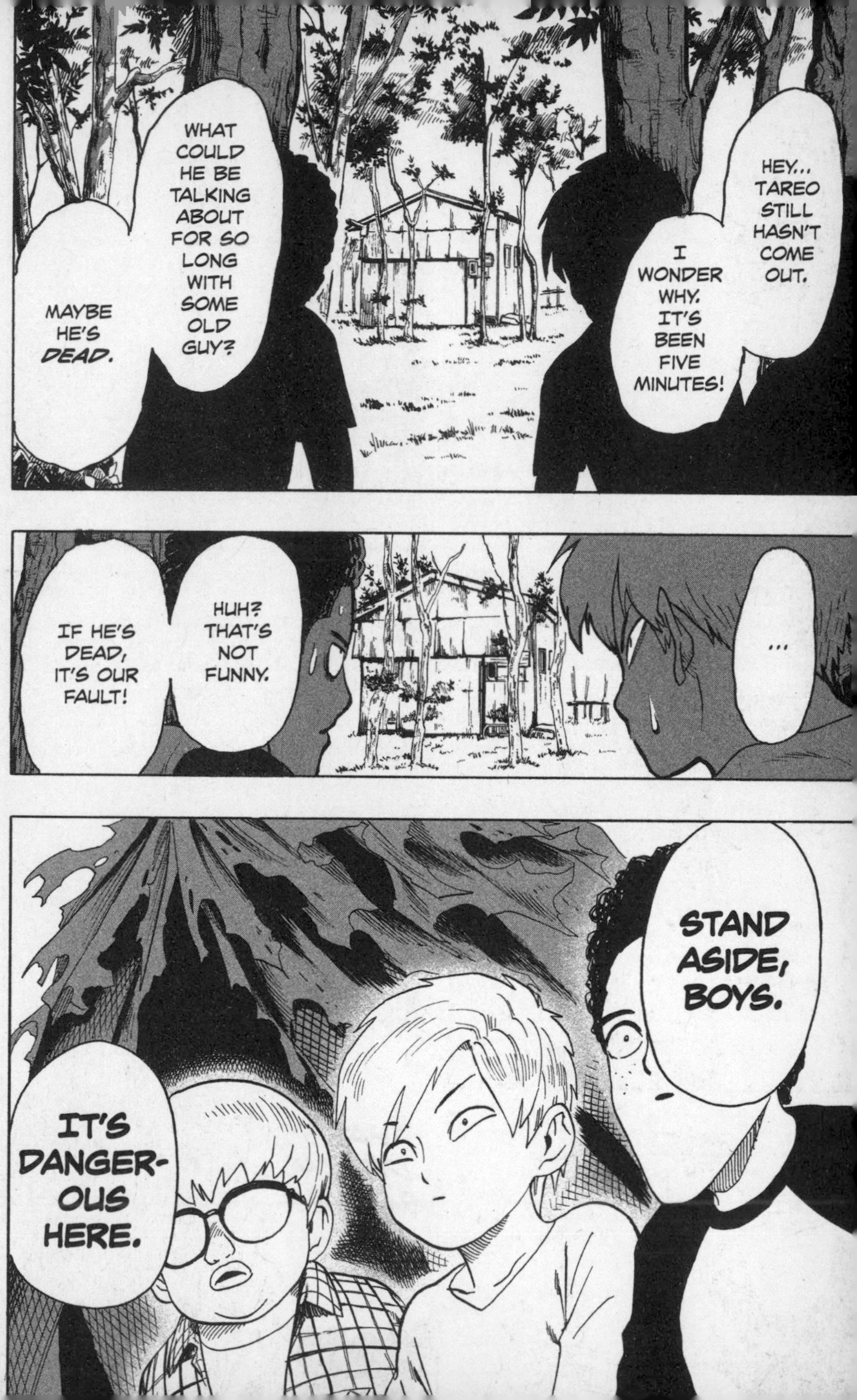
HEY... TAREO STILL HASN'T COME OUT.
I WONDER WHY. IT'S BEEN FIVE MINUTES!
WHAT COULD HE BE TALKING ABOUT FOR SO LONG WITH SOME OLD GUY?
MAYBE HE'S *DEAD*.
...
HUH? THAT'S NOT FUNNY.
IF HE'S DEAD, IT'S OUR FAULT!
STAND ASIDE, BOYS.
IT'S DANGER-OUS HERE.

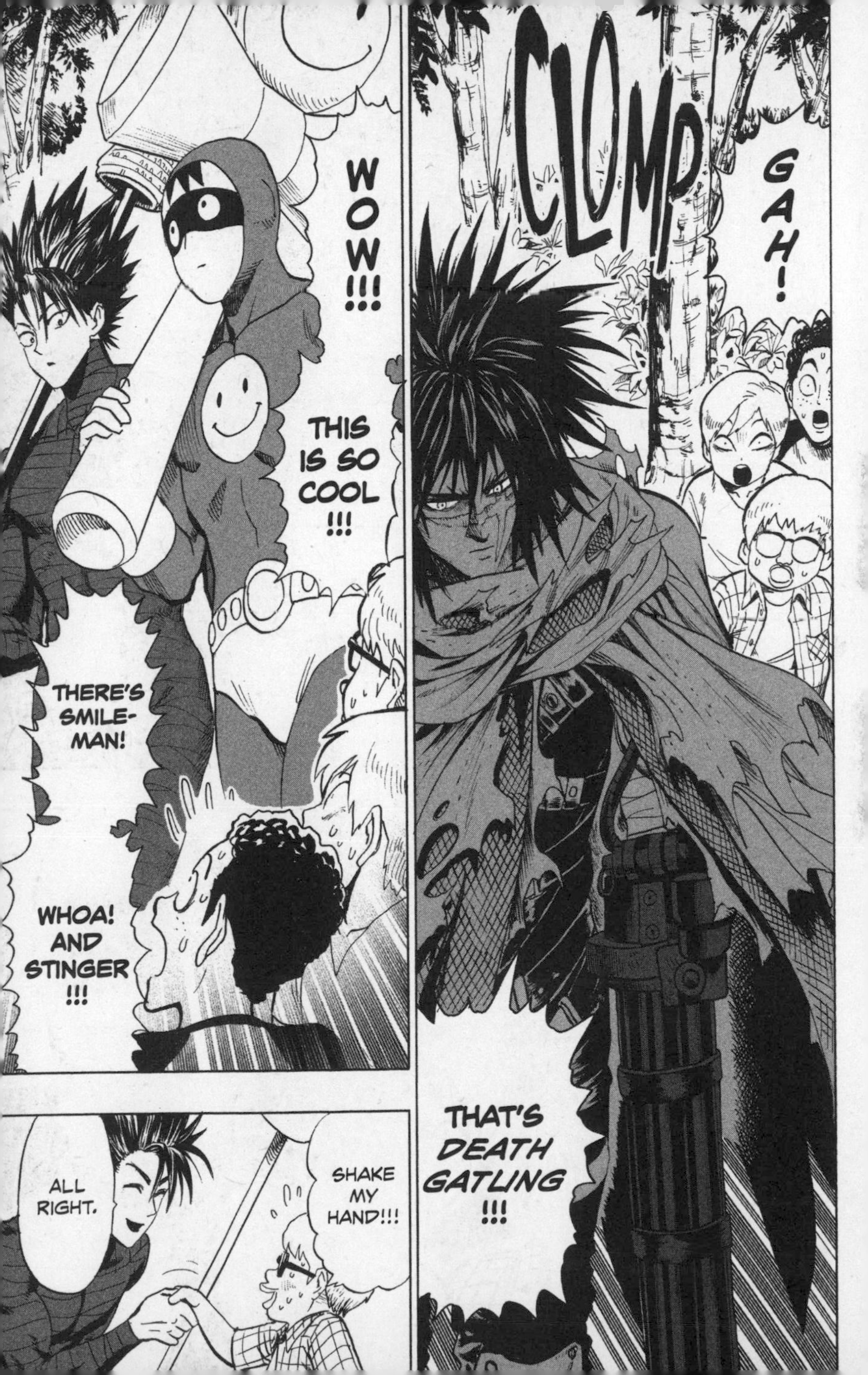
GAH!
CLOMP
THAT'S DEATH GATLING!!!
WOW!!!
THIS IS SO COOL!!!
THERE'S SMILE-MAN!
WHOA! AND STINGER!!!
SHAKE MY HAND!!!
ALL RIGHT.

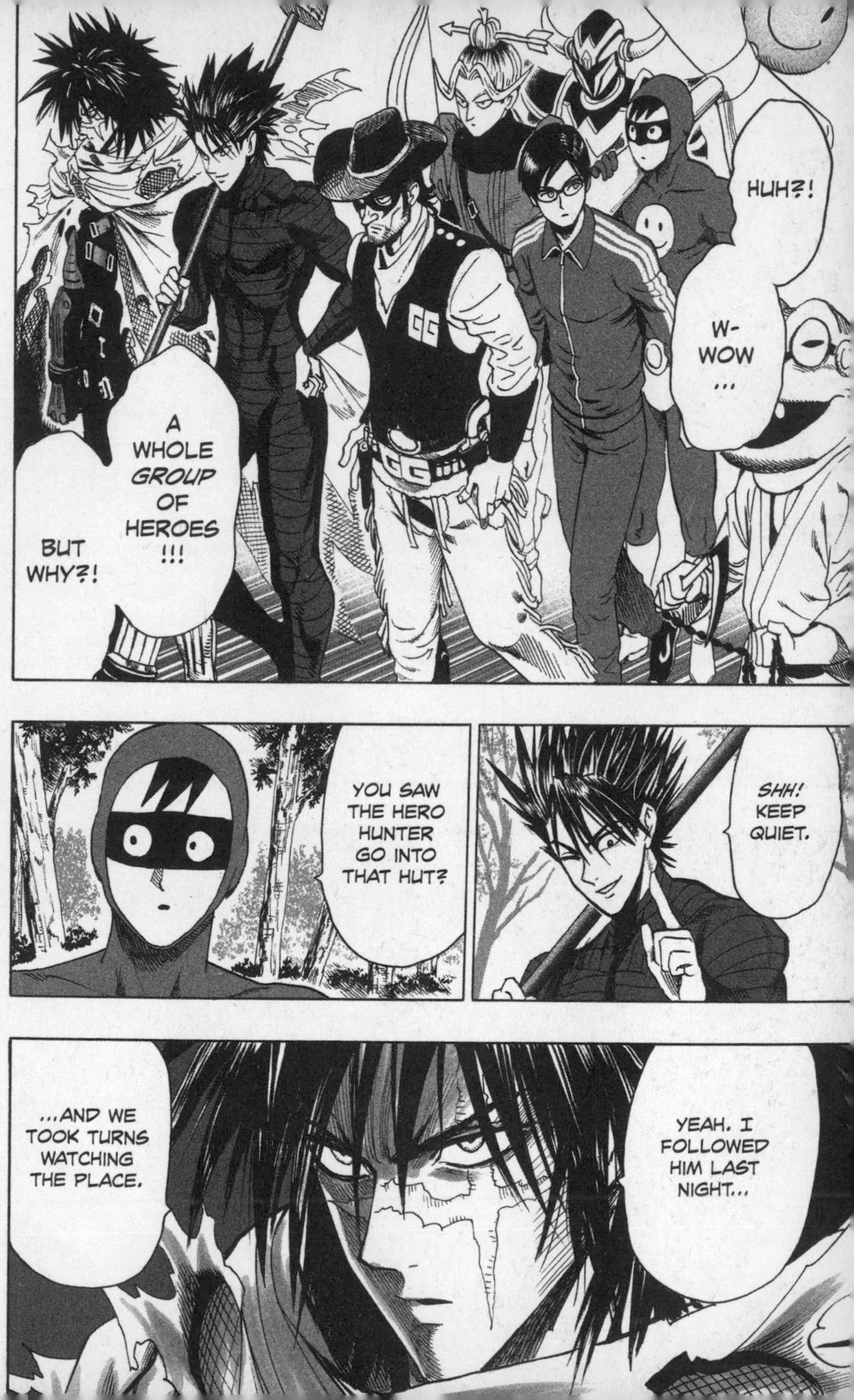
HUH?!
W-WOW...
A WHOLE *GROUP* OF HEROES!!!
BUT WHY?!
SHH! KEEP QUIET.
YOU SAW THE HERO HUNTER GO INTO THAT HUT?
YEAH. I FOLLOWED HIM LAST NIGHT...
...AND WE TOOK TURNS WATCHING THE PLACE.

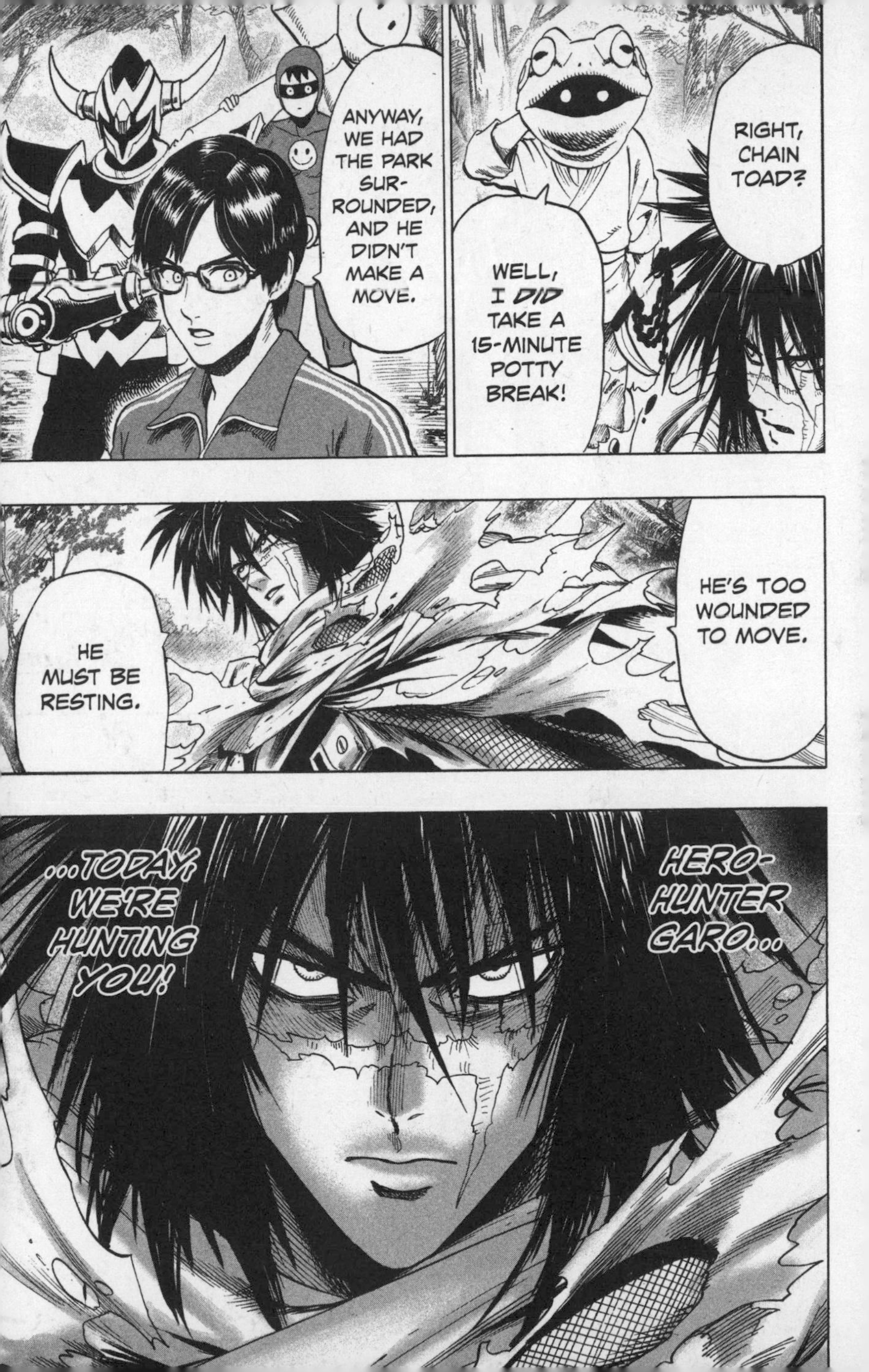
RIGHT, CHAIN TOAD?
WELL, I *DID* TAKE A 15-MINUTE POTTY BREAK!
ANYWAY, WE HAD THE PARK SUR-ROUNDED, AND HE DIDN'T MAKE A MOVE.
HE'S TOO WOUNDED TO MOVE.
HE MUST BE RESTING.
HERO-HUNTER GARO...
...TODAY, WE'RE HUNTING YOU!

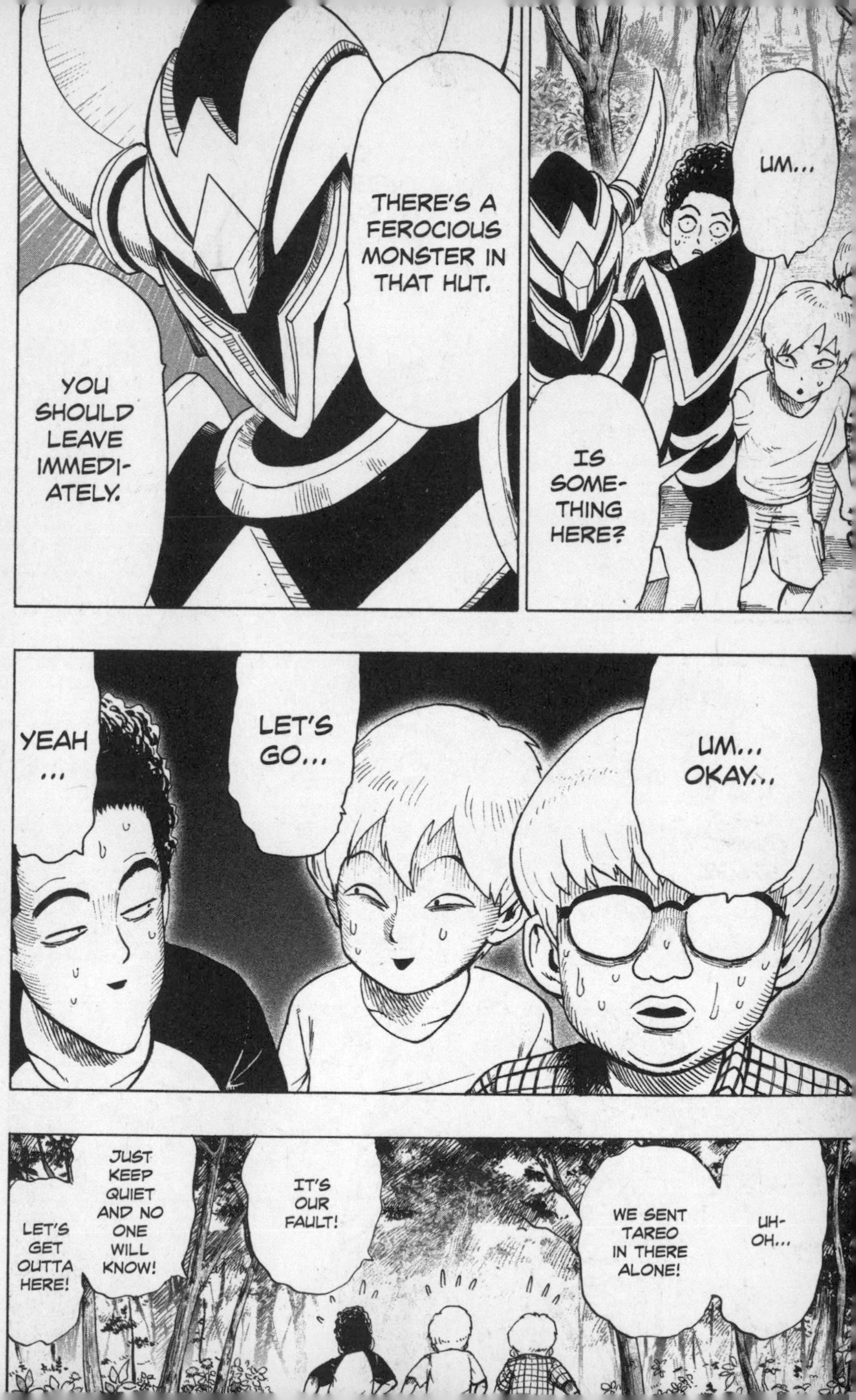
UM...
IS SOMETHING HERE?
THERE'S A FEROCIOUS MONSTER IN THAT HUT.
YOU SHOULD LEAVE IMMEDIATELY.
UM... OKAY...
LET'S GO...
YEAH ...
UH-OH...
WE SENT TAREO IN THERE ALONE!
IT'S OUR FAULT!
JUST KEEP QUIET AND NO ONE WILL KNOW!
LET'S GET OUTTA HERE!

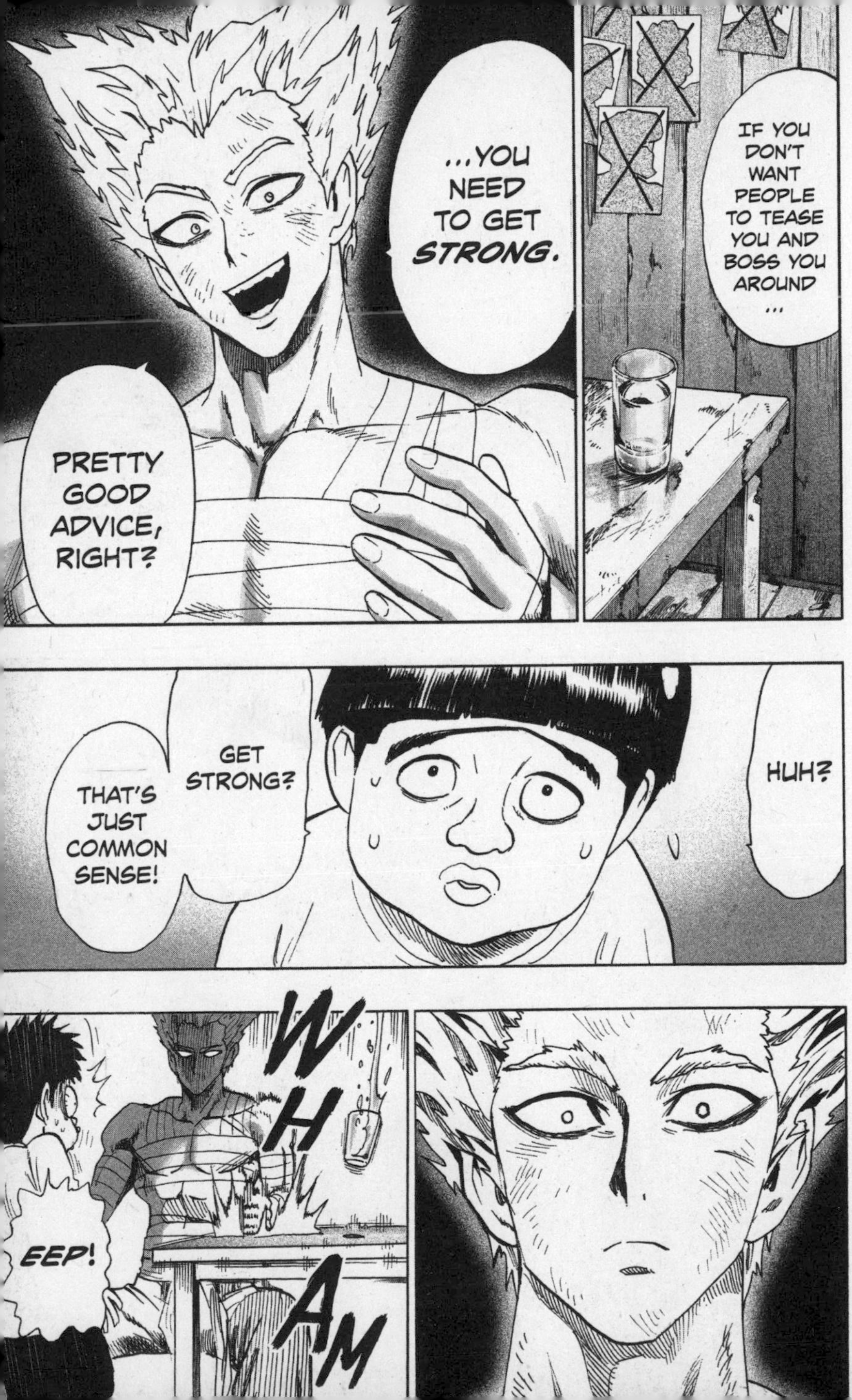
IF YOU DON'T WANT PEOPLE TO TEASE YOU AND BOSS YOU AROUND ...
...YOU NEED TO GET STRONG.
PRETTY GOOD ADVICE, RIGHT?
HUH?
GET STRONG?
THAT'S JUST COMMON SENSE!
WHAM
EEP!

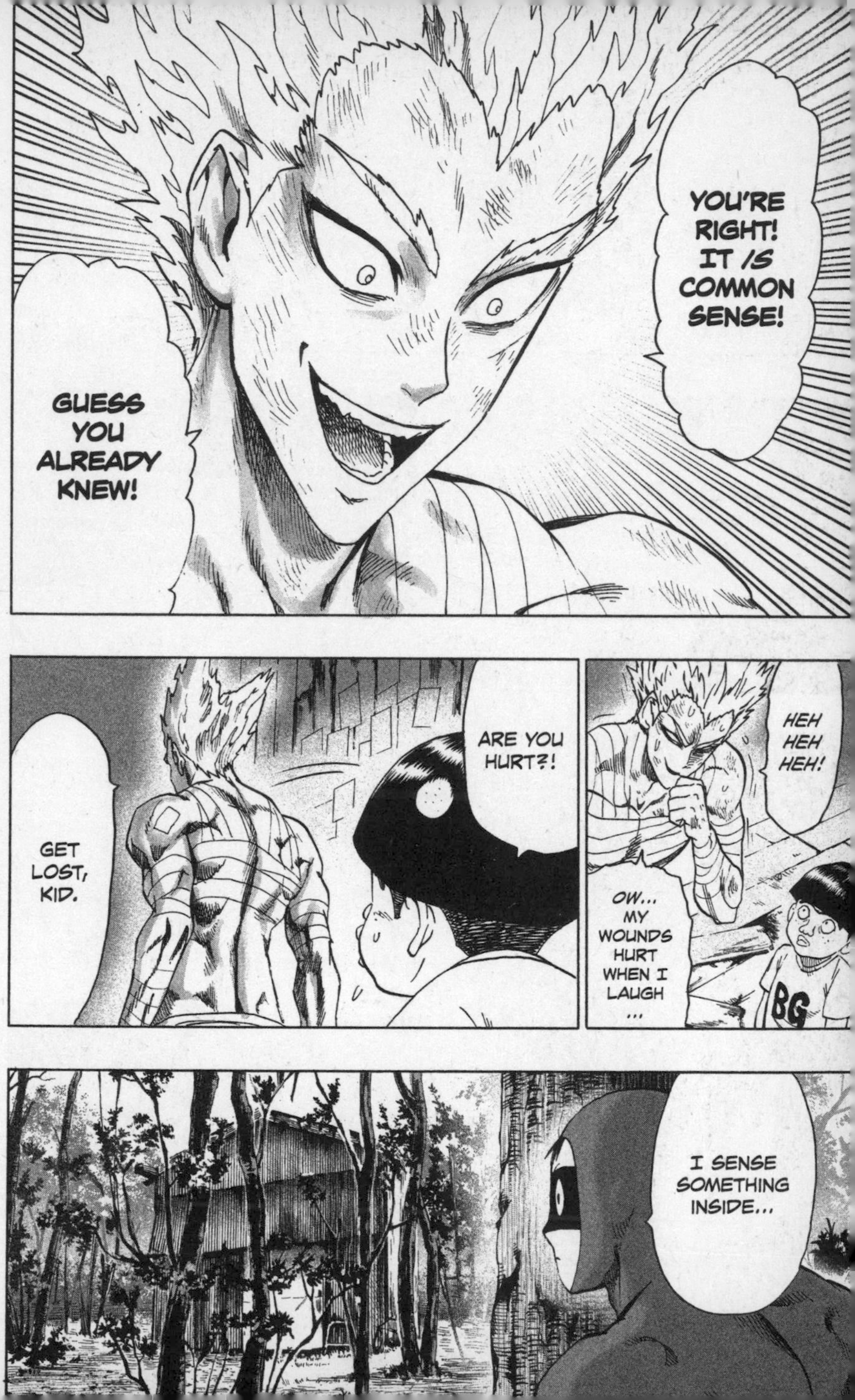
YOU'RE RIGHT! IT *IS* COMMON SENSE!
GUESS YOU ALREADY KNEW!
HEH HEH HEH!
OW... MY WOUNDS HURT WHEN I LAUGH ...
ARE YOU HURT?!
GET LOST, KID.
I SENSE SOMETHING INSIDE...

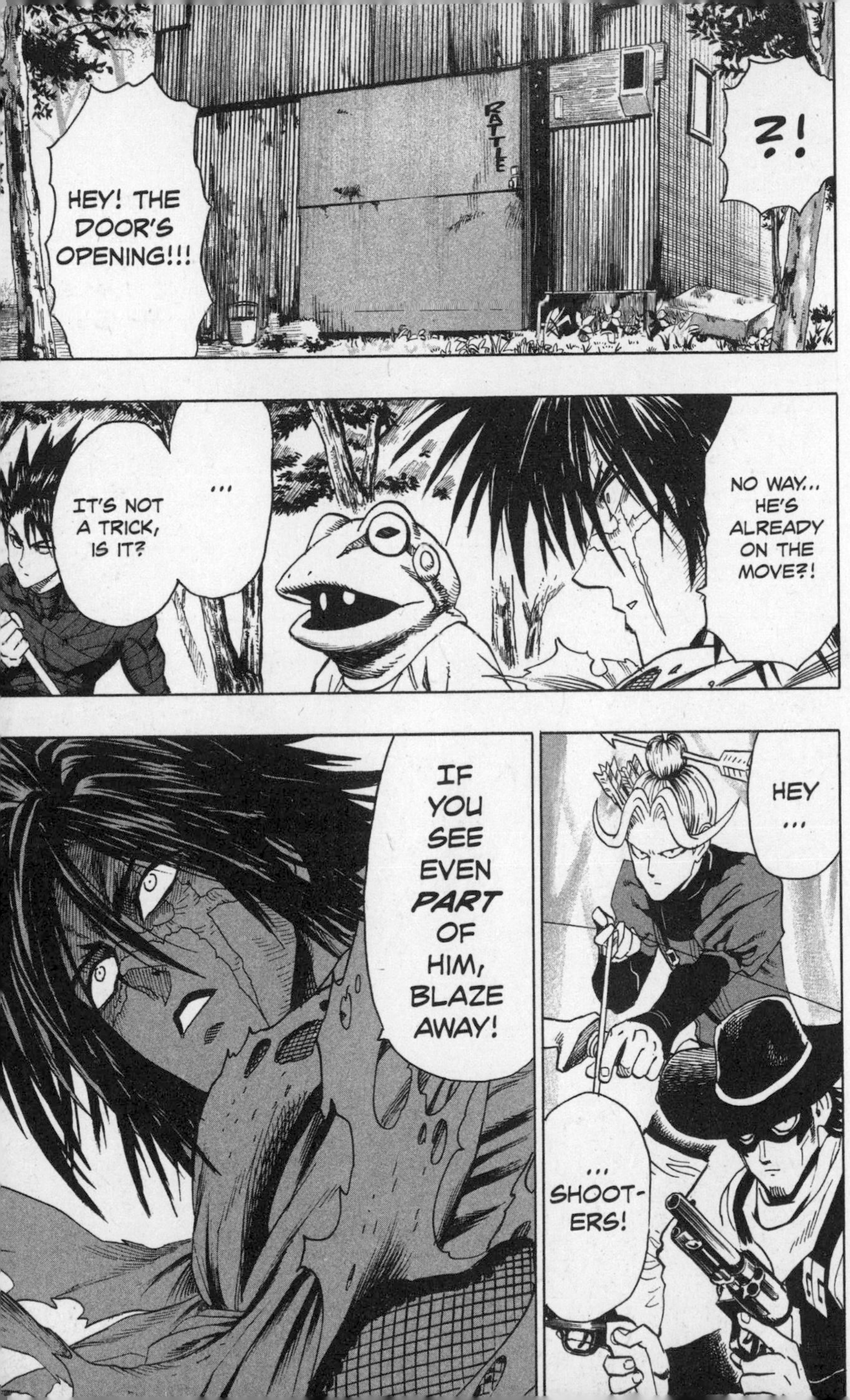
?!
RATTLE
HEY! THE DOOR'S OPENING!!!
NO WAY... HE'S ALREADY ON THE MOVE?!
...
IT'S NOT A TRICK, IS IT?
HEY ...
... SHOOT-ERS!
IF YOU SEE EVEN PART OF HIM, BLAZE AWAY!

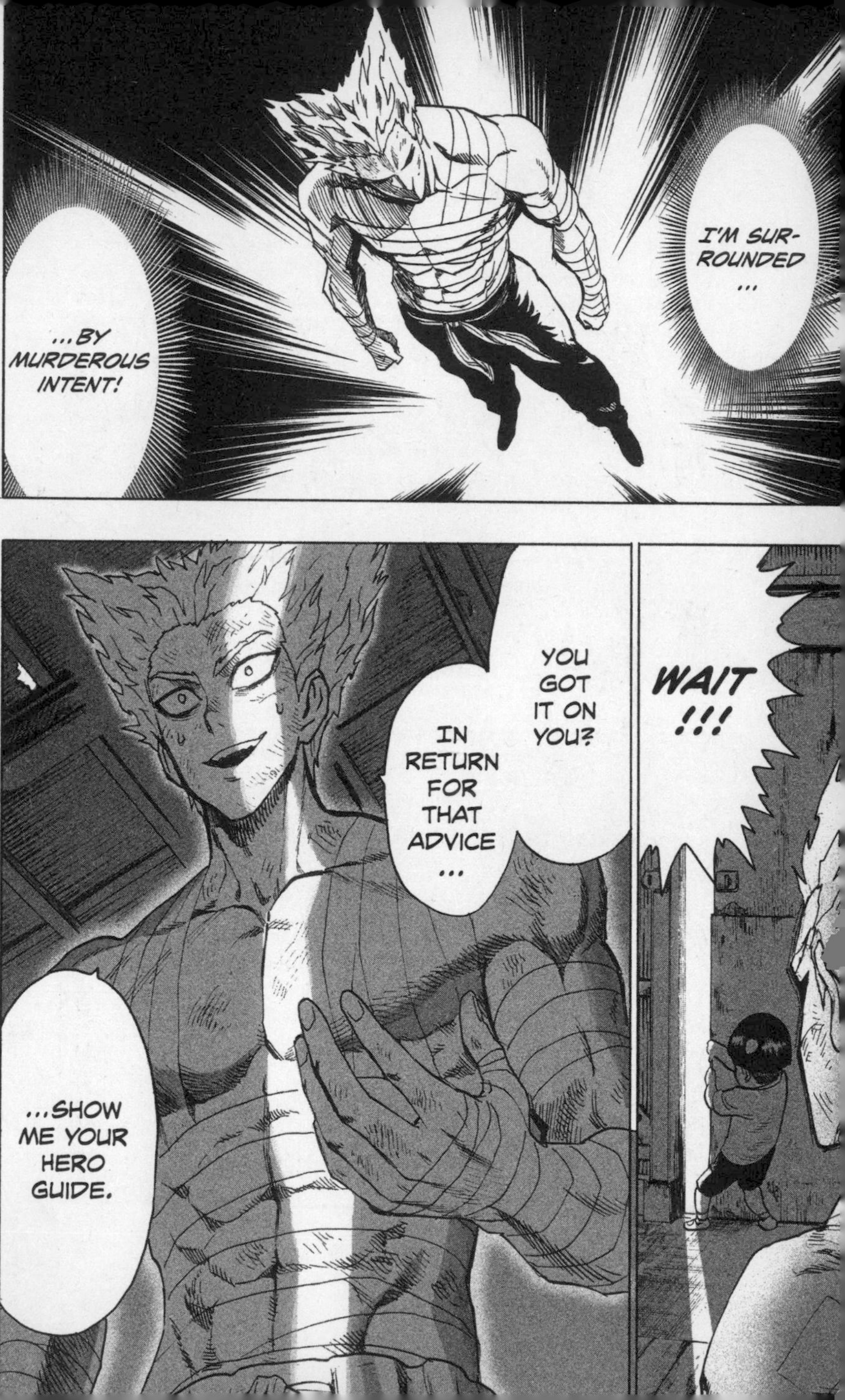
I'M SUR-ROUNDED...
...BY MURDEROUS INTENT!
WAIT!!!
YOU GOT IT ON YOU?
IN RETURN FOR THAT ADVICE...
...SHOW ME YOUR HERO GUIDE.

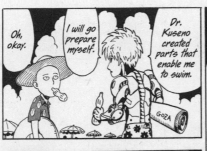

LEARNING TO SWIM

SPLASH
Hm?
I thought you couldn't swim.
You're too heavy.
Dr. Kuseno created parts that enable me to swim.
I will go prepare myself.
Oh, okay.
GOZA
ZSHHH
What's taking so long?
Hey! Genos?!
SPOOSH
Yes?
SWIVEL
SWIVEL
Mas-ter?
Knock it off!
GENOS 19000

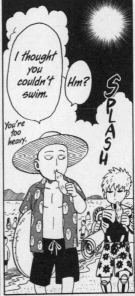

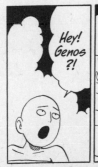

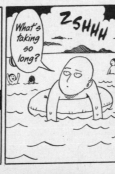

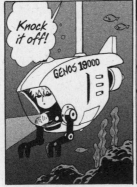

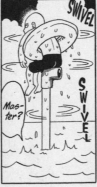

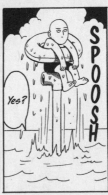

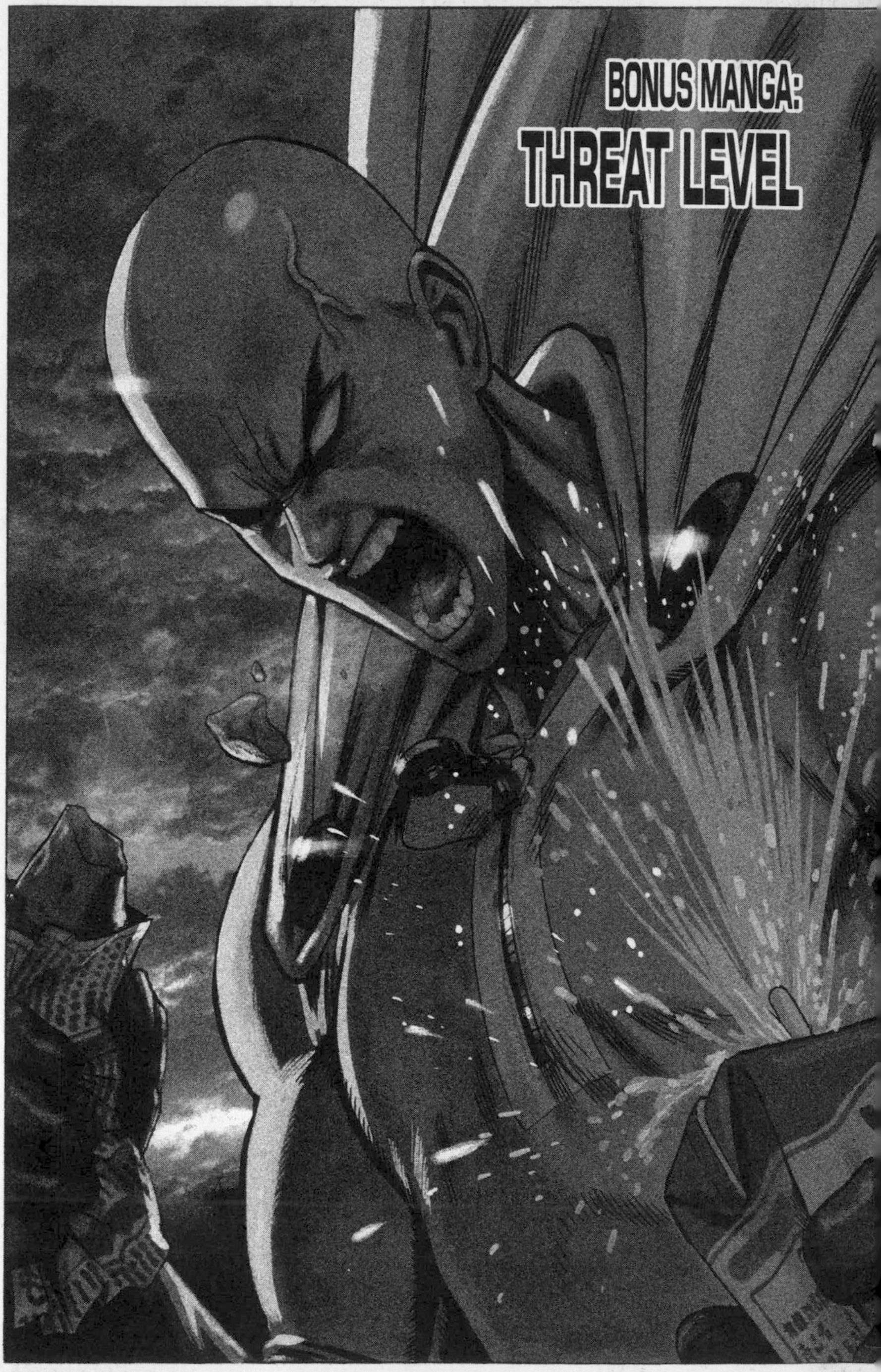
BONUS MANGA:
THREAT LEVEL

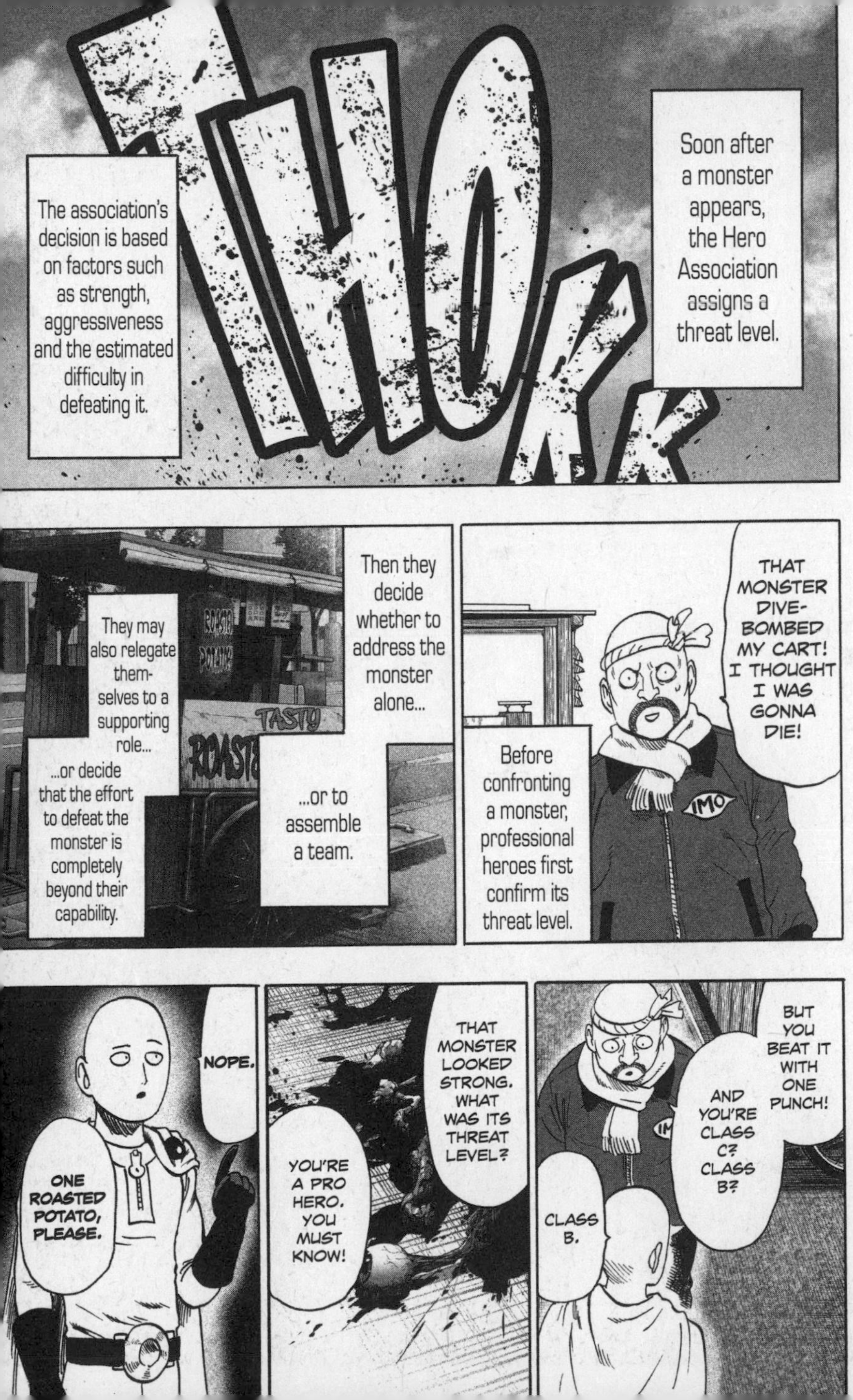
Soon after a monster appears, the Hero Association assigns a threat level.
The association's decision is based on factors such as strength, aggressiveness and the estimated difficulty in defeating it.
THAT MONSTER DIVE-BOMBED MY CART! I THOUGHT I WAS GONNA DIE!
Before confronting a monster, professional heroes first confirm its threat level.
Then they decide whether to address the monster alone...
...or to assemble a team.
They may also relegate them-selves to a supporting role...
...or decide that the effort to defeat the monster is completely beyond their capability.
BUT YOU BEAT IT WITH ONE PUNCH!
AND YOU'RE CLASS C? CLASS B?
CLASS B.
THAT MONSTER LOOKED STRONG. WHAT WAS ITS THREAT LEVEL?
YOU'RE A PRO HERO. YOU MUST KNOW!
NOPE.
ONE ROASTED POTATO, PLEASE.

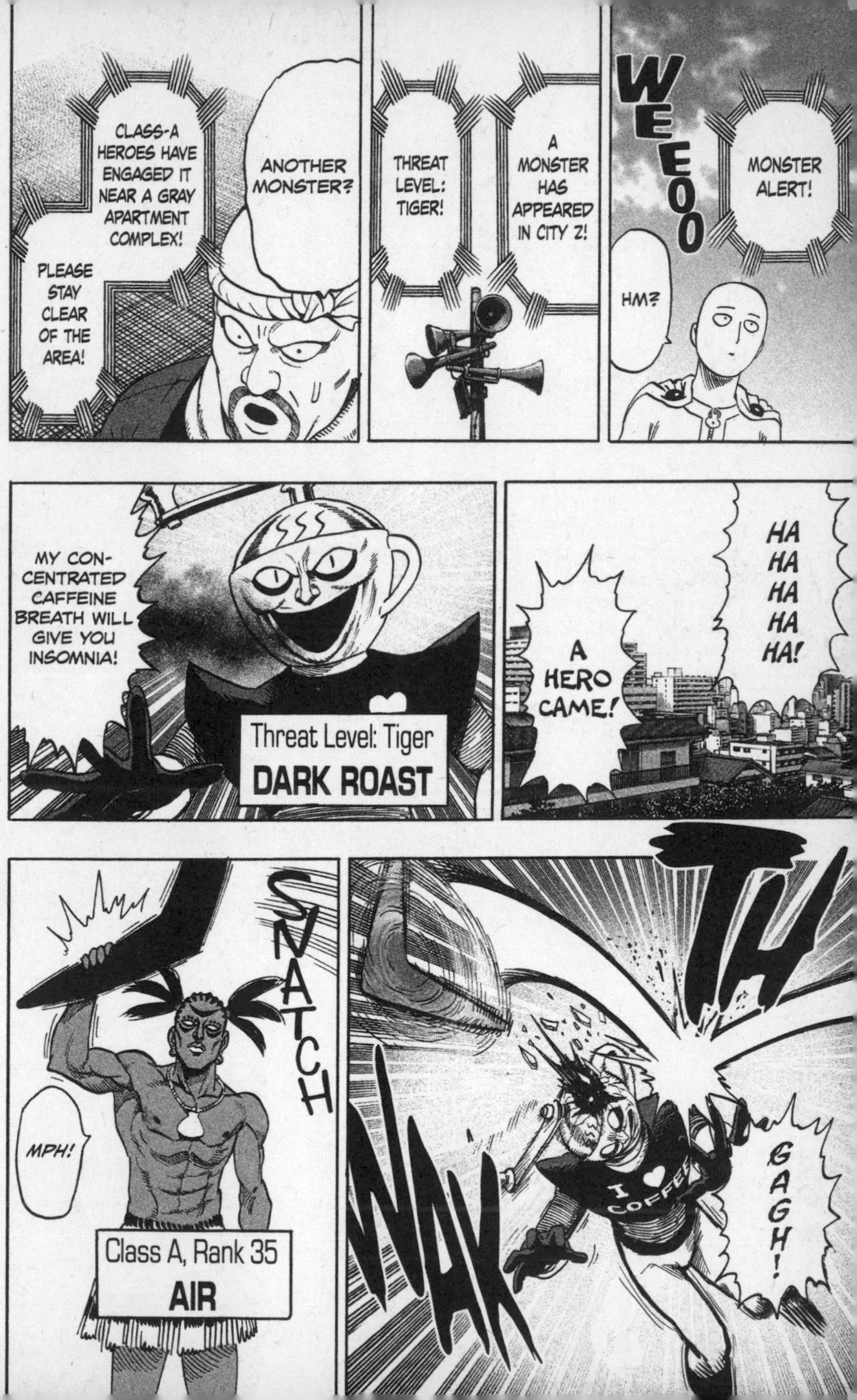
WEEOO
MONSTER ALERT!
HM?
A MONSTER HAS APPEARED IN CITY Z!
THREAT LEVEL: TIGER!
ANOTHER MONSTER?
CLASS-A HEROES HAVE ENGAGED IT NEAR A GRAY APARTMENT COMPLEX!
PLEASE STAY CLEAR OF THE AREA!
HA HA HA HA HA!
A HERO CAME!
MY CON-CENTRATED CAFFEINE BREATH WILL GIVE YOU INSOMNIA!
Threat Level: Tiger
DARK ROAST
THWAK
GAGH!
I ♥ COFFEE
SNATCH
MPH!
Class A, Rank 35
AIR

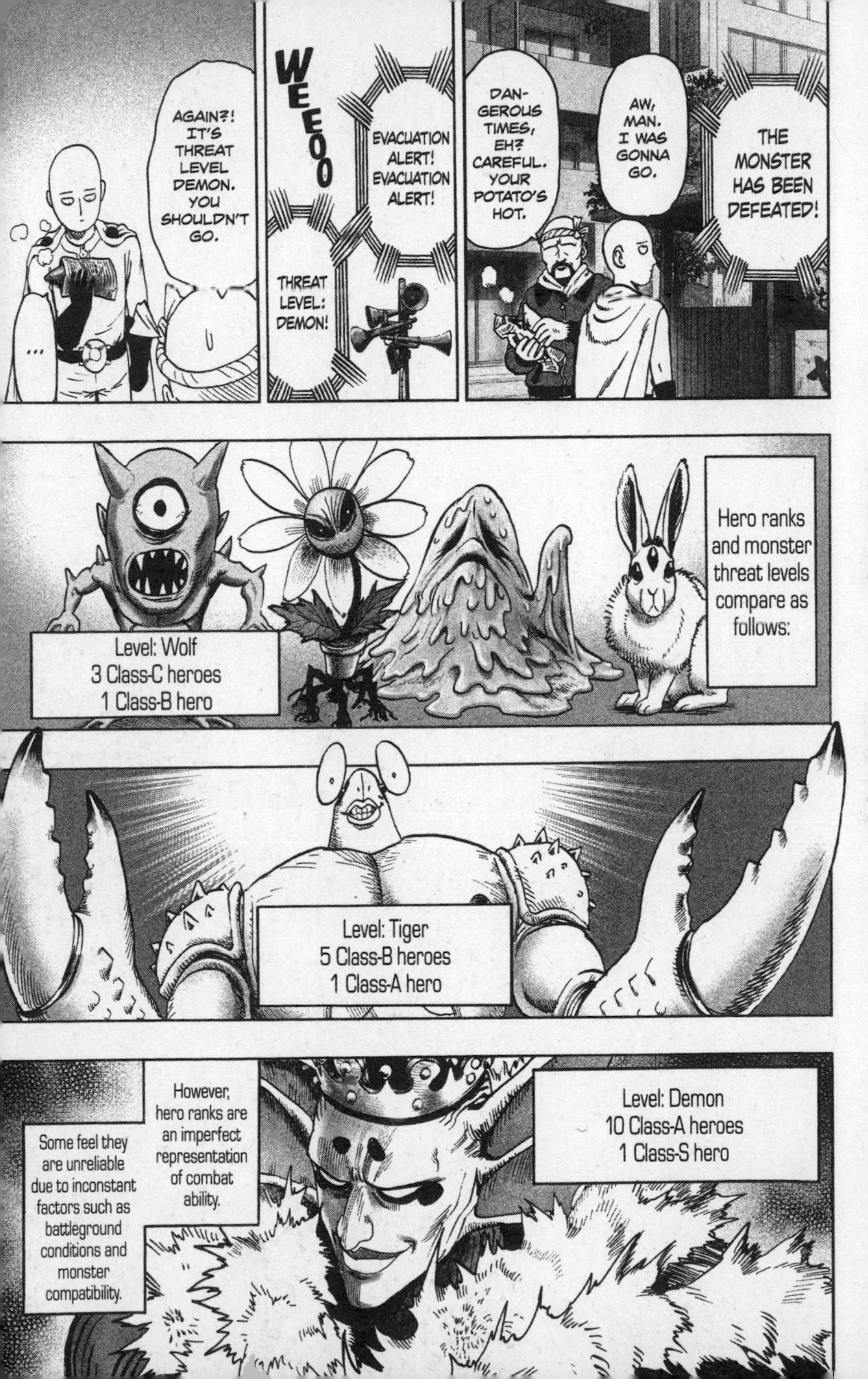
THE MONSTER HAS BEEN DEFEATED!
AW, MAN. I WAS GONNA GO.
DANGEROUS TIMES, EH? CAREFUL. YOUR POTATO'S HOT.
EVACUATION ALERT! EVACUATION ALERT!
WEEOO
THREAT LEVEL: DEMON!
AGAIN?! IT'S THREAT LEVEL DEMON. YOU SHOULDN'T GO.
...
Hero ranks and monster threat levels compare as follows:
Level: Wolf
3 Class-C heroes
1 Class-B hero
Level: Tiger
5 Class-B heroes
1 Class-A hero
Level: Demon
10 Class-A heroes
1 Class-S hero
However, hero ranks are an imperfect representation of combat ability.
Some feel they are unreliable due to inconstant factors such as battleground conditions and monster compatibility.

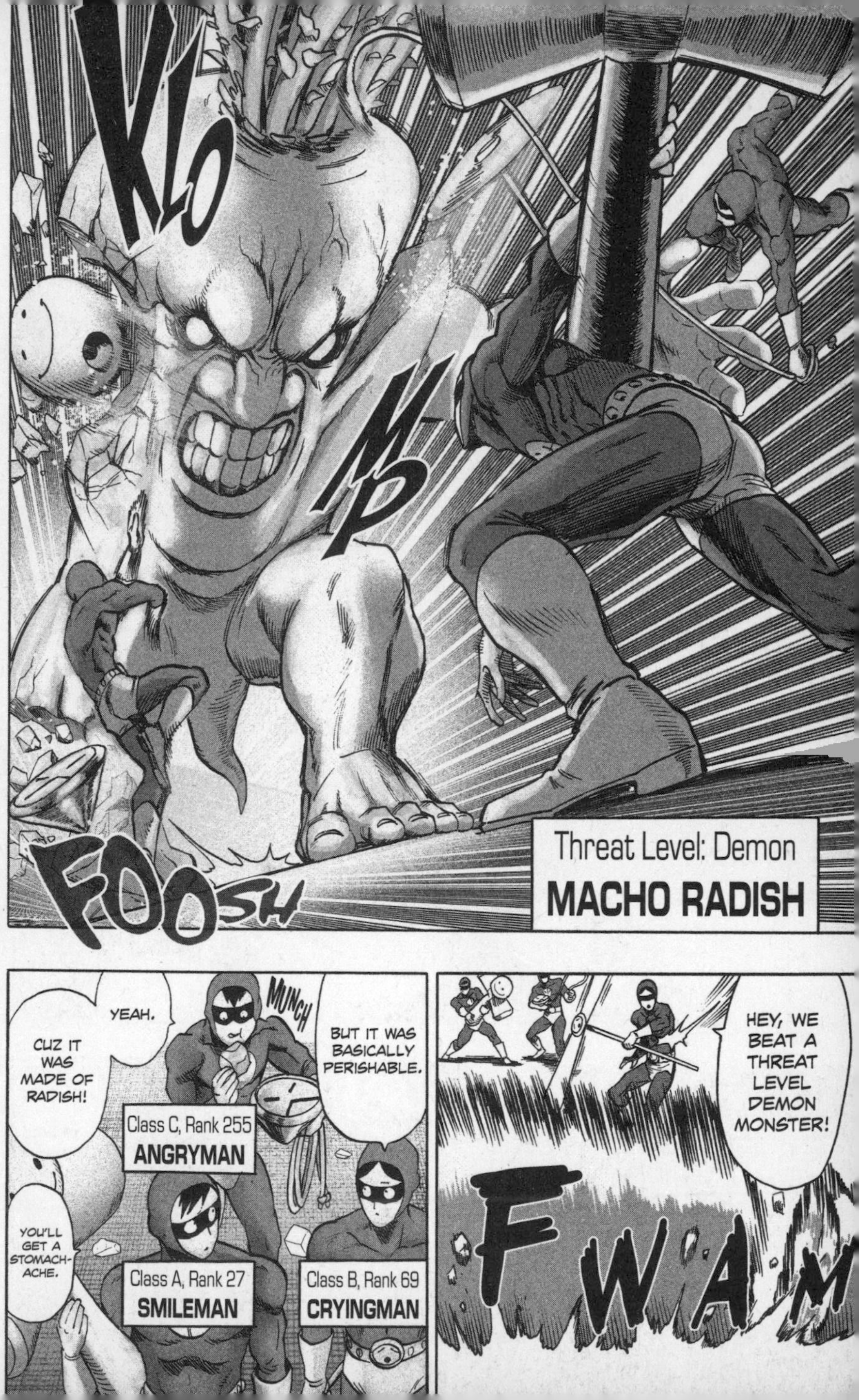
KLOMP
FOOSH
Threat Level: Demon
MACHO RADISH
HEY, WE BEAT A THREAT LEVEL DEMON MONSTER!
FWAM
BUT IT WAS BASICALLY PERISHABLE.
MUNCH
YEAH.
CUZ IT WAS MADE OF RADISH!
Class C, Rank 255
ANGRYMAN
Class B, Rank 69
CRYINGMAN
Class A, Rank 27
SMILEMAN
YOU'LL GET A STOMACH-ACHE.

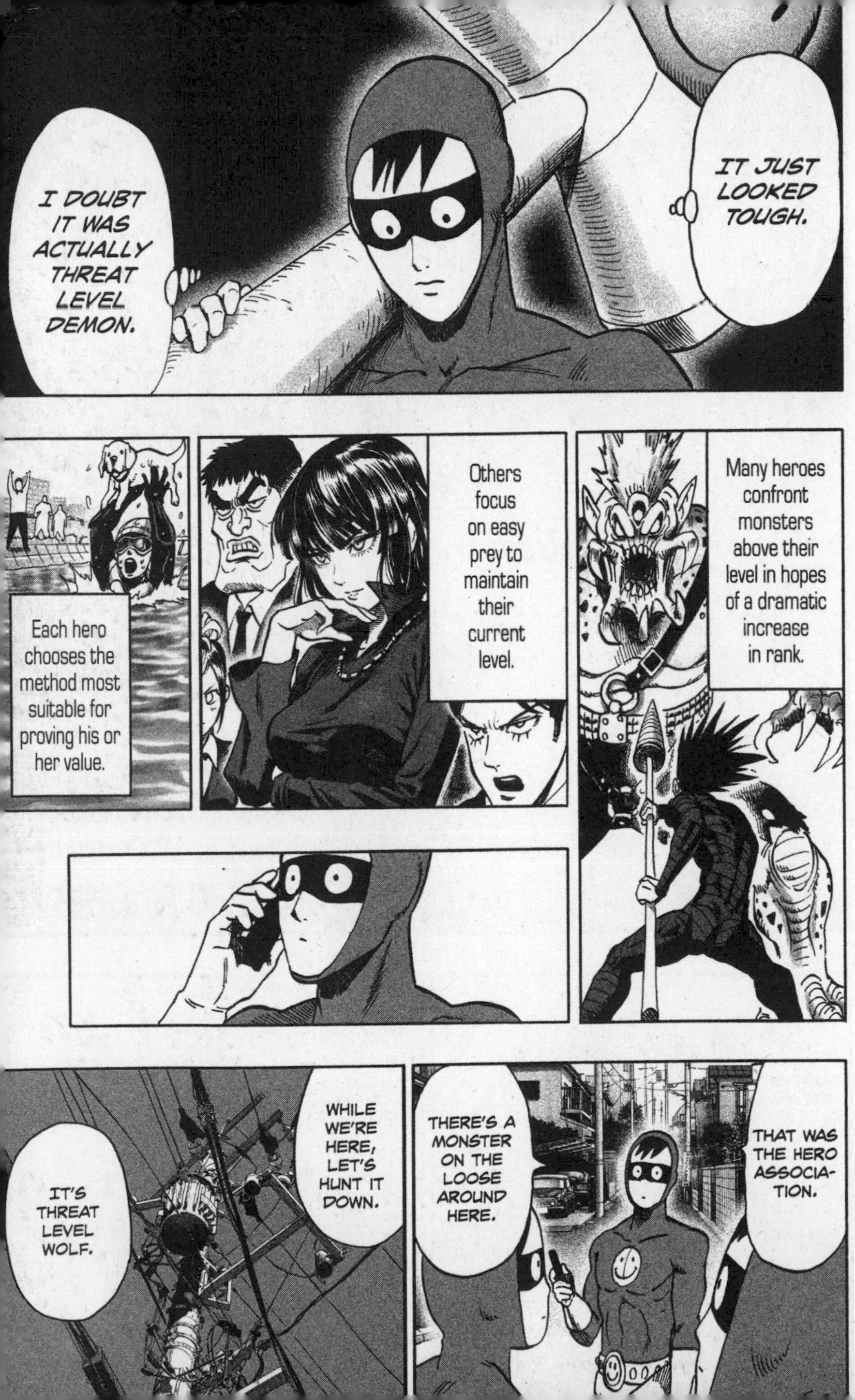
IT JUST LOOKED TOUGH.
I DOUBT IT WAS ACTUALLY THREAT LEVEL DEMON.
Many heroes confront monsters above their level in hopes of a dramatic increase in rank.
Others focus on easy prey to maintain their current level.
Each hero chooses the method most suitable for proving his or her value.
THAT WAS THE HERO ASSOCIATION.
THERE'S A MONSTER ON THE LOOSE AROUND HERE.
WHILE WE'RE HERE, LET'S HUNT IT DOWN.
IT'S THREAT LEVEL WOLF.

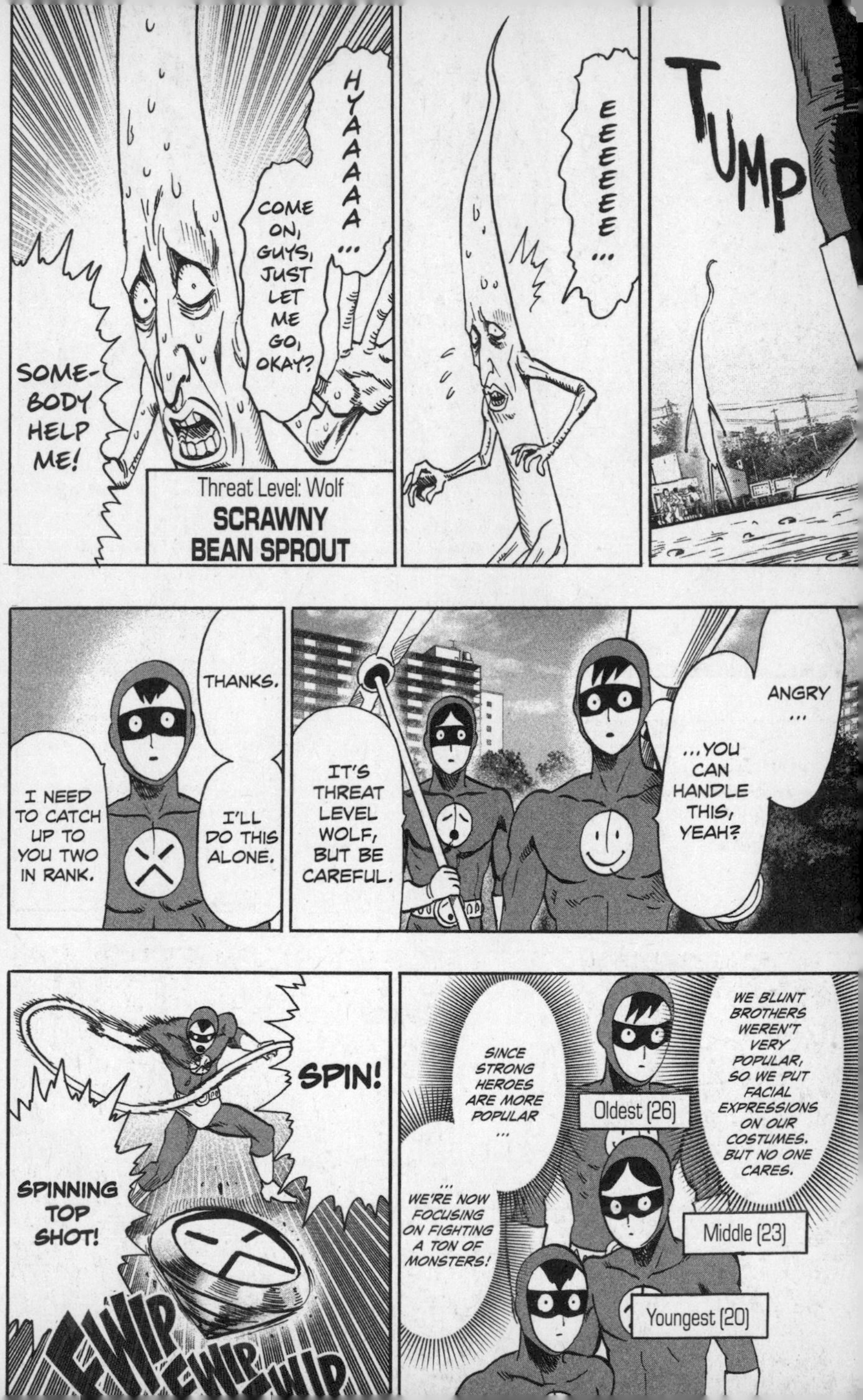
TUMP
EEEEEE...
HYAAAAA...
COME ON, GUYS, JUST LET ME GO, OKAY?
SOME-BODY HELP ME!
Threat Level: Wolf
SCRAWNY BEAN SPROUT
ANGRY...
...YOU CAN HANDLE THIS, YEAH?
IT'S THREAT LEVEL WOLF, BUT BE CAREFUL.
THANKS.
I'LL DO THIS ALONE.
I NEED TO CATCH UP TO YOU TWO IN RANK.
WE BLUNT BROTHERS WEREN'T VERY POPULAR, SO WE PUT FACIAL EXPRESSIONS ON OUR COSTUMES. BUT NO ONE CARES.
SINCE STRONG HEROES ARE MORE POPULAR...
...WE'RE NOW FOCUSING ON FIGHTING A TON OF MONSTERS!
Oldest (26)
Middle (23)
Youngest (20)
SPIN!
SPINNING TOP SHOT!

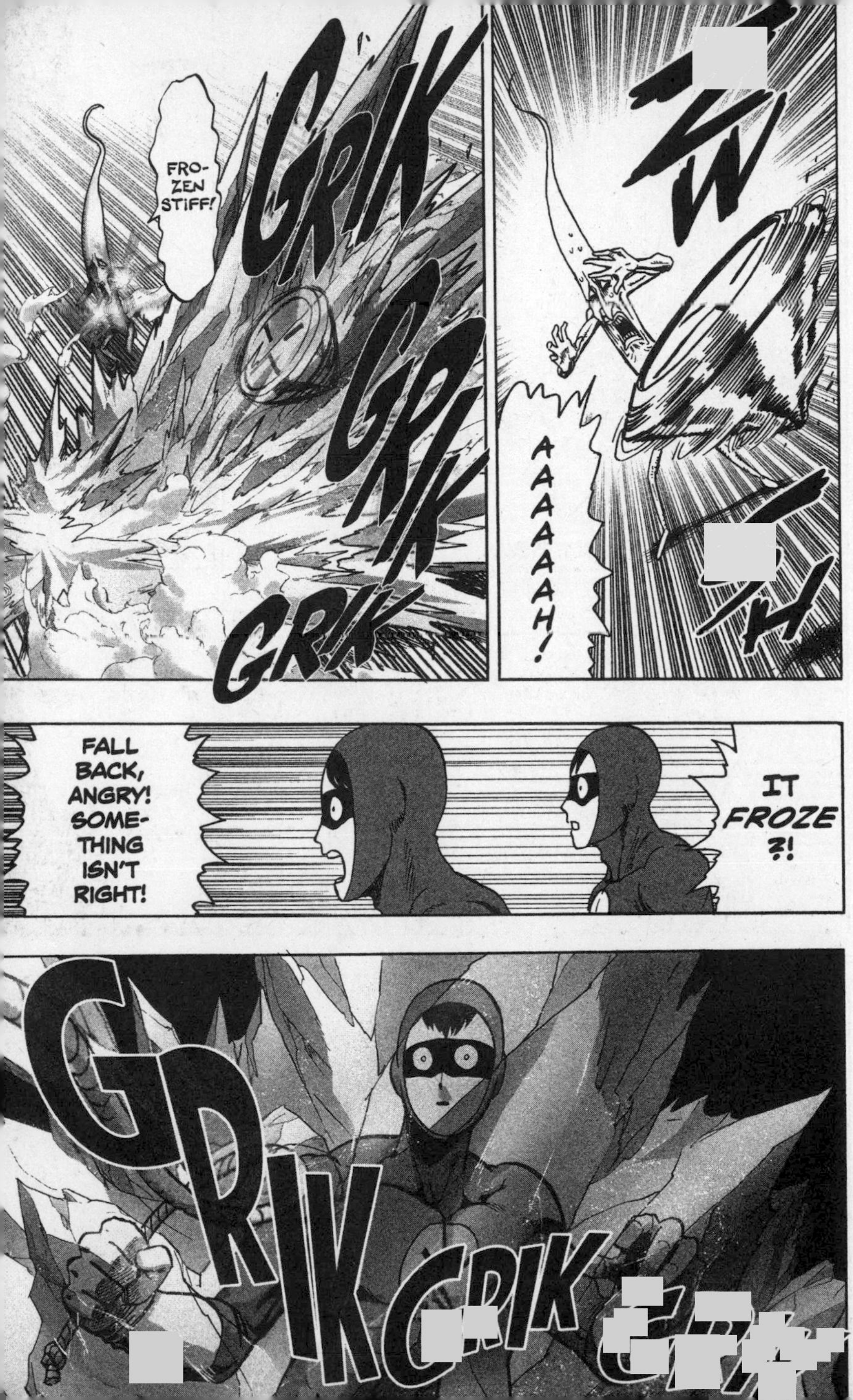
AAAAAAAH!
FRO-ZEN STIFF!
GRIK GRIK GRIK
IT FROZE?!
FALL BACK, ANGRY! SOME-THING ISN'T RIGHT!
GRIK
CRIK

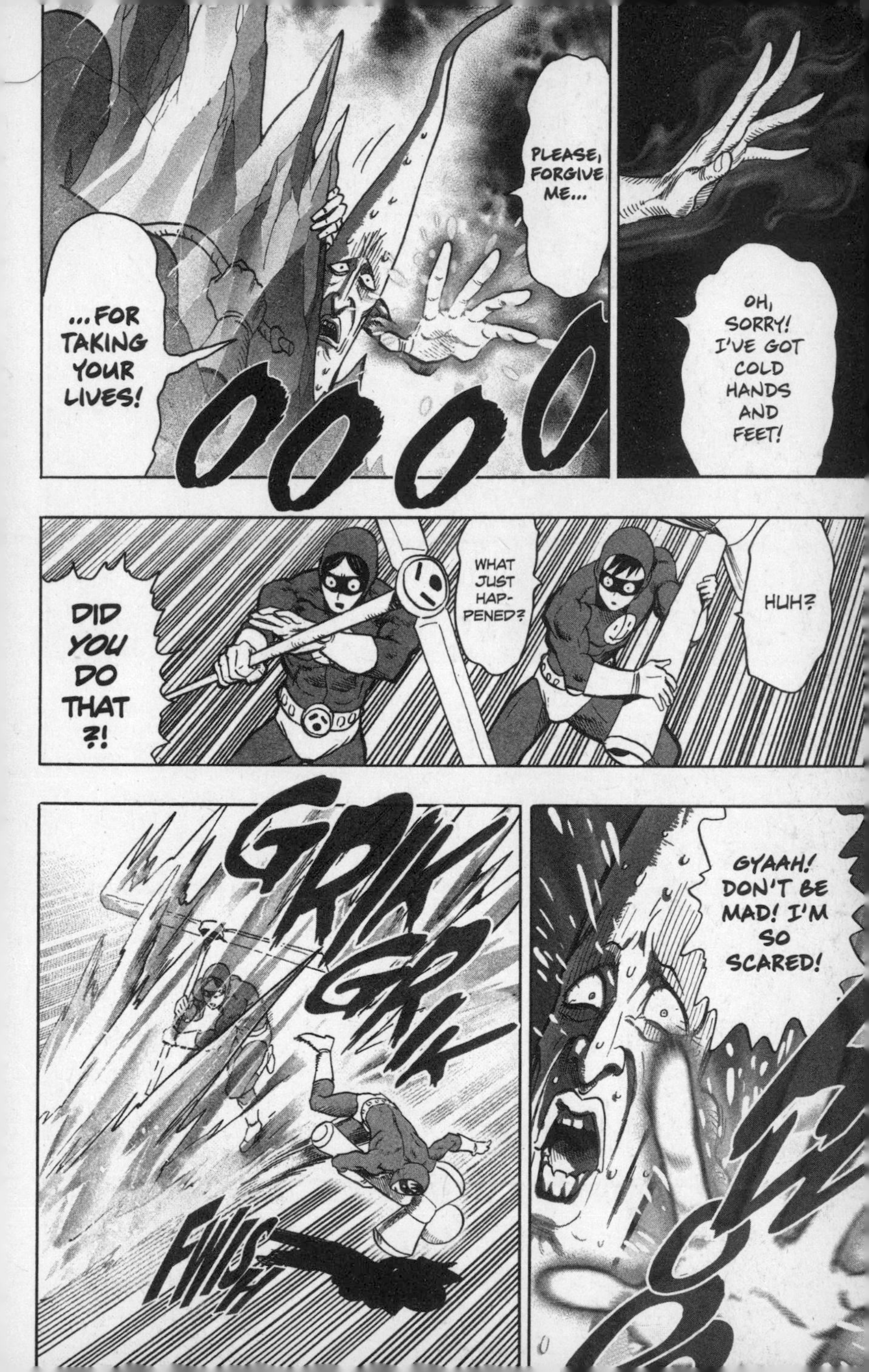
OH, SORRY! I'VE GOT COLD HANDS AND FEET!
PLEASE, FORGIVE ME...
...FOR TAKING YOUR LIVES!
OOOO
HUH?
WHAT JUST HAP-PENED?
DID YOU DO THAT?!
GYAAH! DON'T BE MAD! I'M SO SCARED!
GRIK GRIK
FWISH

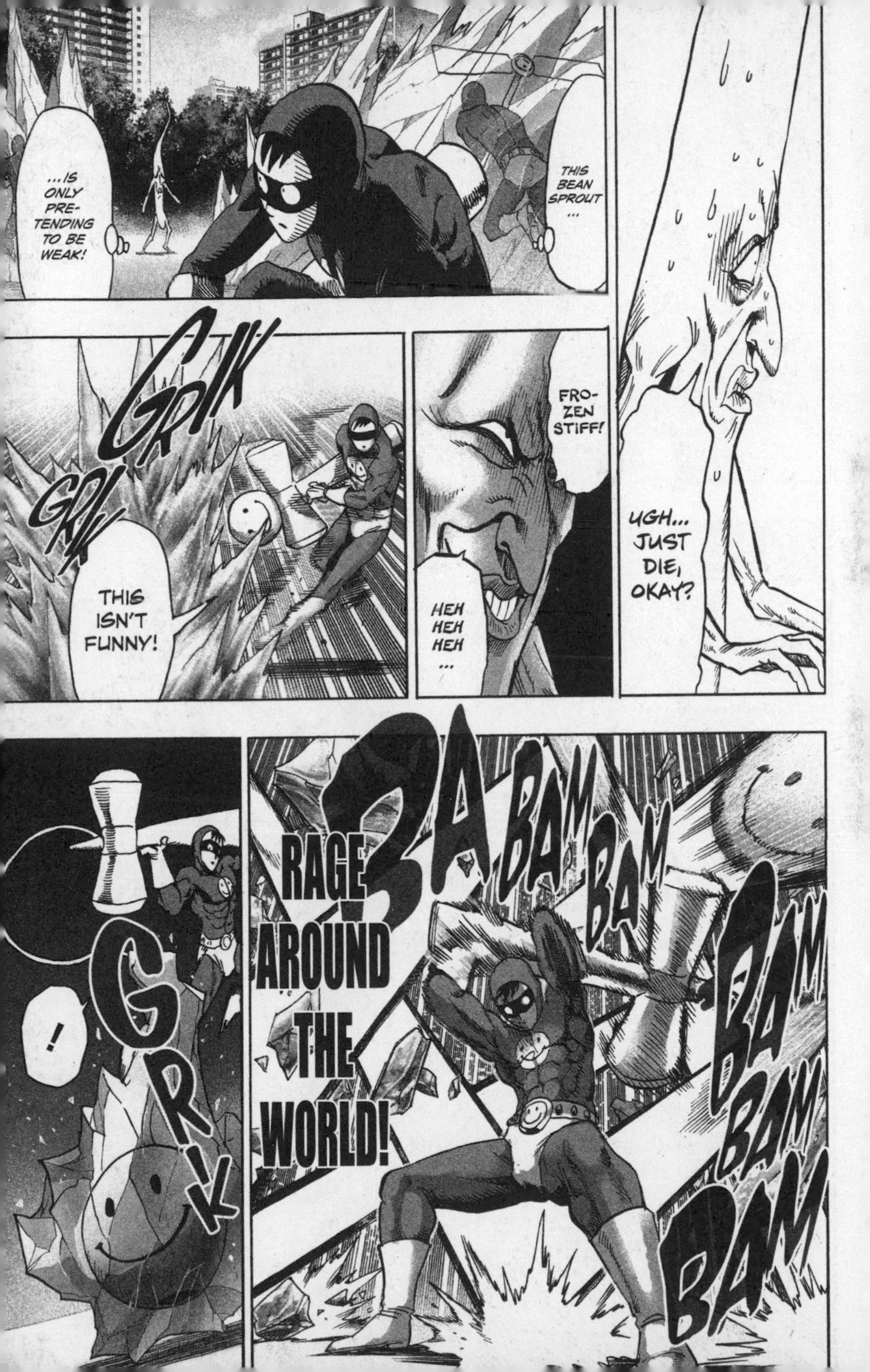
UGH... JUST DIE, OKAY?
THIS BEAN SPROUT ...
...IS ONLY PRE-TENDING TO BE WEAK!
FRO-ZEN STIFF!
HEH HEH HEH ...
GRIK
GRIK
THIS ISN'T FUNNY!
BABAM
BAM
BAM
RAGE AROUND THE WORLD!
BAM
BABAM
BAM
GRIK
!

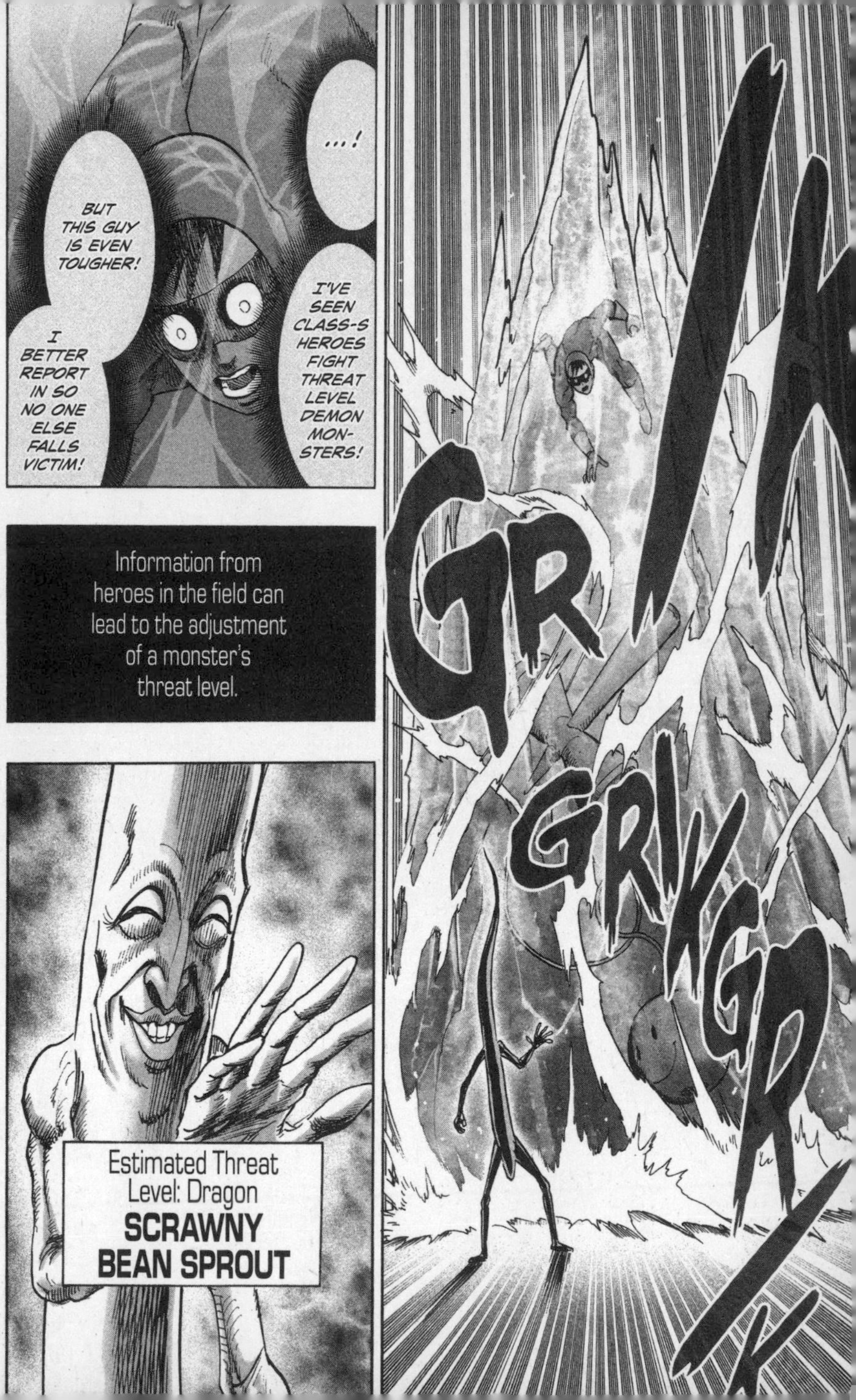
GR
GRKGR
...!
I'VE SEEN CLASS-S HEROES FIGHT THREAT LEVEL DEMON MON-STERS!
BUT THIS GUY IS EVEN TOUGHER!
I BETTER REPORT IN SO NO ONE ELSE FALLS VICTIM!
Information from heroes in the field can lead to the adjustment of a monster's threat level.
Estimated Threat Level: Dragon
SCRAWNY BEAN SPROUT

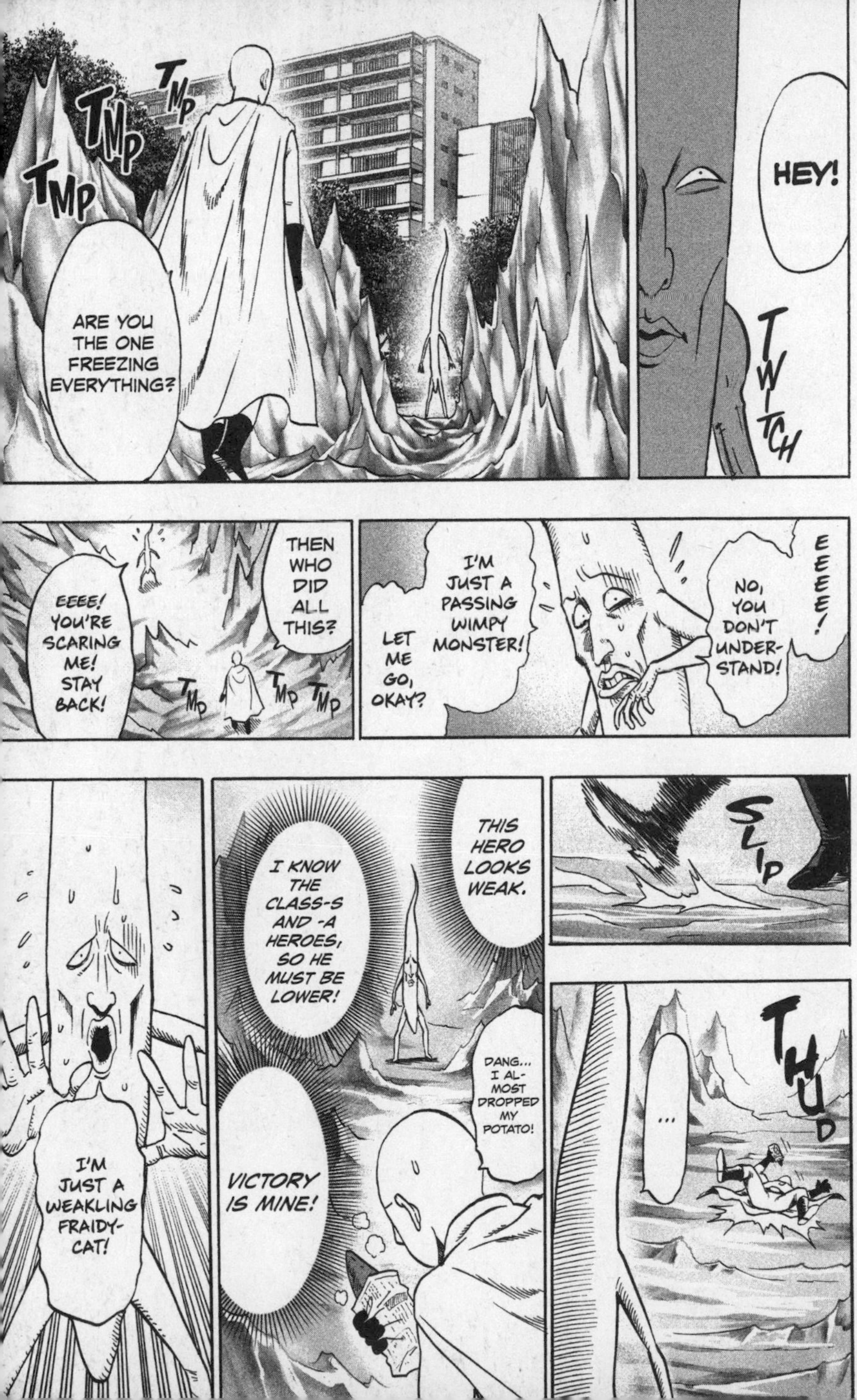
HEY!
TWITCH
TMP
TMP
TMP
ARE YOU THE ONE FREEZING EVERYTHING?
EEEE!
NO, YOU DON'T UNDER-STAND!
I'M JUST A PASSING WIMPY MONSTER!
LET ME GO, OKAY?
THEN WHO DID ALL THIS?
EEEE! YOU'RE SCARING ME! STAY BACK!
TMP TMP TMP
SLIP
THUD
...
THIS HERO LOOKS WEAK.
I KNOW THE CLASS-S AND -A HEROES, SO HE MUST BE LOWER!
DANG... I AL-MOST DROPPED MY POTATO!
VICTORY IS MINE!
I'M JUST A WEAKLING FRAIDY-CAT!

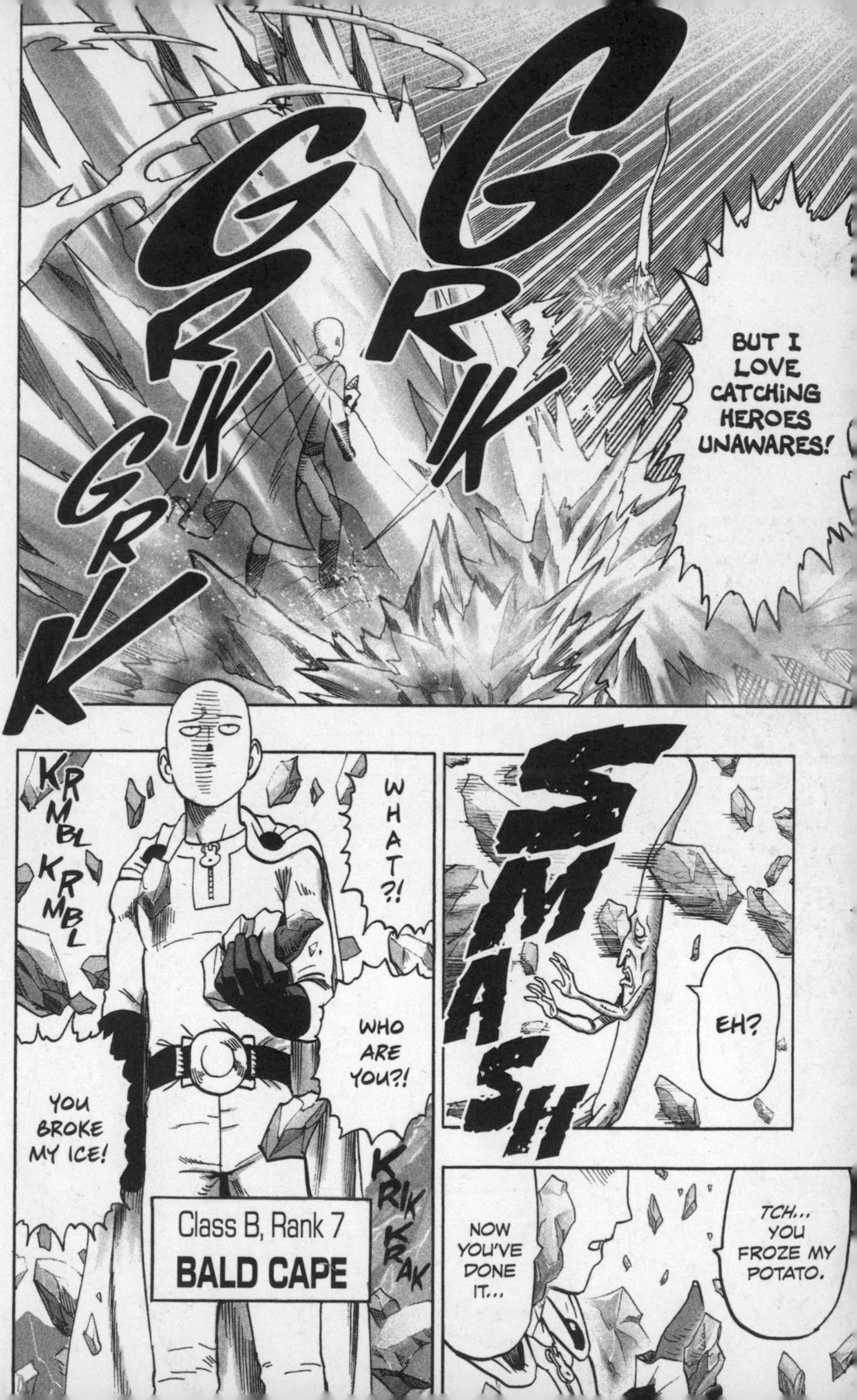

GRIK
GRIK
GRIK
BUT I LOVE CATCHING HEROES UNAWARES!
SMASH
EH?
TCH... YOU FROZE MY POTATO.
NOW YOU'VE DONE IT...
WHAT?!
KRMBL KRMBL
WHO ARE YOU?!
YOU BROKE MY ICE!
Class B, Rank 7
BALD CAPE
KRIK KRAK

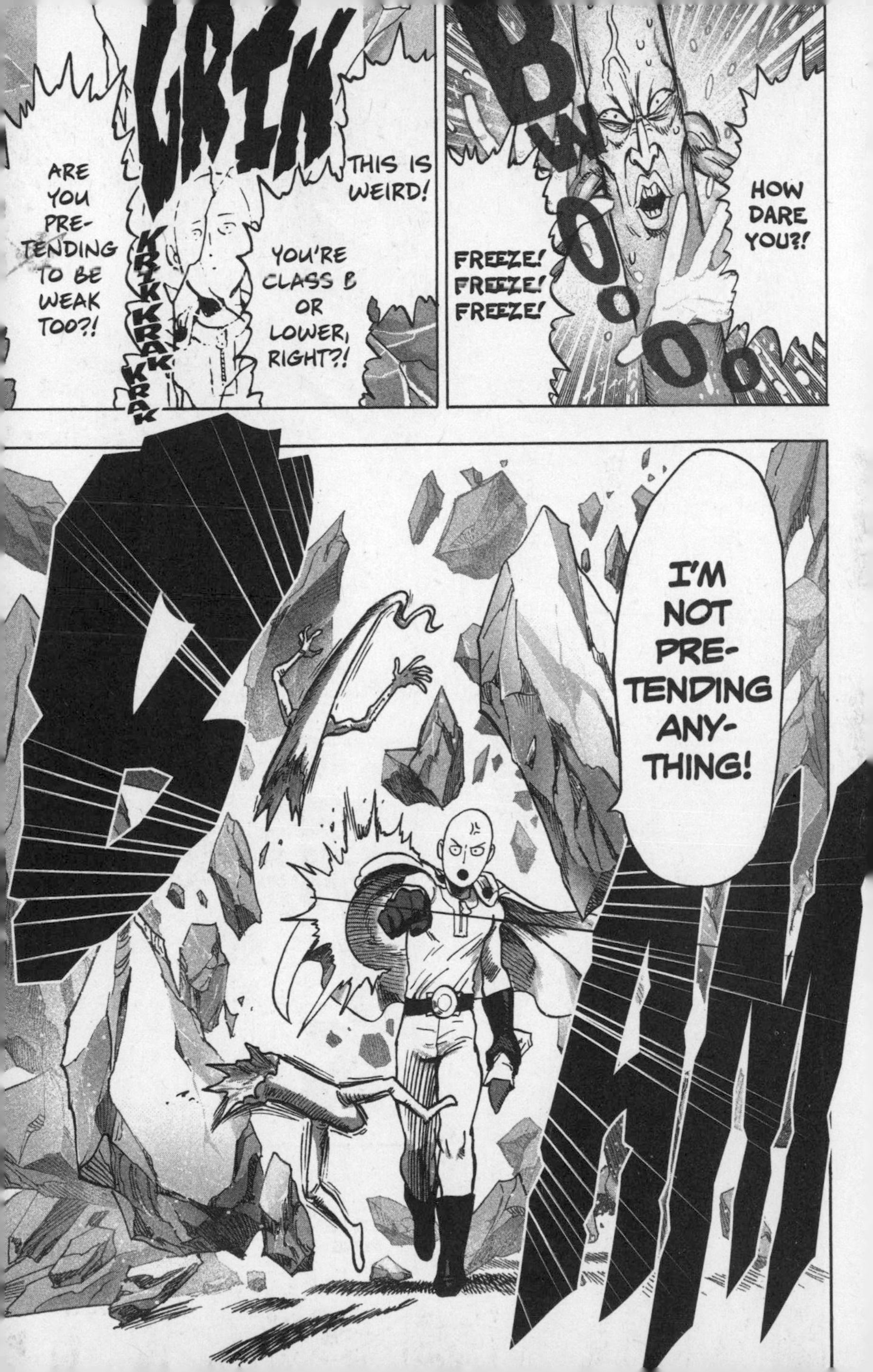
BWOOOO
HOW DARE YOU?!
FREEZE! FREEZE! FREEZE!
GRIK
THIS IS WEIRD!
YOU'RE CLASS B OR LOWER, RIGHT?!
KRIK KRAK KRAK KRAK
ARE YOU PRETENDING TO BE WEAK TOO?!
I'M NOT PRETENDING ANYTHING!

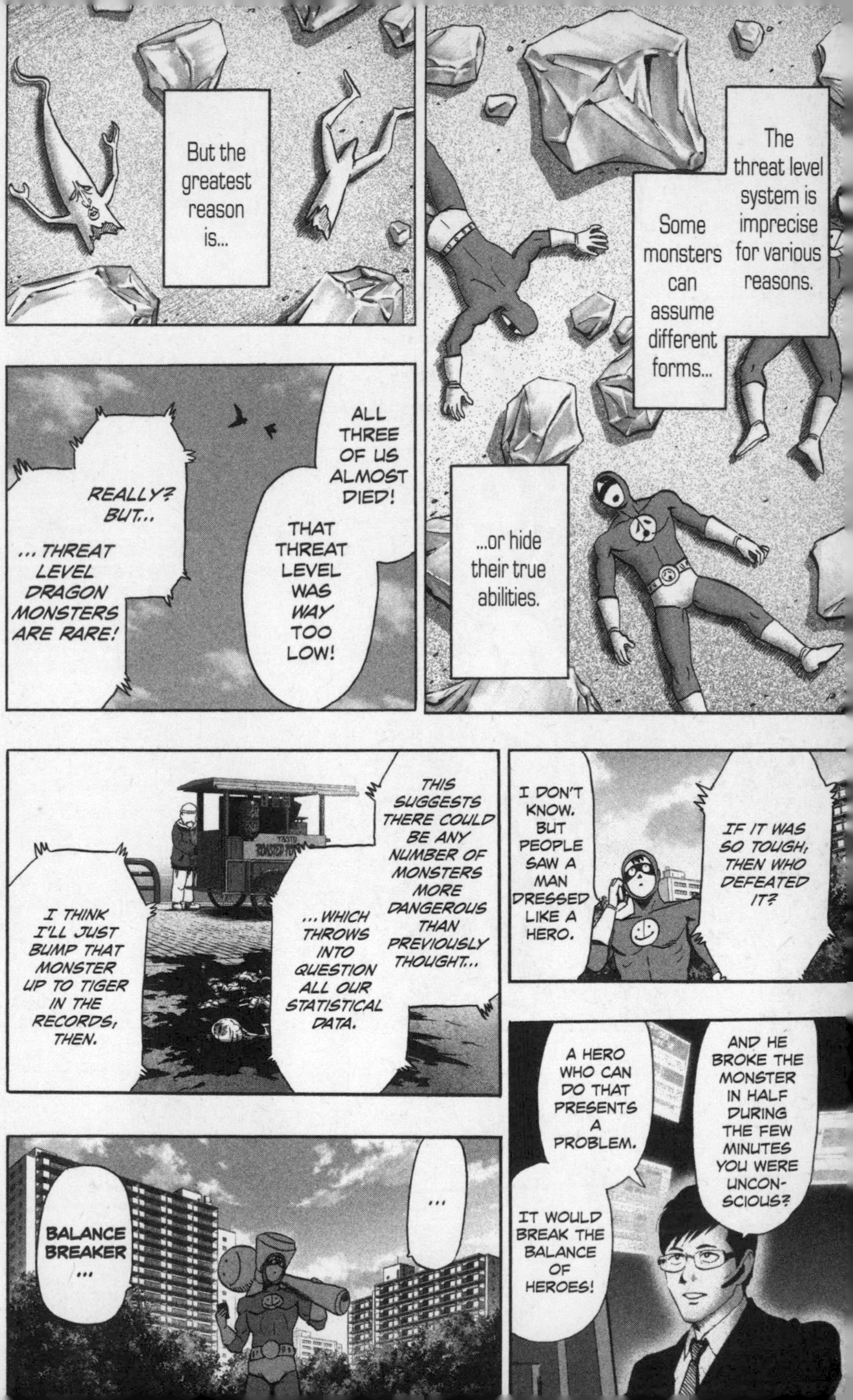
The threat level system is imprecise for various reasons.
Some monsters can assume different forms...
...or hide their true abilities.
But the greatest reason is...
ALL THREE OF US ALMOST DIED!
THAT THREAT LEVEL WAS WAY TOO LOW!
REALLY? BUT...
...THREAT LEVEL DRAGON MONSTERS ARE RARE!
IF IT WAS SO TOUGH, THEN WHO DEFEATED IT?
I DON'T KNOW. BUT PEOPLE SAW A MAN DRESSED LIKE A HERO.
THIS SUGGESTS THERE COULD BE ANY NUMBER OF MONSTERS MORE DANGEROUS THAN PREVIOUSLY THOUGHT...
...WHICH THROWS INTO QUESTION ALL OUR STATISTICAL DATA.
I THINK I'LL JUST BUMP THAT MONSTER UP TO TIGER IN THE RECORDS, THEN.
AND HE BROKE THE MONSTER IN HALF DURING THE FEW MINUTES YOU WERE UNCONSCIOUS?
A HERO WHO CAN DO THAT PRESENTS A PROBLEM.
IT WOULD BREAK THE BALANCE OF HEROES!
...
BALANCE BREAKER...

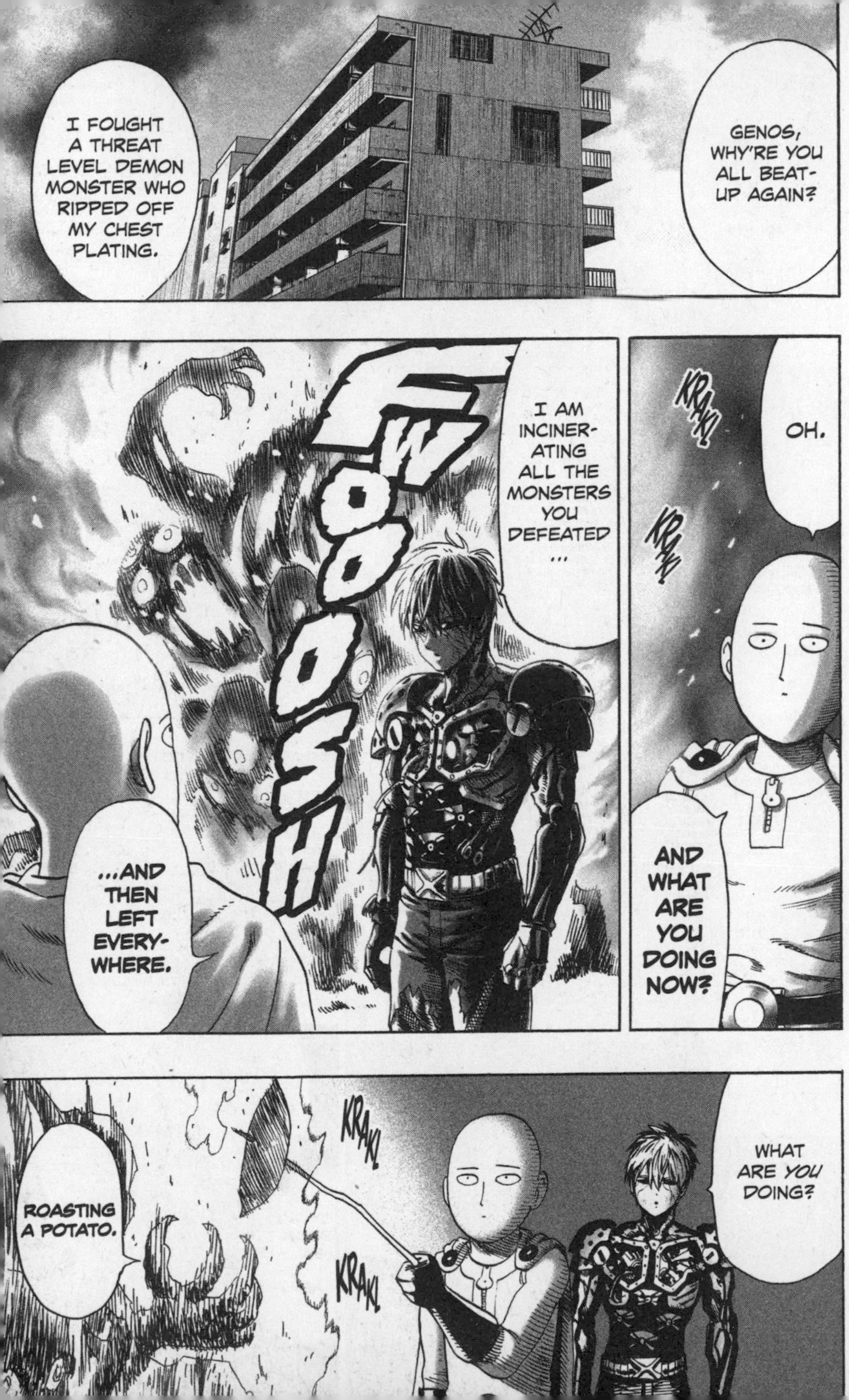
GENOS, WHY'RE YOU ALL BEAT-UP AGAIN?
I FOUGHT A THREAT LEVEL DEMON MONSTER WHO RIPPED OFF MY CHEST PLATING.
KRAK!
OH.
KRAK!
AND WHAT ARE YOU DOING NOW?
I AM INCINER-ATING ALL THE MONSTERS YOU DEFEATED ...
FWOOOSH
...AND THEN LEFT EVERY-WHERE.
WHAT ARE *YOU* DOING?
KRAK!
KRAK!
ROASTING A POTATO.

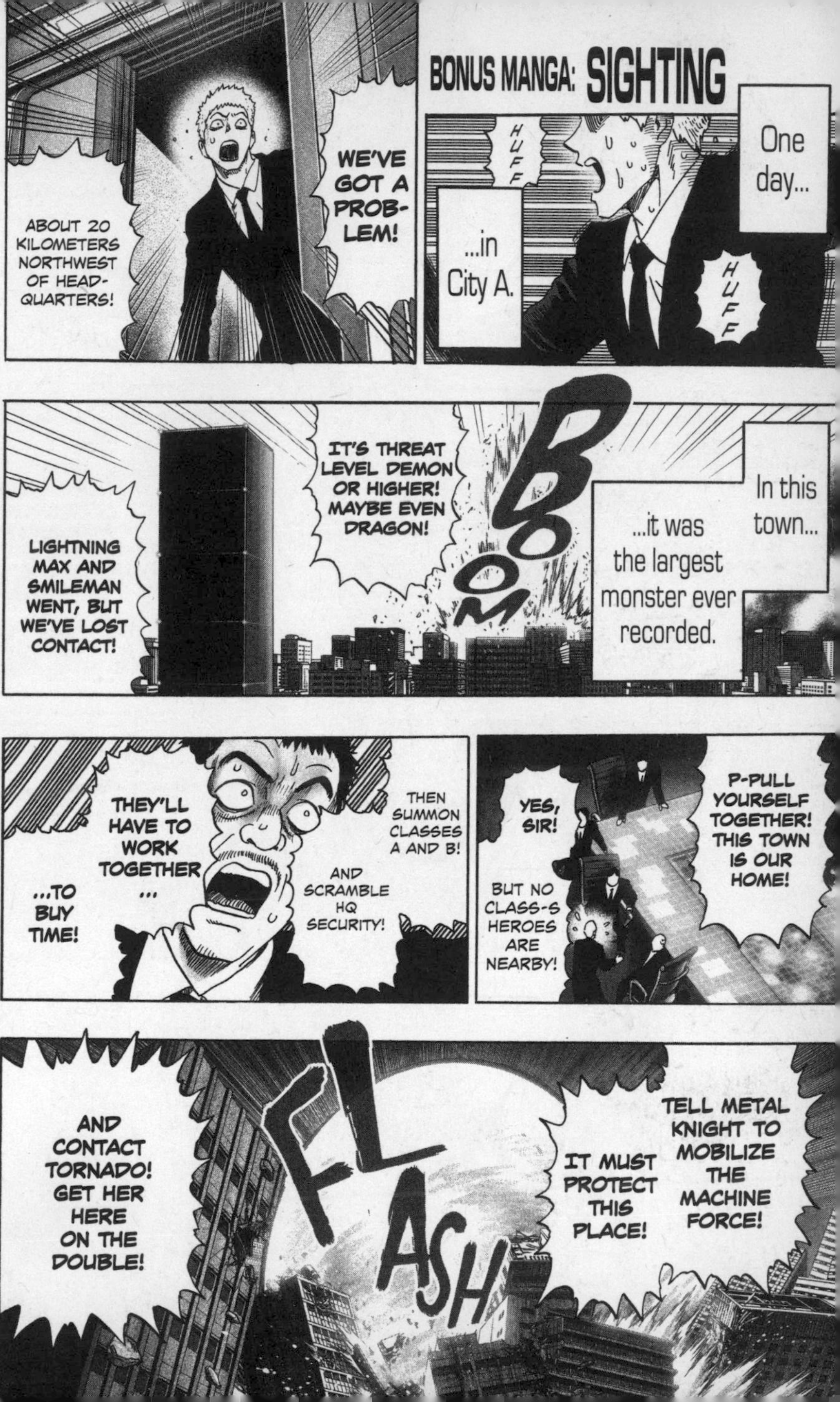
BONUS MANGA: SIGHTING
One day...
...in City A.
HUFF
HUFF
WE'VE GOT A PROB-LEM!
ABOUT 20 KILOMETERS NORTHWEST OF HEAD-QUARTERS!
In this town...
...it was the largest monster ever recorded.
BOOM
IT'S THREAT LEVEL DEMON OR HIGHER! MAYBE EVEN DRAGON!
LIGHTNING MAX AND SMILEMAN WENT, BUT WE'VE LOST CONTACT!
P-PULL YOURSELF TOGETHER! THIS TOWN IS OUR HOME!
YES, SIR!
BUT NO CLASS-S HEROES ARE NEARBY!
THEN SUMMON CLASSES A AND B!
AND SCRAMBLE HQ SECURITY!
THEY'LL HAVE TO WORK TOGETHER...
...TO BUY TIME!
TELL METAL KNIGHT TO MOBILIZE THE MACHINE FORCE!
IT MUST PROTECT THIS PLACE!
FLASH
AND CONTACT TORNADO! GET HER HERE ON THE DOUBLE!

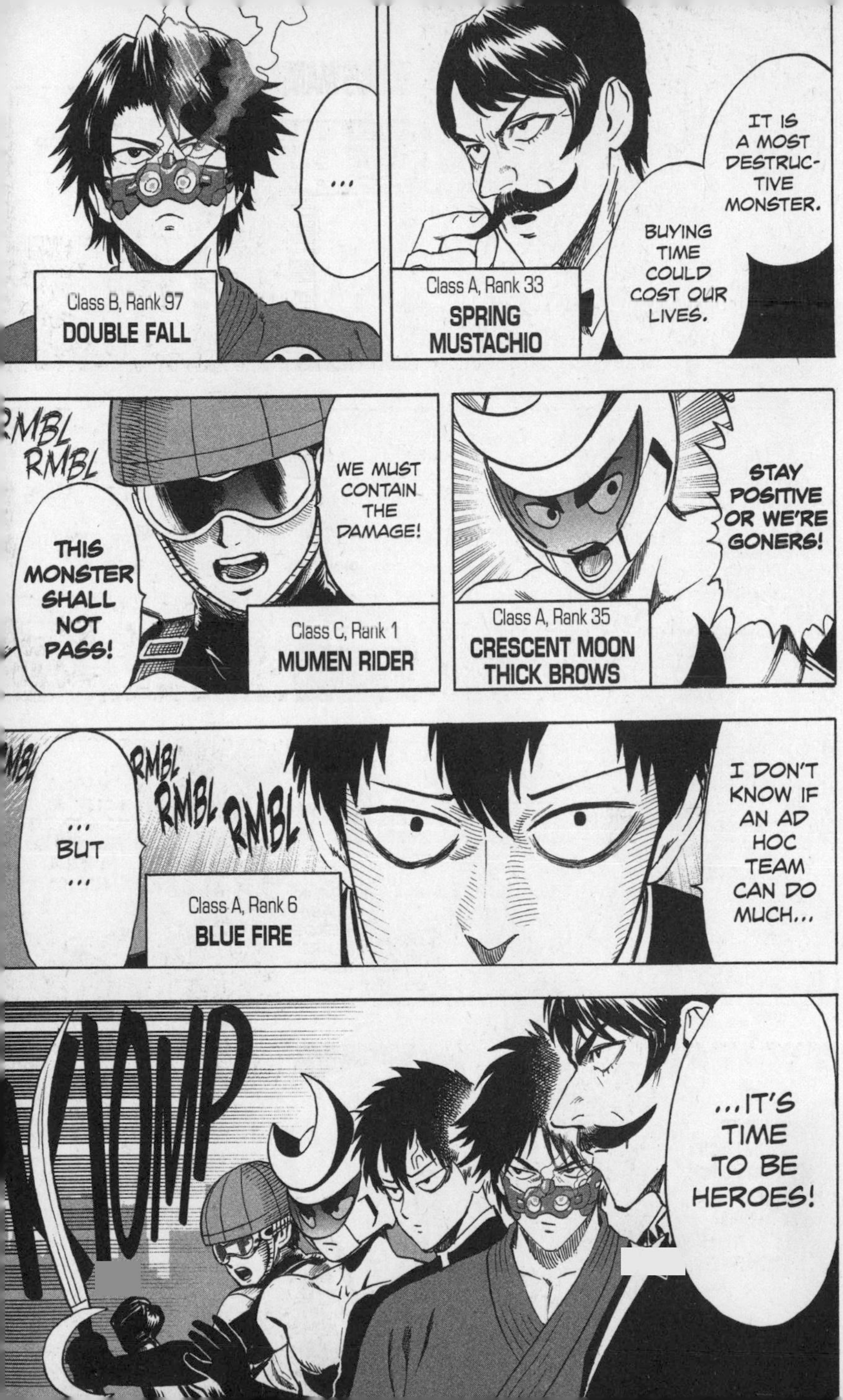
IT IS A MOST DESTRUC-TIVE MONSTER.
BUYING TIME COULD COST OUR LIVES.
Class A, Rank 33
SPRING MUSTACHIO
...
Class B, Rank 97
DOUBLE FALL
STAY POSITIVE OR WE'RE GONERS!
Class A, Rank 35
CRESCENT MOON THICK BROWS
WE MUST CONTAIN THE DAMAGE!
RMBL RMBL
THIS MONSTER SHALL NOT PASS!
Class C, Rank 1
MUMEN RIDER
I DON'T KNOW IF AN AD HOC TEAM CAN DO MUCH...
RMBL RMBL RMBL
MBL
... BUT ...
Class A, Rank 6
BLUE FIRE
...IT'S TIME TO BE HEROES!
TOMP

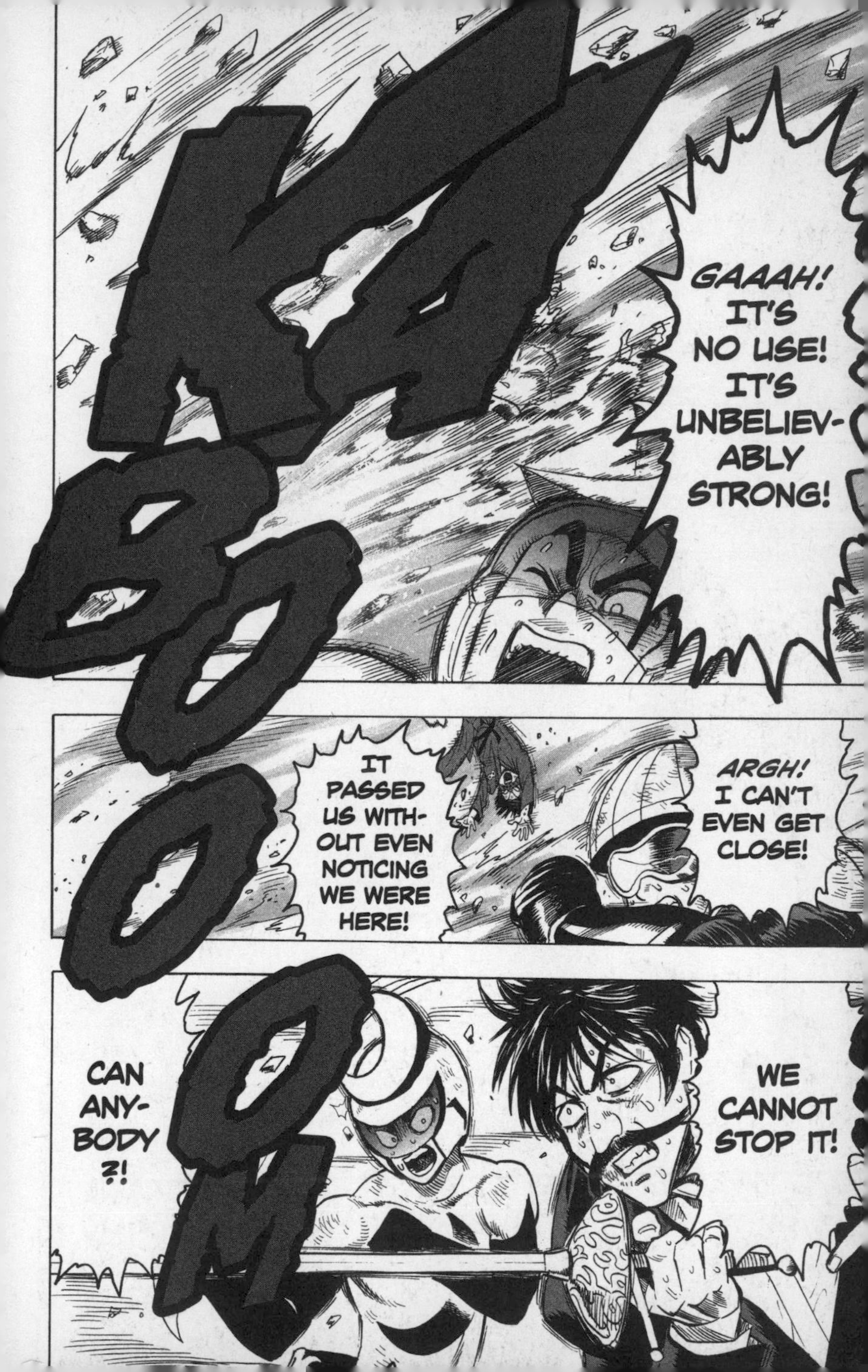
KABOOOM
GAAAH! IT'S NO USE! IT'S UNBELIEV-ABLY STRONG!
ARGH! I CAN'T EVEN GET CLOSE!
IT PASSED US WITH-OUT EVEN NOTICING WE WERE HERE!
WE CANNOT STOP IT!
CAN ANY-BODY ?!

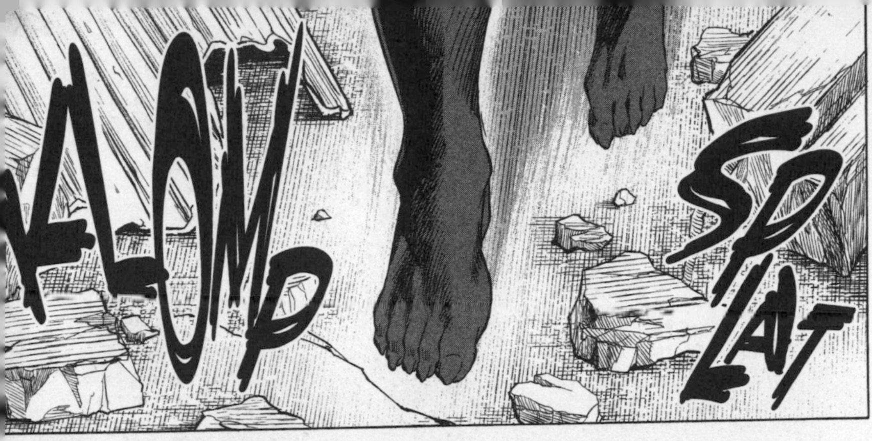
SPLAT
KLOMP
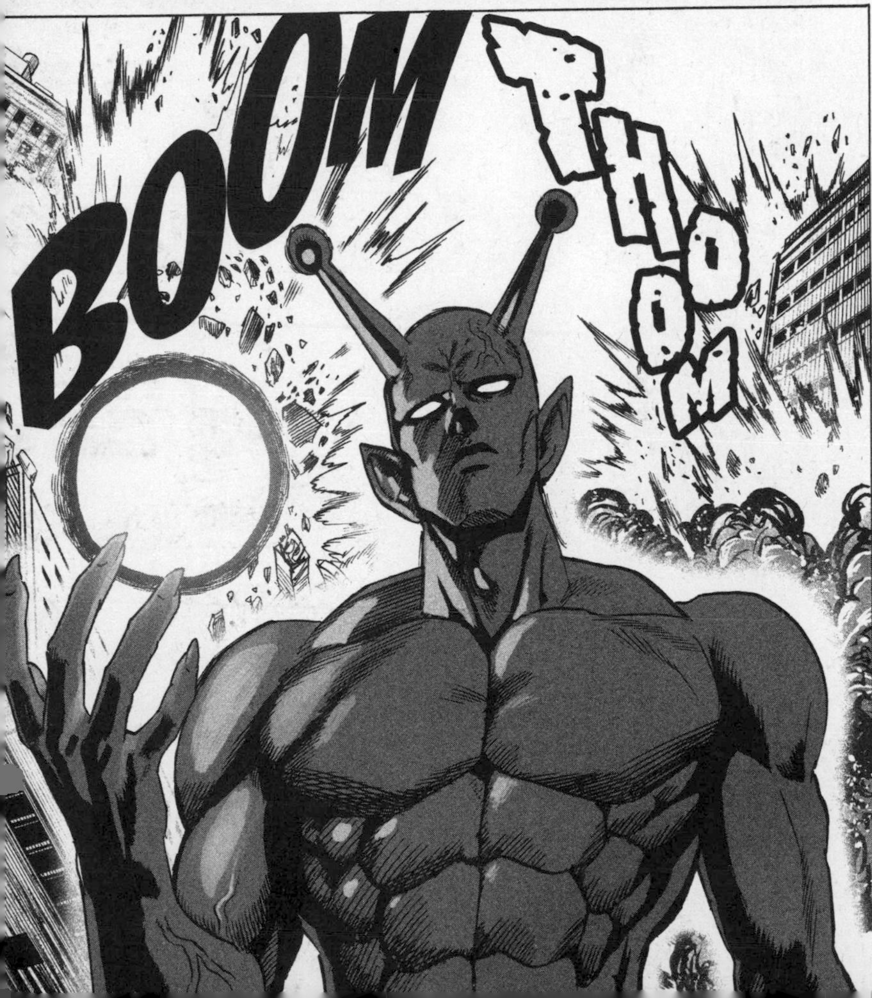
THOOOM
BOOM

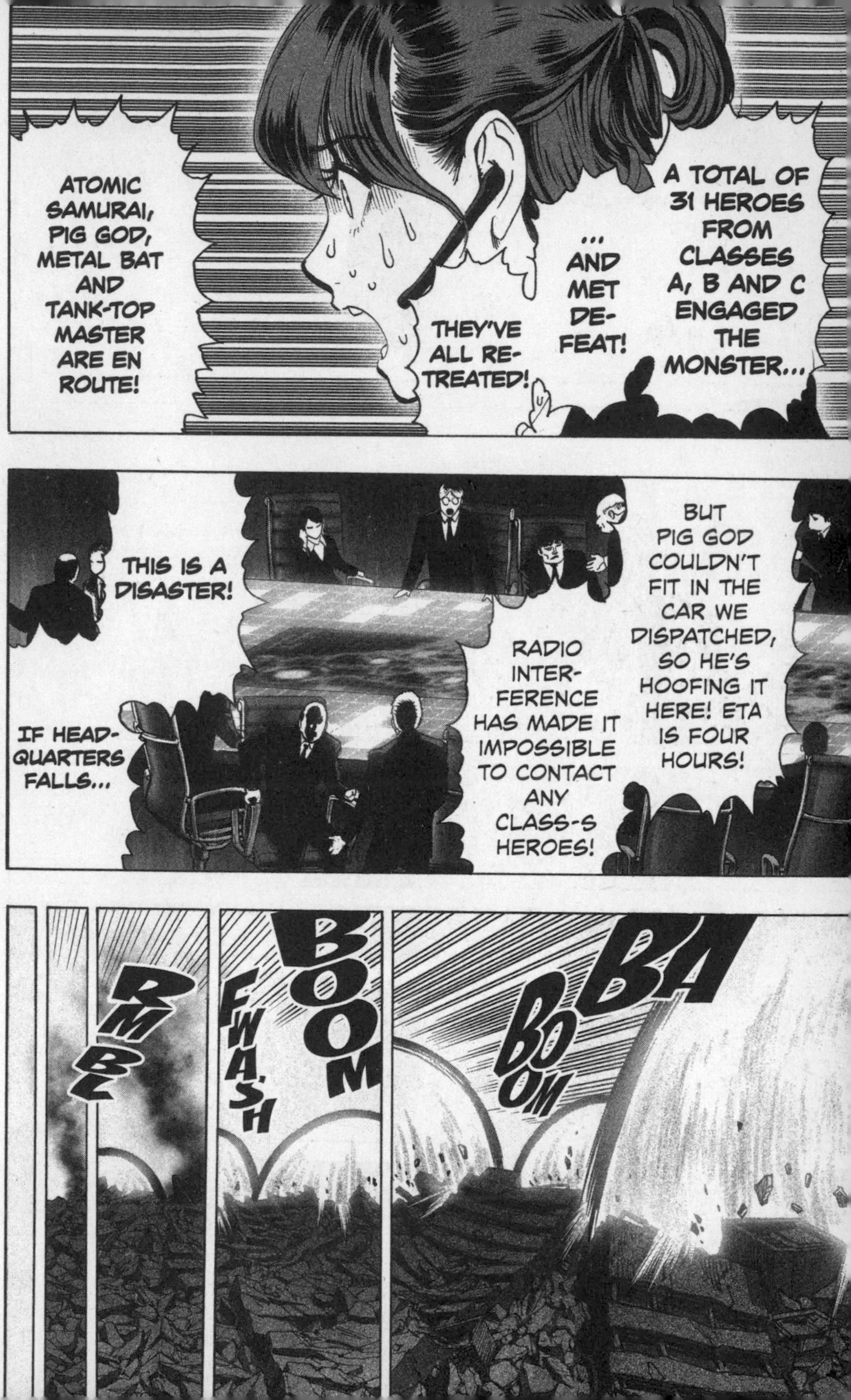
A TOTAL OF 31 HEROES FROM CLASSES A, B AND C ENGAGED THE MONSTER...
...AND MET DEFEAT!
THEY'VE ALL RETREATED!
ATOMIC SAMURAI, PIG GOD, METAL BAT AND TANK-TOP MASTER ARE EN ROUTE!
BUT PIG GOD COULDN'T FIT IN THE CAR WE DISPATCHED, SO HE'S HOOFING IT HERE! ETA IS FOUR HOURS!
RADIO INTERFERENCE HAS MADE IT IMPOSSIBLE TO CONTACT ANY CLASS-S HEROES!
THIS IS A DISASTER!
IF HEADQUARTERS FALLS...
BA
BOBOOM
BOOM
FWASH
RMBL

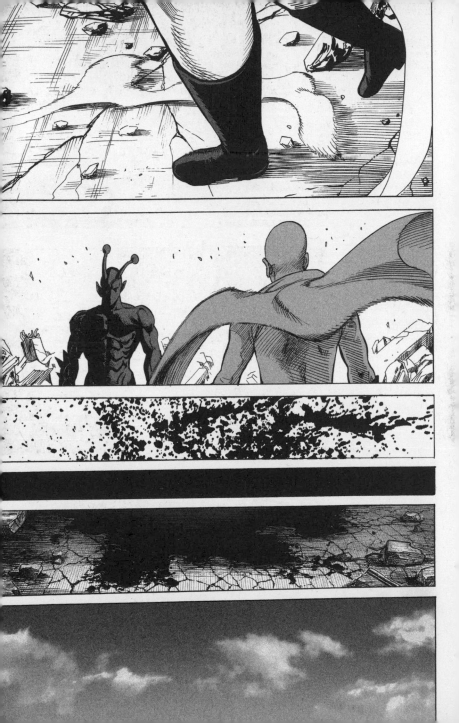

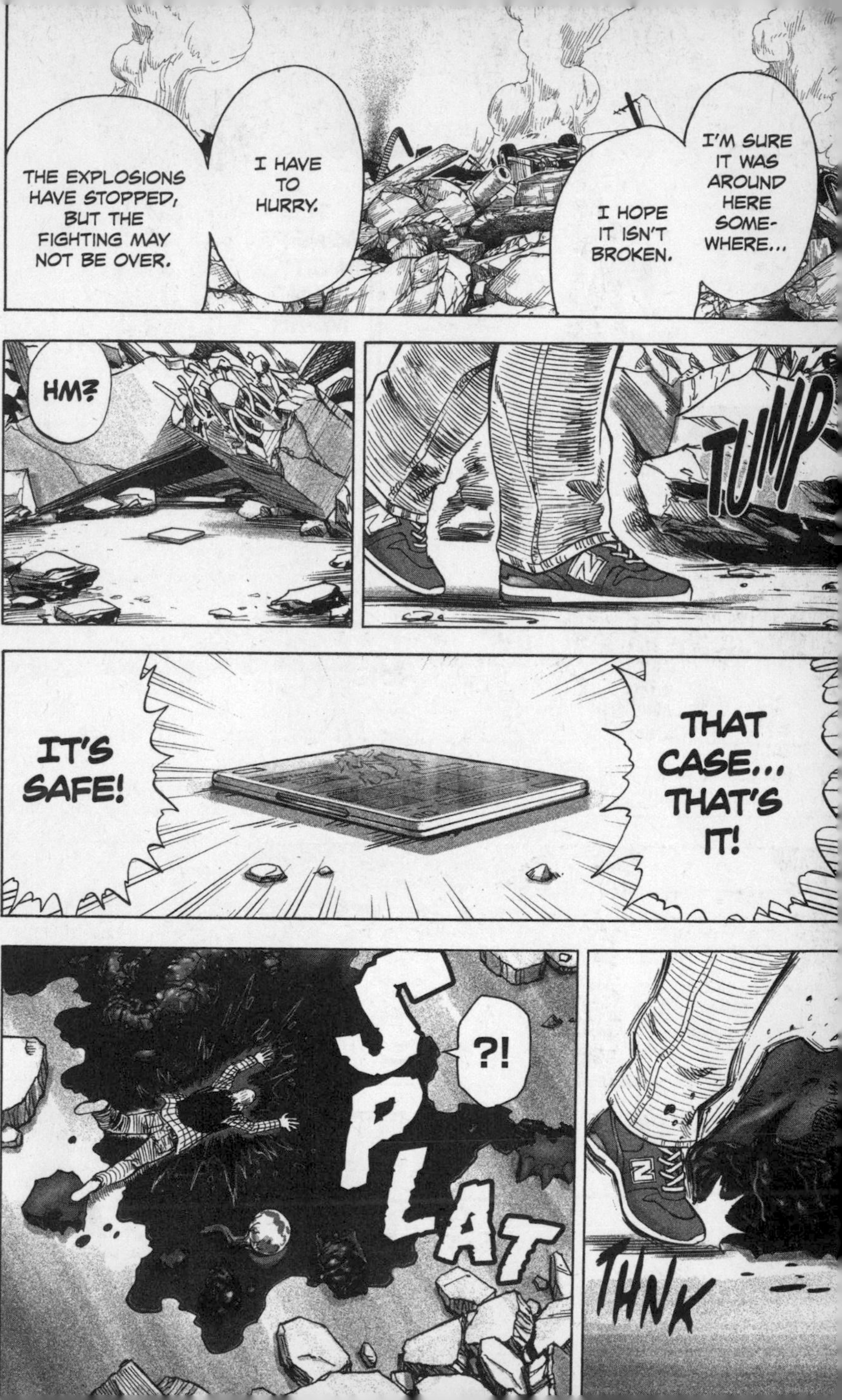
I'M SURE IT WAS AROUND HERE SOME-WHERE...
I HOPE IT ISN'T BROKEN.
I HAVE TO HURRY.
THE EXPLOSIONS HAVE STOPPED, BUT THE FIGHTING MAY NOT BE OVER.
TUMP
HM?
THAT CASE... THAT'S IT!
IT'S SAFE!
THNK
SPLAT
?!

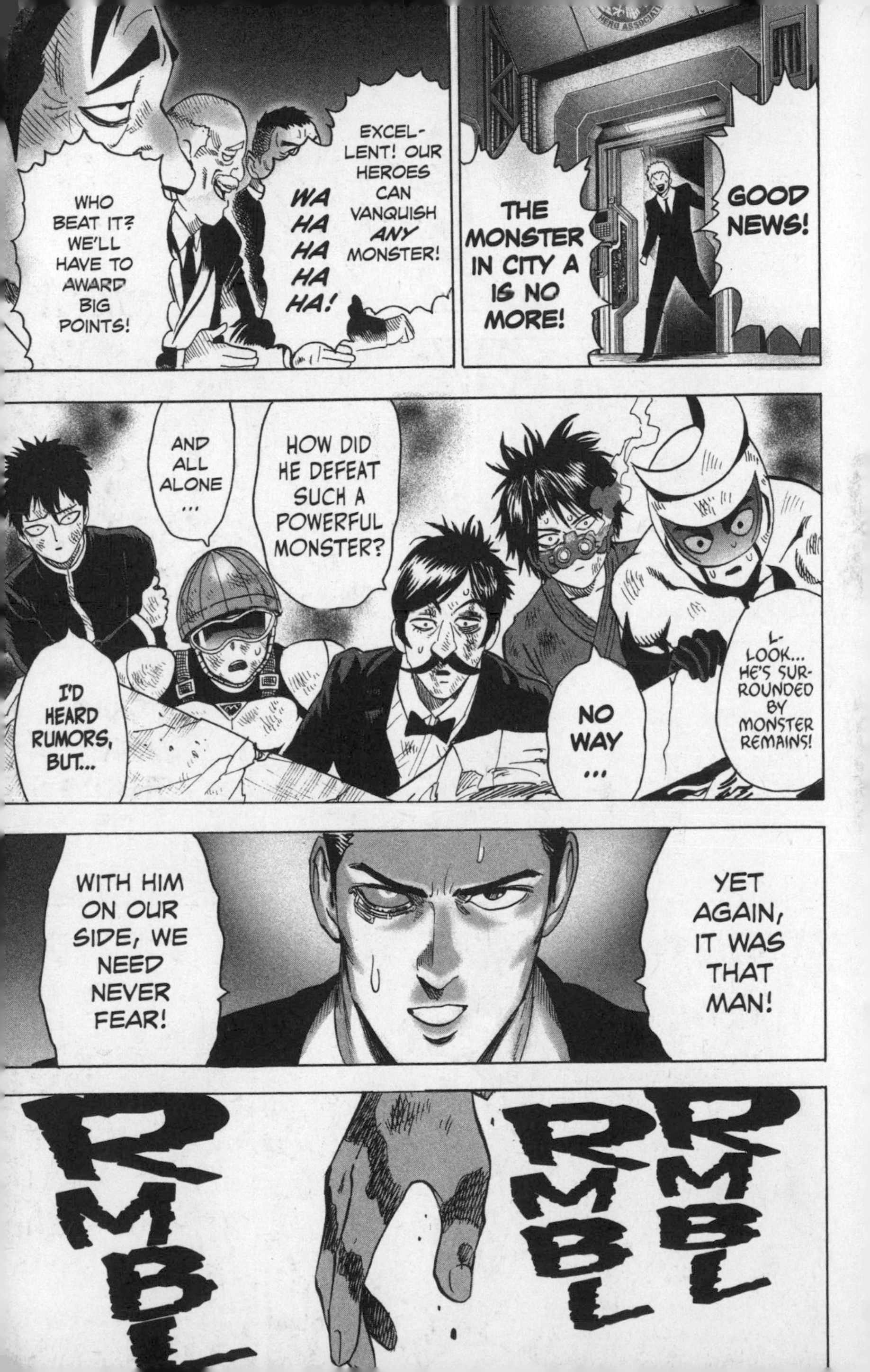
GOOD NEWS!
THE MONSTER IN CITY A IS NO MORE!
EXCEL-LENT! OUR HEROES CAN VANQUISH ANY MONSTER!
WA HA HA HA HA!
WHO BEAT IT? WE'LL HAVE TO AWARD BIG POINTS!
L-LOOK... HE'S SUR-ROUNDED BY MONSTER REMAINS!
NO WAY...
HOW DID HE DEFEAT SUCH A POWERFUL MONSTER?
AND ALL ALONE...
I'D HEARD RUMORS, BUT...
YET AGAIN, IT WAS THAT MAN!
WITH HIM ON OUR SIDE, WE NEED NEVER FEAR!
RMBL
RMBL
RMBL

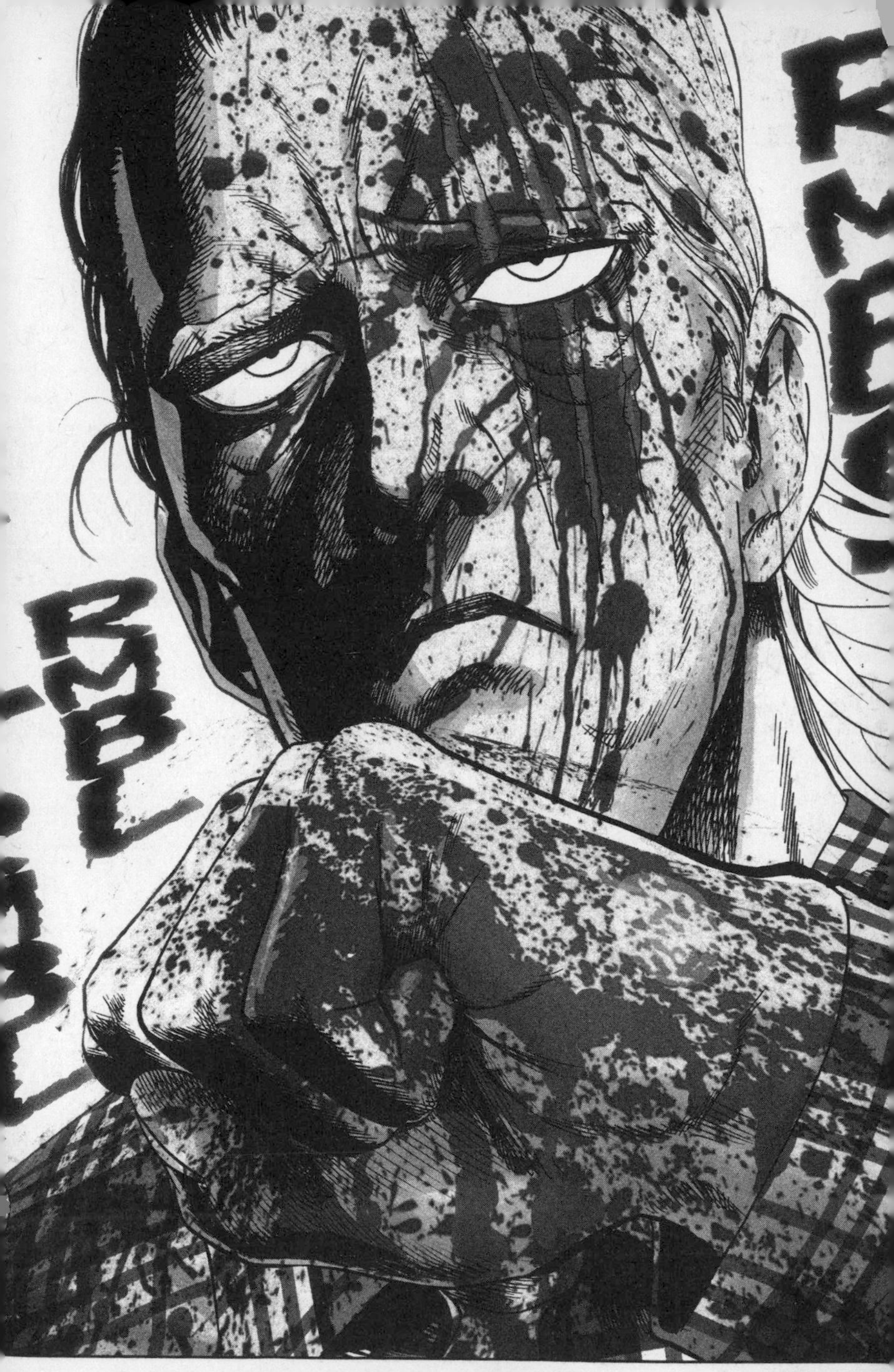
RMBL

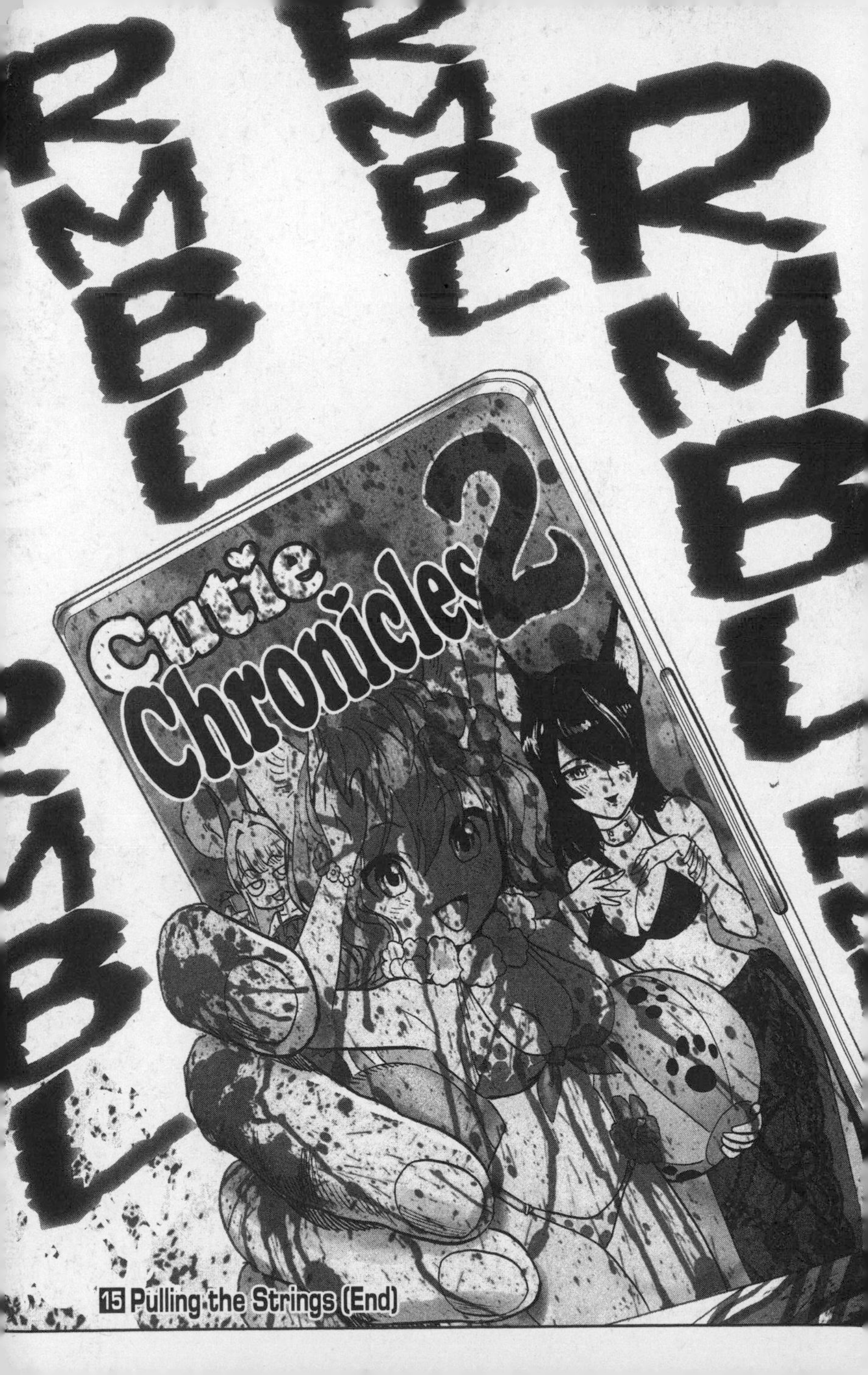
RMBL
RMBL
RMBL
RMBL
Cutie Chronicles 2
15 Pulling the Strings (End)

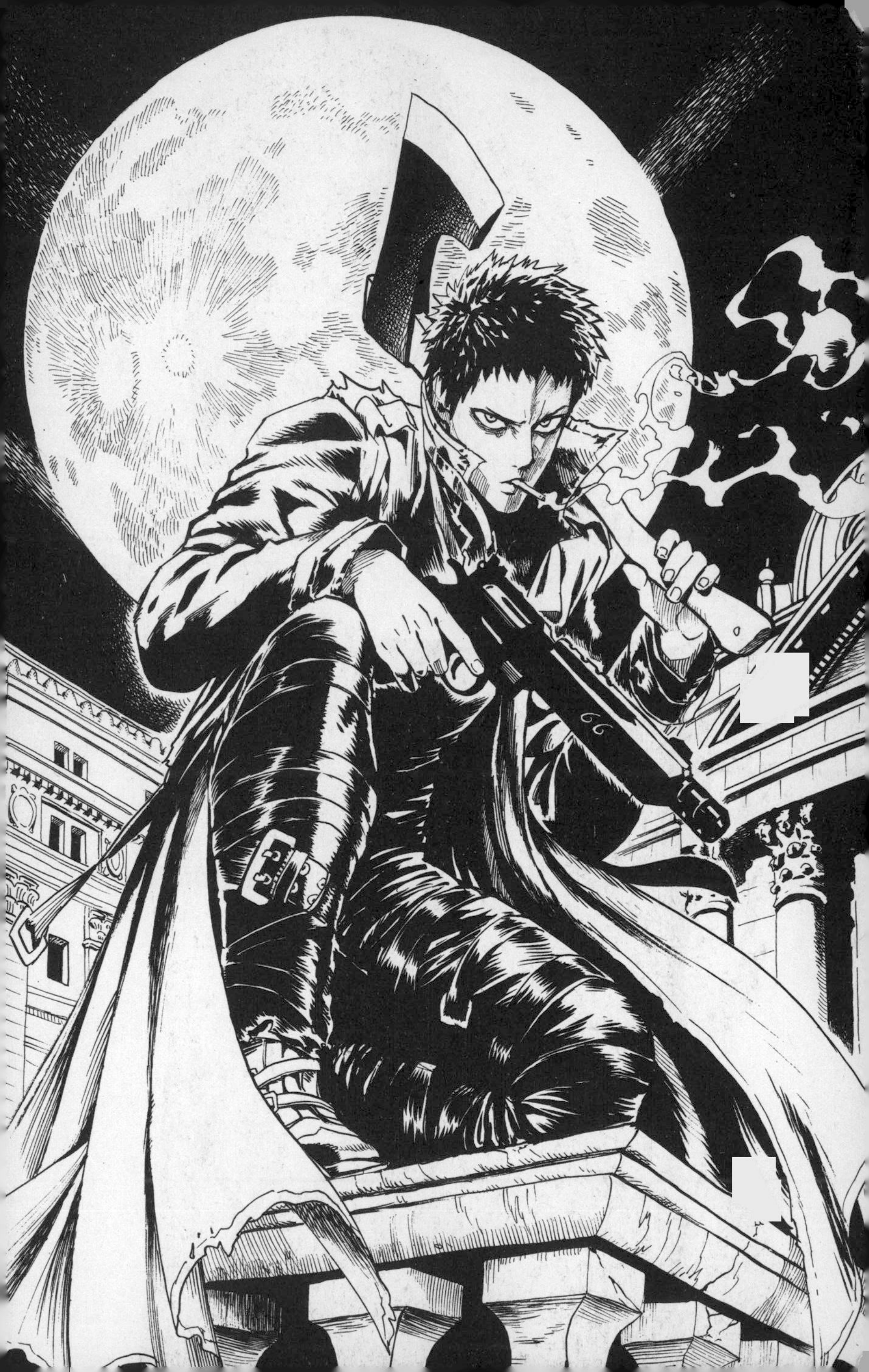

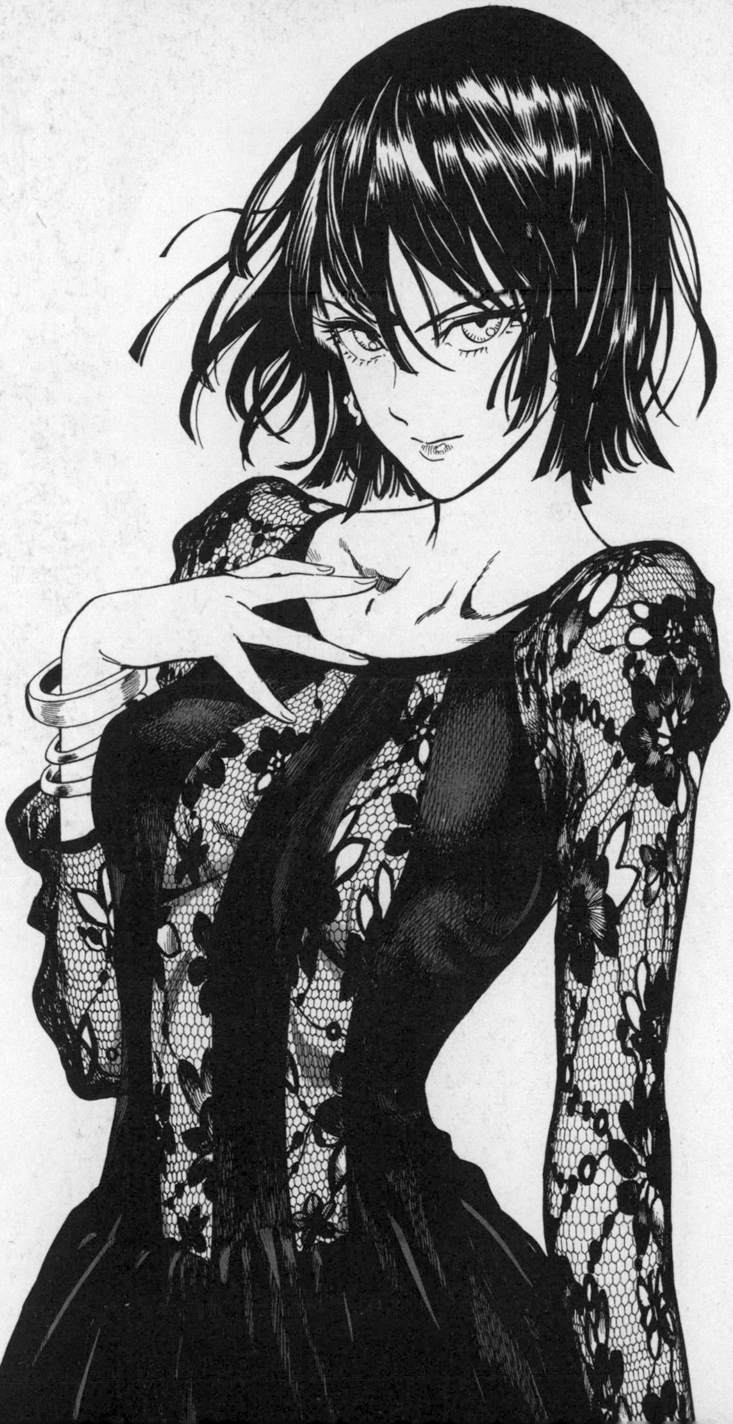

END NOTES

PAGE 18, PANEL 3:
The text on his head and chest means "water."

PAGE 140, PANEL 1:
The text on his chest means "demon."

PAGE 140, PANEL 2:
The text on Saitama's shirt says *dokishisu*, which references one of King's favorite games *Heartthrob Sisters* (*DokiDoki Sisters*).

PAGE 140, PANEL 5:
The text on King's shirt says "I love my house."

Puppy!

15

ONE-PUNCH MAN
VOLUME 15
SHONEN JUMP MANGA EDITION

STORY BY | ONE
ART BY | YUSUKE MURATA

TRANSLATION | JOHN WERRY
TOUCH-UP ART AND LETTERING | JAMES GAUBATZ
DESIGN | SHAWN CARRICO
SHONEN JUMP SERIES EDITOR | JOHN BAE
GRAPHIC NOVEL EDITOR | JENNIFER LEBLANC

ONE-PUNCH MAN © 2012 by ONE, Yusuke Murata
All rights reserved.
First published in Japan in 2012 by SHUEISHA Inc., Tokyo.
English translation rights arranged by SHUEISHA Inc.

The stories, characters and incidents mentioned in this
publication are entirely fictional.

Printed in the U.S.A.

Published by VIZ Media, LLC
P.O. Box 77010
San Francisco, CA 94107

10 9 8 7 6 5 4 3 2 1
First printing, January 2019

VIZ MEDIA
viz.com

SHONEN JUMP
shonenjump.com

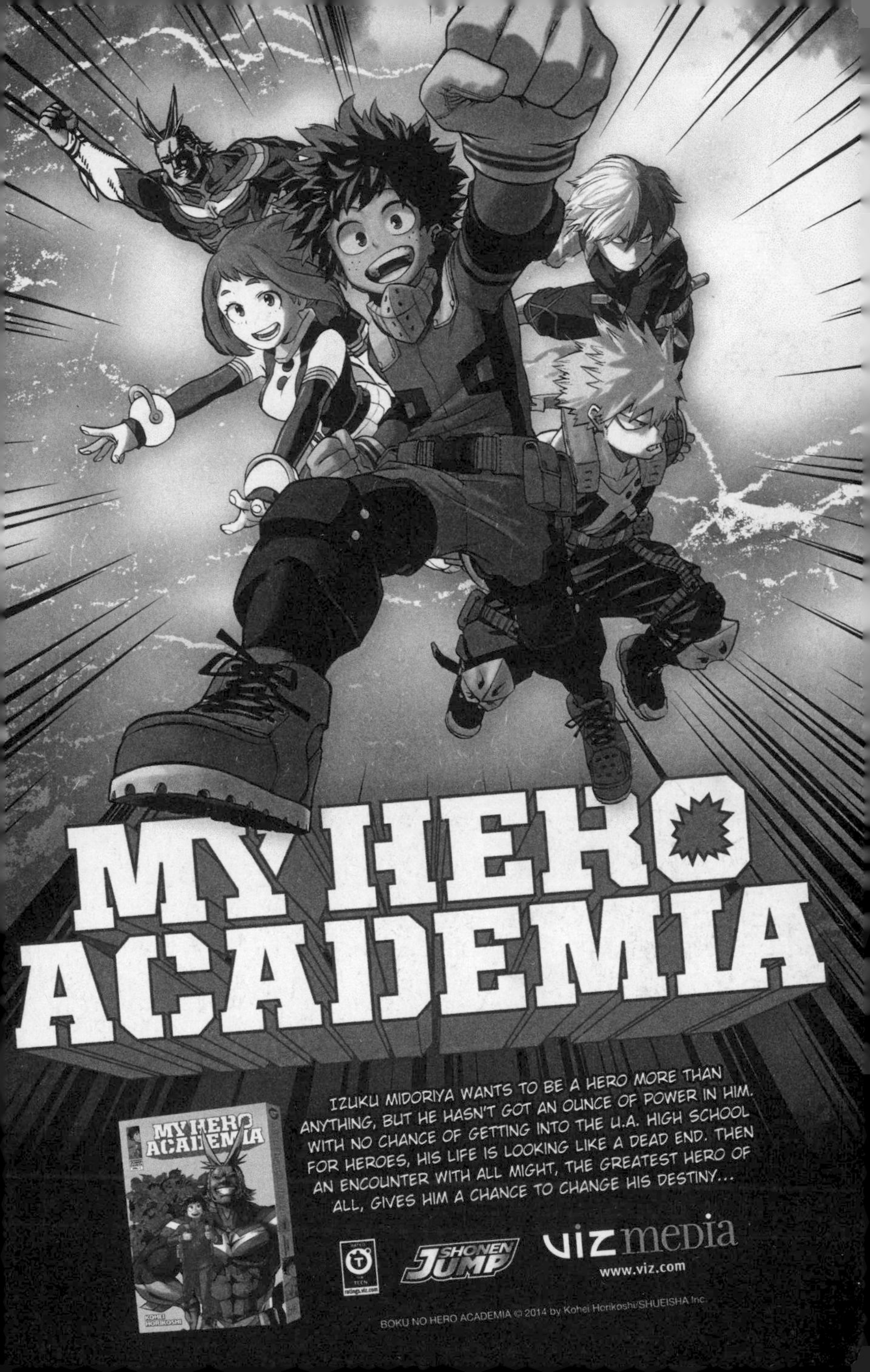
MY HERO ACADEMIA
IZUKU MIDORIYA WANTS TO BE A HERO MORE THAN ANYTHING, BUT HE HASN'T GOT AN OUNCE OF POWER IN HIM. WITH NO CHANCE OF GETTING INTO THE U.A. HIGH SCHOOL FOR HEROES, HIS LIFE IS LOOKING LIKE A DEAD END. THEN AN ENCOUNTER WITH ALL MIGHT, THE GREATEST HERO OF ALL, GIVES HIM A CHANCE TO CHANGE HIS DESTINY...
MY HERO ACADEMIA
KOHEI HORIKOSHI
SHONEN JUMP
VIZ media
www.viz.com
BOKU NO HERO ACADEMIA © 2014 by Kohei Horikoshi/SHUEISHA Inc.

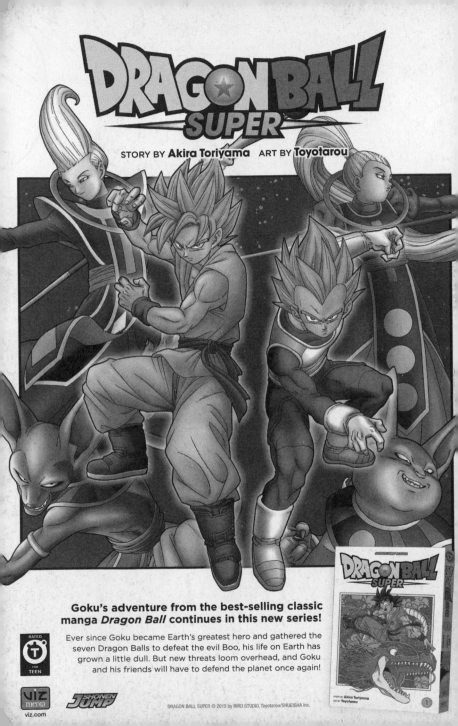

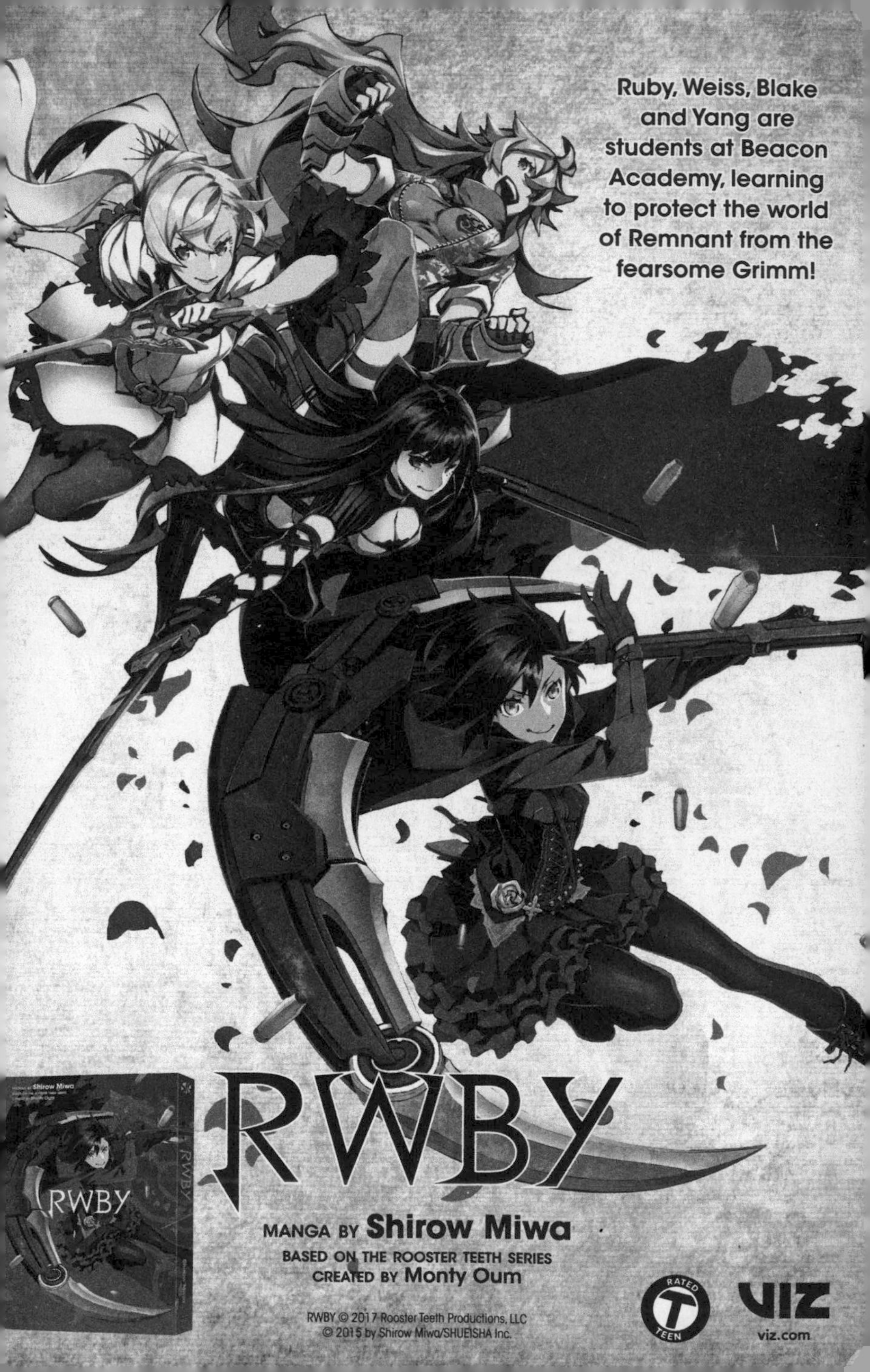
Ruby, Weiss, Blake and Yang are students at Beacon Academy, learning to protect the world of Remnant from the fearsome Grimm!
RWBY
MANGA BY Shirow Miwa
BASED ON THE ROOSTER TEETH SERIES
CREATED BY Monty Oum
RWBY © 2017 Rooster Teeth Productions, LLC
© 2015 by Shirow Miwa/SHUEISHA Inc.
RATED T TEEN
VIZ
viz.com

BORUTO
–NARUTO NEXT GENERATIONS–

CREATOR/SUPERVISOR **Masashi Kishimoto**
ART BY **Mikio Ikemoto** SCRIPT BY **Ukyo Kodachi**

A NEW GENERATION OF NINJA IS HERE!

Naruto was a young shinobi with an incorrigible knack for mischief. He achieved his dream to become the greatest ninja in his village, and now his face sits atop the Hokage monument. But this is not his story... A new generation of ninja is ready to take the stage, led by Naruto's own son, Boruto!

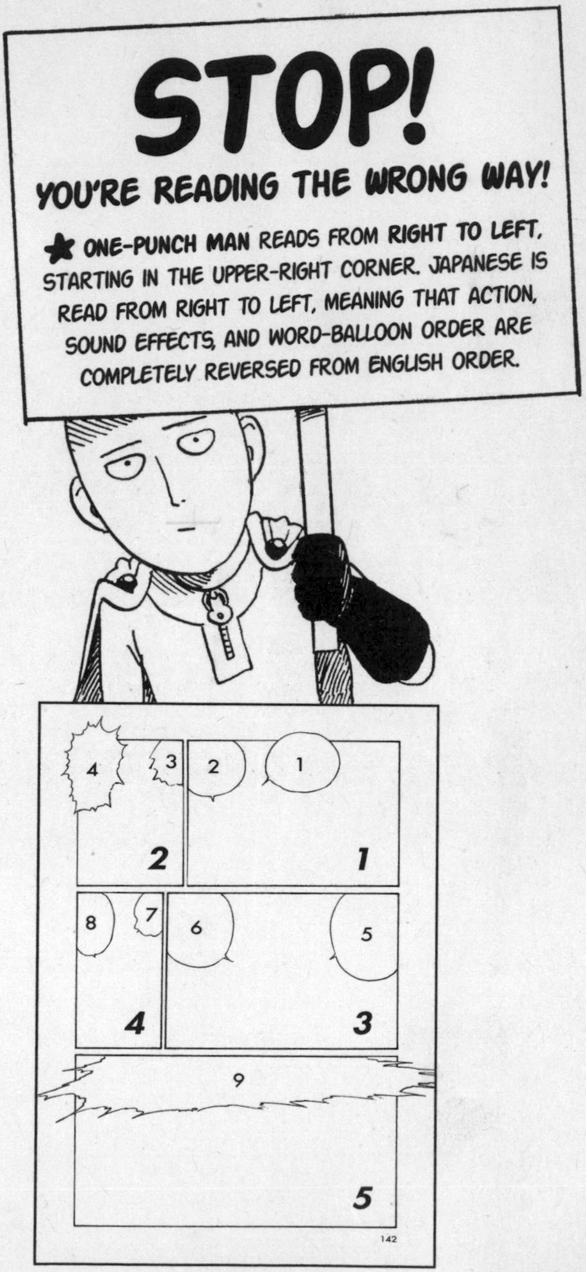
STOP!
YOU'RE READING THE WRONG WAY!
ONE-PUNCH MAN READS FROM RIGHT TO LEFT, STARTING IN THE UPPER-RIGHT CORNER. JAPANESE IS READ FROM RIGHT TO LEFT, MEANING THAT ACTION, SOUND EFFECTS, AND WORD-BALLOON ORDER ARE COMPLETELY REVERSED FROM ENGLISH ORDER.